SIX GO

VALANCOURT CLASSICS

Six Gothic Dramas

De Monfort
Orra
The Dream
The Family Legend
The Phantom
Witchcraft

Joanna Baillie

Selected and introduced by
Christine A. Colón

VALANCOURT BOOKS
CHICAGO

Six Gothic Dramas by Joanna Baillie
First Valancourt Books edition, March 2007

Introduction © 2007 by Christine A. Colón
This edition © 2007 by Valancourt Books

Library of Congress Cataloging-in-Publication Data

Baillie, Joanna, 1762-1851.
    Six gothic dramas / Joanna Baillie ; selected and introduced by Christine A. Colón. (1st Valancourt Books ed.).
            p. cm. -- (Valancourt classics)
        Contents: De Monfort—Orra—The dream—The family legend—The phantom—Witchcraft.
        ISBN 0-9792332-0-8
1. Horror plays, English. 2. Gothic revival (Literature)--Great Britain.
3. English drama--18th century. 4. English drama--19th century. I. Colón, Christine A. II. Series.
        PR4056 .A6 2007
        822/.7 22   2006102843

Published by Valancourt Books
P. O. Box 220511
Chicago, Illinois 60622

Typesetting by James D. Jenkins
Set in Dante MT

10 9 8 7 6 5 4 3 2 1

CONTENTS

INTRODUCTION

Joanna Baillie: Gothic Dramatist

In one of her reminiscences of early childhood Joanna Baillie recalls that despite their differences, one activity drew her and her sister, Agnes, together:

> ...there was one occupation which we both joined in with equal avidity—listening to Ghost stories told us by the sexton of the parish who, frequently came to the house of a winter evening and sat by the Kitchen fire. We always, I dont [sic] know how, contrived to escape from the parlor when we heard that *John Leipen,* so he was called, was in the house. His stories excited us much, and as the house we lived in was said to be haunted by the ghost of a man who had in former years hanged himself in the Garret, we became so frighten'd that we durst not go up stairs alone even in broad day light.[1]

This fascination with ghosts eventually found its way into Baillie's early endeavors at storytelling. Baillie was not a child who enjoyed reading. Despite her sister's attempts to interest her in books, Baillie spent her most enjoyable moments of childhood playing outside. She only discovered the joys of reading upon being confined to her bed after an accident, but as Baillie mentions in her poem "Lines to Agnes Baillie on her Birthday," when she finally did begin to read and to compose stories, her imagination was filled with Gothic images:

> Thy love of tale and story was the stroke
> At which my dormant fancy first awoke,
> And ghosts and witches in my busy brain
> Arose in somber show, a motley train.
> This new-found path attempting, proud was I,
> Lurking approval on thy face to spy,
> Or hear thee say, as grew thy roused attention,
> "What! is this story all thine own invention?"[2]

---

[1] Qtd. in Judith Bailey Slagle, Introduction. *The Collected Letters of Joanna Baillie* (Cranbury, NJ: Associated University Presses, 1999), 4.

[2] Joanna Baillie, "Lines to Agnes Baillie on her Birthday," *The Dramatic and Poetical Works.* (New York: Georg Olms, 1976), 811.

For Baillie, images and stories that would eventually be termed "Gothic" were what initially captured her imagination and prompted her early attempts at storytelling, so it is no surprise that when she, as an adult, enters into her career as a playwright, she relies on these images repeatedly.

Joanna Baillie's Life and Work

Joanna Baillie was born 11 September 1762 in Bothwell, Lanarkshire, Scotland to James Baillie (1722-78), a minister in the parish, and his wife Dorothea Hunter Baillie (1721-1806), the sister of William and John Hunter who both became famous physicians in London. Her twin sister died a few hours after birth, but Baillie did have two older siblings: Agnes (1760-1861), who was to become her lifelong companion, and Matthew (1761-1823), who followed in their uncles' footsteps eventually becoming the Physician Extraordinary to George III. As her reminiscences of childhood reveal, Baillie was not a precocious child who began reading, writing, and planning for a literary career almost as soon as she could walk. Instead, she remembers a childhood full of picking flowers, searching for butterflies and beetles, and wading in the river.[1] Most of the memories she records come from her earliest childhood in Bothwell even though her family did not live there for very long. Her family moved twice in her childhood, first to Hamilton in 1766 when her father became the minister there and then to Glasgow when her father became professor of divinity at the University of Glasgow in 1775. By the time her family moved to Glasgow, Baillie and her sister had already been attending boarding school there for about three years. From the evidence that we have, it would seem that Baillie enjoyed her time at school, for it gave her an even greater scope for her imagination. Lucy Aikin, a friend that Baillie was to make later in her life, recalls Baillie and Agnes talking about these school days where Baillie "used to entertain her companions with an endless string of stories of her own invention" and became "addicted to

---

[1] Baillie, "Lines to Agnes," 811.

clambering on the roof of the house, to act over her scenes alone and in secret."[1]

The Baillie family's time in Glasgow was cut short, for in 1778, James Baillie died. Upon her father's death, Baillie, her mother, and sister went to live at Long Calderwood, a home just outside of Glasgow that was owned by Dorothea's brother William. Matthew left Scotland and traveled to Oxford to attend Balliol College where he had received a fellowship, and after completing his education there, he moved to London to work with his Uncle William. The family remained separated until 1784 when Dorothea along with her two daughters moved to London to keep house for Matthew upon the death of William Hunter. While this move took Baillie away from the Scotland that she loved so deeply, it also took her directly into the center of the literary world in London. Baillie's aunt, Anne Home Hunter (Uncle John's wife), was a published author who not only introduced Baillie to other writers but also inspired her to write for herself. Baillie recalls, "To write as she did was far beyond any attempt of mine, but it turned my thoughts to poetical composition."[2] Baillie had already been composing stories and plays for years, but her aunt seemed to inspire her to move beyond creating simply for her own amusement to consider the possibility of publication. Baillie began working more seriously on poems and plays, and in 1790 her first work, *Poems*, was published anonymously. As Baillie mentions in the preface to a later volume of poetry, *Fugitive Verses*, her early poems were "not noticed by the public, or circulated in any considerable degree," but there was one review that "had spoken of it encouragingly" so Baillie was not entirely dejected.[3] Instead, she seems to have turned her attention to the plays that she had also been composing. In a fragment of a memoir, she recalls the moment she began to think of being a playwright:

> ...seeing a quantity of white paper lying on the floor which from a circumstance needless to mention had been left there...it came into my head that one might write something upon it...that the

---

[1] Lucy Aikin, *Memoirs, Miscellanies and Letters of the Late Lucy Aikin*, ed. Philip Hemery Le Breton (London: Longman, 1864), 9.

[2] Qtd. in Slagle, Introduction, 9.

[3] Joanna Baillie, Preface, *Fugitive Verses* (London: Moxon, 1840), vii.

something might be a play. The play was written or rather composed while my fingers were employed in sprigging muslin for an apron and afterwards transferred to the paper, and though my Brother did not much like such a bent given to my mind, he bestowed upon it so much hearty & manly praise, that my favorite propensity was fixed for ever. I was just two & twenty when we first came to London and this took place I believe the following summer about 9 months afterwards.[1]

As Baillie remembers it, her career as a playwright began in 1785 almost as a whim, but it soon became much more than a whim. With her move to London, Baillie not only had access to the British Museum where she began to read other playwrights extensively,[2] but she also had the opportunity to attend the London theatres and see the greatest actors of the day. And in the next twelve years, Baillie not only begins to write new plays but also to formulate a new and potentially revolutionary theory of drama.

In the late eighteenth and early nineteenth centuries, drama was extremely popular in Britain. Middle and upper class audiences flocked to the theatre, and many of the authors we read today such as Wordsworth, Coleridge, and Byron attempted to write plays that would be produced in the London theatres. Success in the theatre, however, was not easily attainable, for serious drama was confined to three patent theatres: Covent Garden and Drury Lane, which operated from September to June, or Haymarket, which operated in the summers when the other two theatres were closed. With only two major theatres operating for most of the year, the number of plays that could be performed was very limited. In addition, the Licensing Act of 1737 subjected every play to a censor who worked to insure that any controversial subjects, particularly those dealing with politics, religion, or sex, never made it to the stage. All plays were carefully monitored, and with the threat of the French Revolution looming over the consciousness of the nation the censorship of plays became even more intense at the time that Baillie was writing. Finally, the conditions of the two major theatres made it difficult for any serious play to succeed. Covent Garden and Drury Lane could seat around

---

[1] Qtd. in Slagle, Introduction, 8.
[2] Judith Bailey Slagle, *Joanna Baillie: A Literary Life* (Cranbury, NJ: Associated University Presses, 02), 67.

3,000 patrons each. When the size of the theatres was combined with the bad lighting, poor acoustics, and rowdy audiences, it was a wonder than most of the audience could even tell what was being performed on stage. As a result, the acting was often exaggerated, and playwrights tended to rely more and more on spectacle so that the audience members could be entertained by sight even if they could not actually hear what the actors were saying.

This was the world of drama that Baillie desired to enter, but rather than accepting the state of the theatre and crafting the huge spectacles that the audiences desired, Baillie wanted to revolutionize theatre, believing that it could be used more effectively to affect people's lives. She, therefore, worked carefully for the next few years not simply writing plays but also crafting her philosophy of theatre. The results appeared in 1798 with the anonymous publication of *A Series of Plays: in which it is attempted to delineate the stronger passions of the mind—each passion being the subject of a tragedy and a comedy* (commonly called the *Plays on the Passions*). In the Introductory Discourse to this volume, Baillie presents her theories of drama and demonstrates just how carefully she has crafted her ideas.

Building upon the moral philosophy of eighteenth-century thinkers such as the Earl of Shaftesbury, David Hume, and Adam Smith, Baillie focuses her plan for theatre on what she calls "sympathetick curiosity." She believes that all humans are inherently curious about the people around them and argues that "[t]here is, perhaps, no employment which the human mind will with so much avidity pursue, as the discovery of concealed passion, as the tracing the varieties and progress of a perturbed soul."[1] Through drama Baillie desires to harness this tendency and help individuals learn to use it effectively so that they may learn to control the passions that may so easily destroy them. With drama, individuals may "[follow] the great man into his secret closet,...[stand] by the side of his nightly couch, and [hear] those exclamations of the soul which heaven alone may hear."[2] By allowing her audience members to see the minute progress of the passions as they take over an individual's life, Baillie hopes that they will not simply be entertained but also will learn

---

[1] Joanna Baillie, Introductory Discourse, *The Dramatic and Poetical Works* (New York: Georg Olms, 1976), 4.

[2] Baillie, Introductory Discourse, 8.

from the experiences of the fictional characters. She remarks, "[w]e cannot, it is true, amidst [passion's] wild uproar, listen to the voice of reason, and save ourselves from destruction; but we can foresee its coming, we can mark its rising signs, we can know the situations that will most expose us to its rage, and we can shelter our heads from the coming blast."[1] Baillie believes that by observing the characters in her plays, audience members will become more attuned to this process and learn to protect themselves. With volume one of her *Plays on the Passions*, then, Baillie not only enters the London theatre world as a playwright but also presents herself as a theorist who wishes to use drama to help transform individuals.

Unlike Baillie's earlier volume of poetry, Baillie's first volume of *Plays on the Passions* did cause quite a stir. The volume received favorable reviews from many of the leading journals. The critic writing for *Analytical Review*, for instance, declares "So many of the observations in this 'introductory discourse,' such beautiful and familiar illustrations attend them, and so attentively does the author appear to have studied the anatomy of the human mind that we were led to expect in the perusal of his dramas, and we have not been disappointed, many beautiful traits of character, many faithful and affecting touches of nature,"[2] and the writer for *British Critic* goes even further, remarking, "May we not hope that, in the unknown author of these Dramas, exists the long wished-for talent, which is to remove the present opprobrium of our theatres, and supply them with productions of native growth, calculated not for the destruction of idle time, but for the amusement of ages?"[3] The critics recognize that the anonymous author of *Plays on the Passions* is attempting to do something new, and they appreciate how successful she is in presenting her theories and in enacting them in her first three plays. Literary society also began to take notice of Baillie's work. Mary Berry's remarks to a friend in 1799 reveal just how popular the volume was becoming: "This winter, the first question on everybody's lips is, 'Have you read the series of plays?' Everybody talks in the raptures (I always thought they deserved) of the tragedies and of the introduction as of a new and

---

[1] Baillie, Introductory Discourse, 11.

[2] Rev. of *A Series of Plays* Vol. 1, *Analytical Review* 27 (1798): 526.

[3] Rev. of *A Series of Plays* Vol. 1, *British Critic* 13 (1799): 290.

admirable piece of criticism."[1] The volume continued to be popular, going through five editions before 1807, and in 1800 *De Monfort*, the final play in the volume, was performed at Drury Lane with the two leading actors of the time, John Kemble and Sarah Siddons, acting the two major roles.

With this production Baillie's career as a playwright was put to the test. In her Introductory Discourse, Baillie reveals that she intends these plays to be acted on the stage rather than simply read as closet drama, for she believes that the power of drama stems from the fact that "[t]he impressions made by it are communicated, at the same instant of time, to a greater number of individuals than those made by any other species of writing: and they are strengthened in every spectator, by observing their effects upon those who surround him."[2] With the production of *De Monfort*, she was about to discover if her theories would work on the contemporary stage. Critical opinion suggests that they did not. The play was performed for eight nights, which, while being a respectable run for a play at this time, did not live up to the expectations of many. After seeing the play, the writer Elizabeth Inchbald, remarks, "That fine play, supported by the most appropriate acting of Kemble and Siddons, is both dull and highly improbable in the representation,"[3] and years later in 1821 when another production of *De Monfort* was attempted, the writer for *European Magazine* recalls that "[*De Monfort* is] celebrated as being a most powerful production in the vigour of its language, and the weakness of its plot; and celebrated also as failing in dramatic attraction, even when supported by John Kemble and Mrs. Siddons."[4] Many felt that the powerful writing simply did not transfer to the stage, which is perhaps no wonder considering the type of theatre in which it was produced. While *De Monfort* does have some spectacle to entertain the audience, particularly as the play becomes more Gothic in the final act with a gloomy wood, a powerful storm, and an isolated cloister as the settings for the dénouement, most of the play is concerned with following De Monfort's character as he slips

---

[1] Qtd. in Ellen Donkin, *Getting into the Act: Women Playwrights in London 1776-1829*, (New York: Routledge, 1995), 163.

[2] Baillie, Introductory Discourse, 14.

[3] Qtd. in Donkin, 163.

[4] Rev. of *De Monfort*, *European Magazine*, 80 (1821): 567.

deeper and deeper into his hatred for Rezenvelt. The focus here is not on spectacle but rather on the subtle developments of his character that could have been nearly impossible for many of the audience members to follow in such a large theatre.

More recently, scholars such as Ellen Donkin have posited that the success of *De Monfort* on stage was also hindered by the revelation that it was written by a woman, for on 29 April 1800 (right when *De Monfort* opened) *The Dramatic Censor* reported that "the Play in question is now referred to Miss Bailey [*sic*], sister to the physician of that name."[1] According to Donkin, who researched the box office receipts before and after the revelation, "the discovery that the author of *Plays on the Passions* was a woman apparently damaged both the sale of her book and the box-office receipts."[2] This supposition that Baillie's success was hindered by the revelation of her sex is supported by contemporary accounts in two magazines that take the discussion beyond the reception of her play on stage to an exploration of the criticism that she received more generally as a female playwright. Both *Blackwood's Edinburgh Magazine* (1824) and *Fraser's Magazine* (1836) find fault with the *Edinburgh Review* in particular for condemning Baillie simply because she is a woman. The writer of the article in *Blackwood's Edinburgh Magazine* is quite blunt, stating that the journal's "malignant observations" were based on "an unaccountable and unwarrantable aversion to all female authorship."[3] Baillie herself also believed that the revelation of her sex hindered the reception of her plays. In a letter to Sir Walter Scott in 1826, she comments on another female writer's plight and compares it to her own: "She [Miss Head] would fain have kept her name & sex unknown, if her friends would have allowed it, and they were not very wise friends who thwarted her on this point. I speak feelingly on this subject like a burnt child. John *any-body* would have stood higher with the critics than Joanna Baillie. I too was unwisely thwarted on this point."[4] The anonymous author of the *Plays on the*

---

[1] Qtd. in Slagle *A Literary Life*, 89.

[2] Donkin, 165.

[3] "Celebrated Female Writers, No. 1: Joanna Baillie." *Blackwood's Edinburgh Magazine*. 16 (1824): 165.

[4] Joanna Baillie, Letter to Sir Walter Scott: 13 October 1826, *The Collected Letters of Joanna Baillie*, ed. Judith Bailey Slagle (Cranbury, NJ: Associated University Presses, 1999), 439.

Passions may have been lauded as the playwright who could revitalize the London theatre, but Joanna Baillie was chastised for moving out of the feminine sphere and into the masculine world of tragedy.

Mary Ann Stodart in her book *Female Writers: Thoughts on Their Proper Sphere and on Their Powers of Usefulness* (1842) demonstrates the difficulties many readers had once they discovered that the author of the *Plays on the Passions* was a woman. Early in her study she remarks, "It is not within our [women's] province to dive into the deep recesses of the human heart with that myriad-minded man, our own Shakespeare, and to drag into the open day-light the hidden secrets of the soul."[1] Since this is the basis of Baillie's entire project, it is no wonder that later she condemns Baillie for "the undue prominence given to one passion" and is appalled that Baillie expects the audience of *De Monfort* to sympathize with a murderer. Sarah Hale's criticism of 1855 is even more blunt. She remarks, "We prefer that our own sex should rather be admirers of the fame of Joanna Baillie than followers in her own peculiar and chosen sphere."[2] By delving into the complexities of the human mind and showing the terrible effects that unrestrained passions might have, Baillie was entering into the masculine world of tragedy and Shakespeare rather than staying within the "proper" sphere of women writers. An oft quoted remark of Lord Byron (who admired Baillie's plays so much that he advocated for their production) expresses the conflict that her contemporaries had with Baillie, as a woman, choosing her particular project: "When Voltaire was asked why no woman has ever written even a tolerable tragedy, 'Ah (said the Patriarch) the composition of a tragedy requires *testicles*.' If this be true, Lord knows what Joanna Baillie does—I suppose she borrows them."[3] Baillie was treading on masculine territory, and many readers and reviewers had difficulty accepting that.

Despite these setbacks Baillie continued to write, and she soon became an important member of the literary society in Hampstead

---

[1] Mary Ann Stodart, *Female Writers: Thoughts on Their Proper Sphere and on Their Powers of Usefulness* (London, 1842), 88.

[2] Sarah Josepha Hale, *Woman's Record: or, Sketches of All Distinguished Women, from Creation to A. D. 1854* (New York: Harper, 1855), 574.

[3] Qtd. in William D. Brewer, "Joanna Baillie and Lord Byron," *Keats-Shelley Journal*, 44 (1995): 170.

where she, her sister, and her mother had re-located around the time of the publication of *Plays on the Passions*. She became friends with many other writers, such as Sir Walter Scott, Lord Byron, William Wordsworth, Anna Laetitia Barbauld, Maria Edgeworth, and Anna Jameson, and her home became an important destination for many foreign visitors who wished to meet the famous author. While Baillie was obviously frustrated by many of the critical responses to her plays, she continued her project, publishing the second volume of her *Plays on the Passions* in 1802 and the third volume in 1812. She also took time to publish a volume of what she termed *Miscellaneous Plays* in 1804, demonstrating that she could move beyond her original project to craft plays not as exclusively devoted to the passions.

As Baillie continued to write, she also continued to receive harsh criticism, particularly from Francis Jeffrey of the *Edinburgh Review*. In 1803, he writes a review which condemns her overall project, for he believes that "[p]lays have, for the most part, no moral effect at all."[1] While he finds some genius in her work, he asks her to abandon the idea of creating a tragedy and comedy for each passion, feeling that this project is constraining her talents.[2] In 1805 after she does produce a volume of plays separate from that project, he remarks, that the volume is "so decidedly inferior to those which the same writer had produced in pursuance of that plan, that we cannot help regretting that she should ever have thought of abandoning it."[3] Nothing that Baillie writes seems to please Jeffrey, and in 1812 his criticism becomes so harsh that he examines "the causes of [this volume's] failure" for twelve entire pages.[4] Baillie was clearly disheartened by Jeffrey's criticism, asking Scott in 1812, "Think you there is spirit at all in me now to write Plays of any kind, after all that our great Northern Critic hath said of the deplorable dullness & want of interest in those I have already written?"[5]

She was also frustrated that her plays, which she so desperately desired to see on the stage, were not being produced, and in her preface to the third volume of *Plays on the Passions*, Baillie addresses

---

[1] Francis Jeffrey, Rev. of *A Series of Plays* Vol. 2 *Edinburgh Review* 2 (1803): 275.
[2] Francis Jeffrey, Rev. of *A Series of Plays* Vol. 2 *Edinburgh Review* 2 (1803): 286.
[3] Francis Jeffrey, Rev. of *Miscellaneous Plays*, *Edinburgh Review* 5 (1805): 405.
[4] Francis Jeffrey, Rev. of *A Series of Plays* Vol. 3, *Edinburgh Review* 19 (1812): 261.
[5] Baillie, Letter to Sir Walter Scott: 27 May 1812, *Collected Letters*, 303.

this issue, telling her readers that "this will probably be the last volume of plays I shall ever publish."[1] Interestingly, Baillie does not intend to give up her project; she has only decided that the current state of the theatre is not conducive to the types of plays she desires to create. She then proceeds to create a trenchant criticism of the theatre of her day, explaining why serious drama has such a difficult time succeeding in the London theatres. As she discusses why the size of the theatres, the size of the stage, and the lighting effects compel actors to exaggerate their characters and playwrights to focus more on spectacle than on character development, Baillie reveals her commitment to her project. She is not going to capitulate to the current state of the theatre. Instead, she will continue to write according to her project and hope that the theatre will eventually be transformed into a realm where the subtleties of character development will be appreciated by the audiences.

While Baillie's frustration with the London theatres and the criticism from Jeffrey might imply that she was no longer an important force in British literature, that supposition is incorrect. As Baillie herself acknowledges in a letter to Scott, the third volume of her *Plays on the Passions* was "sell[ing] better than any of those that preceded it."[2] Theatre managers and Francis Jeffrey may not have appreciated her project, but the public and many other critics were still entranced. In fact, in 1824 when *Blackwood's Edinburgh Magazine* published an issue on women writers, the editor remarks, "When we resolved on presenting our readers with a succession of Essays on the works and talents of the most distinguished female authors, we did not for a moment hesitate in deciding to whom the right of precedency was due. The name of Joanna Baillie instantly suggested itself to our minds."[3] While much twentieth- and twenty-first-century criticism has focused on the difficulties Baillie faced as a female playwright, she was also what Jeffrey Cox has termed "a consummate insider."[4] The collection of poems that she edited in

---

[1] Baillie, Preface to the Third Volume of *Plays on the Passions. Dramatic and Poetical Works* (New York: Georg Olms, 1976), 231.

[2] Baillie, Letter to Sir Walter Scott: n.d., *Collected Letters*, 297.

[3] "Celebrated Female Writers, No. 1: Joanna Baillie." *Blackwood's Edinburgh Magazine*, 162.

[4] Jeffrey N. Cox, "Baillie, Siddons, Larpent: Gender, Power and Politics in the Theatre of Romanticism." *Women in British Romantic Theatre: Drama, Perfor-*

1823 illustrates just how well connected she was, for she managed to elicit contributions from many of the important writers of the time, such as Sir Walter Scott, Robert Southey, William Wordsworth, George Crabbe, Samuel Rogers, Felicia Hemans, and Anna Laetitia Barbauld. Evidence shows that these writers not only succumbed to her persuasion as an editor but also appreciated the force of her talent as a playwright. After Baillie's death, Mary Russell Mitford was to declare that Baillie was "praised...of all whose praise is best worth having for half a century."[1] While Baillie certainly received criticism during her career, the majority opinion was still very much in favor of her plays.

Baillie's popularity allowed her in the 1820s and 1830s to begin to explore more controversial issues, particularly her thoughts regarding Christianity. While Christianity had always been an important foundation for her project of moral reform, she usually avoided overt discussions of it in her plays, perhaps because religious references were subject to elision by the censor. In 1826, however, she publishes *The Martyr*, which sets out many of her beliefs in the value of Christian principles. In her play, she attempts to refute "the gloomy, cruel, and absurd superstitions" that have been associated with religion and instead to present a picture of "pure Christianity unencumbered with many perplexing and contradictory doctrines which followed, when churchmen had leisure to overlay the sacred Scriptures with a multitude of explanatory dissertations."[2] Throughout her *Plays on the Passions*, Baillie repeatedly asks her audiences to examine the evidence for themselves and make the interpretations that will allow them to transform their own lives without relying on other people's interpretations, and in *The Martyr* Baillie transfers this idea to the truths of Christianity, asking her audience to ignore the various doctrines that have developed over the years and focus instead on the basic truths that they may interpret for themselves.

---

mance, and Society, 1790-1840, ed. Catherine Burroughs (New York: Cambridge University Press, 2000), 32.

[1] Mary Russell Mitford, *Recollections of a Literary Life* (New York: Harper, 1852), 152.

[2] Baillie, Preface to *The Martyr. Dramatic and Poetical Works* (New York: Georg Olms, 1976), 509 and 511.

This focus on the basic truths of Christianity may have been one of the reasons why Sir Alexander Johnstone, the chief justice of Ceylon, had the play translated into Sinhalese so that it could be used to introduce the people of Ceylon to Christianity. He also asked Baillie to compose another play: one tailored more directly to the people of Ceylon. The result was *The Bride*, which Baillie published in 1828. With this play Baillie immerses herself in the complicated issues of imperialism. On the one hand, Baillie hopes that her play will appeal to childlike natives caught in "ignorance and delusion,"[1] but, on the other, she also provides her foreign audience with the same freedom that she allows her British audience: the freedom to make their own interpretations of Scripture without having to depend upon Western interpretations. Baillie's commitment to individual interpretation allows her subvert some of the traditional goals of imperialism with this play. It also compels her to publish a religious tract in 1831 entitled, *A View of the General Tenor of the New Testament Regarding the Nature and Dignity of Jesus Christ* where she asks her readers to examine various passages from the New Testament and determine for themselves whether Christ is truly God. Since her own conclusion reveals her doubts about the doctrine of the trinity, she received quite a bit of criticism for the tract including a few letters from the Bishop of Salisbury, who attempted to change her mind. Baillie, however, held firm to her interpretation, revealing yet again her tenacious desire to stay true to her beliefs rather than to compromise for the sake of conformity or popularity.

Baillie did, however, change her mind about publishing more of her plays, for in 1836 she published three volumes of *Dramas* that encompassed not only her final *Plays on the Passions* but also additional miscellaneous plays. In the preface to the first volume, Baillie reveals that while she still does not find the state of the London theatre conducive to her type of drama, she does not want the burden of editing and publishing her plays to fall upon her heirs.[2] Thirty-eight years had passed since her first volume of *Plays on the Passions* appeared, and after all of the criticism that she had received

---

[1] Baillie, Preface to *The Bride. Dramatic and Poetical Works* (New York: Georg Olms, 1976), 665.

[2] Baillie, Preface to *Romiero. Dramatic and Poetical Works* (New York: Georg Olms, 1976), 312.

Baillie expresses only "diffident hope" that her plays will meet with approval.[1] If she read the review in *Fraser's Magazine*, she must have been encouraged that, for many readers, the volume was a welcome addition to their libraries. The reviewer remarks:

> We dreaded lest our expectations should be disappointed—lest these later plays should prove unworthy the high celebrity of their author—and lest, on rising from the perusal of them, we should find that the early-implanted and long-cherished admiration, which had been inspired by the wonderful creations of the summer of her days and the vigour of her genius, had in any degree suffered check or diminution from the perusal of the feebler efforts of her age. Our alarm was quite superfluous. We might have spared ourselves the pain of these petty, jealous, and mistrustful feelings. The new work has surpassed all that we had expected, or could have ventured to hope for.[2]

This critic's review was not the only positive one she received, for *Blackwood's Magazine*, *Monthly Review*, and *Quarterly Review* all printed positive notices. Even the review in the dreaded *Edinburgh Review* was positive. Baillie's plays still had the power to enchant readers, and she continued to write poetry and edit her plays into her later years, supervising the publication of her complete works until right before her death in February of 1851. When she died, *Harper's New Monthly Magazine* declared her "the most illustrious of the female poets of England" and remarked that "[h]er power of portraying the darker and sterner passions of the human heart has rarely been surpassed."[3]

At her death (fifty-three years after the publication of her first volume of *Plays on the Passions*) Baillie was still recognized as a powerful force in English literature. Why, then, did it take so long for twentieth-century scholars to rediscover her? While she is occasionally mentioned in various studies throughout the twentieth century and is even the subject of a monograph by Margaret Carhart in 1923, her project is usually trivialized. In 1909, Florence MacCunn

---

[1] Baillie, Preface to *Romiero*, 312.
[2] Rev. of *Miscellaneous Plays*, *Fraser's Magazine* 13 (1836): 236.
[3] "Obituary for Joanna Baillie," *Harper's New Monthly Magazine* 2 (1851): 709.

accuses her of "pathetic simplicity."[1] In 1930, Donald Carswell calls her a "literary oddity."[2] In 1963, W. L. Renwick determines that she is not a "real dramatist,"[3] and even as late as 1988, Marilyn Gaull condemns her for being "uneducated and inexperienced."[4] Part of the problem may stem from a selective view of the evidence, focusing on the opinion of critics such as Francis Jeffrey to the exclusion of many other reviewers. Some of the problem may also arise from distaste for her moral project, which is so different from the type of plays produced today. But perhaps what is most problematic for Baillie is that her works fall into several categories that early twentieth-century literary criticism refused to value. She, like other neglected writers such as Charlotte Smith and Felicia Hemans, was a woman writing during a time when good writing came to be defined by the works of the six great male Romanticists: Blake, Wordsworth, Coleridge, Keats, Shelley, and Byron. She was also primarily a dramatist during a time that came to be defined by its poetry. And, finally, she was fascinated by the Gothic, a genre that until very recently was seen as popular and, therefore, second-rate. All may have contributed to her falling into obscurity.

As literary criticism has changed, however, Baillie has entered fully into the discussion. She is now seen as much more than an odd literary footnote. Instead, she has been a key figure in the rediscovery not only of female, Romantic writers but also of Romantic dramatists, and scholars such as Marjean Purinton, Ellen Donkin, and Catherine Burroughs have begun to reveal the great depth that lies within her works as they have explored her ideas on theatre, gender, and psychology. With the recent publication of Baillie's letters and a biography by Judith Bailey Slagle as well as a collection of critical essays on her works edited by Thomas C. Crochunis, Baillie's works are beginning to receive the attention that many of her contemporaries thought was justly deserved. In a letter to Sir Walter Scott written in 1810, Baillie compares his fame to her own

---

[1] Florence MacCunn, *Sir Walter Scott's Friends* (Edinburgh: Blackwoods, 1909), 291.

[2] Donald Carswell, *Scott and His Circle* (New York: Doubleday, 1930), 295.

[3] W. L. Renwick, *English Literature: 1789-1815* (London: Oxford University Press, 1963), 232.

[4] Marilyn Gaull, *English Romanticism: The Human Context* (New York: Norton, 1988), 102.

and wishes that he could "transfer all that [he has] over & above what pleases [him] to a certain friend of [his], who loves it with all her heart."[1] While Baillie's name may not yet have the recognition that Sir Walter Scott's does, the increased attention to her works guarantees that she will not be forgotten.

Joanna Baillie and the Gothic

At the time that Joanna Baillie was writing, Gothic drama in Britain was at its height. Many of Ann Radcliffe's novels were adapted for the stage as were Matthew Lewis's *The Monk*, William Godwin's *Caleb Williams*, and Charles Robert Maturin's *Melmoth the Wanderer*. In fact, in 1798, the same year that Baillie published her first volume of *Plays on the Passions*, Matthew Lewis's *The Castle Spectre*, which was written specifically for the stage, was extremely successful. According to Jeffrey Cox, "[t]he Gothic remained the dominant form of serious popular drama until the rise of the domestic melodrama in the 1820s."[2] While the Gothic with its focus on ruined castles, hidden chambers, stormy nights, and horrific corpses certainly would have appealed to the large audiences of Covent Garden and Drury Lane who were simply looking for spectacle, scholars have repeatedly asked whether the Gothic might actually explore deeper, more significant, issues that would also appeal to this audience at the turn of the century.

Scholars have posited several theories for this appeal, and, interestingly, Baillie's Gothic plays resonate with each of them. One theory is that the interest in Gothic spectacle was directly tied to Edmund Burke's *A Philosophical Enquiry into the Origin of Our Ideas of the Sublime and Beautiful* (1757) in which he discusses the value that the sublime has to shatter the indifference of individuals. Rather than allowing the viewer to be lulled into complacency by the softness of the beautiful, the sublime's delight that comes mixed with terror can wake humanity up to the intensity of life. The Gothic, which compels an audience to derive pleasure from fear, clearly allies itself

---

[1] Baillie, Letter to Sir Walter Scott: 28 November 1810, *Collected Letters*, 275.

[2] Jeffrey N. Cox, "English Gothic Theatre," *The Cambridge Companion to Gothic Fiction*, ed. Jerrold E. Hogle (New York: Cambridge University Press, 2002), 127.

with the idea of the sublime, and for a playwright like Baillie who desperately wishes to stir her audience members' imaginations and compel them to transform their lives, the spectacle of the Gothic sublime would have been appealing. It had the potential to awaken audiences and cause them to act.

Another theory links the appeal of the Gothic to the growing interest in extreme states of mind, a way of exploring the psychological even before twentieth-century constructions of it. Here, Gothic spectacle becomes linked to the internal state of the characters' minds as authors explore how individuals react in times of great stress. As Frederick Burwick mentions, Baillie, through her brother Matthew, not only had access to cutting edge medical thought on the subject (such as his lecture "Anatomy of the Nervous System"), but she also knew of the difficulties that George the Third's physicians went through as he struggled with his periodic bouts of madness.[1] Her *Plays on the Passions*, in particular, allow her to create her own "scientific" theories of the development of the different passions as they lead several of her characters into the world of madness.

Baillie's interest in both of these aspects of the Gothic is clear not only from the images and storylines of her plays but also from her discussions of the purpose of her plays. In her Introductory Discourse, for instance, Baillie references the potential the Gothic has both to awaken her audience and to reveal the inner-workings of the mind. As she explains the interest that all individuals have in the actions of those around them, she focuses firstly on the fascination that compels people to watch horrific events like hangings and torture just to see how the individuals involved will respond. Her final example, then, asks her readers to consider the supernatural, for "[a]mongst the many trials to which the human mind is subjected, that of holding intercourse, real or imaginary, with the world of spirits: of finding itself alone with a being terrific and awful, whose nature and power are unknown, has been justly considered as one of the most severe."[2] For Baillie, these sublime moments provide some

---

[1] Frederick Burwick, "Joanna Baillie, Matthew Baillie, and the Pathology of the Passions," *Joanna Baillie, Romantic Dramatist*, ed. Thomas C. Crochunis (New York: Routledge, 2004), 48-65.

[2] Baillie, Introductory Discourse, 3.

of the best opportunities to catch the attention of individuals and compel them to observe others dealing with extreme passions, for "every man wishes to see one who believes that he sees [a ghost], in all the agitation and wildness of that species of terror."[1] The Gothic, then, provides a perfect means for Baillie to enact her theories of moral reform by combining the audience's fascination with terror and interest in the workings of the mind.

The Gothic also allows Baillie to explore the tremendous social changes that occurred during her lifetime. One of the most popular theories of the Gothic is that it arose as a response to the rapid political and social changes that occurred at the end of the eighteenth century and the beginning of the nineteenth century, and this is not simply a twentieth century supposition. Several of Baillie's contemporaries remarked on the connection. The Marquis de Sade, for instance, saw the Gothic as "the necessary fruits of the revolutionary tremors felt by the whole of Europe" while William Hazlitt remarked that Gothic works "derived part of their interest, no doubt, from the supposed tottering state of all old structures at the time."[2] While the French Revolution obviously turned writers' minds to a new fluidity of class structure and political frameworks, it also provoked new ideas about gender roles as Mary Wollstonecraft expresses in *A Vindication of the Rights of Woman*. All the "old structures" of society were suddenly open for debate. The early nineteenth century, then, was a time of great possibility, but it was also a time of concern as individuals began to wonder how these changes might affect their society. These anxieties are mirrored in the structure of the Gothic, which repeatedly returns to issues of freedom and imprisonment, the abuse of power, the repression of evil deeds, and the desire to transcend the sins of the past. For Baillie, this aspect of the Gothic is just as pertinent as the previous ones, for her plays repeatedly use Gothic images to explore the anxieties that arise as individuals attempt to create roles for themselves in worlds with fluid class structures, changing definitions of masculinity and femininity, shifting political alliances, and evolving ideas of Christianity.

---

[1] Baillie, Introductory Discourse, 3.

[2] Qtd. in Robert Miles, "The 1790s: the Effulgence of Gothic," *The Cambridge Companion to Gothic Fiction*, ed. Jerrold E. Hogle (New York: Cambridge University Press, 2002), 43.

Plays on the Passions

De Monfort (1798)

Baillie's best-known play, *De Monfort*, is the final play in the first
volume of her *Plays on the Passions* (1798). It was first produced at the
Drury Lane Theatre in 1800 with John Kemble as De Monfort and
Sarah Siddons as Jane De Monfort, and it was revived at Drury Lane
in 1821 with Edmund Kean in the role of De Monfort. Throughout the
early nineteenth century, productions were also mounted in various
other cities in Britain and in the United States. In fact, in a letter to
Scott in 1810 Baillie remarks that it was even performed "at a county
fair, in a great waggon [*sic*] along side of the wild beasts."[1] In the
Introductory Discourse to the first volume of *Plays on the Passions*,
Baillie remarks that out of the three plays in the volume *De Monfort*
is the one that "will more clearly discover the nature and intention
of [her] design."[2] With this tragedy, Baillie explores the passion of
hatred as it develops in the mind of De Monfort. She recognizes
the problems that are inherent in her project, asking her readers to
remember "that it is the passion and not the man which is held up
to our execration; and that this and every other bad passion does
more strongly evince its pernicious and dangerous nature, when we
see it thus counteracting and destroying the good gifts of Heaven,
than when it is represented as the suitable associate in the breast of
inmates as dark as itself."[3] Baillie hopes that her readers will be able
to condemn the excessive passion but also understand how easy it is
for even good individuals to be overcome by it. Part of this process
involves the use of soliloquy so that the audience may have deeper
access to the secrets of De Monfort's heart than anyone else in the
play. We are able to see him in those moments that he hides from
everyone else, determine how the passion is developing in his mind,
and sympathize with his struggle.

As we progress deeper and deeper into De Monfort's mind,
we notice that the play becomes decidedly more Gothic. While the
first few acts take place in a realistic country inn and a nobleman's

---

[1] Baillie, Letter to Sir Walter Scott: 28 November 1810, *Collected Letters*, 275.

[2] Baillie, Introductory Discourse, 16.

[3] Baillie, Introductory Discourse, 16.

grand home, the setting at the end of the fourth act shifts to "[a] wild path in a wood, shaded with trees," and the setting for the first scene of the final act is "[t]he inside of a convent chapel, of old Gothic architecture, almost dark: two torches only are seen at a distance, burning over a newly covered grave. Lightning is seen flashing through the windows, and thunder heard, with the sound of wind beating upon the building." As De Monfort becomes more and more consumed by his hatred for Rezenvelt, the world becomes darker and more sinister, mirroring the darkness of his mind. Baillie uses the Gothic, then, to highlight the depths to which De Monfort is sinking.

Baillie also uses the Gothic in this play to explore the various social changes that have set the stage for this crisis. As scholars such as Catherine Burroughs, Marjean Purinton, and Daniel Watkins have remarked, De Monfort's problems do not stem simply from his hatred for Rezenvelt but also from his inability to enact a socially correct definition of masculinity in a world that no longer recognizes worth simply through class status.[1] Much of De Monfort's hatred for Rezenvelt stems from the way Rezenvelt has been able to break through class barriers and achieve a prominence equal to De Monfort's. While Rezenvelt is able to act the role of the affable gentleman and enter easily into high society, De Monfort refuses to be a hypocrite and stifle his hatred, alienating himself from his friends and servants. De Monfort remains true to his feelings, but this fidelity causes his downfall as he allows his hatred to consume him. Rezenvelt's enacting of the masculine role and De Monfort's interpretation of it are placed in direct conflict and result in both of their deaths. These versions of masculinity are also placed in conflict with various versions of femininity. Countess Freburg and Jane De Monfort, in particular, represent two different ways for women to enact their own social roles, and while Jane's version is definitely upheld as the better of the two, even her nurturing presence cannot

---

[1] See Catherine Burroughs, *Closet Stages: Joanna Baillie and the Theater Theory of British Romantic Women Writers* (Philadelphia: University of Pennsylvania Press, 1997); Marjean D. Purinton, *Romantic Ideology Unmasked: The Mentally Constructed Tyrannies in Dramas of William Wordsworth, Lord Byron, Percy Shelley, and Joanna Baillie* (Newark, NJ: U of Delaware P, 1994); and Daniel Watkins, *A Materialist Critique of English Romantic Drama* (Gainesville, FL: University Press of Florida, 1993).

keep De Monfort from committing murder. For a society that was gradually beginning to depend more and more on the influence of the domestic woman to maintain moral standards, Jane De Monfort's failure to save her brother is both surprising and disturbing. As the world in the play becomes progressively more Gothic, Baillie reveals the dangers that may threaten a society in the midst of such great transformations.

Orra (1812)

Orra is the first play in the third volume of Baillie's *Plays on the Passions* (1812), and in it Baillie explores the passion of fear, particularly fear of the supernatural. With that subject, we might expect that *Orra* would be even more explicitly Gothic than Baillie's other plays, and we would be correct. When reading *Orra*, we enter into a medieval world of haunted castles, gloomy woods inhabited by robbers, damsels in distress, ghostly apparitions, and descents into madness. *Orra* is unique amongst Baillie's *Plays on the Passions* in that it is one of only a few that has a female protagonist who must learn to control her passions, but Baillie is clear in her preface that women are not the only ones who suffer from fear. In fact, she even writes an additional tragedy on fear, *The Dream*, because she is "unwilling to appropriate this passion in a serious form to [her] own sex entirely."[1] By using a female protagonist in this play, Baillie allows herself to explore in more depth how the power dynamics inherent in the Gothic affect women. In doing so, Baillie also presents her most explicit criticism of the Gothic or at least how certain readers react to the Gothic. Like Catherine Morland in Jane Austen's *Northanger Abbey*, Orra is obsessed with Gothic stories, and, as Baillie reveals, this obsession allows for her downfall. Rather than using these stories to learn to check her excessive passions, Orra uses them to inflame her passions, delighting in the physical sensations of fear that course through her body with every exciting ghost story. Baillie might use the Gothic throughout her plays, but, as she demonstrates through Orra, she expects her audiences to respond to it properly,

---

[1] Baillie, Preface to the Third Volume of *Plays on the Passions. Dramatic and Poetical Works*, (New York: Georg Olms, 1976), 229.

moving beyond the titillation of fear to an understanding that it might actually be used to convey deeper truths.

One of the deeper truths conveyed in *Orra* is the dangerous disempowerment of women in society. While Baillie may condemn Orra's naïve response to Gothic tales, she also reveals that it is not the Gothic stories that ultimately endanger Orra but rather the Gothic world in which she lives. The ghosts in Orra's world may not be real, but the power dynamics that make the Gothic world so sinister permeate her existence. Ultimately, Orra is at the mercy of the various men who control her life. She simply wishes to remain single and control her own household, but she is not allowed this luxury. When Hughobert, her guardian, misuses his power and imprisons her in a supposedly haunted castle because she refuses to marry his son Glottenbal, she has no recourse, nor does she have any protection when Rudigere, another rival for her affection, accompanies her to the castle and uses her fear to attempt to coerce her into a relationship with him. She has to rely on the agency of another man, Theobald, to rescue her, and even that goes horribly wrong. As a woman living in a world where men have all the power, Orra is forced into madness. While Baillie may use her play to critique how audiences often respond to the Gothic, she also acknowledges the truths of unequal power dynamics that often lie beneath the surface of those same Gothic tales.

The Dream (1812)

With *The Dream*, which follows *Orra* in the third volume of *Plays on the Passions* (1812), Baillie creates a second tragedy on the subject of fear, this time with a male protagonist. As in *Orra*, the readers find themselves in a dark, Gothic, medieval world. Most of the action takes place in a gloomy monastery where monks are haunted by disturbing dreams, where an opened tomb reveals a mysterious skeleton, and where a passing knight is chosen by lot to pay penance for an unknown crime. Baillie uses this setting to create the environment in which Osterloo, the chosen knight, will undergo his test of fear. As the play progresses, however, the readers begin to realize that this test will involve far more than just withstanding the Gothic atmosphere of the monastery, for Baillie uses this Gothic world to explore the dangers of rivalry and revenge that are perhaps an even greater plague than the one raging through the village. Like *Orra*, *The Dream* reveals that even when the Gothic exteriors are swept away through explanations, the Gothic core of repressed guilt, uncontrolled anger, and vicious revenge remains.

As readers, we gradually come to realize that the seemingly supernatural events that have led to Osterloo's imprisonment may have been carefully orchestrated so that the prior could enact his revenge upon Osterloo for killing the prior's brother years before. While Osterloo, as a valiant soldier, is ready and willing to withstand any physical torture the monks may devise for his penance, he is not ready to face the reality of the crime he committed so many years before, nor is he ready to face the eternal punishment that is awaiting him after death. These are the fears that haunt him and ultimately cause his death. While the focus of this play is definitely upon Osterloo as he struggles to control his fear, Baillie also widens the scope to consider the type of world that has forced Osterloo into this position. Even though Osterloo committed murder in his rivalry with the prior's brother for the woman they both loved, he is actually presented more sympathetically than the prior, who in his quest for revenge ignores not only the laws of his land but also the tenet of Christian forgiveness for those who are penitent. As the supposed spiritual leader of the monastery, the prior is woefully inadequate, becoming consumed with the secular world's obsession with revenge. Baillie uses the Gothic in this play to reveal the truth of a world in which the secular values of revenge and rivalry have come to replace Christian love and forgiveness.

Miscellaneous Plays

The Family Legend (1810)

Originally conceived in 1805 as an addition to Baillie's second edition of *Miscellaneous Plays*, *The Family Legend* became well known in 1810 when it was produced in Edinburgh with Daniel Terry, Henry Siddons, and Harriet Siddons in the lead roles. Sir Walter Scott was very influential in getting the play produced, not only submitting it to Henry Siddons for his consideration but also guiding it through production. Baillie appreciated Scott's efforts, remarking, "I cannot express to you how much I am gratified & obliged by the warm-hearted, Brotherly interest you take in the success of my Family Legend."[1] After her frustrations with the lukewarm reception the production of *De Monfort* received, she was probably relieved to have a good friend watching over the play in her absence. When the reviews came in, she was even more relieved, for the play was a success. Because the play deals with Scottish themes, Baillie seems particularly pleased that it did well in her homeland. Replying to a letter from Scott detailing the play's successful debut, Baillie responds, "You have indeed sent me a loud & hearty cheer from my native land, and I feel it at my heart sensibly & dearly. The applause of the most brilliant London Theatre I could not so feel."[2] With *The Family Legend*, Baillie uses the Gothic in a new way to explore her own country's heritage, and much of the scholarly criticism on the play has revolved around how she presents that heritage. By representing a past where violence is in the process of destroying the way of life that the Scots hold dear, is Baillie making a conservative move that justifies England's control over Scotland, or is she using her homeland to represent a more universal danger represented by the unrestrained violence of the masculine sphere?

Throughout the play, the Gothic is used to highlight the flaws of the masculine sphere that may very well destroy this nation. Members of the Maclean clan not only gather in a dark, Gothic cave as they plot to destroy their chief's virtuous wife, but they also invoke seers' visions of strange lights to convince Maclean to turn his wife over to them. For Maclean, the Gothic visions become a good excuse to hide his cowardice as he chooses his clan over his wife. While Helen's only "crime" is being a Campbell rather than a Maclean, her virtue cannot withstand the clan loyalty and the violence that the clan members use to preserve it. As in so many Gothic tales, she becomes the innocent victim of a patriarchal society in which women are used simply as pawns between men. While the early Gothic images may seem harmless enough (for dark caves and strange lights certainly cannot hurt anyone), the image of Helen perched on a rock waiting helplessly for the tide to come and

---

[1] Baillie, Letter to Sir Walter Scott: 21 October 1809, *Collected Letters*, 245.
[2] Baillie, Letter to Sir Walter Scott: 4 February 1810, *Collected Letters*, 250.

drown her demonstrates that, for the women caught up in it, the dangers of the Gothic world go far beyond signs and wonders.

Even when Helen is rescued and returned to her father's house, she still remains a pawn in this deadly game as her father veils her and uses the moment of her unveiling to reveal Maclean's guilt and to begin again the cycle of clan violence that Helen's marriage to Maclean was meant to avert. Helen may be virtuous, but her virtue is not enough to protect either her or this nation. Ultimately, the only hope in this play comes from Sir Hubert De Grey, who is the only man to repudiate senseless violence, placing the care of Helen and her child above the desire for revenge. As in *Orra*, Baillie uses the Gothic to reveal the dangerous violence that lurks below the façade of civility in society, but with *The Family Legend* Baillie takes the story one step further, showing how it endangers not only powerless women but also entire nations.

The Phantom (1836)

The Phantom, published in the second volume of Baillie's *Dramas* (1836), is a musical drama set in Scotland. While known primarily as a playwright, Baillie also wrote many lyrics, which appeared in George Thomson's collections of Scottish, Welsh, and Irish songs, and she placed songs throughout several of her plays. While *The Phantom* begins with joyous singing at a highland wedding, however, the play soon becomes more sinister when the ghost of Emma Graham appears. Interestingly, Baillie's use of the ghost in the play is different from her use of the supernatural in her other plays. In each of her other Gothic plays, the audience may deduce explanations for the supernatural events even if the characters do not. In *The Phantom*, however, Emma Graham's appearance as a ghost cannot be explained away. It is truly a supernatural occurrence.

On the surface, Emma's ghost does not appear to be very threatening. Emma has previously been described as the perfect example of kind and gracious femininity, and the ghost does nothing to disprove this, simply asking Alice to travel to Glasgow, find a paper that has been hidden in Emma's room, and read it. Despite her non-threatening appearance, however, Emma is still a phantom, and even a "blessed spirit" carries with it the tradition of many unholy apparitions. Emma's ghost may not be as horrific as Matthew Lewis's Bleeding Nun, one of her literary ancestors, but she does share some dangerous similarities with her. Just as the Bleeding Nun needs Raymond to put her spirit to rest by burying her bones, Emma needs Alice to find the document and read it. Once the paper is read, another similarity is revealed, for like the nun, Emma has had an improper romance. Emma's "crime" is certainly not as monstrous as the Bleeding Nun's, for the nun not only abandons the cloister and lives in debauchery with her lover but also eventually murders him when she transfers her affections to his brother. Emma never acts on her desires; but, ironically, the results are the same, for at the conclusion of the play, we discover that Emma has, in a sense, murdered Basil, her fiancé. By the end of the play, we realize that this woman, who has been described by everyone as a perfect domestic angel, has unwittingly brought confusion, despair and death to the people who love her. By combining the image of the domestic angel with the Gothic symbol of the phantom, Baillie, living in a world where the domestic woman was increasingly seen as the moral center of society, questions whether this figure actually has the power to transform her world for the better.

Through her use of the ghost, Baillie also highlights the political and religious tensions that were rampant both in Scotland and in the rest of Britain in the early nineteenth century. From the beginning of the play, Baillie emphasizes the division between Highlanders and Lowlanders, divisions that, historically, were enhanced by the general sense of fear many English and Lowlanders had of Highlanders after the battle of Culloden, by the political differences between the Jacobites and those who were loyal to the crown, by the religious differences between the Catholics and Protestants, and by the economic differences that allowed many Lowlanders to flourish while many Highlanders could barely eke out an existence. By leading Alice to the document that declares Emma's secret engagement to Basil Gordon, Emma's ghost is the catalyst that brings all of these issues to the forefront.

Emma's doomed engagement is not simply an example of a daughter subverting the power of her father; instead, it symbolizes the dangers of the controversies that are tearing Scotland apart. The fact that Basil's surname is Gordon implies that he is from a Highland

clan: a clan that had contributed a large contingent of men to fight
for the Jacobite cause at Culloden. His Catholicism connects him
not only to the Jacobites but also more generally to the anti-Catholic
sentiments of many in Britain in the early nineteenth century, which
tended to flare up any time Britain was at war with a Catholic nation.
Baillie highlights these prejudices between Protestants and Catholics
by having the crowd watching Emma's funeral procession speculate
about her relationship with Basil. While they acknowledge that Basil
has been "brave and soldierly" in the foreign wars (as were many
Highlanders who proudly served in the Highland regiments), they
still call him a "rank Romanist" and compare Emma's friendship with
him to sitting next to Satan. Basil symbolizes all that these Lowland
Protestants have learned to hate. While the Gothic is often used to
demonstrate the dangers of Catholicism (Baillie, herself, presents
this view in *Ethwald* and *The Dream*), here it demonstrates the need
for tolerance. It also reveals the conflicts in Scotland and in the rest
of Britain that will need more than the power of a domestic angel to
resolve them.

Witchcraft (1836)

Witchcraft was published in the third volume of Baillie's *Dramas*
(1836), and like *The Family Legend* and *The Phantom*, it takes place
in Scotland. The play was inspired by a scene from Scott's *Bride of
Lammermuir* in which old, poverty-stricken women wonder why the
Devil has never approached them and tempted them to serve him.
After failing to convince Scott to tackle the subject in more depth,
Baillie decided to write the work herself, desiring to explore how
poor, powerless women might actually believe themselves to be
in the service of Satan. Apparently, the process of writing the play
was not a smooth one, for in a letter to William Sotheby in 1825,
she declares, "…my matter of witchcraft having gone on slowly &
vilely, no speed or progress to signify, my broom stick being a very
broom-stick fit to be set behind the door instead of careering it to
the clouds."[1] Some of Baillie's struggles with the play might have
derived from the fact that it is very different from her other plays.
This one is not only written in prose, but it also makes extensive

---

[1] Baillie, Letter to William Sotheby: 5 November 1825, *Collected Letters*, 213.

use of Scottish dialect with several of the major characters being lower-class countrywomen. In her use of the Gothic, though, Baillie continues to explore many of the themes that we have seen expressed in her previous Gothic plays, particularly demonstrating the powerlessness of women in a patriarchal society.

For many of the women in this play, witchcraft is a temptation, for it will supposedly grant them the power that they lack in their society. For the lower-class women, a pact with Satan would not only provide them with sustenance but also allow them to torture their more well to do neighbors who have scorned them. For Annabella, witchcraft would allow her to triumph over her romantic rival. While all of these women attempt to use witchcraft in various ways to gain power, Baillie reveals that its dangers lie not in the supposed communication with the Devil but rather in the patriarchal society that denies them any power and then corrupts and destroys them when they attempt to empower themselves. Ironically, in their attempts to achieve power, these women can only strike at others who are only slightly better off than they are; they cannot affect any real change in the power structure. Indeed, their actions actually end up victimizing other women.

Violet becomes the symbol of this victimization, for the accusation of witchcraft against her comes not only from Annabella planting evidence against her but also from her appearance with the supposed ghost of her father on the moor where Mary Macmurren, Elspy Low, and Grizeld Bane have apparently contacted Satan. While the end of the play is not as bloody as it could have been since Violet and Mary escape being hanged as witches, it is still a disturbing conclusion to the story, for these women survive only through the actions of various men: actions, which (while generally honorable) are often dependent upon random coincidences. These women have no power to save themselves but must wait for the loving father, loyal male servant, or earnest male legislator to save them. Yes, the crime of witchcraft has been revoked at the end of the play, but the social dynamics that made it such an appealing option for some women remain. Through her use of the Gothic in this play, Baillie reveals that while individuals may fear visitation by witches, ghostly apparitions, and supernatural storms, the real dangers may actually lie in the mundane world of economics and politics.

Conclusion

While the evidence suggests that Baillie continually drew upon the Gothic for her inspiration, many of her contemporaries would have cringed at the idea of linking Baillie with the Gothic. Most serious writers of the time worked diligently to distance their works from the supposed excesses of Gothic literature. In fact, as we have already seen, some of Baillie's reviewers actually saw her type of drama as an antidote to the popular plays of the day, which were very often Gothic plays. Baillie was expected to return British drama to the weighty seriousness of Shakespeare, not to embrace the ridiculous spectacle of ghosts and corpses. Leaving aside the question of whether Shakespeare was perhaps more Gothic than the reviewers would like to acknowledge (for he did make occasional use of both ghosts and corpses), we are left with the question of whether Baillie's plays are Gothic (as many scholars today read them) or an antidote to the Gothic (as many of her contemporaries read them).

In his discussion of Baillie's Gothic plays, Michael Gamer posits that Baillie's treatment of the Gothic is complex, for while she uses it to appeal to her audiences, she does not want them simply to focus on the spectacle. Instead, she attempts to "[transform the supernatural] into a tool for audience reform and edification."[1] Baillie, on the one hand, embraces the Gothic as a way of directing her audience's attention to the passions and the struggles of her characters, but, on the other hand, she also moves beyond simple Gothic effects and encourages her audience to do so as well. In addition, as Baillie attempts to convey her moral project, she repeatedly varies how she utilizes the Gothic. Sometimes, the Gothic becomes a manifestation of the deterioration of a character's mind or an exploration of the tensions that arise as a result of political, economic, and social change. At other times, it represents the supernatural realm as a warning against evil deeds or even as a temptation to evil that the characters must learn to avoid. Baillie even uses the Gothic to reveal the dangers of being too intrigued by the Gothic. In each play, the Gothic takes on new roles as Baillie experiments with the power

---

[1] Michael Gamer, "National Supernaturalism: Joanna Baillie, Germany, and the Gothic Drama," *Theatre Survey* 38.2 (1997): 82.

the Gothic has to capture her audience and highlight her themes. By exploring Baillie's experimentation, then, we can begin to see the value of the Gothic in ways that her reviewers did not even imagine.

CHRISTINE A. COLÓN
Wheaton, Illinois
July 5, 2006

CHRISTINE A. COLÓN is Assistant Professor of English at Wheaton College in Wheaton, Illinois, where she teaches courses on women writers, Victorian literature, and British drama. She is the author of articles and book chapters on Anne Brontë, Jane Austen, Christina Rossetti, and Joanna Baillie.

NOTE ON THE TEXTS

THE texts used in the present edition are taken from the 1851 edition of *The Dramatic and Poetical Works of Joanna Baillie* published at London by Longman, Brown, Green, and Longmans. This was the final edition overseen by Baillie, and published the same year as her death. Baillie made a number of revisions to some of her plays over the years, some of which she indicates in footnotes in this edition. Many of the changes are minor, such as changes in punctuation and capitalization, although she occasionally revises entire scenes.

Four of the plays collected in this volume have not appeared in new editions since 1851; the principal goal of this edition, therefore, is to make these texts available to students and readers in an accessible, affordable edition. As this edition does not seek to serve as an "authoritative" edition of the texts, textual variants among the different editions are not noted here. Those interested in comparing the various editions are advised to consult the facsimile reprints issued by Garland Publishing in 1976-77 and Georg Olms Verlag in 1976, all of which are readily obtainable at most major research libraries.

DE MONFORT:

A TRAGEDY.

PERSONS OF THE DRAMA.

MEN.

DE MONFORT.
REZENVELT.
COUNT FREBERG, *friend to* DE MONFORT *and* REZENVELT.
MANUEL, *servant to* DE MONFORT.
JEROME, DE MONFORT'S *old landlord.*
CONRAD, *an artful knave.*
BERNARD, *a monk.*
    Monks, gentlemen, officers, page, *&c. &c.*

WOMEN.

JANE DE MONFORT, *sister to* DE MONFORT.
COUNTESS FREBERG, *wife to* FREBERG.
THERESA, *servant to the* COUNTESS.
    Abbess, nuns, and a lay sister, ladies, *&c.*

Scene, a town in Germany.

ACT I.

SCENE I.

Jerome's house. A large old-fashioned chamber.

Jer. (speaking without). This way, good masters.

Enter Jerome, *bearing a light, and followed by* Manuel, *and servants carrying luggage.*

      Rest your burthens here.
This spacious room will please the marquis best.
He takes me unawares; but ill prepar'd:
If he had sent, e'en though a hasty notice,
I had been glad.
Man.   Be not disturb'd, good Jerome;
Thy house is in most admirable order;
And they who travel o' cold winter nights
Think homeliest quarters good.
Jer. He is not far behind?
Man.   A little way.
  (To the servants.) Go you and wait below till he arrive.
Jer. (shaking Manuel *by the hand).*
  Indeed, my friend, I'm glad to see you here;
  Yet marvel wherefore.
Man. I marvel wherefore too, my honest Jerome:
  But here we are; pri'thee be kind to us.
Jer. Most heartily I will. I love your master:
  He is a quiet and a lib'ral man:
  A better inmate never cross'd my door.
Man. Ah! but he is not now the man he was.
  Lib'ral he'll be. God grant he may be quiet.
Jer. What has befallen him?
Man.   I cannot tell thee;
  But, faith, there is no living with him now.
Jer. And yet, methinks, if I remember well
  You were about to quit his service, Manuel,
  When last he left this house. You grumbled then.

Man. I've been upon the eve of leaving him
    These ten long years; for many times he is
    So difficult, capricious, and distrustful,
    He galls my nature—yet, I know not how,
    A secret kindness binds me to him still.
Jer. Some who offend from a suspicious nature,
    Will afterwards such fair confession make
    As turns e'en the offence into a favour.
Man. Yes, some indeed do so; so will not he:
    He'd rather die than such confession make.
Jer. Ay, thou art right; for now I call to mind
    That once he wrong'd me with unjust suspicion,
    When first he came to lodge beneath my roof;
    And when it so fell out that I was prov'd
    Most guiltless of the fault, I truly thought
    He would have made profession of regret.
    But silent, haughty, and ungraciously
    He bore himself as one offended still.
    Yet shortly after, when unwittingly
    I did him some slight service, o' the sudden
    He overpower'd me with his grateful thanks;
    And would not be restrain'd from pressing on me
    A noble recompense. I understood
    His o'erstrain'd gratitude and bounty well,
    And took it as he meant.
Man.   'Tis often thus.
    I would have left him many years ago,
    But that with all his faults there sometimes come
    Such bursts of natural goodness from his heart,
    As might engage a harder churl than I
    To serve him still.—And then his sister too;
    A noble dame, who should have been a queen:
    The meanest of her hinds, at her command,
    Had fought like lions for her, and the poor,
    E'en o'er their bread of poverty, had bless'd her—
    She would have griev'd if I had left my lord.
Jer. Comes she along with him?

Man. No, he departed all unknown to her,
    Meaning to keep conceal'd his secret route;
    But well I knew it would afflict her much,
    And therefore left a little nameless billet,
    Which after our departure, as I guess,
    Would fall into her hands, and tell her all.
    What could I do! O 'tis a noble lady!
Jer. All this is strange—something disturbs his mind—
    Belike he is in love.
Man.   No, Jerome, no.
    Once on a time I serv'd a noble master,
    Whose youth was blasted with untoward love,
    And he, with hope and fear and jealousy
    For ever toss'd, led an unquiet life:
    Yet, when unruffled by the passing fit,
    His pale wan face such gentle sadness wore
    As mov'd a kindly heart to pity him.
    But Monfort, even in his calmest hour,
    Still bears that gloomy sternness in his eye
    Which powerfully repels all sympathy.
    O no! good Jerome, no, it is not love.
Jer. Hear I not horses trampling at the gate?

                                       [Listening.

    He is arrived—stay thou—I had forgot—
    A plague upon't! my head is so confus'd—
    I will return i' the instant to receive him.

                                      [Exit hastily.

       [A great bustle without. Exit MANUEL *with lights, and
       returns again, lighting in* DE MONFORT, *as if just alighted
       from his journey.*
Man. Your ancient host, my lord, receives you gladly,
    And your apartment will be soon prepar'd.
De Mon. 'Tis well.
Man. Where shall I place the chest you gave in charge?
    So please you, say, my lord.
De Mon. (*throwing himself into a chair*). Wheree'er thou wilt.
Man. I would not move that luggage till you came.

                             [Pointing to certain things.

De Mon. Move what thou wilt, and trouble me no more.

> [MANUEL, *with the assistance of other servants, sets about
> putting the things in order, and* DE MONFORT *remains
> sitting in a thoughtful posture.*

Enter JEROME, *bearing wine, &c. on a salver. As he approaches* DE
MONFORT, MANUEL *pulls him by the sleeve.*

Man. (*aside to* JEROME). No, do not now; he will not be disturb'd.

Jer. What! not to bid him welcome to my house,
    And offer some refreshment?

Man.   No, good Jerome.
    Softly a little while: I pri'thee do.

> [JEROME *walks softly on tiptoe, till he gets behind* DE
> MONFORT, *then peeping on one side to see his face.*

Jer. (*aside to* MANUEL). Ah, Manuel, what an alter'd man is here!
    His eyes are hollow, and his cheeks are pale—
    He left this house a comely gentleman.

De Mon. Who whispers there?

Man.   'Tis your old landlord, sir.

Jer. I joy to see you here—I crave your pardon—
    I fear I do intrude—

De Mon. No, my kind host, I am obliged to thee.

Jer. How fares it with your honour?

De Mon. Well enough.

Jer. Here is a little of the fav'rite wine
    That you were wont to praise. Pray honour me.

                                   [*Fills a glass.*

De Mon. (*after drinking*). I thank you, Jerome, 'tis delicious.

Jer. Ay, my dear wife did ever make it so.

De Mon. And how does she?

Jer.   Alas, my lord! she's dead.

De Mon. Well, then she is at rest.

Jer.   How well, my lord?

De Mon. Is she not with the dead, the quiet dead,
    Where all is peace? Not e'en the impious wretch,
    Who tears the coffin from its earthy vault,

And strews the mould'ring ashes to the wind,
Can break their rest.

Jer. Woe's me! I thought you would have griev'd for her.
She was a kindly soul! Before she died,
When pining sickness bent her cheerless head,
She set my house in order—
And but the morning ere she breath'd her last,
Bade me preserve some flaskets of this wine,
That should the Lord de Monfort come again
His cup might sparkle still.

[DE MONFORT *walks across the stage, and wipes his eyes.*
Indeed I fear I have distress'd you, sir;
I surely thought you would be griev'd for her.

De Mon. (*taking* JEROME's *hand*). I am, my friend. How long has she
been dead?

Jer. Two sad long years.

De Mon.   Would she were living still!
I was too troublesome, too heedless of her.

Jer. O no! she lov'd to serve you.

[*Loud knocking without.*

De Mon. What fool comes here, at such untimely hours,
To make this cursed noise? (*To* MANUEL.) Go to the gate.

[*Exit* MANUEL.

All sober citizens are gone to bed;
It is some drunkards on their nightly rounds,
Who mean it but in sport.

Jer. I hear unusual voices—here they come.

Re-enter MANUEL, *showing in* COUNT FREBERG *and his lady,*
with a mask in her hand.

Freb. (*running to embrace* DE MON.)
My dearest Monfort! most unlook'd for pleasure!
Do I indeed embrace thee here again?
I saw thy servant standing by the gate,
His face recall'd, and learnt the joyful tidings!
Welcome, thrice welcome here!

De Mon. I thank thee, Freberg, for this friendly visit,
    And this fair lady too.

                        [Bowing to the lady.

Lady.   I fear, my lord,
    We do intrude at an untimely hour:
    But now, returning from a midnight mask,
    My husband did insist that we should enter.
Freb. No, say not so; no hour untimely call,
    Which doth together bring long absent friends.
    Dear Monfort, why hast thou so slily play'd,
    Coming upon us thus so suddenly?
De Mon. O! many varied thoughts do cross our brain,
    Which touch the will, but leave the memory trackless;
    And yet a strange compounded motive make,
    Wherefore a man should bend his evening walk
    To th' east or west, the forest or the field.
    Is it not often so?
Freb. I ask no more, happy to see you here
    From any motive. There is one behind,
    Whose presence would have been a double bliss:
    Ah! how is she? The noble Jane De Monfort.
De Mon. (*confused*). She is—I have—I left my sister well.
Lady. (*to* FREBERG). My Freberg, you are heedless of respect.
    You surely mean to say the Lady Jane.
Freb. Respect! No, madam; Princess, Empress, Queen,
    Could not denote a creature so exalted
    As this plain appellation doth,
    The noble Jane De Monfort.
Lady. (*turning from him displeased to* DE MON.)
    You are fatigued, my lord; you want repose;
    Say, should we not retire?
Freb.   Ha! is it so?
    My friend, your face is pale; have you been ill?
De Mon. No, Freberg, no; I think I have been well.
Freb. (*shaking his head*). I fear thou hast not, Monfort—Let it pass.
    We'll re-establish thee: we'll banish pain.
    I will collect some rare, some cheerful friends,
    And we shall spend together glorious hours,

That gods might envy. Little time so spent
Doth far outvalue all our life beside.
This is indeed our life, our waking life,
The rest dull breathing sleep.

De Mon. Thus, it is true, from the sad years of life
We sometimes do short hours, yea minutes strike,
Keen, blissful, bright, never to be forgotten;
Which, through the dreary gloom of time o'erpast,
Shine like fair sunny spots on a wild waste.
But few they are, as few the heaven-fir'd souls
Whose magic power creates them. Bless'd art thou,
If, in the ample circle of thy friends,
Thou canst but boast a few.

Freb. Judge for thyself: in truth I do not boast.
There is amongst my friends, my later friends,
A most accomplish'd stranger: new to Amberg;
But just arriv'd, and will ere long depart:
I met him in Franconia two years since.
He is so full of pleasant anecdote,
So rich, so gay, so poignant is his wit,
Time vanishes before him as he speaks,
And ruddy morning through the lattice peeps
Ere night seems well begun.

De Mon.   How is he call'd?

Freb. I will surprise thee with a welcome face:
I will not tell thee now.

Lady. (*to* De Mon.) I have, my lord, a small request to make,
And must not be denied. I too may boast
Of some good friends, and beauteous country-women:
To-morrow night I open wide my doors
To all the fair and gay: beneath my roof
Music, and dance, and revelry shall reign:
I pray you come and grace it with your presence.

De Mon. You honour me too much to be denied.

Lady. I thank you, sir; and in return for this,
We shall withdraw, and leave you to repose.

Freb. Must it be so? Good night—sweet sleep to thee! (*to* De
Monfort.)

De Mon. (*to* FREB.) Good night. (*To lady.*)

       Good night, fair lady.

Lady.   Farewell!

       [*Exeunt* FREBERG *and lady.*

De Mon. (*to* JER.) I thought Count Freberg had been now in France.

Jer. He meant to go, as I have been inform'd.

De Mon. Well, well, prepare my bed; I will to rest.

          [*Exit* JEROME.

De Mon. (*aside*). I know not how it is, my heart stands back,
 And meets not this man's love.—Friends! rarest friends!
 Rather than share his undiscerning praise
 With every table-wit, and book-form'd sage,
 And paltry poet puling to the moon,
 I'd court from him proscription, yea abuse,
 And think it proud distinction.

           [*Exit.*

SCENE II.

A small apartment in JEROME'*s house: a table and breakfast set out. Enter* DE MONFORT, *followed by* MANUEL, *and sits down by the table, with a cheerful face.*

De Mon. Manuel, this morning's sun shines pleasantly:
 These old apartments too are light and cheerful.
 Our landlord's kindness has reviv'd me much:
 He serves as though he lov'd me. This pure air
 Braces the listless nerves, and warms the blood:
 I feel in freedom here.

     [*Filling a cup of coffee, and drinking.*

Man.   Ah! sure, my lord,
 No air is purer than the air at home.

De Mon. Here can I wander with assured steps,
 Nor dread, at every winding of the path,
 Lest an abhorred serpent cross my way,
 To move—(*stopping short.*)

Man. What says your honour?
There are no serpents in our pleasant fields.
De Mon. Thinkst thou there are no serpents in the world,
But those who slide along the grassy sod,
And sting the luckless foot that presses them?
There are who in the path of social life
Do bask their spotted skins in Fortune's sun,
And sting the soul—Ay, till its healthful frame
Is chang'd to secret, fest'ring, sore disease,
So deadly is the wound.
Man. Heav'n guard your honour from such horrid scath!
They are but rare, I hope!
De Mon. (*shaking his head*).
We mark the hollow eye, the wasted frame,
The gait disturb'd of wealthy honour'd men,
But do not know the cause.
Man. 'Tis very true. God keep you well, my lord!
De Mon. I thank thee, Manuel, I am very well.
I shall be gay too, by the setting sun.
I go to revel it with sprightly dames,
And drive the night away.

[*Filling another cup, and drinking.*

Man. I should be glad to see your honour gay.
De Mon. And thou too shalt be gay. There, honest Manuel,
Put these broad pieces in thy leathern purse,
And take at night a cheerful jovial glass.
Here is one too, for Bremer; he loves wine:
And one for Jaques: be joyful altogether.

Enter Servant.

Ser. My lord, I met e'en now, a short way off,
Your countryman the Marquis Rezenvelt.
De Mon. (*starting from his seat, and letting the cup fall from his hand*).
Whom sayst thou?
Ser. Marquis Rezenvelt, an' please you.
De Mon. Thou liest—it is not so—it is impossible!
Ser. I saw him with these eyes, plain as yourself.

De Mon. Fool! 'tis some passing stranger thou hast seen,
  And with a hideous likeness been deceiv'd.
Ser. No other stranger could deceive my sight.
De Mon. (*dashing his clenched hand violently upon the table, and
  overturning every thing*).
  Heaven blast thy sight! it lights on nothing good.
Ser. I surely thought no harm to look upon him.
De Mon. What, dost thou still insist? He must it be?
  Does it so please thee well?
  (*Servant endeavours to speak.*) Hold thy damn'd tongue!
  By heaven I'll kill thee! (*Going furiously up to him.*)
Man. (*in a soothing voice*).
  Nay, harm him not, my lord; he speaks the truth;
  I've met his groom, who told me certainly
  His lord is here. I should have told you so,
  But thought, perhaps, it might displease your honour.
De Mon. (*becoming all at once calm, and turning sternly to* MANUEL.)
  And how dar'st thou
  To think it would displease me?
  What is't to me who leaves or enters Amberg?
  But it displeases me, yea e'en to frenzy,
  That every idle fool must hither come,
  To break my leisure with the paltry tidings
  Of all the cursed things he stares upon.
      [*Servant attempts to speak*—DE MONFORT *stamps with his foot.*
  Take thine ill-favour'd visage from my sight,
  And speak of it no more.
                                          [*Exit Servant.*
  And go thou too; I choose to be alone.
                                          [*Exit* MANUEL.
      [DE MONFORT *goes to the door by which they went out;
      opens it, and looks.*
  But is he gone indeed? Yes, he is gone.
      [*Goes to the opposite door, opens it, and looks: then gives
      loose to all the fury of gesture, and walks up and down in
      great agitation.*
  It is too much: by heaven it is too much!
  He haunts me—stings me—like a devil haunts—

He'll make a raving maniac of me—Villain!
The air wherein thou drawst thy fulsome breath
Is poison to me—Oceans shall divide us! (*Pauses.*)
But no; thou thinkst I fear thee, cursed reptile;
And hast a pleasure in the damned thought.
Though my heart's blood should curdle at thy sight,
I'll stay and face thee still.

> [*Knocking at the chamber door.*
Ha! who knocks there?

Freberg. (*without*). It is thy friend, De Monfort.
De Mon. (*opening the door*). Enter, then.

Enter FREBERG.

Freb. (*taking his hand kindly*).
How art thou now? How hast thou pass'd the night?
Has kindly sleep refresh'd thee?
De Mon. Yes, I have lost an hour or two in sleep,
And so should be refresh'd.
Freb.   And art thou not?
Thy looks speak not of rest. Thou art disturb'd.
De Mon. No, somewhat ruffled from a foolish cause,
Which soon will pass away.
Freb. (*shaking his head*). Ah no, De Monfort! something in thy face
Tells me another tale. Then wrong me not:
If any secret grief distract thy soul,
Here am I all devoted to thy love:
Open thy heart to me. What troubles thee?
De Mon. I have no grief: distress me not, my friend.
Freb. Nay, do not call me so. Wert thou my friend,
Wouldst thou not open all thine inmost soul,
And bid me share its every consciousness?
De Mon. Freberg, thou knowst not man; not nature's man,
But only him who, in smooth studied works
Of polish'd sages, shines deceitfully
In all the splendid foppery of virtue.
That man was never born whose secret soul,
With all its motley treasure of dark thoughts,

Foul fantasies, vain musings, and wild dreams,
Was ever open'd to another's scan.
Away, away! it is delusion all.

Freb. Well, be reserved then; perhaps I'm wrong.

De Mon. How goes the hour?

Freb. 'Tis early still; a long day lies before us;
Let us enjoy it. Come along with me;
I'll introduce you to my pleasant friend.

De Mon. Your pleasant friend?

Freb.   Yes, him of whom I spake.

[*Taking his hand.*

There is no good I would not share with thee;
And this man's company, to minds like thine,
Is the best banquet feast I could bestow.
But I will speak in mystery no more;
It is thy townsman, noble Rezenvelt.

[De Mon. *pulls his hand hastily from* Freberg, *and shrinks back.*

Ha! what is this?
Art thou pain-stricken, Monfort?
Nay, on my life, thou rather seemst offended:
Does it displease thee that I call him friend?

De Mon. No, all men are thy friends.

Freb. No, say not all men. But thou art offended.
I see it well. I thought to do thee pleasure.
But if his presence be not welcome here,
He shall not join our company to-day.

De Mon. What dost thou mean to say? What is't to me
Whether I meet with such a thing as Rezenvelt
To-day, to-morrow, every day, or never?

Freb. In truth, I thought you had been well with him;
He prais'd you much.

De Mon. I thank him for his praise—Come, let us move:
This chamber is confin'd and airless grown.

[*Starting.*

I hear a stranger's voice!

Freb.   'Tis Rezenvelt.
Let him be told that we are gone abroad.

De Mon. (*proudly*). No! let him enter. Who waits there? Ho! Manuel!

Enter MANUEL.

What stranger speaks below?
Man.   The Marquis Rezenvelt.
I have not told him that you are within.
De Mon. (angrily). And wherefore didst thou not? Let him ascend.
                 [*A long pause.* DE MONFORT *walking up and down with a
                 quick pace.*

Enter REZENVELT, *who runs freely up to* DE MONFORT.

Rez. (to DE MON.) My noble marquis, welcome!
De Mon.   Sir, I thank you.
Rez. (to FREB.) My gentle friend, well met. Abroad so early?
Freb. It is indeed an early hour for me.
How sits thy last night's revel on thy spirits?
Rez. O, light as ever. On my way to you,
E'en now, I learnt De Monfort was arriv'd,
And turn'd my steps aside; so here I am.
                               [*Bowing gaily to* DE MONFORT.
De Mon. (proudly.) I thank you, sir; you do me too much honour.
Rez. Nay, say not so; not too much honour surely,
Unless, indeed, 'tis more than pleases you.
De Mon. (confused). Having no previous notice of your coming,
I look'd not for it.
Rez. Ay, true indeed; when I approach you next,
I'll send a herald to proclaim my coming,
And bow to you by sound of trumpet, marquis.
De Mon. (to FREB., *turning haughtily from* REZENVELT *with affected
indifference).* How does your cheerful friend, that good old
man?
Freb. My cheerful friend? I know not whom you mean.
De Mon. Count Waterlan.
Freb.   I know not one so nam'd.
De Mon. (very confused). O pardon me—it was at Basle I knew him.
Freb. You have not yet inquir'd for honest Reisdale.
I met him as I came, and mention'd you.
He seem'd amaz'd; and fain he would have learnt

What cause procur'd us so much happiness.
He question'd hard, and hardly would believe;
I could not satisfy his strong desire.
Rez. And know you not what brings De Monfort here?
Freb. Truly I do not.
Rez.   O! 'tis love of me.
I have but two short days in Amberg been,
And here with postman's speed he follows me,
Finding his home so dull and tiresome grown.
Freb. (*to* DE MON.) Is Rezenvelt so sadly miss'd with you?
Your town so chang'd?
De Mon.   Not altogether so;
Some witlings and jest-mongers still remain
For fools to laugh at.
Rez. But he laughs not, and therefore he is wise.
He ever frowns on them with sullen brow
Contemptuous; therefore he is very wise;
Nay, daily frets his most refined soul
With their poor folly to its inmost core;
Therefore he is most eminently wise.
Freb. Fy, Rezenvelt! you are too early gay.
Such spirits rise but with the ev'ning glass:
They suit not placid morn.
        [*To* DE MONFORT, *who, after walking impatiently up and
        down, comes close to his ear and lays hold of his arm.*
                         What would you Monfort?
De Mon. Nothing—what is't o'clock?
No, no—I had forgot—'tis early still.
                         [*Turns away again.*
Freb. (*to* REZ.) Waltser informs me that you have agreed
To read his verses o'er, and tell the truth.
It is a dangerous task.
Rez.   Yet I'll be honest:
I can but lose his favour and a feast.
        [*Whilst they speak,* DE MONFORT *walks up and down
        impatiently and irresolute: at last pulls the bell violently.*

Enter Servant.

De Mon. (*to ser.*) What dost thou want?

Ser. I thought your honour rung.

De Mon. I have forgot—stay. Are my horses saddled?

Ser. I thought, my lord, you would not ride to-day,
   After so long a journey.

De Mon. (*impatiently*). Well—'tis good.
   Begone!—I want thee not.

[*Exit servant.*

Rez. (*smiling significantly*).
   I humbly crave your pardon, gentle marquis.
   It grieves me that I cannot stay with you,
   And make my visit of a friendly length.
   I trust your goodness will excuse me now;
   Another time I shall be less unkind.
   (*To* FREBERG.) Will you not go with me?

Freb. Excuse me, Monfort, I'll return again.

[*Exeunt* REZENVELT *and* FREBERG.

De Mon. (*alone, tossing his arms distractedly*).
   Hell hath no greater torment for th' accurs'd
   Than this man's presence gives—
   Abhorred fiend! he hath a pleasure too,
   A damned pleasure in the pain he gives!
   Oh! the side glance of that detested eye!
   That conscious smile! that full insulting lip!
   It touches every nerve: it makes me mad.
   What, does it please thee? Dost thou woo my hate?
   Hate shalt thou have! determin'd, deadly hate,
   Which shall awake no smile. Malignant villain!
   The venom of thy mind is rank and devilish,
   And thin the film that hides it.
   Thy hateful visage ever spoke thy worth:
   I loath'd thee when a boy.
   That men should be besotted with him thus!
   And Freberg likewise so bewitched is,
   That like a hireling flatt'rer at his heels
   He meanly paces, off'ring brutish praise.
   O! I could curse him too!

[*Exit.*

ACT II.

SCENE I.

A very splendid apartment in Count Freberg's *house, fancifully decorated. A wide folding-door opened, shows another magnificent room lighted up to receive company. Enter through the folding doors the Count and Countess, richly dressed.*

Freb. (*looking round*). In truth, I like those decorations well:
    They suit those lofty walls. And here, my love,
    The gay profusion of a woman's fancy
    Is well display'd. Noble simplicity
    Becomes us less, on such a night as this,
    Than gaudy show.
Lady. Is it not noble then? (*He shakes his head.*) I thought it so;
    And as I know you love simplicity,
    I did intend it should be simple too.
Freb. Be satisfied, I pray; we want to-night
    A cheerful banquet-house, and not a temple.
    How runs the hour?
Lady. It is not late, but soon we shall be rous'd
    With the loud entry of our frolic guests.

Enter a Page, richly dressed.

Page. Madam, there is a lady in your hall,
    Who begs to be admitted to your presence.
Lady. Is it not one of our invited friends?
Page. No, far unlike to them; it is a stranger.
Lady. How looks her countenance?
Page. So queenly, so commanding, and so noble,
    I shrunk at first in awe; but when she smil'd,
    For so she did to see me thus abash'd,
    Methought I could have compass'd sea and land
    To do her bidding.
Lady.   Is she young or old?

Page. Neither, if right I guess; but she is fair:
    For Time hath laid his hand so gently on her,
    As he too had been aw'd.
Lady.   The foolish stripling!
    She has bewitch'd thee. Is she large in stature?
Page. So stately and so graceful is her form,
    I thought at first her stature was gigantic;
    But on a near approach I found, in truth,
    She scarcely does surpass the middle size.
Lady. What is her garb?
Page. I cannot well describe the fashion of it.
    She is not deck'd in any gallant trim,
    But seems to me clad in the usual weeds
    Of high habitual state; for as she moves
    Wide flows her robe in many a waving fold,
    As I have seen unfurled banners play
    With a soft breeze.
Lady.   Thine eyes deceive thee, boy;
    It is an apparition thou hast seen.
Freb. (*starting from his seat, where he has been sitting during the
conversation between the lady and the page*).
    It is an apparition he has seen,
    Or it is Jane De Monfort.
                            [*Exit, hastily.*
Lady (*displeased*). No; such description surely suits not her.
    Did she inquire for me?
Page. She ask'd to see the lady of Count Freberg.
Lady. Perhaps it is not she—I fear it is—
    Ha! here they come. He has but guess'd too well.

      Enter FREBERG, *leading in* JANE DE MONFORT.

Freb. (*presenting her to lady*).
    Here, madam, welcome a most worthy guest.
Lady. Madam, a thousand welcomes! Pardon me;
    I could not guess who honour'd me so far;
    I should not else have waited coldly here.

Jane. I thank you for this welcome, gentle countess.
    But take those kind excuses back again;
    I am a bold intruder on this hour,
    And am entitled to no ceremony.
    I came in quest of a dear truant friend,
    But Freberg has inform'd me—
    (*To* FREBERG.) And he is well, you say?
Freb. Yes, well, but joyless.
Jane. It is the usual temper of his mind;
    It opens not, but with the thrilling touch
    Of some strong heart-string o' the sudden press'd.
Freb. It may be so, I've known him otherwise:
    He is suspicious grown.
Jane. Not so, Count Freberg; Monfort is too noble.
    Say rather, that he is a man in grief,
    Wearing at times a strange and scowling eye;
    And thou, less generous than beseems a friend,
    Hast thought too hardly of him.
Freb. (*bowing with great respect*). So will I say;
    I'll own nor word nor will, that can offend you.
Lady. De Monfort is engag'd to grace our feast:
    Ere long you'll see him here.
Jane. I thank you truly, but this homely dress
    Suits not the splendour of such scenes as these.
Freb. (*pointing to her dress*). Such artless and majestic elegance,
    So exquisitely just, so nobly simple,
    Will make the gorgeous blush.
Jane (*smiling*). Nay, nay, be more consistent, courteous knight,
    And do not praise a plain and simple guise
    With such profusion of unsimple words.
    I cannot join your company to-night.
Lady. Not stay to see your brother?
Jane. Therefore it is I would not, gentle hostess.
    Here will he find all that can woo the heart
    To joy and sweet forgetfulness of pain;
    The sight of me would wake his feeling mind
    To other thoughts. I am no doating mistress;
    No fond distracted wife, who must forthwith

Rush to his arms and weep. I am his sister:
The eldest daughter of his father's house:
Calm and unwearied is my love for him;
And having found him, patiently I'll wait,
Nor greet him in the hour of social joy,
To dash his mirth with tears.—
The night wears on; permit me to withdraw.

Freb. Nay, do not, do not injure us so far!
Disguise thyself, and join our friendly train.

Jane. You wear not masks to-night.

Lady. We wear not masks, but you may be conceal'd
Behind the double foldings of a veil.

Jane (after pausing to consider). In truth, I feel a little so inclin'd.
Methinks unknown, I e'en might speak to him,
And gently prove the temper of his mind;
But for the means I must become your debtor.

[*To lady.*

Lady. Who waits? (*Enter her woman*). Attend this lady to my wardrobe,
And do what she commands you.

[*Exeunt* JANE *and waiting-woman.*

Freb. (*looking after* JANE, *as she goes out, with admiration*).
Oh! what a soul she bears! See how she steps!
Nought but the native dignity of worth
E'er taught the moving form such noble grace.

Lady. Such lofty mien, and high assumed gait,
I've seen ere now, and men have call'd it pride.

Freb. No, 'faith! thou never didst, but oft indeed
The paltry imitation thou hast seen.
(*Looking at her.*) How hang those trappings on thy motley gown?
They seem like garlands on a May-day queen,
Which hinds have dress'd in sport.

[*Lady turns away displeased.*

Freb. Nay, do not frown; I spoke it but in haste;
For thou art lovely still in every garb.
But see, the guests assemble.

Enter groups of well-dressed people, who pay their compliments to FREBERG
*and his lady; and, followed by her, pass into the inner apartment, where
more company appear assembling, as if by another entry.*

Freb. (who remains on the front of the stage with a friend or two).
    How loud the hum of this gay-meeting crowd!
    'Tis like a bee-swarm in the noonday sun.
    Music will quell the sound. Who waits without?
    Music strike up.
             [*Music, and when it ceases, enter from the inner apartment*
             REZENVELT, *with several gentlemen, all richly dressed.*
Freb. (to those just entered). What, lively gallants, quit the field so soon?
    Are there no beauties in that moving crowd
    To fix your fancy?
Rez. Ay, marry are there! men of ev'ry fancy
    May in that moving crowd some fair one find
    To suit their taste, though whimsical and strange,
    As ever fancy own'd.
    Beauty of every cast and shade is there,
    From the perfection of a faultless form,
    Down to the common, brown, unnoted maid,
    Who looks but pretty in her Sunday gown.
1st gent. There is, indeed, a gay variety.
Rez. And if the liberality of nature
    Suffices not, there's store of grafted charms,
    Blending in one the sweets of many plants,
    So obstinately, strangely opposite,
    As would have well defied all other art
    But female cultivation. Aged youth,
    With borrowed locks, in rosy chaplets bound,
    Clothes her dim eye, parch'd lips, and skinny cheek
    In most unlovely softness:
    And youthful age, with fat round trackless face,
    The downcast look of contemplation deep
    Most pensively assumes.
    Is it not even so? The native prude,
    With forced laugh, and merriment uncouth,
    Plays off the wild coquette's successful charms

With most unskilful pains; and the coquette,
In temporary crust of cold reserve,
Fixes her studied looks upon the ground,
Forbiddingly demure.

Freb. Fy! thou art too severe.

Rez. Say, rather, gentle.
　　I 'faith! the very dwarfs attempt to charm
　　With lofty airs of puny majesty;
　　While potent damsels, of a portly make,
　　Totter like nurslings, and demand the aid
　　Of gentle sympathy.
　　From all those diverse modes of dire assault,
　　He owns a heart of hardest adamant,
　　Who shall escape to-night.

Freb. (*to* DE MON., *who has entered during* REZENVELT'*s speech, and
　　heard the greatest part of it*). Ha, ha, ha, ha!
　　How pleasantly he gives his wit the rein,
　　Yet guides its wild career!

　　　　　　　　　　　　　　　　[DE MON. *is silent.*

Rez. (*smiling archly*). What, think you, Freberg, the same powerful spell
　　Of transformation reigns o'er all to-night?
　　Or that De Monfort is a woman turn'd,—
　　So widely from his native self to swerve,
　　As grace my folly with a smile of his?

De Mon. Nay, think not, Rezenvelt, there is no smile
　　I can bestow on thee. There is a smile,
　　A smile of nature too, which I can spare,
　　And yet, perhaps, thou wilt not thank me for it.

　　　　　　　　　　　　　　　　[*Smiles contemptuously.*

Rez. Not thank thee! It were surely most ungrateful
　　No thanks to pay for nobly giving me
　　What, well we see, has cost thee so much pain.
　　For nature hath her smiles of birth more painful
　　Than bitt'rest execrations.

Freb. These idle words will lead us to disquiet:
　　Forbear, forbear, my friends! Go, Rezenvelt,
　　Accept the challenge of those lovely dames,

Who through the portal come with bolder steps
To claim your notice.

Enter a group of ladies from the other apartment, who walk slowly across the bottom of the stage, and return to it again. Rez. shrugs up his shoulders, as if unwilling to go.

1st gent. (*to* Rez.) Behold in sable veil a lady comes,
    Whose noble air doth challenge fancy's skill
    To suit it with a countenance as goodly.
               [Pointing to Jane De Mon., *who now enters in a thick black veil.*
Rez. Yes, this way lies attraction. (*To* Freb.)
    With permission—

                      [Going up to Jane.

    Fair lady, though within that envious shroud
    Your beauty deigns not to enlighten us,
    We bid you welcome, and our beauties here
    Will welcome you the more for such concealment.
    With the permission of our noble host—
            [Taking her hand, and leading her to the front of the stage.
Jane. (*to* Freb.) Pardon me this presumption, courteous sir:
    I thus appear (*pointing to her veil*), not careless of respect
    Unto the generous lady of the feast.
    Beneath this veil no beauty shrouded is,
    That, now, or pain, or pleasure can bestow.
    Within the friendly cover of its shade
    I only wish, unknown, again to see
    One who, alas! is heedless of my pain.
De Mon. Yes, it is ever thus. Undo that veil,
    And give thy count'nance to the cheerful light.
    Men now all soft and female beauty scorn,
    And mock the gentle cares which aim to please.
    It is most damnable! undo thy veil,
    And think of him no more.
Jane. I know it well: e'en to a proverb grown,
    Is lovers' faith, and I had borne such slight:
    But he, who has, alas! forsaken me,

Was the companion of my early days,
My cradle's mate, mine infant play-fellow.
Within our op'ning minds, with riper years,
The love of praise and gen'rous virtue sprung:
Through varied life our pride, our joys were one;
At the same tale we wept: he is my brother.

De Mon. And he forsook thee?—No, I dare not curse him:
My heart upbraids me with a crime like his.

Jane. Ah! do not thus distress a feeling heart.
All sisters are not to the soul entwin'd
With equal bands; thine has not watch'd for thee,
Wept for thee, cheer'd thee, shar'd thy weal and woe,
As I have done for him.

De Mon. (*eagerly*).   Ah! has she not?
By heav'n the sum of all thy kindly deeds
Were but as chaff pois'd against massy gold,
Compar'd to that which I do owe her love.
Oh, pardon me! I mean not to offend—
I am too warm—but she of whom I speak
Is the dear sister of my earliest love;
In noble, virtuous worth to none a second:
And though behind those sable folds were hid
As fair a face as ever woman own'd,
Still would I say she is as fair as thou.
How oft amidst the beauty-blazing throng,
I've proudly to th' inquiring stranger told
Her name and lineage! yet within her house,
The virgin mother of an orphan race
Her dying parents left, this noble woman
Did, like a Roman matron, proudly sit,
Despising all the blandishments of love;
While many a youth his hopeless love conceal'd,
Or, humbly distant, woo'd her like a queen.
Forgive, I pray you! O forgive this boasting!
In faith! I mean you no discourtesy.

Jane (*off her guard, in a soft natural tone of voice*).
Oh, no! nor do me any.

De Mon. What voice speaks now? Withdraw, withdraw this shade!
    For if thy face bear semblance to thy voice,
    I'll fall and worship thee. Pray! pray undo!
        [*Puts forth his hand eagerly to snatch away the veil, whilst
        she shrinks back, and* REZENVELT *steps between to prevent
        him.*
Rez. Stand off: no hand shall lift this sacred veil.
De Mon. What, dost thou think De Monfort fall'n so low,
    That there may live a man beneath heav'n's roof,
    Who dares to say, he shall not?
Rez. He lives who dares to say—
Jane (*throwing back her veil, much alarmed, and rushing between them*).
    Forbear, forbear!

        [REZENVELT, *very much struck, steps back respectfully, and makes
        her a low bow.* DE MONFORT *stands for a while motionless,
        gazing upon her, till she, looking expressively to him, extends her
        arms, and he, rushing into them, bursts into tears.* FREBERG *seems
        very much pleased. The company then advancing from the inner
        apartment, gather about them, and the scene closes.*

SCENE II.

DE MONFORT's *apartments. Enter* DE MONFORT, *with a disordered air,
and his hand pressed upon his forehead, followed by* JANE.

De Mon. No more, my sister, urge me not again:
    My secret troubles cannot be reveal'd.
    From all participation of its thoughts
    My heart recoils: I pray thee be contented.
Jane. What, must I, like a distant humble friend,
    Observe thy restless eye, and gait disturb'd,
    In timid silence, whilst with yearning heart
    I turn aside to weep? O no! De Monfort!
    A nobler task thy nobler mind will give;
    Thy true entrusted friend I still shall be.
De Mon. Ah, Jane, forbear! I cannot e'en to thee.

Jane. Then, fy upon it! fy upon it, Monfort!
    There was a time when e'en with murder stain'd,
    Had it been possible that such dire deed
    Could e'er have been the crime of one so piteous,
    Thou wouldst have told it me.
De Mon. So would I now—but ask of this no more.
    All other trouble but the one I feel
    I had disclos'd to thee. I pray thee spare me.
    It is the secret weakness of my nature.
Jane. Then secret let it be; I urge no farther.
    The eldest of our valiant father's hopes,
    So sadly orphan'd, side by side we stood,
    Like two young trees, whose boughs in early strength
    Screen the weak saplings of the rising grove,
    And brave the storm together—
    I have so long, as if by nature's right,
    Thy bosom's inmate and adviser been,
    I thought through life I should have so remain'd,
    Nor ever known a change. Forgive me, Monfort,
    A humbler station will I take by thee:
    The close attendant of thy wand'ring steps;
    The cheerer of this home, with strangers sought;
    The soother of those griefs I must not know:
    This is mine office now: I ask no more.
De Mon. Oh, Jane! thou dost constrain me with thy love!
    Would I could tell it thee!
Jane. Thou shalt not tell me. Nay I'll stop mine ears,
    Nor from the yearnings of affection wring
    What shrinks from utt'rance. Let it pass, my brother.
    I'll stay by thee; I'll cheer thee, comfort thee:
    Pursue with thee the study of some art,
    Or nobler science, that compels the mind
    To steady thought progressive, driving forth
    All floating, wild, unhappy fantasies;
    Till thou, with brow unclouded, smil'st again;
    Like one who, from dark visions of the night,
    When th' active soul within its lifeless cell
    Holds it own world, with dreadful fancy press'd

    Of some dire, terrible, or murd'rous deed,
    Wakes to the dawning morn, and blesses heaven.
De Mon. It will not pass away; 'twill haunt me still.
Jane. Ah! say not so, for I will haunt thee too;
    And be to it so close an adversary,
    That, though I wrestle darkling with the fiend,
    I shall o'ercome it.
De Mon.   Thou most gen'rous woman!
    Why do I treat thee thus? It should not be—
    And yet I cannot—O that cursed villain!
    He will not let me be the man I would.
Jane. What sayst thou, brother? Oh! what words are these?
    They have awak'd my soul to dreadful thoughts.
    I do beseech thee, speak!
         [*He shakes his head, and turns from her; she following him.*
    By the affection thou didst ever bear me;
    By the dear mem'ry of our infant days;
    By kindred living ties, ay, and by those
    Who sleep i' the tomb, and cannot call to thee,
    I do conjure thee, speak!
         [*He waves her off with his hand and covers his face with the*
         other, still turning from her.
               Ah! wilt thou not?
    (*Assuming dignity.*) Then, if affection, most unwearied love,
    Tried early, long, and never wanting found,
    O'er gen'rous man hath more authority,
    More rightful power than crown or sceptre give,
    I do command thee.
         [*He throws himself into a chair, greatly agitated.*
    De Monfort, do not thus resist my love.
    Here I entreat thee on my bended knees.
                       [*Kneeling.*
    Alas! my brother!
         [DE MONFORT *starts up, and catching her in his arms, raises*
         her up, then placing her in the chair, kneels at her feet.
De Mon. Thus let him kneel who should the abased be,
    And at thine honour'd feet confession make!
    I'll tell thee all—but, oh! thou wilt despise me.

For in my breast a raging passion burns,
To which thy soul no sympathy will own—
A passion which hath made my nightly couch
A place of torment; and the light of day,
With the gay intercourse of social man,
Feel like th' oppressive airless pestilence.
O Jane! thou wilt despise me.

Jane.   Say not so:
I never can despise thee, gentle brother.
A lover's jealousy and hopeless pangs
No kindly heart contemns.

De Mon.   A lover, sayst thou?
No, it is hate! black, lasting, deadly hate!
Which thus hath driven me forth from kindred peace,
From social pleasure, from my native home,
To be a sullen wand'rer on the earth,
Avoiding all men, cursing and accurs'd.

Jane. De Monfort, this is fiend-like, frightful, terrible!
What being, by th' Almighty Father form'd,
Of flesh and blood, created even as thou,
Could in thy breast such horrid tempest wake,
Who art thyself his fellow?
Unknit thy brows, and spread those wrath-clench'd hands.
Some sprite accurs'd within thy bosom mates
To work thy ruin. Strive with it, my brother!
Strive bravely with it; drive it from thy breast;
'Tis the degrader of a noble heart:
Curse it, and bid it part.

De Mon. It will not part. (*His hand on his breast.*) I've lodg'd it here
too long:
With my first cares I felt its rankling touch;
I loath'd him when a boy.

Jane. Whom didst thou say?

De Mon.   Oh! that detested Rezenvelt!
E'en in our early sports, like two young whelps
Of hostile breed, instinctively reverse,
Each 'gainst the other pitch'd his ready pledge,
And frown'd defiance. As we onward pass'd

From youth to man's estate, his narrow art
And envious gibing malice, poorly veil'd
In the affected carelessness of mirth,
Still more detestable and odious grew.
There is no living being on this earth
Who can conceive the malice of his soul,
With all his gay and damned merriment,
To those, by fortune or by merit plac'd
Above his paltry self. When, low in fortune,
He look'd upon the state of prosp'rous men,
As nightly birds, rous'd from their murky holes,
Do scowl and chatter at the light of day,
I could endure it; even as we bear
Th' impotent bite of some half-trodden worm,
I could endure it. But when honours came,
And wealth and new-got titles fed his pride;
Whilst flatt'ring knaves did trumpet forth his praise,
And grov'ling idiots grinn'd applauses on him;
Oh! then I could no longer suffer it!
It drove me frantic.—What! what would I give!
What would I give to crush the bloated toad,
So rankly do I loathe him!

Jane. And would thy hatred crush the very man
Who gave to thee that life he might have ta'en;
That life which thou so rashly didst expose
To aim at his? Oh! this is horrible!

De Mon. Ha! thou hast heard it, then? From all the world,
But most of all from thee, I thought it hid.

Jane. I heard a secret whisper, and resolv'd
Upon the instant to return to thee.
Didst thou receive my letter?

De Mon. I did! I did! 'twas that which drove me hither.
I could not bear to meet thine eye again.

Jane. Alas! that, tempted by a sister's tears,
I ever left thy house! These few past months,
These absent months, have brought us all this woe.
Had I remain'd with thee it had not been.
And yet, methinks, it should not move you thus.

You dar'd him to the field; both bravely fought;
He more adroit disarm'd you; courteously
Return'd the forfeit sword, which, so return'd,
You did refuse to use against him more;
And then, as says report, you parted friends.

De Mon. When he disarm'd this curs'd, this worthless hand
Of its most worthless weapon, he but spar'd
From dev'lish pride, which now derives a bliss
In seeing me thus fetter'd, sham'd, subjected
With the vile favour of his poor forbearance;
While he securely sits with gibing brow,
And basely bates me like a muzzled cur
Who cannot turn again.—
Until that day, till that accursed day,
I knew not half the torment of this hell,
  Which burns within my breast. Heaven's lightnings blast him!

Jane. O this is horrible! Forbear, forbear!
Lest heaven's vengeance light upon thy head,
For this most impious wish.

De Mon.   Then let it light.
Torments more fell than I have felt already
It cannot send. To be annihilated,
What all men shrink from; to be dust, be nothing,
Were bliss to me, compar'd to what I am!

Jane. Oh! wouldst thou kill me with these dreadful words?

De Mon. (*raising his hands to heaven*).
Let me but once upon his ruin look,
Then close mine eyes for ever!

            [JANE, *in great distress, staggers back, and supports herself*
            upon the side scene. DE MON., *alarmed, runs up to her with*
            a softened voice.

Ha! how is this? thou'rt ill; thou'rt very pale.
What have I done to thee? Alas, alas!
I meant not to distress thee.—O my sister!

Jane. (*shaking her head*). I cannot speak to thee.

De Mon.   I have kill'd thee.
Turn, turn thee not away! look on me still!

    Oh! droop not thus, my life, my pride, my sister;
    Look on me yet again.
Jane.   Thou too, De Monfort,
    In better days, wert wont to be my pride.
De Mon. I am a wretch, most wretched in myself,
    And still more wretched in the pain I give.
    O curse that villain! that detested villain!
    He has spread mis'ry o'er my fated life:
    He will undo us all.
Jane. I've held my warfare through a troubled world,
    And borne with steady mind my share of ill;
    For thou wert then the helpmate of my toil.
    But now the wane of life comes darkly on,
    And hideous passion tears me from thy heart,
    Blasting thy worth.—I cannot strive with this.
De Mon. (*affectionately*). What shall I do?
Jane.   Call up thy noble spirit;
    Rouse all the gen'rous energy of virtue;
    And with the strength of heaven-endued man,
    Repel the hideous foe. Be great; be valiant.
    O, if thou couldst! e'en shrouded as thou art
    In all the sad infirmities of nature,
    What a most noble creature wouldst thou be!
De Mon. Ay, if I could: alas! alas! I cannot.
    Jane. Thou canst, thou mayst, thou wilt.
    We shall not part till I have turn'd thy soul.

Enter MANUEL.

De Mon. Ha! some one enters. Wherefore com'st thou here?
Man. Count Freberg waits your leisure.
De Mon. (*angrily*). Begone, begone!—I cannot see him now.
                                    [*Exit* MANUEL.
Jane. Come to my closet; free from all intrusion,
    I'll school thee there; and thou again shalt be
    My willing pupil, and my gen'rous friend,
    The noble Monfort I have lov'd so long,
    And must not, will not lose.

De Mon. Do as thou wilt; I will not grieve thee more.

[*Exeunt.*

ACT III.

SCENE I.[1]

COUNTESS FREBERG' *s dressing-room. Enter the Countess dispirited and out of humour, and throws herself into a chair: enter, by the opposite side,* THERESA.

Ther. Madam, I am afraid you are unwell:
　　What is the matter? does your head ache?
Lady (peevishly). 　　　　　　　　　　No,
　　'Tis not my head: concern thyself no more
　　With what concerns not thee.
Ther. Go you abroad to-night?
Lady. Yes, thinkest thou I'll stay and fret at home?
Ther. Then please to say what you would choose to wear:—
　　One of your newest robes?
Lady. 　　　　　　　　I hate them all.
Ther. Surely that purple scarf became you well,
　　With all those wreaths of richly-hanging flowers.
　　Did I not overhear them say, last night,
　　As from the crowded ball-room ladies pass'd,
　　How gay and handsome, in her costly dress,
　　The Countess Freberg look'd?
Lady. 　　　　　　　　Didst thou o'erhear it?
Ther. I did, and more than this.
Lady. Well, all are not so greatly prejudic'd;
　　All do not think me like a May-day queen,
　　Which peasants deck in sport.
Ther. 　　　　　　　　And who said this?

---

[1] This scene has been very much altered from what it was in the former editions of this play, and scene fifth of the last act will be found to be almost entirely changed. These alterations, though of no great importance, are, I hope, upon the whole, improvements. [Baillie's note.]

Lady (*putting her handkerchief to her eyes*). E'en my good lord, Theresa.

Ther. He said it but in jest. He loves you well.

Lady. I know as well as thou he loves me well.
   But what of that! he takes in me no pride:
   Elsewhere his praise and admiration go,
   And Jane De Monfort is not mortal woman.

Ther. The wondrous character this lady bears
   For worth and excellence: from early youth
   The friend and mother of her younger sisters,
   Now greatly married, as I have been told,
   From her most prudent care, may well excuse
   The admiration of so good a man
   As my good master is. And then, dear madam,
   I must confess, when I myself did hear
   How she was come through the rough winter's storm,
   To seek and comfort an unhappy brother,
   My heart beat kindly to her.

Lady. Ay, ay, there is a charm in this I find:
   But wherefore may she not have come as well
   Through wintry storms to seek a lover too?

Ther. No, madam, no, I could not think of this.

Lady. That would reduce her in your eyes, mayhap,
   To woman's level.—Now I see my vengeance!
   I'll tell it round that she is hither come,
   Under pretence of finding out De Monfort,
   To meet with Rezenvelt. When Freberg hears it,
   'Twill help, I ween, to break this magic charm.

Ther. And say what is not, madam?

Lady. How canst thou know that I shall say what is not?
   'Tis like enough I shall but speak the truth.

Ther. Ah, no! there is—

Lady. Well, hold thy foolish tongue.
                [*Freberg's voice is heard without. After hesitating.*
   I will not see him now.
                                                              [*Exit.*
            [*Enter* FREBERG *by the opposite side, passing on hastily.*

Ther. Pardon, my lord; I fear you are in haste.
   Yet must I crave that you will give to me

The books my lady mention'd to you: she
Has charg'd me to remind you.

Freb.   I'm in haste.

                              [*Passing on.*

Ther. Pray you, my lord: your countess wants them much:
    The Lady Jane De Monfort ask'd them of her.

Freb. (*returning instantly*). Are they for her? I knew not this before.
    I will, then, search them out immediately.
    There is nought good or precious in my keeping,
    That is not dearly honour'd by her use.

Ther. My lord, what would your gentle countess say,
    If she o'erheard her own request neglected,
    Until supported by a name more potent?

Freb. Thinkst thou she is a fool, my good Theresa,
    Vainly to please herself with childish thoughts
    Of matching what is matchless—Jane De Monfort?
    Thinkst thou she is a fool, and cannot see,
    That love and admiration often thrive
    Though far apart?

                    [*Re-enter lady with great violence.*

Lady. I am a fool, not to have seen full well,
    That thy best pleasure in o'er-rating so
    This lofty stranger, is to humble me,
    And cast a dark'ning shadow o'er my head.
    Ay, wherefore dost thou stare upon me thus?
    Art thou asham'd that I have thus surpris'd thee?
    Well mayst thou be so!

Freb.   True; thou rightly sayst.
    Well may I be asham'd: not for the praise
    Which I have ever openly bestow'd
    On Monfort's noble sister; but that thus,
    Like a poor mean and jealous listener,
    She should be found, who is Count Freberg's wife.

Lady. Oh, I am lost and ruin'd! hated, scorn'd!

                              [*Pretending to faint.*

Freb. Alas, I have been too rough!

                    [*Taking her hand and kissing it tenderly.*

My gentle love! my own, my only love!
See, she revives again. How art thou, love?
Support her to her chamber, good Theresa.
I'll sit and watch by her. I've been too rough.

[*Exeunt; lady supported by* FREB. *and* THER.

SCENE II.

DE MONFORT *discovered sitting by a table reading. After a little time he lays down his book, and continues in a thoughtful posture. Enter to him* JANE DE MONFORT.

Jane. Thanks, gentle brother.—

[*Pointing to the book.*
    Thy willing mind has rightly been employ'd:
    Did not thy heart warm at the fair display
    Of peace and concord and forgiving love?
De Mon. I know resentment may to love be turn'd,
    Though keen and lasting, into love as strong:
    And fiercest rivals in th' ensanguin'd field
    Have cast their brandish'd weapons to the ground,
    Joining their mailed breasts in close embrace,
    With gen'rous impulse fir'd. I know right well
    The darkest, fellest wrongs have been forgiven
    Seventy times o'er from blessed heav'nly love:
    I've heard of things like these; I've heard and wept.
    But what is this to me?
Jane.   All, all, my brother!
    It bids thee too that noble precept learn,
    To love thine enemy.
De Mon. Th' uplifted stroke that would a wretch destroy,
    Gorg'd with my richest spoil, stain'd with my blood,
    I would arrest, and cry, "Hold! hold! have mercy."
    But when the man most adverse to my nature,
    Who e'en from childhood hath, with rude malevolence,
    Withheld the fair respect all paid beside,
    Turning my very praise into derision,

    › Who galls and presses me where'er I go,
       Would claim the gen'rous feelings of my heart,
       Nature herself doth lift her voice aloud,
       And cry, "It is impossible!"
Jane. (*shaking her head*). Ah, Monfort, Monfort!
De Mon. I can forgive th' envenom'd reptile's sting,
       But hate his loathsome self.
Jane. And canst thou do no more for love of heaven?
De Mon. Alas! I cannot now so school my mind
       As holy men have taught, nor search it truly:
       But this, my Jane, I'll do for love of thee;
       And more it is than crowns could win me to,
       Or any power but thine. I'll see the man.
       Th' indignant risings of abhorrent nature;
       The stern contraction of my scowling brows,
       That like the plant whose closing leaves do shrink
       At hostile touch, still knit at his approach;
       The crooked curving lip, by instinct taught,
       In imitation of disgustful things,
       To pout and swell, I strictly will repress;
       And meet him with a tamed countenance,
       E'en as a townsman, who would live at peace,
       And pay him the respect his station claims.
       I'll crave his pardon too for all offence
       My dark and wayward temper may have done.
       Nay more, I will confess myself his debtor
       For the forbearance I have curs'd so oft:
       Life spar'd by him, more horrid than the grave
       With all its dark corruption! This I'll do.
       Will it suffice thee? More than this I cannot.
Jane. No more than this do I require of thee
       In outward act, though in thy heart, my friend,
       I hop'd a better change, and yet will hope.
       I told thee Freberg had propos'd a meeting.
De Mon. I know it well.
Jane.   And Rezenvelt consents.
       He meets you here; so far he shows respect.
De Mon. Well, let it be; the sooner past the better.

Jane. I'm glad to hear you say so, for, in truth,
    He has propos'd for it an early hour.
    'Tis almost near his time; I came to tell you.
De Mon. What, comes he here so soon? shame on his speed!
    It is not decent thus to rush upon me.
    He loves the secret pleasure he will feel
    To see me thus subdued.
Jane. O say not so! he comes with heart sincere.
De Mon. Could we not meet elsewhere? from home—i' the fields,
    Where other men—must I alone receive him?
    Where is your agent, Freberg, and his friends,
    That I must meet him here?
                          [*Walks up and down, very much disturbed.*
    Now! didst thou say?—how goes the hour?—e'en now!
    I would some other friend were first arriv'd.
Jane. See, to thy wish come Freberg and his dame.
De Mon. His lady too! why comes he not alone?
    Must all the world upon our meeting stare?

                Enter COUNT FREBERG *and his* COUNTESS.

Freb. A happy morrow to my noble marquis,
    And his most noble sister!
Jane.   Gen'rous Freberg,
    Your face, methinks, forebodes a happy morn,
    Open and cheerful. What of Rezenvelt?
Freb. I left him at his home, prepar'd to follow:
    He'll soon appear. (*To* DE MONFORT.) And now, my worthy
    friend,
    Give me your hand; this happy change delights me.
                [DE MONFORT *gives him his hand coldly, and they walk to*
                the bottom of the stage together, in earnest discourse, whilst
                JANE *and the Countess remain in the front.*
Lady. My dearest madam, will you pardon me?
    I know Count Freberg's bus'ness with De Monfort,
    And had a strong desire to visit you,
    So much I wish the honour of your friendship;
    For he retains no secret from mine ear.

Jane (*archly*). Knowing your prudence—you are welcome, madam;
>So shall Count Freberg's lady ever be.

>>[DE MONFORT *and* FREBERG *returning towards the front of*
>>*the stage, still engaged in discourse.*

Freb. He is indeed a man, within whose breast
>Firm rectitude and honour hold their seat,
>Though unadorned with that dignity
>Which were their fittest garb. Now, on my life!
>I know no truer heart than Rezenvelt.

De Mon. Well, Freberg, well, there needs not all this pains
>To garnish out his worth: let it suffice;
>I am resolv'd I will respect the man,
>As his fair station and repute demand.
>Methinks I see not at your jolly feasts
>The youthful knight, who sang so pleasantly.

Freb. A pleasant circumstance detains him hence;
>Pleasant to those who love high gen'rous deeds
>Above the middle pitch of common minds;
>And, though I have been sworn to secrecy,
>Yet must I tell it thee.
>This knight is near akin to Rezenvelt,
>To whom an old relation, short while dead,
>A good estate bequeathed, some leagues distant.
>But Rezenvelt, now rich in fortune's store,
>Disdain'd the sordid love of further gain,
>And gen'rously the rich bequest resign'd
>To this young man, blood of the same degree
>To the deceas'd, and low in fortune's gifts,
>Who is from hence to take possession of it:
>Was it not nobly done?

De Mon.   'Twas right and honourable.
>This morning is oppressive, warm, and heavy:
>There hangs a foggy closeness in the air;
>Dost thou not feel it?

Freb. O no! to think upon a gen'rous deed
>Expands my soul, and makes me lightly breathe.

De Mon. Who gives the feast to-night? His name escapes me.
>You say I am invited.

Freb.   Old Count Waterlan.
    In honour of your townsman's gen'rous gift,
    He spreads the board.
De Mon. He is too old to revel with the gay.
Freb. But not too old is he to honour virtue.
    I shall partake of it with open soul;
    For, on my honest faith, of living men
    I know not one, for talents, honour, worth,
    That I should rank superior to Rezenvelt.
De Mon. How virtuous he hath been in three short days!
Freb. Nay, longer, marquis; but my friendship rests
    Upon the good report of other men,
    And that has told me much.

> [DE MONFORT *aside, going some steps hastily from* FREBERG,
> *and rending his cloak with agitation as he goes.*

    Would he were come! by heav'n I would he were!
    This fool besets me so.

> [*Suddenly correcting himself, and joining the ladies,*
> *who have retired to the bottom of the stage, he speaks to*
> COUNTESS FREBERG *with affected cheerfulness.*

    The sprightly dames of Amberg rise by times,
    Untarnish'd with the vigils of the night.
Lady. Praise us not rashly, 'tis not always so.
De Mon. He does not rashly praise who praises you;
    For he were dull indeed—

> [*Stopping short, as if he heard something.*

Lady.   How dull indeed?
De Mon. I should have said—It has escap'd me now—

> [*Listening again, as if he heard something.*

Jane (to DE MON.) What, hear you aught?
De Mon. (hastily).   'Tis nothing.
Lady (to DE MON.) Nay, do not let me lose it so, my lord.
    Some fair one has bewitch'd your memory,
    And robs me of the half-form'd compliment.
Jane. Half-utter'd praise is to the curious mind
    As to the eye half-veiled beauty is,

More precious than the whole. Pray pardon him.
Some one approaches.

[Listening.

Freb. No, no, it is a servant who ascends;
    He will not come so soon.
De Mon. (off his guard). 'Tis Rezenvelt: I heard his well-known foot,
    From the first staircase, mounting step by step.
Freb. How quick an ear thou hast for distant sound!
    I heard him not.

[DE MONFORT looks embarrassed, and is silent.

Enter REZENVELT.

[DE MONFORT, recovering himself, goes up to receive
REZENVELT, who meets him with a cheerful countenance.

De Mon. (to REZ.) I am, my lord, beholden to you greatly.
    This ready visit makes me much your debtor.
Rez. Then may such debts between us, noble marquis,
    Be oft incurr'd, and often paid again!
    (To JANE.) Madam, I am devoted to your service,
    And ev'ry wish of yours commands my will.
    (To Countess.) Lady, good morning. (To FREB.) Well, my gentle
    friend,
    You see I have not linger'd long behind.
Freb. No, thou art sooner than I look'd for thee.
Rez. A willing heart adds feather to the heel,
    And makes the clown a winged Mercury.
De Mon. Then let me say, that, with a grateful mind,
    I do receive these tokens of good will;
    And must regret, that, in my wayward moods,
    I have too oft forgot the due regard
    Your rank and talents claim.
Rez.   No, no, De Monfort,
    You have but rightly curb'd a wanton spirit,
    Which makes me too neglectful of respect.
    Let us be friends, and think of this no more.
Freb. Ay, let it rest with the departed shades
    Of things which are no more; whilst lovely concord,

Follow'd by friendship sweet, and firm esteem,
Your future days enrich. O heavenly friendship!
Thou dost exalt the sluggish souls of men,
By thee conjoin'd, to great and glorious deeds;
As two dark clouds, when mix'd in middle air,
With vivid lightnings flash, and roar sublime.
Talk not of what is past, but future love.

De Mon. (*with dignity*).

No, Freberg, no, it must not. (*To* REZENVELT.) No, my lord,
I will not offer you an hand of concord,
And poorly hide the motives which constrain me.
I would that, not alone, these present friends,
But ev'ry soul in Amberg were assembled,
That I, before them all, might here declare
I owe my spared life to your forbearance.
(*Holding out his hand.*) Take this from one who boasts no
feeling warmth,
But never will deceive.

> [JANE *smiles upon* DE MONFORT *with great approbation,*
> *and* REZENVELT *runs up to him with open arms.*

Rez. Away with hands! I'll have thee to my breast.
Thou art, upon my faith, a noble spirit!

De Mon. (*shrinking back from him*).

Nay, if you please, I am not so prepar'd—
My nature is of temperature too cold—
I pray you pardon me (JANE'*s countenance changes*).
But take this hand, the token of respect;
The token of a will inclin'd to concord;
The token of a mind, that bears within
A sense impressive of the debt it owes you:
And cursed be its power, unnerv'd its strength,
If e'er again it shall be lifted up
To do you any harm!

Rez. Well, be it so, De Monfort, I'm contented;
I'll take thy hand, since I can have no more.
(*Carelessly.*) I take of worthy men whate'er they give.
Their heart I gladly take, if not their hand;
If that too is withheld, a courteous word,

Or the civility of placid looks:
And, if e'en these are too great favours deem'd,
'Faith, I can set me down contentedly
With plain and homely greeting, or "God save ye!"
De Mon. (aside, starting away from him some paces).
By the good light, he makes a jest of it!

> [JANE *seems greatly distressed, and* FREBERG *endeavours to cheer her.*

Freb. (to JANE*).* Cheer up, my noble friend; all will go well;
For friendship is no plant of hasty growth.
Though rooted in esteem's deep soil, the slow
And gradual culture of kind intercourse
Must bring it to perfection.
(*To the Countess.*) My love, the morning, now, is far advanc'd;
Our friends elsewhere expect us; take your leave.
Lady (to JANE*).* Farewell, dear madam, till the evening hour.
Freb. (to DE MON.) Good day, De Monfort. (*To* JANE.) Most devoutly
yours.
Rez. (to FREB.) Go not too fast, for I will follow you.

> [*Exeunt* FREBERG *and his lady.*

(*To* JANE.) The Lady Jane is yet a stranger here:
She might, perhaps, in this your ancient city
Find somewhat worth her notice.
Jane. I thank you, marquis, I am much engag'd;
I go not out to-day.
Rez. Then fare ye well! I see I cannot now
Be the proud man who shall escort you forth,
And show to all the world my proudest boast,
The notice and respect of Jane de Monfort.
De Mon. (aside impatiently). He says farewell, and goes not!
Jane (to REZ.) You do me honour.
Rez. Madam, adieu! (*To* JANE.) Good morning, noble marquis.

> [JANE *and* DE MONFORT *look expressively to one another, without speaking, and then exeunt severally.*

ACT IV.

SCENE I.

A hall or antechamber, with the folding doors of an inner apartment open, which discovers the guests rising from a banquet. They enter and pass over the stage, and exeunt; and after them enter Rezenvelt *and* Freberg.

Freb. Alas, my Rezenvelt!
    I vainly hop'd the hand of gentle peace,
    From this day's reconciliation sprung,
    These rude unseemly jarrings had subdu'd;
    But I have mark'd, e'en at the social board,
    Such looks, such words, such tones, such untold things,
    Too plainly told, 'twixt you and Monfort pass,
    That I must now despair.
    Yet who could think, two minds so much refin'd,
    So near in excellence, should be remov'd,
    So far remov'd, in gen'rous sympathy?
Rez. Ay, far remov'd indeed!
Freb. And yet, methought, he made a noble effort,
    And with a manly plainness bravely told
    The galling debt he owes to your forbearance.
Rez. 'Faith! so he did, and so did I receive it;
    When, with spread arms, and heart e'en mov'd to tears,
    I frankly proffer'd him a friend's embrace:
    And, I declare, had he as such receiv'd it,
    I from that very moment had forborne
    All opposition, pride-provoking jest,
    Contemning carelessness, and all offence;
    And had caress'd him as a worthy heart,
    From native weakness such indulgence claiming.
    But since he proudly thinks that cold respect,
    The formal tokens of his lordly favour,
    So precious are, that I would sue for them
    As fair distinction in the public eye,
    Forgetting former wrongs, I spurn it all.
    And but that I do bear that noble woman,

His worthy, his incomparable sister,
Such fix'd, profound regard, I would expose him;
And, as a mighty bull, in senseless rage,
Rous'd at the baiter's will, with wretched rags
Of ire-provoking scarlet, chafes and bellows,
I'd make him at small cost of paltry wit,
With all his deep and manly faculties,
The scorn and laugh of fools.

Freb. For heaven's sake, my friend, restrain your wrath!
For what has Monfort done of wrong to you,
Or you to him, bating one foolish quarrel,
Which you confess from slight occasion rose,
That in your breasts such dark resentment dwells,
So fix'd, so hopeless?

Rez. O! from our youth he has distinguish'd me
With ev'ry mark of hatred and disgust.
For e'en in boyish sports I still oppos'd
His proud pretensions to pre-eminence;
Nor would I to his ripen'd greatness give
That fulsome adulation of applause
A senseless crowd bestow'd. Though poor in fortune,
I still would smile at vain assuming wealth:
But when unlook'd-for fate on me bestow'd
Riches and splendour equal to his own,
Though I, in truth, despise such poor distinction,
Feeling inclin'd to be at peace with him,
And with all men beside, I curb'd my spirit,
And sought to soothe him. Then, with spiteful rage,
From small offence he rear'd a quarrel with me,
And dar'd me to the field. The rest you know.
In short, I still have been th' opposing rock,
O'er which the stream of his o'erflowing pride
Hath foam'd and fretted. Seest thou how it is?

Freb. Too well I see, and warn thee to beware.
Such streams have oft, by swelling floods surcharg'd,
Borne down, with sudden and impetuous force,
The yet unshaken stone of opposition,

    Which had for ages stopp'd their flowing course.
    I pray thee, friend, beware.
Rez. Thou canst not mean—he will not murder me?
Freb. What a proud heart, with such dark passion toss'd,
    May, in the anguish of its thoughts, conceive,
    I will not dare to say.
Rez.   Ha, ha! thou knowst him not.
    Full often have I mark'd it in his youth,
    And could have almost lov'd him for the weakness:
    He's form'd with such antipathy, by nature,
    To all infliction of corporeal pain,
    To wounding life, e'en to the sight of blood,
    He cannot if he would.
Freb.   Then fie upon thee!
    It is not gen'rous to provoke him thus.
    But let us part: we'll talk of this again.
    Something approaches.—We are here too long.
Rez. Well, then, to-morrow I'll attend your call.
    Here lies my way. Good night.

                                       [*Exit.*

Enter CONRAD.

Con. Forgive, I pray, my lord, a stranger's boldness.
    I have presum'd to wait your leisure here,
    Though at so late an hour.
Freb.   But who art thou?
Con. My name is Conrad, sir,
    A humble suitor to your honour's goodness,
    Who is the more embolden'd to presume,
    In that De Monfort's brave and noble marquis
    Is so much fam'd for good and gen'rous deeds.
Freb. You are mistaken, I am not the man.
Con. Then, pardon me: I thought I could not err;
    That mien so dignified, that piercing eye
    Assur'd me it was he.
Freb. My name is not De Monfort, courteous stranger;
    But, if you have a favour to request,
    I may, with him, perhaps, befriend your suit.

Con. I thank your honour, but I have a friend
Who will commend me to De Monfort's favour:
The Marquis Rezenvelt has known me long,
Who, says report, will soon become his brother.
Freb. If thou wouldst seek thy ruin from De Monfort,
The name of Rezenvelt employ, and prosper;
But, if aught good, use any name but his.
Con. How may this be?
Freb.   I cannot now explain.
Early to-morrow call upon Count Freberg;
So am I call'd, each burgher knows my house,
And there instruct me how to do you service.
Good night.

                                        [*Exit.*

Con. (*alone*). Well, this mistake may be of service to me:
And yet my bus'ness I will not unfold
To this mild, ready, promise-making courtier;
I've been by such too oft deceiv'd already.
But if such violent enmity exist
Between De Monfort and this Rezenvelt,
He'll prove my advocate by opposition.
For if De Monfort would reject my suit,
Being the man whom Rezenvelt esteems,
Being the man he hates, a cord as strong,
Will he not favour me? I'll think of this.

                                        [*Exit.*

SCENE II.

A lower apartment in JEROME's *house, with a wide folding glass door, looking into a garden, where the trees and shrubs are brown and leafless. Enter* DE MONFORT *with a thoughtful frowning aspect, and paces slowly across the stage,* JEROME *following behind him, with a timid step.* DE MONFORT *hearing him, turns suddenly about.*

De Mon. (*angrily*). Who follows me to this sequester'd room?

Jer. I have presum'd, my lord. 'Tis somewhat late:
    I am inform'd you eat at home to-night;
    Here is a list of all the dainty fare
    My busy search has found; please to peruse it.
De Mon. Leave me: begone! Put hemlock in thy soup,
    Or deadly night-shade, or rank hellebore,
    And I will mess upon it.
Jer.   Heaven forbid!
    Your honour's life is all too precious, sure.
De Mon. (*sternly*). Did I not say begone?
Jer. Pardon, my lord, I'm old, and oft forget.

                                   [*Exit.*

De Mon. (*looking after him, as if his heart smote him*).
    Why will they thus mistime their foolish zeal,
    That I must be so stern?
    O, that I were upon some desert coast!
    Where howling tempests and the lashing tide
    Would stun me into deep and senseless quiet;
    As the storm-beaten trav'ller droops his head,
    In heavy, dull, lethargic weariness,
    And, 'mid the roar of jarring elements,
    Sleeps to awake no more.
    What am I grown? all things are hateful to me.

Enter MANUEL.

(*Stamping with his foot.*) Who bids thee break upon my privacy?
Man. Nay, good my lord! I heard you speak aloud,
    And dreamt not surely that you were alone.
De Mon. What, dost thou watch, and pin thine ears to holes,
    To catch those exclamations of the soul,
    Which heaven alone should hear? Who hir'd thee, pray?
    Who basely hir'd thee for a task like this?
Man. My lord, I cannot hold. For fifteen years,
    Long-troubled years, I have your servant been,
    Nor hath the proudest lord in all the realm,
    With firmer, with more honourable faith
    His sov'reign serv'd, than I have served you;

But if my honesty be doubted now,
Let him who is more faithful take my place,
And serve you better.

De Mon. Well, be it as thou wilt. Away with thee!
Thy loud-mouth'd boasting is no rule for me
To judge thy merit by.

Enter JEROME *hastily, and pulls* MANUEL *away.*

Jer. Come, Manuel, come away; thou art not wise.
The stranger must depart and come again,
For now his honour will not be disturb'd.

[*Exit* MANUEL *sulkily.*

De Mon. A stranger, saidst thou?

[*Drops his handkerchief.*

Jer. I did, good sir, but he shall go away;
You shall not be disturb'd.

[*Stooping to lift the handkerchief.*

You have dropp'd somewhat.

De Mon. (*preventing him*). Nay, do not stoop, my friend, I pray thee not!
Thou art too old to stoop.
I'm much indebted to thee.—Take this ring—
I love thee better than I seem to do.
I pray thee do it—thank me not.—What stranger?

Jer. A man who does most earnestly intreat
To see your honour; but I know him not.

De Mon. Then let him enter.

[*Exit* JEROME.

A pause. Enter CONRAD.

De Mon. You are the stranger who would speak with me?

Con. I am so far unfortunate, my lord.
That, though my fortune on your favour hangs,
I am to you a stranger.

De Mon. How may this be? what can I do for you?

Con. Since thus your lordship does so frankly ask
The tiresome preface of apology
I will forbear, and tell my tale at once,
In plodding drudgery I've spent my youth,

A careful penman in another's office;
And now, my master and employer dead,
They seek to set a stripling o'er my head,
And leave me on to drudge, e'en to old age,
Because I have no friend to take my part.
It is an office in your native town,
For I am come from thence, and I am told
You can procure it for me. Thus, my lord,
From the repute of goodness which you bear,
I have presum'd to beg.

De Mon. They have befool'd thee with a false report.

Con. Alas! I see it is in vain to plead,
Your mind is prepossess'd against a wretch,
Who has, unfortunately for his weal,
Offended the revengeful Rezenvelt.

De Mon. What dost thou say?

Con. What I, perhaps, had better leave unsaid.
Who will believe my wrongs if I complain?
I am a stranger, Rezenvelt my foe,
Who will believe my wrongs?

De Mon. (*eagerly catching him by the coat*). I will believe them!
Though they were base as basest, vilest deeds,
In ancient record told, I would believe them!
Let not the smallest atom of unworthiness
That he has put upon thee be conceal'd.
Speak boldly, tell it all; for, by the light!
I'll be thy friend, I'll be thy warmest friend,
If he has done thee wrong.

Con. Nay, pardon me, it were not well advis'd,
If I should speak so freely of the man
Who will so soon your nearest kinsman be.

De Mon. What canst thou mean by this?

Con.   That Marquis Rezenvelt
Has pledg'd his faith unto your noble sister,
And soon will be the husband of her choice.
So I am told, and so the world believes.

De Mon. 'Tis false! 'tis basely false!
What wretch could drop from his envenom'd tongue

A tale so damn'd?—It chokes my breath—
(*Stamping with his foot.*) What wretch did tell it thee?
Con. Nay, every one with whom I have convers'd
Has held the same discourse. I judge it not.
But you, my lord, who with the lady dwell.
You best can tell what her deportment speaks;
Whether her conduct and unguarded words
Belie such rumour.
          [De Monfort *pauses, staggers backwards, and sinks into a*
          chair; then starting up hastily.
De Mon. Where am I now? 'midst all the cursed thoughts,
That on my soul like stinging scorpions prey'd,
This never came before——Oh, if it be!
The thought will drive me mad.—Was it for this
She urg'd her warm request on bended knee?
Alas! I wept, and thought of sister's love,
No damned love like this.
Fell devil! 'tis hell itself has lent thee aid
To work such sorcery! (*Pauses.*) I'll not believe it.
I must have proof clear as the noon-day sun
For such foul charge as this! Who waits without?
                    [*Paces up and down, furiously agitated.*
Con. (*aside*). What have I done? I've carried this too far.
I've rous'd a fierce ungovernable madman.

Enter JEROME.

De Mon. (*in a loud angry voice*). Where did she go, at such an early hour,
And with such slight attendance?
Jer. Of whom inquires your honour?
De Mon. Why, of your lady. Said I not my sister?
Jer. The Lady Jane, your sister?
De Mon. (*in a faltering voice*). Yes, I did call her so.
Jer. In truth, I cannot tell you where she went.
E'en now, from the short beechen walk hard-by,
I saw her through the garden-gate return.
The Marquis Rezenvelt, and Freberg's countess,
Are in her company. This way they come,

    As being nearer to the back apartments;
    But I shall stop them, if it be your will,
    And bid them enter here.

De Mon. No, stop them not. I will remain unseen,
    And mark them as they pass. Draw back a little.

> [CONRAD *seems alarmed, and steals off unnoticed.* DE
> MONFORT *grasps* JEROME *tightly by the hand, and drawing
> back with him two or three steps, not to be seen from the gar-
> den, waits in silence, with his eyes fixed on the glass door.*

De Mon. I hear their footsteps on the grating sand:
    How like the croaking of a carrion bird,
    That hateful voice sounds to the distant ear!
    And now she speaks—her voice sounds cheerly too—
    Curs'd be their mirth!—
    Now, now, they come; keep closer still! keep steady!

> [*Taking hold of* JEROME *with both hands.*

Jer. My lord, you tremble much.

De Mon. What, do I shake?

Jer. You do, in truth, and your teeth chatter too.

De Mon. See! see they come! he strutting by her side.

> [JANE, REZENVELT, *and* COUNTESS FREBERG *appear
> through the glass door, pursuing their way up a short walk
> leading to the other wing of the house.*

    See, his audacious face he turns to hers;
    Utt'ring with confidence some nauseous jest.
    And she endures it too—Oh! this looks vilely!
    Ha! mark that courteous motion of his arm!—
    What does he mean?—he dares not take her hand!
    (*Pauses and looks eagerly.*) By heaven and hell he does!

> [*Letting go his hold of* JEROME, *he throws out his hands
> vehemently, and thereby pushes him against the scene.*

Jer. Oh! I am stunn'd! my head is crack'd in twain:
    Your honour does forget how old I am.

De Mon. Well, well, the wall is harder than I wist.
    Begone, and whine within.

> [*Exit* JEROME, *with a sad rueful countenance.*
> [DE MONFORT *comes forward to the front of the stage, and
> makes a long pause expressive of great agony of mind.*

It must be so: each passing circumstance;
Her hasty journey here; her keen distress
Whene'er my soul's abhorrence I express'd;
Ay, and that damned reconciliation,
With tears extorted from me: Oh, too well!
All, all too well bespeak the shameful tale.
I should have thought of heaven and hell conjoin'd,
The morning star mix'd with infernal fire,
Ere I had thought of this—
Hell's blackest magic, in the midnight hour,
With horrid spells and incantation dire,
Such combination opposite unseemly,
Of fair and loathsome, excellent and base,
Did ne'er produce—But every thing is possible,
So as it may my misery enhance!
Oh! I did love her with such pride of soul!
When other men, in gay pursuit of love,
Each beauty follow'd, by her side I stay'd;
Far prouder of a brother's station there,
Than all the favours favour'd lovers boast.
We quarrell'd once, and when I could no more
The alter'd coldness of her eye endure,
I slipp'd o' tip-toe to her chamber-door;
And when she ask'd who gently knock'd—Oh! oh!
Who could have thought of this?

> [*Throws himself into a chair, covers his face with his hand,
> and bursts into tears. After some time, he starts up from his
> seat furiously.*

Hell's direst torment seize the infernal villain!
Detested of my soul! I will have vengeance!
I'll crush thy swelling pride—I'll still thy vaunting—
I'll do a deed of blood!—Why shrink I thus?
If by some spell or magic sympathy,
Piercing the lifeless figure on that wall
Could pierce his bosom too, would I not cast it?

> [*Throwing a dagger against the wall.*

Shall groans and blood affright me? No, I'll do it.
Though gasping life beneath my pressure heav'd,

And my soul shudder'd at the horrid brink,
I would not flinch.—Fie, this recoiling nature!
O that his sever'd limbs were strew'd in air,
So as I saw it not!

Enter REZENVELT *behind from the glass door.* DE MONFORT *turns round,
and on seeing him, starts back, then drawing his sword, rushes furiously
upon him.*

Detested robber! now all forms are over;
Now open villainy, now open hate!
Defend thy life!
Rez.   De Monfort, thou art mad.
De Mon. Speak not, but draw. Now for thy hated life!
          [*They fight:* REZENVELT *parries his thrusts with great skill,
          and at last disarms him.*
Then take my life, black fiend, for hell assists thee.
Rez. No, Monfort, but I'll take away your sword,
Not as a mark of disrespect to you,
But for your safety. By to-morrow's eve
I'll call on you myself and give it back;
And then, if I am charg'd with any wrong,
I'll justify myself. Farewell, strange man!

                                                        [*Exit.*
          [DE MONFORT *stands for some time quite motionless, like
          one stupified. Enters to him a servant: he starts.*
De Mon. Ha! who art thou?
Ser.   'Tis I, an' please your honour.
De Mon. (*staring wildly at him*). Ha! who art thou?
Ser. Your servant Jacques.
De Mon.   Indeed I knew thee not.
Now leave me, and when Rezenvelt is gone,
Return and let me know.
Ser.   He's gone already.
De Mon. How! is he gone so soon?
Ser.   His servant told me,
He was in haste to go; as night comes on,
And at the evening hour he purposes
To visit some old friend, whose lonely mansion

Stands a short mile beyond the farther wood,
In which a convent is of holy nuns,
Who chaunt this night a requiem to the soul
Of a departed sister. For so well
He loves such solemn music, he has order'd
His horses onward by the usual road,
Meaning on foot to cross the wood alone.
So says his knave. Good may it do him, sooth!
I would not walk through those wild dells alone
For all his wealth. For there, as I have heard,
Foul murders have been done, and ravens scream;
And things unearthly, stalking through the night,
Have scar'd the lonely trav'ller from his wits.

                [DE MONFORT *stands fixed in thought.*
I've ta'en your steed, an' please you, from the field,
And wait your farther orders.

                    [DE MONFORT *heeds him not.*
His hoofs are sound, and where the saddle gall'd,
Begins to mend. What further must be done?

                  [DE MONFORT *still heeds him not.*
His honour heeds me not. Why should I stay?
De Mon. (*eagerly, as he is going*). He goes alone, saidst thou?
Ser. His servant told me so.
De Mon.   And at what hour?
Ser. He 'parts from Amberg by the fall of eve.
Save you, my lord! how chang'd your count'nance is!
Are you not well?
De Mon.   Yes, I am well: begone,
And wait my orders by the city wall:
I'll wend that way, and speak to thee again.

                        [*Exit servant.*
    [DE MONFORT *walks rapidly two or three times across the
    stage; then seizes his dagger from the wall, looks steadfastly
    at its point, and exit hastily.*

SCENE III.

Moonlight. A wild path in a wood, shaded with trees. Enter De Monfort, *with a strong expression of disquiet, mixed with fear, upon his face, looking behind him, and bending his ear to the ground, as if he listened to something.*

De Mon. How hollow groans the earth beneath my tread!
　　Is there an echo here? Methinks it sounds
　　As though some heavy footstep follow'd me.
　　I will advance no farther.
　　Deep settled shadows rest across the path,
　　And thickly-tangled boughs o'erhang this spot.
　　O that a tenfold gloom did cover it,
　　That 'mid the murky darkness I might strike!
　　As in the wild confusion of a dream,
　　Things horrid, bloody, terrible do pass,
　　As though they pass'd not; nor impress the mind
　　With the fix'd clearness of reality.
　　　　　　　　　　[*An owl is heard screaming near him.*
　　(*Starting.*) What sound is that?
　　　　　　　　　　[*Listens, and the owl cries again.*
　　It is the screech-owl's cry.
　　Foul bird of night! what spirit guides thee here?
　　Art thou instinctive drawn to scenes of horror?
　　I've heard of this.
　　　　　　　　　　[*Pauses and listens.*
　　How those fall'n leaves so rustle on the path,
　　With whisp'ring noise, as though the earth around me
　　Did utter secret things.
　　The distant river, too, bears to mine ear
　　A dismal wailing. O mysterious night!
　　Thou art not silent; many tongues hast thou.
　　A distant gath'ring blast sounds through the wood,
　　And dark clouds fleetly hasten o'er the sky:
　　O! that a storm would rise, a raging storm;
　　Amidst the roar of warring elements
　　I'd lift my hand and strike! but this pale light,

The calm distinctness of each stilly thing,
Is terrible (*starting*). Footsteps, and near me too!
He comes! he comes! I'll watch him farther on—
I cannot do it here.

[*Exit.*

Enter REZENVELT, *and continues his way slowly from the bottom of the
stage: as he advances to the front, the owl screams, he stops and listens,
and the owl screams again.*

Rez. Ha! does the night-bird greet me on my way?
How much his hooting is in harmony
With such a scene as this! I like it well.
Oft when a boy, at the still twilight hour,
I've leant my back against some knotted oak,
And loudly mimick'd him, till to my call
He answer would return, and, through the gloom,
We friendly converse held.
Between me and the star-bespangled sky,
Those aged oaks their crossing branches wave,
And through them looks the pale and placid moon.
How like a crocodile, or winged snake,
Yon sailing cloud bears on its dusky length!
And now transformed by the passing wind,
Methinks it seems a flying Pegasus.
Ay, but a shapeless band of blacker hue
Comes swiftly after.—
A hollow murm'ring wind sounds through the trees;
I hear it from afar; this bodes a storm.
I must not linger here—

[*A bell heard at some distance.*
The convent bell.
'Tis distant still: it tells their hour of prayer.
It sends a solemn sound upon the breeze,
That, to a fearful superstitious mind,
In such a scene, would like a death-knell come.

[*Exit.*

ACT V.

SCENE I.

The inside of a convent chapel, of old Gothic architecture, almost dark: two torches only are seen at a distance, burning over a newly covered[1] grave. Lightning is seen flashing through the windows, and thunder heard, with the sound of wind beating upon the building. Enter two monks.

1st monk. The storm increases: hark how dismally
    It howls along the cloisters. How goes time?
2nd monk. It is the hour: I hear them near at hand:
    And when the solemn requiem has been sung
    For the departed sister, we'll retire.
    Yet, should this tempest still more violent grow,
    We'll beg a friendly shelter till the morn.
1st monk. See, the procession enters: let us join.
        [*The organ strikes up a solemn prelude. Enter a procession
        of nuns, with the abbess, bearing torches. After compassing
        the grave twice, and remaining there some time, the organ
        plays a grand dirge, while they stand round the grave.*

SONG BY THE NUNS.

Departed soul, whose poor remains
This hallow'd lowly grave contains;
Whose passing storm of life is o'er,
Whose pains and sorrows are no more;
Bless'd be thou with the bless'd above,
Where all is joy, and purity, and love!

Let HIM, in might and mercy dread,
Lord of the living and the dead;
In whom the stars of heav'n rejoice,

---

[1] I have put above newly covered instead of new-made grave, as it stands in the former editions, because I wish not to give the idea of a funeral procession, but merely that of a hymn or requiem sung over the grave of a person who has been recently buried.

And the ocean lifts its voice;
Thy spirit, purified, to glory raise,
To sing with holy saints his everlasting praise!

Departed soul, who in this earthly scene
Hast our lowly sister been,
Swift be thy way to where the blessed dwell!
Until we meet thee there, farewell! farewell!

*Enter a young pensioner, with a wild terrified look, her hair and dress all
scattered, and rushes forward amongst them.*

Abb. Why com'st thou here, with such disorder'd looks,
    To break upon our sad solemnity?
Pen. Oh! I did hear through the receding blast,
    Such horrid cries! they made my blood run chill.
Abb. 'Tis but the varied voices of the storm,
    Which many times will sound like distant screams:
    It has deceiv'd thee.
Pen. O no, for twice it call'd, so loudly call'd,
    With horrid strength, beyond the pitch of nature;
    And murder! murder! was the dreadful cry.
    A third time it return'd with feeble strength,
    But o' the sudden ceas'd, as though the words
    Were smother'd rudely in the grappled throat,
    And all was still again, save the wild blast
    Which at a distance growl'd.—
    Oh! it will never from my mind depart!
    That dreadful cry, all i' the instant still'd:
    For then, so near, some horrid deed was done,
    And none to rescue.
Abb. Where didst thou hear it?
Pen.   In the higher cells,
    As now a window, open'd by the storm,
    I did attempt to close.
1st monk. I wish our brother Bernard were arriv'd;
    He is upon his way.

Abb. Be not alarm'd; it still may be deception.
　　'Tis meet we finish our solemnity,
　　Nor show neglect unto the honour'd dead.
　　　　　[*Gives a sign, and the organ plays again: just as it ceases, a
　　　　　loud knocking is heard without.*
Abb. Ha! who may this be? hush!

　　　　　　　　　　　　　　　　[*Knocking heard again.*
2d monk. It is the knock of one in furious haste.
　　Hush! hush! What footsteps come? Ha! brother Bernard.

　　　　　Enter BERNARD *bearing a lantern.*

1st monk. See, what a look he wears of stiffen'd fear!
　　Where hast thou been, good brother?
Bern. I've seen a horrid sight!
All gathering round him and speaking at once. What hast thou seen?
Bern. As on I hasten'd, bearing thus my light,
　　Across the path, not fifty paces off,
　　I saw a murder'd corse, stretch'd on his back,
　　Smear'd with new blood, as though but freshly slain.
Abb. A man or woman was't?
Bern. 　　　　　　　　　　A man, a man!
Abb. Didst thou examine if within its breast
　　There yet were lodg'd some small remains of life?
　　Was it quite dead?
Bern. 　　　　　　　　Nought in the grave is deader.
　　I look'd but once, yet life did never lodge
　　In any form so laid.
　　A chilly horror seiz'd me, and I fled.
1st monk. And does the face seem all unknown to thee?
Bern. The face! I would not on the face have look'd
　　For e'en a kingdom's wealth, for all the world!
　　O no! the bloody neck, the bloody neck!
　　　　　[*Shaking his head and shuddering with horror. Loud
　　　　　knocking heard without.*
Sist. Good mercy! who comes next?
Bern. 　　　　　　　　　　Not far behind
　　I left our brother Thomas on the road;

But then he did repent him as he went,
And threatened to return.
2d monk.   See, here he comes.

Enter Brother THOMAS, *with a wild terrified look.*

1st monk. How wild he looks!
Bern. (*going up to him eagerly*). What, hast thou seen it too?
Thom. Yes, yes! it glared upon me as it pass'd.
Bern. What glared upon thee?
                    [*All gathering round* THOMAS, *and speaking at once.*
O! what hast thou seen?
Thom. As striving with the blast I onward came,
Turning my feeble lantern from the wind,
Its light upon a dreadful visage gleam'd,
Which paus'd and look'd upon me as it pass'd;
But such a look, such wildness of despair,
Such horror-strained features, never yet
Did earthly visage show. I shrank and shudder'd.
If a damn'd spirit may to earth return,
I've seen it.
Bern.   Was there any blood upon it?
Thom. Nay, as it pass'd, I did not see its form;
Nought but the horrid face.
Bern. It is the murderer.
1st monk.   What way went it?
Thom. I durst not look till I had pass'd it far.
Then turning round, upon the rising bank,
I saw, between me and the paly sky,
A dusky form, tossing and agitated.
I stopp'd to mark it; but, in truth, I found
'Twas but a sapling bending to the wind,
And so I onward hied, and look'd no more.
1st monk. But we must look to't; we must follow it:
Our duty so commands. (*To* 2d monk.) Will you go, brother?
(*To* BERNARD.) And you, good Bernard?
Bern. If I needs must go.
1st monk. Come, we must all go.

Abb. Heaven be with you, then!

[*Exeunt monks.*

Pen. Amen! amen! Good heav'n, be with us all!
      O what a dreadful night!
Abb. Daughters, retire; peace to the peaceful dead!
      Our solemn ceremony now is finish'd.

[*Exeunt.*

SCENE II.

*A large room in the convent, very dark. Enter the abbess, young pensioner
bearing a light, and several nuns; she sets down the light on a table at the
bottom of the stage, so that the room is still very gloomy.*

Abb. They have been longer absent than I thought:
      I fear he has escap'd them.
1st nun. Heaven forbid!
Pen. No, no, found out foul murder ever is,
      And the foul murderer too.
2d nun. The good Saint Francis will direct their search;
      The blood so near this holy convent shed
      For threefold vengeance calls.
Abb. I hear a noise within the inner court—
      They are return'd (*listening*); and Bernard's voice I hear:
      They are return'd.
Pen.   Why do I tremble so?
      It is not I who ought to tremble thus.
2d nun. I hear them at the door.
Bern. (*without*). Open the door, I pray thee, brother Thomas;
      I cannot now unhand the prisoner.
(*All speak together, shrinking back from the door, and staring upon one
      another.*) He is with them!
            [*A folding door at the bottom of the stage is opened, and enter*
            BERNARD, THOMAS, *and the other two monks, carrying
            lanterns in their hands, and bringing in* DE MONFORT. *They
            are likewise followed by other monks. As they lead forward*
            DE MONFORT, *the light is turned away, so that he is seen*

obscurely; but when they come to the front of the stage, they
turn the light side of their lanterns on him at once, and his
face is seen in all the strengthened horror of despair, with his
hands and clothes bloody.

(*Abbess and nuns speak at once, and start back*). Holy saints be with us!

Bern. (*to abb.*) Behold the man of blood!

Abb. Of misery too; I cannot look upon him.

Bern. (*to nuns*). Nay, holy sisters, turn not thus away.
    Speak to him, if, perchance, he will regard you:
    For from his mouth we have no utt'rance heard,
    Save one deep groan and smother'd exclamation,
    When first we seiz'd him.

Abb. (*to* De Mon.) Most miserable man, how art thou thus?

                              [*Pauses.*

    Thy tongue is silent, but those bloody hands
    Do witness horrid things. What is thy name?

De Mon. (*roused, looks steadfastly at the abbess for some time; then*
    speaking in a short hurried voice). I have no name.

Abb. (*to* Bern.) Do it thyself; I'll speak to him no more.

Pen. O holy saints! that this should be the man
    Who did against his fellow lift the stroke,
    Whilst he so loudly call'd.—
    Still in my ears it rings: O murder! murder!

De Mon. (*starting*). He calls again!

Pen. No, he did call, but now his voice is still'd.
    'Tis past.

De Mon.   'Tis past.

Pen. Yes, it is past! art thou not he who did it?

        [De Monfort *utters a deep groan, and is supported from*
        falling by the monks. A noise is heard without.

Abb. What noise is this of heavy lumb'ring steps,
    Like men who with a weighty burthen come?

Bern. It is the body: I have orders given
    That here it should be laid.

        [*Enter men bearing the body of* Rezenvelt, *covered with a*
        white cloth, and set it down in the middle of the room: they
        then uncover it. De Monfort *stands fixed and motionless*

with horror, only that a sudden shivering seems to pass over
him when they uncover the corpse. The abbess and nuns
shrink back and retire to some distance, all the rest fixing
their eyes steadfastly upon DE MONFORT. *A long pause.*

Bern. (to DE MON.)

Seest thou the lifeless corpse, those bloody wounds?
See how he lies, who but so shortly since
A living creature was, with all the powers
Of sense, and motion, and humanity!
Oh! what a heart had he who did this deed!

1st *monk (looking at the body).*

How hard those teeth against the lips are press'd,
As though he struggled still!

2nd *monk.* The hands too, clench'd: nature's last fearful effort.

[DE MONFORT *still stands motionless. Brother* THOMAS
then goes to the body, and raising up the head a little, turns
it towards DE MONFORT.

Thom. Knowst thou this ghastly face?

De Mon. (putting his hands before his face in violent perturbation).

Oh, do not! do not! Veil it from my sight!
Put me to any agony but this!

Thom. Ha! dost thou then confess the dreadful deed?

Hast thou against the laws of awful heaven
Such horrid murder done? What fiend could tempt thee?

[*Pauses, and looks steadfastly at* DE MONFORT.

De Mon. I hear thy words, but do not hear their sense—

Hast thou not cover'd it?

Bern. (to THOM.) Forbear, my brother, for thou seest right well

He is not in a state to answer thee.
Let us retire and leave him for awhile.
These windows are with iron grated o'er;
He is secur'd, and other duty calls.

Thom. Then let it be.

Bern. (to monks, &c.) Come, let us all depart.

[*Exeunt abbess and nuns, followed by the monks, one monk*
lingering a little behind.

De Mon. All gone! *(Perceiving the monk.)* O stay thou here!

Monk.   It must not be.

De Mon. I'll give thee gold; I'll make thee rich in gold,
If thou wilt stay e'en but a little while.

Monk. I must not, must not, stay.

De Mon.   I do conjure thee!

Monk. I dare not stay with thee.

[*Going.*

De Mon.   And wilt thou go?

[*Catching hold of him eagerly.*

O! throw thy cloak upon this grizly form!
The unclos'd eyes do stare upon me still.
O do not leave me thus!

[*Monk covers the body, and exit.*

De Mon. (*alone, looking at the covered body, but at a distance*).
Alone with thee! but thou art nothing now.
'Tis done, 'tis number'd with the things o'erpast;
Would! would it were to come!—
What fated end, what darkly gathering cloud
Will close on all this horror?
O that dire madness would unloose my thoughts,
And fill my mind with wildest fantasies,
Dark, restless, terrible! aught, aught but this!

[*Pauses and shudders.*

How with convulsive life he heav'd beneath me,
E'en with the death's wound gor'd! O horrid, horrid!
Methinks I feel him still.—What sound is that?
I heard a smother'd groan.—It is impossible!

[*Looking steadfastly at the body.*

It moves! it moves! the cloth doth heave and swell.
It moves again! I cannot suffer this—
Whate'er it be, I will uncover it.

[*Runs to the corpse, and tears off the cloth in despair.*

All still beneath.
Nought is there here but fix'd and grizly death,
How sternly fixed! Oh! those glazed eyes!
They look upon me still.

[*Shrinks back with horror.*

Come, madness! come unto me, senseless death!
I cannot suffer this! Here, rocky wall,
Scatter these brains, or dull them!

> [*Runs furiously, and dashing his head against the wall, falls upon the floor.*

Enter two monks hastily.

1st monk. See: wretched man, he hath destroy'd himself.
2d monk. He does but faint. Let us remove him hence.
1st monk. We did not well to leave him here alone.
2d monk. Come, let us bear him to the open air.

> [*Exeunt, bearing out* DE MONFORT.

SCENE III.

Before the gates of the convent. Enter JANE DE MONFORT, FREBERG, *and* MANUEL. *As they are proceeding towards the gate, Jane stops short and shrinks back.*

Freb. Ha! wherefore? has a sudden illness seiz'd thee?
Jane. No, no, my friend.—And yet I am very faint—
I dread to enter here.
Man.   Ay, so I thought:
For, when between the trees, that abbey tower
First show'd its top, I saw your count'nance change.
But breathe a little here: I'll go before,
And make inquiry at the nearest gate.
Freb. Do so, good Manuel.

> [MANUEL *goes and knocks at the gate.*

Courage, dear madam: all may yet be well.
Rezenvelt's servant, frighten'd with the storm,
And seeing that his master join'd him not,
As by appointment, at the forest's edge,
Might be alarm'd, and give too ready ear
To an unfounded rumour.
He saw it not; he came not here himself.

Jane (looking eagerly to the gate, where MANUEL *talks with the porter).*
    Ha! see, he talks with some one earnestly.
    And seest thou not that motion of his hands?
    He stands like one who hears a horrid tale.
    Almighty God!

                        [MANUEL *goes into the convent.*
             He comes not back; he enters.

Freb. Bear up, my noble friend.

Jane. I will, I will! But this suspense is dreadful.

       [*A long pause.* MANUEL *re-enters from the convent, and
       comes forward slowly with a sad countenance.*
    Is this the face of one who bears good tidings?
    O God! his face doth tell the horrid fact:
    There is nought doubtful here.

Freb.   How is it, Manuel?

Man. I've seen him through a crevice in his door:
    It is indeed my master.

                      [*Bursting into tears.*
       [JANE *faints, and is supported by* FREBERG.—*Enter abbess
       and several nuns from the convent, who gather about her,
       and apply remedies. She recovers.*

1st nun. The life returns again.

2d nun. Yes, she revives.

Abb. (to FREB.) Let me entreat this noble lady's leave
    To lead her in. She seems in great distress:
    We would with holy kindness soothe her woe,
    And do by her the deeds of christian love.

Freb. Madam, your goodness has my grateful thanks.

                [*Exeunt, supporting* JANE *into the convent.*

SCENE IV.

DE MONFORT *is discovered sitting in a thoughtful posture. He remains so for some time. His face afterwards begins to appear agitated, like one whose mind is harrowed with the severest thoughts; then, starting from his seat, he clasps his hands together, and holds them up to heaven.*

De Mon. O that I ne'er had known the light of day!
  That filmy darkness on mine eyes had hung,
  And clos'd me out from the fair face of nature!
  O that my mind in mental darkness pent,
  Had no perception, no distinction known,
  Of fair or foul, perfection or defect,
  Nor thought conceiv'd of proud pre-eminence!
  O that it had! O that I had been form'd
  An idiot from the birth! a senseless changeling,
  Who eats his glutton's meal with greedy haste,
  Nor knows the hand which feeds him.—
                    [*Pauses; then in a calmer sorrowful voice.*
  What am I now? how ends the day of life?
  For end it must; and terrible this gloom,
  This storm of horrors that surrounds its close.
  This little term of nature's agony
  Will soon be o'er, and what is past is past;
  But shall I then, on the dark lap of earth
  Lay me to rest, in still unconsciousness,
  Like senseless clod that doth no pressure feel
  From wearing foot of daily passenger;
  Like a steep'd rock o'er which the breaking waves
  Bellow and foam unheard? O would I could!

Enter MANUEL, *who springs forward to his master, but is checked upon perceiving* DE MONFORT *draw back and look sternly at him.*

Man. My lord, my master! O my dearest master!
                [DE MONFORT *still looks at him without speaking.*
  Nay, do not thus regard me, good my lord!
  Speak to me: am I not your faithful Manuel?

De Mon. (in a hasty broken voice). Art thou alone?

Man. No, sir, the Lady Jane is on her way;
   She is not far behind.

De Mon. (tossing his arm over his head in an agony).
                     This is too much! all I can bear but this!
   It must not be.—Run and prevent her coming.
   Say, he who is detain'd a prisoner here
   Is one to her unknown. I now am nothing.
   I am a man of holy claims bereft;
   Out of the pale of social kindred cast;
   Nameless and horrible.—
   Tell her De Monfort far from hence is gone
   Into a desolate and distant land,
   Ne'er to return again. Fly, tell her this;
   For we must meet no more.

Enter JANE DE MONFORT, *bursting into the chamber and followed by*
   FREBERG, *abbess, and several nuns.*

Jane. We must! we must! My brother, O my brother!
         [DE MONFORT *turns away his head and hides his face with*
         his arm. JANE *stops short, and, making a great effort, turns*
         to FREBERG, *and the others who followed her, and with an*
         air of dignity stretches out her hand, beckoning them to
         retire. All retire but FREBERG, *who seems to hesitate.*
   And thou too, Freberg: call it not unkind.
            [*Exit* FREBERG: JANE *and* DE MONFORT *only remain.*

Jane. My hapless Monfort!
         [DE MONFORT *turns round and looks sorrowfully upon her;*
         she opens her arms to him, and he, rushing into them, hides
         his face upon her breast, and weeps.

Jane. Ay, give thy sorrow vent; here mayst thou weep.

De Mon. (in broken accents). Oh! this, my sister, makes me feel again
   The kindness of affection.
   My mind has in a dreadful storm been tost;
   Horrid and dark—I thought to weep no more—
   I've done a deed—But I am human still.

Jane. I know thy suff'rings: leave thy sorrow free!
    Thou art with one who never did upbraid;
    Who mourns, who loves thee still.
De Mon. Ah! sayst thou so? no, no; it should not be.
    (*Shrinking from her.*) I am a foul and bloody murderer,
    For such embrace unmeet: O leave me! leave me!
    Disgrace and public shame abide me now;
    And all, alas! who do my kindred own,
    The direful portion share.—Away, away!
    Shall a disgrac'd and public criminal
    Degrade thy name, and claim affinity
    To noble worth like thine?—I have no name—
    I'm nothing now, not e'en to thee: depart.
           [*She takes his hand, and grasping it firmly, speaks with a*
           determined voice.
Jane. De Monfort, hand in hand we have enjoy'd
    The playful term of infancy together;
    And in the rougher path of ripen'd years
    We've been each other's stay. Dark low'rs our fate,
    And terrible the storm that gathers o'er us;
    But nothing, till that latest agony
    Which severs thee from nature, shall unloose
    This fix'd and sacred hold. In thy dark prison-house;
    In the terrific face of armed law;
    Yea, on the scaffold, if it needs must be,
    I never will forsake thee.
De Mon. (*looking at her with admiration.*)
    Heav'n bless thy gen'rous soul, my noble Jane!
    I thought to sink beneath this load of ill,
    Depress'd with infamy and open shame;
    I thought to sink in abject wretchedness:
    But for thy sake I'll rouse my manhood up,
    And meet it bravely; no unseemly weakness,
    I feel my rising strength, shall blot my end,
    To clothe thy cheek with shame.
Jane. Yes, thou art noble still.
De Mon. With thee I am; who were not so with thee?
    But, ah! my sister, short will be the term:

Death's stroke will come, and in that state beyond,
Where things unutterable wait the soul,
New from its earthly tenement discharg'd,
We shall be sever'd far.
Far as the spotless purity of virtue
Is from the murd'rer's guilt, far shall we be.
This is the gulf of dread uncertainty
From which the soul recoils.

Jane. The God who made thee is a God of mercy:
Think upon this.

De Mon. (*shaking his head*). No, no! this blood! this blood!

Jane. Yes, e'en the sin of blood may be forgiv'n,
When humble penitence hath once aton'd.

De Mon. (*eagerly*). What, after terms of lengthen'd misery,
Imprison'd anguish of tormented spirits,
Shall I again, a renovated soul,
Into the blessed family of the good
Admittance have? Thinkst thou that this may be?
Speak, if thou canst: O speak me comfort here!
For dreadful fancies, like an armed host,
Have push'd me to despair. It is most horrible—
O speak of hope! if any hope there be.

[JANE *is silent, and looks sorrowfully upon him; then
clasping her hands, and turning her eyes to heaven, seems
to mutter a prayer.*

De Mon. Ha! dost thou pray for me? heav'n hear thy prayer!
I fain would kneel.—Alas! I dare not do it.

Jane. Not so! all by th' Almighty Father form'd,
May in their deepest misery call on Him.
Come kneel with me, my brother.

[*She kneels and prays to herself; he kneels by her, and
clasps his hands fervently, but speaks not. A noise of chains
clanking is heard without, and they both rise.*

De Mon. Hearest thou that noise? They come to interrupt us.

Jane. (*moving towards a side door*). Then let us enter here.

De Mon. (*catching hold of her with a look of horror*).
Not there—not there—the corpse—the bloody corpse!

Jane. What, lies he there?—Unhappy Rezenvelt!

De Mon. A sudden thought has come across my mind;
    How came it not before? Unhappy Rezenvelt!
    Sayst thou but this?
Jane. What should I say? he was an honest man;
    I still have thought him such, as such lament him.

                      [DE MONFORT *utters a deep groan.*
    What means this heavy groan?
De Mon.   It hath a meaning.

*Enter abbess and monks, with two officers of justice carrying fetters in their
hands to put upon* DE MONFORT.

Jane (*starting.*) What men are these?
1st off. Lady, we are the servants of the law,
    And bear with us a power, which doth constrain
    To bind with fetters this our prisoner.

                    [*Pointing to* DE MONFORT.
Jane. A stranger uncondemn'd? this cannot be.
1st off. As yet, indeed, he is by law unjudg'd,
    But is so far condemn'd by circumstance,
    That law, or custom sacred held as law,
    Doth fully warrant us, and it must be.
Jane. Nay, say not so; he has no power t'escape:
    Distress hath bound him with a heavy chain;
    There is no need of yours.
1st off. We must perform our office.
Jane. O! do not offer this indignity!
1st off. Is it indignity in sacred law
    To bind a murderer? (*To* 2d *off.*) Come, do thy work.
Jane. Harsh are thy words, and stern thy harden'd brow;
    Dark is thine eye; but all some pity have
    Unto the last extreme of misery.
    I do beseech thee! if thou art a man—

                      [*Kneeling to him.*
        [DE MONFORT, *roused at this, runs up to* JANE, *and raises
        her hastily from the ground: then stretches himself up
        proudly.*

De Mon. (*to* JANE). Stand thou erect in native dignity;
And bend to none on earth the suppliant knee,
Though cloth'd in power imperial. To my heart
It gives a feller gripe than many irons.
(*Holding out his hands.*) Here, officers of law, bind on those
shackles;
And, if they are too light, bring heavier chains,
Add iron to iron; load, crush me to the ground:
Nay, heap ten thousand weight upon my breast,
For that were best of all.

> [*A long pause, whilst they put irons upon him. After they are on,* JANE *looks at him sorrowfully, and lets her head sink on her breast.* DE MONFORT *stretches out his hand, looks at them, and then at* JANE; *crosses them over his breast, and endeavours to suppress his feelings.*[1]

1st off. (*to* DE MONFORT). I have it, too, in charge to move you hence,
Into another chamber more secure.
De Mon. Well, I am ready, sir.

> [*Approaching* JANE, *whom the abbess is endeavouring to comfort, but to no purpose.*

Ah! wherefore thus, most honour'd and most dear?
Shrink not at the accoutrements of ill,
Daring the thing itself.

> [*Endeavouring to look cheerful.*

Wilt thou permit me with a gyved hand?

> [*She gives him her hand, which he raises to his lips.*

This was my proudest office.

> [*Exeunt,* DE MONFORT *leading out* JANE.

---

[1] Should this play ever be acted, perhaps it would be better that the curtain should drop here; since here the story may be considered as completed, and what comes after, prolongs the piece too much when our interest for the fate of De Monfort is at an end. [Baillie's note].

SCENE V.

An apartment in the convent, opening into another room, whose low arched door is seen at the bottom of the stage. In one corner a monk is seen kneeling. Enter another monk, who, on perceiving him, stops till he rises from his knees, and then goes eagerly up to him.

1st monk. How is the prisoner?
2d monk (*pointing to the door*).
   He is within, and the strong hand of death
   Is dealing with him.
1st monk.   How is this, good brother?
   Methought he brav'd it with a manly spirit;
   And led, with shackled hands, his sister forth,
   Like one resolv'd to bear misfortune bravely.
2d monk. Yes, with heroic courage, for a while
   He seem'd inspir'd; but soon depress'd again,
   Remorse and dark despair o'erwhelm'd his soul:
   And, from the violent working of his mind,
   Some stream of life within his breast has burst;
   For many a time, within a little space,
   The ruddy tide has rush'd into his mouth.
   God grant his pains be short!
1st monk.   How does the lady?
2d monk. She sits and bears his head upon her lap.
   Wiping the cold drops from his ghastly face
   With such a look of tender wretchedness,
   It wrings the heart to see her.
   How goes the night?
1st monk. It wears, methinks, upon the midnight hour.
   It is a dark and fearful night; the moon
   Is wrapp'd in sable clouds; the chill blast sounds
   Like dismal lamentations. Ay, who knows
   What voices mix with the dark midnight winds?
   Nay, as I pass'd that yawning cavern's mouth,
   A whisp'ring sound, unearthly, reach'd my ear,
   And o'er my head a chilly coldness crept.
   Are there not wicked fiends and damned sprites,

Whom yawning charnels, and th' unfathom'd depths
Of secret darkness, at this fearful hour,
Do upwards send, to watch, unseen, around
The murd'rer's death-bed, at his fatal term,
Ready to hail with dire and horrid welcome,
Their future mate?—I do believe there are.

2d monk. Peace, peace! a God of wisdom and of mercy,
Veils from our sight—Ha! hear that heavy groan.

[A groan heard within.

1st monk. It is the dying man.

[Another groan.

2d monk. God grant him rest!

[Listening at the door.

I hear him struggling in the gripe of death.
O piteous heaven!

[Goes from the door. Enter Brother THOMAS from the chamber.

How now, good brother?

Thom. Retire, my friends. O many a bed of death
With all its pangs and horrors I have seen,
But never aught like this! Retire, my friends!
The death-bell will its awful signal give,
When he has breath'd his last.
I would move hence, but I am weak and faint:
Let me a moment on thy shoulder lean.
Oh, weak and mortal man!

[Leans on 2d monk: a pause.

Enter BERNARD from the chamber.

2d monk. (to BERN.) How is your penitent?
Bern. He is with HIM who made him; HIM, who knows
The soul of man: before whose awful presence
Th' unsceptred tyrant stands despoil'd and helpless,
Like an unclothed babe.

[Bell tolls.

The dismal sound!
Retire, and pray for the blood-stained soul:
May heav'n have mercy on him!

[*Bell tolls again.*
[*Exeunt.*

SCENE VI.

A hall or large room in the convent. The bodies of DE MONFORT *and* REZENVELT *are discovered laid out upon a low table or platform, covered with black.* FREBERG, BERNARD, *abbess, monks, and nuns attending.*

Abb. (*to* FREB.) Here must they lie, my lord, until we know
  Respecting this the order of the law.
Freb. And you have wisely done, my rev'rend mother.
    [*Goes to the table, and looks at the bodies, but without uncovering
    them.*
  Unhappy men! ye, both in nature rich,
  With talents and with virtues were endued.
  Ye should have lov'd, yet deadly rancour came,
  And in the prime and manhood of your days
  Ye sleep in horrid death. O direful hate!
  What shame and wretchedness his portion is,
  Who, for a secret inmate, harbours thee!
  And who shall call him blameless, who excites,
  Ungen'rously excites, with careless scorn,
  Such baleful passion in a brother's breast,
  Whom heav'n commands to love? Low are ye laid:
  Still all contention now.—Low are ye laid:
  I lov'd you both, and mourn your hapless fall.
Abb. They were your friends, my lord?
Freb. I lov'd them both. How does the Lady Jane?
Abb. She bears misfortune with intrepid soul.
  I never saw in woman, bow'd with grief,
  Such moving dignity.
Freb.   Ay, still the same.
  I've known her long: of worth most excellent;

But in the day of woe she ever rose
Upon the mind with added majesty,
As the dark mountain more sublimely tow'rs
Mantled in clouds and storm.

Enter MANUEL *and* JEROME.

Man. (*pointing*). Here, my good Jerome, here's a piteous sight.
Jer. A piteous sight! yet I will look upon him:
    I'll see his face in death. Alas, alas!
    I've seen him move a noble gentleman!
    And when with vexing passion undisturb'd,
    He look'd most graciously.
        [*Lifts up in mistake the cloth from the body of* REZENVELT, *and
        starts back with horror.*
    Oh! this was the bloody work! Oh! oh, oh, oh!
    That human hands could do it!
                        [*Drops the cloth again.*
Man. That is the murder'd corpse; here lies De Monfort.
                   [*Going to uncover the other body.*
Jer. (*turning away his head*). No, no! I cannot look upon him now.
Man. Didst thou not come to see him?
Jer. Fy! cover him—inter him in the dark—
    Let no one look upon him.
Bern. (*to* JER.) Well dost thou show the abhorrence nature feels
    For deeds of blood, and I commend thee well.
    In the most ruthless heart compassion wakes
    For one, who, from the hand of fellow man,
    Hath felt such cruelty.
               [*Uncovering the body of* REZENVELT.
    This is the murder'd corse:
             [*Uncovering the body of* DE MONFORT.
          But see, I pray!
    Here lies the murderer. What thinkst thou here?
    Look on those features, thou hast seen them oft,
    With the last dreadful conflict of despair,
    So fix'd in horrid strength.
    See those knit brows; those hollow sunken eyes;

The sharpen'd nose, with nostrils all distent;
That writhed mouth, where yet the teeth appear,
In agony, to gnash the nether lip.
Thinkst thou, less painful than the murd'rer's knife
Was such a death as this?
Ay, and how changed too those matted locks!

Jer. Merciful heaven! his hair is grizly grown,
Chang'd to white age, that was, but two days since,
Black as the raven's plume. How may this be?

Bern. Such change, from violent conflict of the mind,
Will sometimes come.

Jer.   Alas, alas! most wretched!
Thou wert too good to do a cruel deed,
And so it kill'd thee. Thou hast suffer'd for it.
God rest thy soul! I needs must touch thy hand,
And bid thee long farewell.

> [*Laying his hand on* DE MONFORT.

Bern. Draw back, draw back: see where the lady comes.

Enter JANE DE MONFORT. FREBERG, *who has been for some time retired
by himself at the bottom of the stage, now steps forward to lead her in, but
checks himself on seeing the fixed sorrow of her countenance, and draws
back respectfully.* JANE *advances to the table, and looks attentively at the
covered bodies.* MANUEL *points out the body of* DE MONFORT, *and she
gives a gentle inclination of the head, to signify that she understands him.
She then bends tenderly over it, without speaking.*

Man. (*to* JANE, *as she raises her head*). Oh, madam, my good lord!

Jane. Well says thy love, my good and faithful Manuel:
But we must mourn in silence.

Man. Alas! the times that I have followed him!

Jane. Forbear, my faithful Manuel. For this love
Thou hast my grateful thanks; and here's my hand:
Thou hast lov'd him, and I'll remember thee.
Where'er I am, in whate'er spot of earth
I linger out the remnant of my days,
I will remember thee.

Man. Nay, by the living God! where'er you are,
    There will I be. I'll prove a trusty servant:
    I'll follow you, even to the world's end.
    My master's gone; and I indeed am mean,
    Yet will I show the strength of nobler men,
    Should any dare upon your honour'd worth
    To put the slightest wrong. Leave you, dear lady!
    Kill me, but say not this!

                            [*Throwing himself at her feet.*

Jane (raising him). Well, then! be thou my servant, and my friend.
    Art thou, good Jerome, too, in kindness come?
    I see thou art. How goes it with thine age?

Jer. Ah, madam! woe and weakness dwell with age:
    Would I could serve you with a young man's strength!
    I'd spend my life for you.

Jane.   Thanks, worthy Jerome.
    O! who hath said, the wretched have no friends?

Freb. In every sensible and gen'rous breast
    Affliction finds a friend; but unto thee,
    Thou most exalted and most honourable,
    The heart in warmest adoration bows,
    And even a worship pays.

Jane. Nay, Freberg! Freberg! grieve me not, my friend.
    He, to whose ear my praise most welcome was,
    Hears it no more! and, oh, our piteous lot!
    What tongue will talk of him? Alas, alas!
    This more than all will bow me to the earth;
    I feel my misery here.
    The voice of praise was wont to name us both:
    I had no greater pride.

        [*Covers her face with her hands, and bursts into tears. Here they
        all hang about her:* FREBERG *supporting her tenderly,* MANUEL
        embracing her knees, and old Jerome catching hold of her robe
        affectionately.* BERNARD, *abbess, monks, and nuns likewise gather
        round her, with looks of sympathy. Enter two officers of Law.*

1st off.   Where is the prisoner?
    Into our hands he straight must be consign'd.

Bern. He is not subject now to human laws;
    The prison that awaits him is the grave.
1st off. Ha! sayst thou so? there is foul play in this.
Man. (*to off.*) Hold thy unrighteous tongue, or hie thee hence,
    Nor in the presence of this honour'd dame,
    Utter the slightest meaning of reproach.
1st off. I am an officer on duty call'd,
    And have authority to say, "How died he?"
             [*Here* JANE *shakes off the weakness of grief, and repressing*
             MANUEL, *who is about to reply to the officer, steps forward*
             with dignity.
Jane. Tell them by whose authority you come,
    He died that death which best becomes a man,
    Who is with keenest sense of conscious ill
    And deep remorse assail'd, a wounded spirit.
    A death that kills the noble and the brave,
    And only them. He had no other wound.
1st off. And shall I trust to this?
Jane.   Do as thou wilt:
    To one who can suspect my simple word
    I have no more reply. Fulfil thine office.
1st off. No, lady. I believe your honour'd word,
    And will no further search.
Jane. I thank your courtesy: thanks, thanks to all;
    My rev'rend mother, and ye honour'd maids;
    Ye holy men, and you, my faithful friends;
    The blessing of the afflicted rest with you!
    And He, who to the wretched is most piteous,
    Will recompense you.—Freberg, thou art good;
    Remove the body of the friend you lov'd:
    'Tis Rezenvelt I mean. Take thou this charge:
    'Tis meet, that with his noble ancestors
    He lie entomb'd in honourable state.
    And now I have a sad request to make,
    Nor will these holy sisters scorn my boon;
    That I, within these sacred cloister walls,
    May raise a humble, nameless tomb to him,
    Who, but for one dark passion, one dire deed,

Had claim'd a record of as noble worth,
As e'er enrich'd the sculptur'd pedestal.[1]

[*Exeunt.*

---

[1] *Note.*—The last three lines of the last speech are not intended to give the reader a true character of *De Monfort,* whom I have endeavoured to represent throughout the play as, notwithstanding his other good qualities, proud, suspicious, and susceptible of envy, but only to express the partial sentiments of an affectionate sister, naturally more inclined to praise him from the misfortune into which he had fallen. [Baillie's note.]

ORRA,

A TRAGEDY,

IN FIVE ACTS.

PERSONS OF THE DRAMA.

MEN.

HUGHOBERT, *Count of Aldenberg.*

GLOTTENBAL, *his son.*

THEOBALD OF FALKENSTEIN, *a nobleman of reduced fortune, and co-burgher of Basle.*

RUDIGERE, *a knight, and commander of one of the free companies returned from the wars, and bastard of a branch of the family of* ALDENBERG.

HARTMAN, *friend of* THEOBALD, *and Banneret of Basle.*

URSTON, *a confessor.*

FRANKO, *chief of a band of outlaws.*

MAURICE, *an agent of* RUDIGERE'S.

Soldiers, vassals, outlaws, &c.

WOMEN.

ORRA, *heiress of another branch of the family of* ALDENBERG, *and ward to* HUGHOBERT.

Eleanora, *wife to* HUGHOBERT.

Cathrina, }
Alice, } *ladies attending on* ORRA.

Scene, Switzerland, *in the canton of* Basle, *and afterwards on the borders of the Black Forest in* Suabia.

Time, *towards the end of the* 14th *century.*

ACT I.

SCENE I.

An open space before the walls of a castle, with wild mountains beyond it; enter GLOTTENBAL, *armed as from the lists, but bare-headed and in disorder, and his arms soiled with earth or sand, which an Attendant is now and then brushing off, whilst another follows bearing his helmet; with him enters* MAURICE, *followed by* RUDIGERE, *who is also armed, and keeps by himself, pacing to and fro at the bottom of the stage, whilst the others come forward.*

Glot. (speaking as he enters, loud and boastingly).
    Ay, let him triumph in his paltry honours,
    Won by mere trick and accident. Good faith!
    It were a shame to call it strength or skill,
    Were it not, Rudigere?
                    [*Calling to* RUDIGERE, *who answers not.*
Maur. His brow is dark, his tongue is lock'd, my lord;
    There come no words from him; he bears it not
    So manfully as thou dost, noble Glottenbal.
Glot. Fy on't! I mind it not.
Maur. And wherefore shouldst thou? This same Theobald,
    Count and co-burgher—mixture most unseemly
    Of base and noble,—know we not right well
    What powers assist him? Mark'd you not, my lord,
    How he did turn him to the witchy north,
    When first he mounted; making his fierce steed,
    That paw'd and rear'd and shook its harness'd neck
    In generous pride, bend meekly to the earth
    Its maned crest, like one who made obeisance?
Glot. Ha! didst thou really see it?
Maur.   Yes, brave Glottenbal,
    I did right truly; and besides myself,
    Many observ'd it.
Glot.   Then 'tis manifest
    How all this foil hath been. Who e'er before
    Saw one with such advantage of the field,

Lose it so shamefully? By my good fay!
Barring foul play and other dev'lish turns,
I'd keep my courser's back with any lord,
Or knight, or squire, that e'er bestrode a steed.
Thinkst thou not, honest Maurice, that I could?
Maur. Who doubts it, good my lord? This Falkenstein
      Is but a clown to you.
Glot.   Well let him boast.
      Boasting I scorn; but I will shortly show him
      What these good arms, with no foul play against them,
      Can honestly achieve.
Maur. Yes, good my lord; but choose you well your day:
      A moonless Friday luck did never bring
      To honest combatant.
Glot. Ha! blessing on thee! I ne'er thought of this:
      Now it is clear how our mischance befell.
      Be sure thou tell to every one thou meetst,
      Friday and a dark moon suit Theobald.
      Ho there! Sir Rudigere! hearst thou not this?
Rud. (as he goes off, aside to MAUR.)
      Flatter the fool awhile and let me go,
      I cannot join thee now.
                                                    [*Exit.*

Glot. (looking after RUD.) Is he so crestfallen?
Maur. He lacks your noble spirit.
Glot.   Fye upon't!
      I heed it not. Yet, by my sword and spurs!
      'Twas a foul turn, that for my rival earn'd
      A branch of victory from Orra's hand.
Maur. Ay, foul indeed! My blood boil'd high to see it.
      Look where he proudly comes.

      Enter THEOBALD *armed, with attendants, having a green sprig
                  stuck in his helmet.*

Glot. (going up to THEOBALD). Comest thou to face me so?
      Audacious burgher!
      The Lady Orra's favour suits thee not,

> Though for a time thou hast upon me gain'd
> A seeming 'vantage.

Theo. A seeming 'vantage!—Then it is not true,
 That thou, unhors'd, layst rolling in the dust,
 Asking for quarter?—Let me crave thy pardon;
 Some strange delusion hung upon our sight
 That we believed it so.

Glot.   Off with thy taunts!
 And pull that sprig from its audacious perch:
 The favour of a dame too high for thee.

Theo. Too high indeed; and hadst thou also added,
 Too good, too fair, I had assented to it.
 Yet, be it known unto your courteous worth,
 That were this spring a queen's gift, or receiv'd
 From the brown hand of some poor mountain maid;
 Yea, or bestow'd upon my rambling head,
 As in the hairy sides of browsing kid
 The wild rose sticks a spray, unpriz'd, unbidden,
 I would not give it thee.

Glot. Dost thou so face me out? Then I will have it.

         [*Snatching at it with rage.*

     Enter HARTMAN.

Hart. (*separating them*). What! Malice! after fighting in the lists
 As noble courteous knights!

Glot. (*to* HARTMAN). Go, paltry banneret! Such friends as thou
 Become such lords as he, whose ruin'd state
 Seeks the base fellowship of restless burghers;
 Thinking to humble still, with envious spite,
 The great and noble houses of the land.
 I know ye well, and I defy you both,
 With all your damned witchery to boot.

    [*Exit grumbling, followed by* MAURICE, *&c. Manent*
    THEOPALD *and* HARTMAN.

Theo. How fierce the creature is, and full of folly!
 Like a shent cur to his own door retired,
 That bristles up his furious back, and there

Each passenger annoys.—And this is he,
Whom sordid and ambitious Hughobert,
The guardian in the selfish father sunk,
Destines for Orra's husband.—O foul shame!
The carrion-crow and royal eagle join'd,
Make not so cross a match.—But thinkst thou, Hartman,
She will submit to it?

Hart. That may be as thou pleasest, Falkenstein.

Theo. Away with mockery!

Hart.   I mock thee not.

Theo. Nay, banneret, thou dost, Saving this favour,
Which every victor in these listed combats
From ladies' hands receives, nor then regards
As more than due and stated courtesy,
She ne'er hath honour'd me with word or look
Such hope to warrant.

Hart.   Wait not thou for looks.

Theo. Thou wouldst not have me to a dame like this,
With rich domains and titled rights encompass'd,
These simple limbs, girt in their soldier's gear,
My barren hills and ruin'd tower present,
And say, "Accept—these will I nobly give
In fair exchange for thee and all thy wealth."
No, Rudolph Hartman, woo the maid thyself,
If thou hast courage for it.

Hart. Yes, Theobald of Falkenstein, I will,
And win her too; but all for thy behoof.
And when I do present, as thou hast said,
Those simple limbs, girt in their soldier's gear,
Adding thy barren hills and ruin'd tower,
With some few items more of gen'rous worth,
And native sense and manly fortitude,
I'll give her in return for all that she
Or any maid can in such barter yield,
Its fair and ample worth.

Theo.   So dost thou reckon.

Hart. And so will Orra. Do not shake thy head.
I know the maid: for still she has receiv'd me

As one who knew her noble father well,
And in the bloody field in which he died
Fought by his side, with kind familiarity:
And her stern guardian, viewing these grey hairs
And this rough visage with no jealous eye
Hath still admitted it.—I'll woo her for thee.

Theo. I do in truth believe thou meanst me well.

Hart. And this is all thou sayst? Cold frozen words!
What has bewitch'd thee, man? Is she not fair?

Theo. O fair indeed as woman need be form'd
To please and be belov'd! Though, to speak honestly,
I've fairer seen; yet such a form as Orra's
For ever in my busy fancy dwells,
Whene'er I think of wiving my lone state.
It is not this; she has too many lures;
Why wilt thou urge me on to meet her scorn?
I am not worthy of her.

Hart. (*pushing him away with gentle anger*).
Go to! I praised thy modesty short-while,
And now with dull and senseless perseverance,
Thou wouldst o'erlay me with it. Go thy ways!
If through thy fault, thus shrinking from the onset,
She should with this untoward cub be match'd,
'Twill haunt thy conscience like a damning sin,
And may it gnaw thee shrewdly!

                                        [*Exeunt.*

SCENE II.

A small apartment in the castle. Enter RUDIGERE *musing gloomily, and
    muttering to himself some time before he speaks aloud.*

Rud. No, no; it is to formless air dissolv'd,
    This cherish'd hope, this vision of my brain!
            [*Pacing to and fro, and then stopping and musing as before.*
    I daily stood contrasted in her sight
    With an ungainly fool; and when she smiled,
    Methought—But wherefore still upon this thought,

Which was perhaps but a delusion then,
Brood I with ceaseless torment? Never, never!
O never more on me, from Orra's eye,
Approving glance shall light, or gentle look!
This day's disgrace mars all my goodly dreams.
My path to greatness is at once shut up.
Still in the dust my grov'ling fortune lies.

[*Striking his breast in despair.*

Tame thine aspiring spirit, luckless wretch!
There is no hope for thee!
And shall I tame it? No, by saints and devils!
The laws have cast me off from every claim
Of house and kindred, and within my veins
Turn'd noble blood to baseness and reproach:
I'll cast them off: why should they be to me
A bar, and no protection?

[*Pacing again to and fro, and muttering low for some time
before he speaks aloud.*

Ay; this may still within my toils enthral her;
This is the secret weakness of her mind
On which I'll clutch my hold.

Enter CATHRINA *behind him, laying her hand upon him.*

Cath.   Ha! speakst thou to thyself?
Rud. (*starting*). I did not speak.
Cath. Thou didst; thy busy mind gave sound to thoughts
    Which thou didst utter with a thick harsh voice,
    Like one who speaks in sleep. Tell me their meaning.
Rud. And dost thou so presume? Be wise; be humble.

[*After a pause.*

    Has Orra oft of late requested thee
    To tell her stories of the restless dead;
    Of spectres rising at the midnight watch
    By the lone trav'ller's bed?
Cath. Wherefore of late dost thou so oft inquire
    Of what she says and does?

Rud. Be wise, and answer what I ask of thee;
    This is thy duty now.

Cath. Alas, alas! I know that one false step
    Has o'er me set a stern and ruthless master.

Rud. No, madam; 'tis thy grave and virtuous seeming;
    Thy saint-like carriage, rigid and demure,
    On which thy high repute so long has stood,
    Endowing thee with right of censorship
    O'er every simple maid, whose cheerful youth
    Wears not so thick a mask, that o'er thee sets
    This ruthless master. Hereon rests my power:
    I might expose, and therefore I command thee.

Cath. Hush, hush! approaching steps!
                    They'll find me here!
    I'll do whate'er thou wilt.

Rud. It is but Maurice: hie thee to thy closet,
    Where I will shortly come to thee. Be thou
    My faithful agent in a weighty matter,
    On which I now am bent, and I will prove
    Thy stay and shelter from the world's contempt.

Cath. Maurice to find me here! Where shall I hide me?

Rud. Nowhere, but boldly pass him as he enters.
    I'll find some good excuse; he will be silent:
    He is my agent also.

Cath.   Dost thou trust him?

Rud. Avarice his master is, as shame is thine:
    Therefore I trust to deal with both.—Away!

      Enter MAURICE, *passing* CATHRINA *as she goes out.*

Maur. What, doth the grave and virtuous Cathrina
    Vouchsafe to give thee of her company?

Rud. Yes, rigid saint! she has bestow'd upon me
    Some grave advice to bear with pious meekness
    My late discomfiture.

Maur.   Ay, and she call'd it,
    I could be sworn! heaven's judgment on thy pride.

Rud. E'en so: thou'st guess'd it.—Shall we to the ramparts
And meet the western breeze?

                                                    [*Exeunt.*

SCENE III.

A spacious apartment. Enter HUGHOBERT *and* URSTON.

Hugh. (*speaking with angry gesticulation as he enters*).
    I feed and clothe these drones, and in return
    They cheat, deceive, abuse me; nay, belike,
    Laugh in their sleeve the while. By their advice,
    This cursed tournay I proclaim'd; for still
    They puff'd me up with praises of my son—
    His grace, his skill in arms, his horsemanship—
    Count Falkenstein to him was but a clown—
    And so in Orra's eyes to give him honour,
    Full surely did I think—I'll hang them all:
    I'll starve them in a dungeon shut from light:
    I'll heap my boards no more with dainty fare
    To feed false flatterers.
Urst.   That indeed were wise:
    But art thou sure, when men shall speak the truth,
    That thou wilt feed them for it? I but hinted
    In gentle words to thee, that Glottenbal
    Was praised with partial or affected zeal,
    And thou receiv'dst it angrily.
Hugh. Ay, true indeed: but thou didst speak of him
    As one bereft of all capacity.
    Now though, God wot! I look on his defects
    With no blind love, and even in my ire
    Will sometimes call him fool; yet ne'ertheless,
    He still has parts and talents, though obscur'd
    By some untoward failings.—Heaven be praised!
    He wants not strength at least and well turn'd limbs,
    Had they but taught him how to use them. Knaves!
    They have neglected him.

Enter GLOTTENBAL, *who draws back on seeing his father.*

> Advance, young sir: art thou afraid of me,
> That thus thou shrinkest like a skulking thief
> To make disgrace the more apparent on thee?

Glot. Yes, call it then disgrace, or what you please;
> Had not my lance's point somewhat awry
> Glanced on his shield—

Hugh.   E'en so; I doubt it not;
> Thy lance's point, and every thing about thee
> Hath glanced awry. Go, rid my house, I say,
> Of all those feasting flatterers that deceive thee;
> They harbour here no more: dismiss them quickly.

Glot. Do it yourself, my lord; you are, I trow,
> Angry enough to do it sharply.

Hugh. (*turning to* URSTON). Faith!
> He gibes me fairly here; there's reason in't;
> Fools speak not thus. (*To* GLOTTENBAL.) Go to! if I am angry,
> Thou art a graceless son to tell me so.

Glot. Have you not bid me still to speak the truth?

Hugh. (*to* URSTON). Again thou hearst he makes an apt reply.

Urst. He wants not words.

Hugh. Nor meaning neither, father.

Enter ELEANORA.

> Well, dame; where hast thou been?

El.   I came from Orra.

Hugh. Hast thou been pleading in our son's excuse?
> And how did she receive it?

El. I tried to do it, but her present humour
> Is jest and merriment. She is behind me,
> Stopping to stroke a hound, that in the corridor
> Came to her fawningly to be caress'd.

Glot. (*listening*). Ay, she is coming; light and quick her steps;
> So sound they when her spirits are unruly:
> But I am bold; she shall not mock me now.

Enter ORRA, *tripping gaily, and playing with the folds of her scarf.*

Methinks you trip it briskly, gentle dame.
Orra. Does it offend you, noble knight?
Glot.   Go to!
   I know your meaning. Wherefore smile you so?
Orra. Because, good sooth! with tired and aching sides
   I have not power to laugh.
Glot. Full well I know why thou so merry art.
   Thou thinkst of him to whom thou gav'st that sprig
   Of hopeful green, his rusty casque to grace,
   While at thy feet his honour'd glave he laid.
Orra. Nay, rather say, of him, who at my feet,
   From his proud courser's back, more gallantly
   Laid his most precious self: then stole away,
   Through modesty, unthank'd, nor left behind
   Of all his gear that flutter'd in the dust,
   Or glove, or band, or fragment of torn hose,
   For dear remembrance-sake, that in my sleeve
   I might have placed it. O! thou wrongst me much,
   To think my merriment a ref'rence hath
   To any one but him. (*Laughing.*)
El. Nay, Orra; these wild fits of uncurb'd laughter,
   Athwart the gloomy tenor of your mind,
   As it has low'r'd of late, so keenly cast,
   Unsuited seem and strange.
Orra. O nothing strange, my gentle Eleanora!
   Didst thou ne'er see the swallow's veering breast,
   Winging the air beneath some murky cloud
   In the sunn'd glimpses of a stormy day,
   Shiver in silv'ry brightness:
   Or boatman's oar, as vivid lightning flash
   In the faint gleam, that like a spirit's path
   Tracks the still waters of some sullen lake:
   Or lonely tower, from its brown mass of woods,
   Give to the parting of a wintry sun
   One hasty glance in mockery of the night
   Closing in darkness round it?—Gentle friend!

Chide not her mirth, who was sad yesterday,
And may be so to-morrow.

Glot. And wherefore art thou sad, unless it is
From thine own wayward humour? Other dames,
Were they so courted, would be gay and happy.

Orra. Wayward it needs must be, since I am sad
When such perfection woos me.

Pray, good Glottenbal,
How didst thou learn with such a wondrous grace
So high in air to toss thine armed heels,
And clutch with outspread hands the slipp'ry sand?
I was the more amaz'd at thy dexterity,
As this, of all thy many gallant feats
Before-hand promised, most modestly
Thou didst forbear to mention.

Glot.   Gibe away!
I care not for thy gibing. With fair lists,
And no black arts against me—

Hugh. (*advancing angrily from the bottom of the stage to* GLOTTENBAL).
Hold thy peace!
(*To* ORRA.) And, madam, be at least somewhat restrain'd
In your unruly humour.

Orra. Pardon, my lord; I knew not you were near me.
My humour is unruly; with your leave,
I will retire till I have curb'd it better.
(*To* ELEANORA.) I would not lose your company, sweet
countess.

El. We'll go together, then.

[*Exeunt* ORRA *and* ELEANORA. *Manet* HUGHOBERT ; *who
paces angrily about the stage, while* GLOTTENBAL *stands on
the front, thumping his legs with his sheathed rapier.*

Hugh. There is no striving with a forward girl,
Nor pushing on a fool. My harass'd life
Day after day more irksome grows. Curs'd bane!
I'll toil no more for this untoward match.

Enter RUDIGERE, *stealing behind, and listening.*

Rud. You are disturb'd, my lord.

Hugh. What, is it thou? I am disturb'd in sooth.

Rud. Ay, Orra has been here; and some light words
    Of girlish levity have mov'd you. How!
    Toil for this match no more! What else remains,
    If this should be abandon'd, noble Aldenberg,
    That can be worth your toil?

Hugh. I'll match the cub elsewhere.

Rud. What call ye matching?

Hugh. Surely for him some other virtuous maid
    Of high descent, though not so richly dower'd,
    May be obtain'd.

Rud.   Within your walls, perhaps,
    Some waiting gentlewoman, who perchance
    May be some fifty generations back
    Descended from a king, he will himself
    Ere long obtain, without your aid, my lord.

Hugh. Thou mak'st me mad! the dolt! the senseless dolt!
    What can I do for him? I cannot force
    A noble maid entrusted to my care:
    I, the sole guardian of her helpless youth!

Rud. That were indeed unfit; but there are means
    To make her yield consent.

Hugh. Then by my faith, good friend, I'll call thee wizard,
    If thou canst find them out. What means already,
    Short of compulsion, have we left untried?
    And now the term of my authority
    Wears to its close.

Rud. I know it well; and therefore powerful means,
    And of quick operation, must be sought.

Hugh. Speak plainly to me.

Rud.   I've watch'd her long.
    I've seen her cheek, flush'd with the rosy glow
    Of jocund spirits, deadly pale become
    At tale of nightly sprite or apparition,
    Such as all hear, 'tis true, with greedy ears,
    Saying, "Saints save us!" but forget as quickly.
    I've marked her long; she has with all her shrewdness

And playful merriment, a gloomy fancy,
That broods within itself on fearful things.
Hugh. And what doth this avail us?
Rud.   Hear me out.
Your ancient castle in the Suabian forest
Hath, as too well you know, belonging to it,
Or false or true, frightful reports. There hold her
Strictly confin'd in sombre banishment;
And doubt not but she will, ere long, full gladly
Her freedom purchase at the price you name.
Hugh. On what pretence can I confine her there?
It were most odious.
Rud.   Can pretence be wanting?
Has she not favour shown to Theobald,
Who in your neighbourhood, with his sworn friend
The Banneret of Basle, suspiciously
Prolongs his stay? A poor and paltry count,
Unmeet to match with her. And want ye then
A reason for removing her with speed
To some remoter quarter? Out upon it!
You are too scrupulous.
Hugh. Thy scheme is good, but cruel.
> [GLOTTENBAL *has been drawing nearer to them, and
> attending to the last part of their discourse.*

Glot. O much I like it, dearly wicked Rudigere!
She then will turn her mind to other thoughts
Than scornful gibes at me.
Hugh. I to her father swore I would protect her:
I must fulfil his will.
Rud. And, in that will, her father did desire
She might be match'd with this your only son:
Therefore you're firmly bound all means to use
That may the end attain.
Hugh. Walk forth with me, we'll talk of this at large.
> [*Exeunt* HUGH. *and* RUD. *Manet* GLOTTENBAL, *who comes
> forward from the bottom of the stage with the action of a
> knight advancing to the charge.*

Glot. Yes, thus it is; I have the sleight o't now;
    And were the combat yet to come, I'd show them
    I'm not a whit behind the bravest knight,
    Cross luck excepted.

Enter MAURICE.

Maur. My lord, indulge us of your courtesy.
Glot. In what, I pray?
Maur.   Did not Fernando tell you?
    We are all met within our social bower;
    And I have wager'd on your head, that none
    But you alone, within the count's domains,
    Can to the bottom drain the chased horn.
    Come do not linger here when glory calls you.
Glot. Thinkst thou that Theobald could drink so stoutly?
Maur. He, paltry chief! he herds with sober burghers;
    A goblet, half its size, would conquer him.

                                                    [*Exeunt.*

ACT II.

SCENE I.

A garden with trees, and shrubs, &c. ORRA, THEOBALD, *and* HARTMAN, *are discovered in a shaded walk at the bottom of the stage, speaking in dumb show, which they cross, disappearing behind the trees; and are presently followed by* CATHRINA *and* ALICE, *who continue walking there.* ORRA, THEO., *and* HART. *then appear again, entering near the front of the stage.*

Orra (talking to HART. *as she enters).*
    And so, since fate has made me, woe the day!
    That poor and good-for-nothing, helpless being.
    Woman yclept, I must consign myself
    With all my lands and rights into the hands
    Of some proud man, and say, "Take all, I pray,

And do me in return the grace and favour
To be my master."
Hart. Nay, gentle lady, you constrain my words.
And load them with a meaning harsh and foreign
To what they truly bear.—A master! No;
A valiant gentle mate, who in the field
Or in the council will maintain your right:
A noble, equal partner.
Orra (shaking her head).   Well I know,
In such a partnership, the share of power
Allotted to the wife. See, noble Falkenstein
Hath silent been the while, nor spoke one word
In aid of all your specious arguments.
(*To* THEO.) What's your advice, my lord?
Theo.   Ah, noble Orra,
'Twere like self-murder to give honest counsel;
Then urge me not. I frankly do confess
I should be more heroic than I am.
Orra. Right well I see thy head approves my plan,
And by-and-bye so will thy gen'rous heart.
In short, I would, without another's leave,
Improve the low condition of my peasants,
And cherish them in peace. E'en now, methinks,
Each little cottage of my native vale
Swells out its earthen sides, up-heaves its roof,
Like to a hillock mov'd by lab'ring mole,
And with green trail-weeds clamb'ring up its walls,
Roses and ev'ry gay and fragrant plant,
Before my fancy stands, a fairy bower:
Ay, and within it too do fairies dwell.
          [*Looking playfully through her fingers like a show-glass.*
Peep through its wreathed window, if indeed
The flowers grow not too close, and there within
Thou'lt see some half a dozen rosy brats
Eating from wooden bowls their dainty milk;—
Those are my mountain elves. Seest thou not
Their very forms distinctly?

Theo. Distinctly; and most beautiful the sight!
    A sight which sweetly stirreth in the heart
    Feelings that gladden and ennoble it,
    Dancing like sun-beams on the rippled sea;
    A blessed picture! Foul befall the man
    Whose narrow, selfish soul would shade or mar it!
Hart. To this right heartily I say Amen!
    But if there be a man whose gen'rous soul

                                   [Turning to ORRA.

    Like ardour fills; who would with thee pursue
    Thy gen'rous plan; who would his harness don—
Orra (putting her hand on him in gentle interruption).
    Nay, valiant banneret, who would, an't please you,
    His harness doff: all feuds, all strife forbear,
    All military rivalship, all lust
    Of added power, and live in steady quietness,
    A mild and fost'ring lord. Know you of one
    That would so share my task?—You answer not;
    And your brave friend, methinks, casts on the ground
    A thoughtful look: wots he of such a lord?

                                      [To THEO.

Theo. Wot I of such a lord? No, noble Orra,
    I do not; nor does Hartman, though perhaps
    His friendship may betray his judgment. No;
    None such exist: we are all fierce, contentious,
    Restless and proud, and prone to vengeful feuds;
    The very distant sound of war excites us,
    Like the curb'd courser list'ning to the chase,
    Who paws, and frets, and bites the rein. Trust none
    To cross thy gentle, but most princely purpose,
    Who hath on head a circling helmet worn,
    Or ever grasp'd a glave.—But ne'ertheless
    There is—I know a man.—Might I be bold?
Orra. Being so honest, boldness is your right.
Theo. Permitted then, I'll say, I know a man,
    Though most unworthy Orra's lord to be,
    Who, as her champion, friend, devoted soldier,
    Might yet commend himself; and, so received,

Who would at her command, for her defence
His sword right proudly draw. An honour'd sword,
Like that which at the gate of Paradise
From steps profane the blessed region guarded.

Orra. Thanks to the gen'rous knight! I also know
The man thou wouldst commend; and when my state
Such service needeth, to no sword but his
Will I that service owe.

Theo. Most noble Orra! greatly is he honour'd;
And will not murmur that a higher wish,
Too high, and too presumptuous, is repress'd.

> [*Kissing her hand with great respect.*

Orra. Nay, Rudolph Hartman, clear that cloudy brow,
And look on Falkenstein and on myself
As two co-burghers of thy native city
(For such I mean ere long to be), and claiming
From thee, as cadets from an elder born,
Thy cheering equal kindness.

Enter a Servant.

Serv. The count is now at leisure to receive
The lord of Falkenstein, and Rudolph Hartman.

Hart. We shall attend him shortly.

> [*Exit servant.*

    (*Aside to* THEO.) Must we now
Our purpos'd suit to some pretended matter
Of slighter import change?

Theo. (*to* HART. *aside*). Assuredly.—
Madam, I take my leave with all devotion.

Hart. I with all friendly wishes.

> [*Exeunt* THEO. *and* HART. CATHRINA *and* ALICE *now advance
> through the shrubs, &c. at the bottom of the stage, while* ORRA
> *remains, wrapped in thought, on the front.*

Cath. Madam, you're thoughtful; something occupies
Your busy mind.

Orra. What was't we talk'd of, when the worthy banneret
With Falkenstein upon our converse broke?

Cath. How we should spend our time, when in your castle
    You shall maintain your state in ancient splendour,
    With all your vassals round you.
Orra. Ay, so it was.
Al.   And you did say, my lady,
    It should not be a cold unsocial grandeur:
    That you would keep, the while, a merry house.
Orra. O doubt it not! I'll gather round my board
    All that heav'n sends to me of way-worn folks,
    And noble travellers, and neighb'ring friends,
    Both young and old. Within my ample hall,
    The worn-out man of arms (of whom too many,
    Nobly descended, rove like reckless vagrants
    From one proud chieftain's castle to another,
    Half chid, half honour'd) shall o' tiptoe tread,
    Tossing his grey locks from his wrinkled brow
    With cheerful freedom, as he boasts his feats
    Of days gone by.—Music we'll have; and oft
    The bick'ring dance upon our oaken floors
    Shall, thund'ring loud, strike on the distant ear
    Of 'nighted trav'llers, who shall gladly bend
    Their doubtful footsteps tow'rds the cheering din.
    Solemn, and grave, and cloister'd, and demure
    We shall not be. Will this content ye, damsels?
Al. O passing well! 'twill be a pleasant life;
    Free from all stern subjection; blithe and fanciful;
    We'll do whate'er we list.
Cath. That right and prudent is, I hope thou meanest.
Al. Why ever so suspicious and so strict?
    How couldst thou think I had another meaning?
    (*To* ORRA.) And shall we ramble in the woods full oft
    With hound and horn?—that is my dearest joy.
Orra. Thou runn'st me fast, good Alice. Do not doubt
    This shall be wanting to us. Ev'ry season
    Shall have its suited pastime: even Winter
    In its deep noon, when mountains piled with snow,
    And chok'd up valleys from our mansion bar
    All entrance, and nor guest, nor traveller

Sounds at our gate; the empty hall forsaking,
In some warm chamber, by the crackling fire
We'll hold our little, snug, domestic court,
Plying our work with song and tale between.

Cath. And stories too, I ween, of ghosts and spirits,
And things unearthly, that on Michael's eve
Rise from the yawning tombs.

Orra. Thou thinkest then one night o' th' year is truly
More horrid than the rest.

Cath. Perhaps 'tis only silly superstition:
But yet it is well known the count's brave father
Would rather on a glacier's point have lain,
By angry tempests rock'd, than on that night
Sunk in a downy couch in Brunier's castle.

Orra. How, pray? What fearful thing did scare him so?

Cath. Hast thou ne'er heard the story of Count Hugo,
His ancestor, who slew the hunter-knight?

Orra (*eagerly*). Tell it, I pray thee.

Al. Cathrina, tell it not; it is not right:
Such stories ever change her cheerful spirits
To gloomy pensiveness; her rosy bloom
To the wan colour of a shrouded corse.

(*To* ORRA.) What pleasure is there, lady, when thy hand,
Cold as the valley's ice, with hasty grasp
Seizes on her who speaks, while thy shrunk form
Cow'ring and shiv'ring stands with keen turn'd ear
To catch what follows of the pausing tale?

Orra. And let me cow'ring stand, and be my touch
The valley's ice: there is a pleasure in it.

Al. Sayst thou indeed there is a pleasure in it?

Orra. Yea, when the cold blood shoots through every vein:
When every pore upon my shrunken skin
A knotted knoll becomes, and to mine ears
Strange inward sounds awake, and to mine eyes
Rush stranger tears, there is a joy in fear.

             [*Catching hold of* CATHRINA.

Tell it, Cathrina, for the life within me
Beats thick, and stirs to hear
He slew the hunter-knight?

Cath. Since I must tell it, then, the story goes
That grim Count Aldenberg, the ancestor
Of Hughobert, and also of yourself,
From hatred or from envy, to his castle
A noble knight, who hunted in the forest,
Well the Black Forest named, basely decoy'd,
And there, within his chamber, murder'd him—

Orra. Merciful Heaven! and in my veins there runs
A murderer's blood. Saidst thou not, murder'd him?

Cath. Ay; as he lay asleep, at dead of night.

Orra. A deed most horrible!

Cath. It was on Michael's eve; and since that time,
The neighb'ring hinds oft hear the midnight yell
Of spectre-hounds, and see the spectre shapes
Of huntsmen on their sable steeds, with still
A noble hunter riding in their van
To cheer the chase, shown by the moon's pale beams,
When wanes its horn in long October nights.

Orra. This hath been often seen?

Cath.   Ay, so they say.
But, as the story goes, on Michael's eve,
And on that night alone of all the year,
The hunter-knight himself, having a horn
Thrice sounded at the gate, the castle enters;
And, in the very chamber where he died,
Calls on his murd'rer, or in his default
Some true descendant of his house, to loose
His spirit from its torment; for his body
Is laid i' the earth unbless'd, and none can tell
The spot of its interment.

Orra. Call on some true descendant of his race!
It were to such a fearful interview.
But in that chamber, on that night alone—
Hath he elsewhere to any of the race
Appeared? or hath he power——

Al.   Nay, nay, forbear:
    See how she looks. (*To* ORRA.) I fear thou art not well.
Orra. There is a sickly faintness come upon me.
Al. And didst thou say there is a joy in fear?
Orra. My mind of late has strange impressions ta'en.
    I know not how it is.
Al.   A few nights since,
    Stealing o' tiptoe, softly through your chamber,
    Towards my own—
Orra. O heaven defend us! didst thou see aught there?
Al. Only your sleeping self. But you appear'd
    Distress'd and troubled in your dreams; and once
    I thought to wake you ere I left the chamber,
    But I forbore.
Orra.   And glad I am thou didst.
    It is not dreams I fear; for still with me
    There is an indistinctness o'er them cast,
    Like the dull gloom of misty twilight, where
    Before mine eyes pass all incongruous things,
    Huge, horrible, and strange, on which I stare
    As idiots do upon this changeful world,
    With nor surprise nor speculation. No;
    Dreams I fear not: it is the dreadful waking,
    When, in deep midnight stillness, the roused fancy
    Takes up th' imperfect shadows of its sleep,
    Like a marr'd speech snatch'd from a bungler's mouth,
    Shaping their forms distinctively and vivid
    To visions horrible:—this is my bane;—
    It is the dreadful waking that I fear.
Al. Well, speak of other things. There in good time
    Your ghostly father comes with quicken'd steps,
    Like one who bears some tidings good or ill.
    Heaven grant they may be good!

Enter URSTON.

Orra. Father, you seem disturb'd.

Urst. Daughter, I am in truth disturb'd. The count
　　　All o' the sudden, being much enraged
　　　That Falkenstein still lingers near these walls,
　　　Resolves to send thee hence, to be awhile
　　　In banishment detain'd, till on his son
　　　Thou lookst with better favour.

Orra.　　　　　　　　　　　　Ay, indeed!
　　　That is to say perpetual banishment:
　　　A sentence light or heavy, as the place
　　　Is sweet or irksome he would send me to.

Urst. He will contrive to make it, doubt him not,
　　　Irksome enough. Therefore I would advise thee
　　　To feign at least, but for a little time,
　　　A disposition to obey his wishes.
　　　He's stern, but not relentless; and his dame,
　　　The gentle Eleanor, will still befriend you,
　　　When fit occasion serves.

Orra.　　　　　　　　　　What saidst thou, father?
　　　To feign a disposition to obey!
　　　I did mistake thy words.

Urst.　　　　　　　　　　No, gentle daughter;
　　　So press'd, thou mayest feign and yet be blameless.
　　　A trusty guardian's faith with thee he holds not,
　　　And therefore thou art free to meet his wrongs
　　　With what defence thou hast.

Orra (*proudly*). Nay, pardon me; I, with an unshorn crown,
　　　Must hold the truth in plain simplicity,
　　　And am in nice distinctions most unskilful.

Urst. Lady, have I deserv'd this sharpness? oft
　　　Thine infant hand has strok'd this shaven crown:
　　　Thou'st ne'er till now reproach'd it.

Orra (*bursting into tears*). Pardon, O pardon me, my gentle Urston!
　　　Pardon a wayward child, whose eager temper
　　　Doth sometimes mar the kindness of her heart.
　　　Father, am I forgiven? (*Hanging on him.*)

Urst.　　　　　　　　　　Thou art, thou art:
　　　Thou art forgiven; more than forgiven, my child.

Orra. Then lead me to the count, I will myself
    Learn his stern purpose.
Urst.   In the hall he is,
    Seated in state, and waiting to receive you.

                                        [*Exeunt.*

SCENE III.

A spacious apartment, or baron's hall, with a chair of state. HUGHOBERT,
ELEANORA, *and* GLOTTENBAL *enter near the front, speaking as they enter;
and afterwards enter Vassals and Attendants, who range themselves at the
bottom of the stage.*

Hugh. Cease, dame! I will not hear; thou striv'st in vain
    With thy weak pleadings. Orra hence must go
    Within the hour, unless she will engage
    Her plighted word to marry Glottenbal.
Glot. Ay, and a mighty hardship, by the mass!
Hugh. I've summon'd her in solemn form before me,
    That these my vassals should my act approve,
    Knowing my right of guardianship; and also
    That her late father, in his dying moments,
    Did will she should be married to my son;
    Which will, she now must promise to obey,
    Or take the consequence.
El.   But why so hasty?
Hugh. Why, sayst thou? Falkenstein still in these parts
    Lingers with sly intent. Even now he left me,
    After an interview of small importance,
    Which he and Hartman, as a blind pretence
    For seeing Orra, formally requested.
    I say again she must forthwith obey me,
    Or take the consequence of wayward will.
El. Nay, not for Orra do I now entreat
    So much as for thyself. Bethink thee well
    What honour thou shalt have, when it is known
    Thy ward from thy protecting roof was sent;
    Thou who shouldst be to her a friend, a father.

Hugh. But do I send her unprotected? No!
    Brave Rudigere conducts her with a band
    Of trusty spearmen. In her new abode
    She will be safe as here.
El.   Ha! Rudigere!
    Putst thou such trust in him? Alas, my lord!
    His heart is full of cunning and deceit.
    Wilt thou to him the flower of all thy race
    Rashly intrust? O be advised, my lord!
Hugh. Thy ghostly father tells thee so, I doubt not.
    Another priest confesses Rudigere,
    And Urston likes him not. But canst thou think,
    With aught but honest purpose, he would chose
    From all her women the severe Cathrina,
    So strictly virtuous, for her companion?
    This puts all doubt to silence. Say no more,
    Else I shall think thou pleadst against my son,
    More with a step-dame's than a mother's feelings.
Glot. Ay, marry does she, father! And forsooth!
    Regards me as a fool. No marvel then
    That Orra scorns me; being taught by her,—
    How should she else?—So to consider me!
Hugh. (*to* GLOTTENBAL). Tut! hold thy tongue.
El. He wrongs me much, my lord.
Hugh. No more, for here she comes.

Enter ORRA, *attended by* URSTON, ALICE *and* CATHRINA, *whilst*
HUGHOBERT *seats himself in his chair of state, the vassals, &c. ranging*
                themselves on each side.

Hugh. (*to* ORRA). Madam and ward, placed under mine authority,
    And to my charge committed by my kinsman,
    Ulric of Aldenberg, thy noble father:
    Having all gentle means essay'd to win thee
    To the fulfilment of his dying will,
    That did decree his heiress should be married
    With Glottenbal my heir; I solemnly
    Now call upon thee, ere that rougher means

Be used for this good end, to promise truly
Thou wilt, within a short and stated time,
Before the altar give thy plighted faith
To this my only son. I wait thine answer.
Orra of Aldenberg, wilt thou do this?

Orra. Count of the same, my lord and guardian,
   I will not.

Hugh.   Have a care, thou froward maid!
   'Tis thy last opportunity: ere long
   Thou shalt, within a dreary dwelling pent,
   Count thy dull hours, told by the dead man's watch,
   And wish thou hadst not been so proudly wilful.

Orra. And let my dull hours by the dead man's watch
   Be told; yea, make me too the dead man's mate,
   My dwelling place the nailed coffin; still
   I would prefer it to the living lord
   Your goodness offers me.

Hugh.   Art thou bewitch'd?
   Is he not young, well featured and well form'd?
   And dost thou put him in thy estimation
   With bones and sheeted clay?
   Beyond endurance is thy stubborn spirit.
   Right well thy father knew that all thy sex
   Stubborn and headstrong are; therefore, in wisdom,
   He vested me with power that might compel thee
   To what he will'd should be.

Orra.   O not in wisdom!
   Say rather in that weak, but gen'rous faith,
   Which said to him, the cope of heaven would fall
   And smother in its cradle his swath'd babe,
   Rather than thou. his mate in arms, his kinsman,
   Who by his side in many a field had fought,
   Shouldst take advantage of his confidence
   For sordid ends.——
                         My brave and noble father!
   A voice comes from thy grave and cries against it,
   And bids me to be bold. Thine awful form

Rises before me,—and that look of anguish
On thy dark brow!—O no! I blame thee not.

Hugh. Thou seemst beside thyself with such wild gestures
And strangely-flashing eyes. Repress these fancies,
And to plain reason listen. Thou hast said,
For sordid ends I have advantage ta'en.
Since thy brave father's death, by war and compact,
Thou of thy lands hast lost a third; whilst I,
By happy fortune, in my heir's behalf,
Have doubled my domains to what they were
When Ulric chose him as a match for thee.

Orra. O, and what speaketh this, but that my father
Domains regarded not; and thought a man
Such as the son should be of such a man
As thou to him appear'dst, a match more honourable
Than one of ampler state. Take thou from Glottenbal
The largely added lands of which thou boastest,
And put, in lieu thereof, into his stores
Some weight of manly sense and gen'rous worth,
And I will say thou keepst faith with thy friend:
But as it is, although a king's domains
Increas'd thy wealth, thou poorly wouldst deceive him.

Hugh. (*rising from his chair in anger*).
Now, madam, be all counsel on this matter
Between us closed. Prepare thee for thy journey.

El. Nay, good my lord! consider.

Hugh. (*to* ELEANORA).   What, again!
Have I not said thou hast an alien's heart
From me and mine. Learn to respect my will:
—Be silent, as becomes a youthful dame.

Urst. For a few days may she not still remain?

Hugh. No, priest; not for an hour. It is my pleasure
That she for Brunier's castle do set forth
Without delay.

Orra (*with a faint starting movement*).
In Brunier's castle!

Hugh.   Ay;
    And doth this change the colour of thy cheek,
    And give thy alter'd voice a feebler sound?

                                    [*Aside to* GLOTTENBAL.

    She shrinks, now to her, boy; this is thy time.
Glot. (*to* ORRA). Unless thou wilt, thou needst not go at all.
    There is full many a maiden would right gladly
    Accept the terms we offer, and remain.
    (*A pause.*) Wilt thou not answer me?
Orra.   I heard thee not.—
    I heard thy voice, but not thy words. What saidst thou?
Glot. I say, there's many a maiden would right gladly
    Accept the terms we offer, and remain.
    The daughter of a king hath match'd ere now
    With mine inferior. We are link'd together
    As 'twere by right and natural property.
    And as I've said before I say again,
    I love thee too: what more couldst thou desire?
Orra. I thank thee for thy courtship, though uncouth;
    For it confirms my purpose: and my strength
    Grows as thou speakst, firm like the deep-bas'd rock.
    (*To* HUGHOBERT). Now for my journey when you will, my lord!
    I'm ready.
Hugh.   Be it so! on thine own head
    Rest all the blame!

                                    [*Going from her.*

    Perverse past all belief!

                                    [*Turning round to her sternly.*

    Orra of Aldenberg, wilt thou obey me?
Orra. Count of that noble house, with all respect,
    Again I say I will not.

            [*Exit* HUGHOBERT *in anger, followed by* GLOTTENBAL,
            URSTON, *&c. Manent only* ELEANORA, CATHRINA, ALICE,
            and ORRA, *who keeps up with stately pride till* HUGHOBERT
            *and all attendants are gone out, and then throwing herself
            into the arms of* ELEANORA, *gives vent to her feelings.*

El. Sweet Orra! be not so depress'd; thou goest
  For a short term, soon to return again;
  The banishment is mine, who stays behind.
  But I will beg of heaven with ceaseless prayers
  To have thee soon restored: and, when I dare,
  Will plead with Hughobert in thy behalf;
  He is not always stern.
Orra. Thanks, gentle friend! Thy voice to me doth ring
  Like the last tones of kindly nature; dearly
  In my remembrance shall they rest.—What sounds,
  What sights, what horrid intercourse I may,
  Ere we shall meet again, be doom'd to prove,
  High heaven alone doth know.—If that indeed
  We e'er shall meet again!

        [*Falls on her neck and weeps.*
El. Nay, nay! come to my chamber. There awhile
  Compose your spirits. Be not so depress'd.

           [*Exeunt.*
  [RUDIGERE, *who has appeared, during the last part of the*
  above scene, at the bottom of the stage, half concealed, as if
  upon the watch, now comes forward, speaking as he advances.
  Hold firm her pride till fairly from these walls
  Our journey is begun; then fortune hail!
  Thy favours are secured.

        [*Looking off the stage.*

  Ho, Maurice there!

    Enter MAURICE.

  My faithful Maurice, I would speak with thee.
  I leave thee here behind me; to thy care,
  My int'rests I commit; be it thy charge
  To counteract thy lady's influence,
  Who will entreat her lord the term to shorten
  Of Orra's absence, maiming thus my plan,
  Which must, belike, have time to be effected.
  Be vigilant, be artful; and be sure
  Thy services I amply will repay.

Maur. Ay, thou hast said so, and I have believ'd thee.

Rud. And dost thou doubt?

Maur. No; yet meantime, good sooth!
    If somewhat of thy bounty I might finger,
    'Twere well: I like to have some actual proof.
    Didst thou not promise it?

Rud.   'Tis true I did,
    But other pressing calls have drain'd my means.

Maur. And other pressing calls my ebbing faith
    May also drain, and change my promis'd purpose.

Rud. Go to! I know thou art a greedy leech,
    Though ne'ertheless thou lov'st me.
                    [*Taking a small case from his pocket, which he opens.*
    Seest thou here?
    I have no coin; but look upon these jewels:
    I took them from a knight I slew in battle.
    When I am Orra's lord, thou shalt receive,
    Were it ten thousand crowns, whate'er their worth
    Shall by a skilful lapidary be
    In honesty esteem'd.
                                    [*Gives him the jewels.*

Maur. I thank thee, but methinks their lustre's dim.
    I've seen the stones before upon thy breast
    In gala days, but never heard thee boast
    They were of so much value.

Rud. I was too prudent: I had lost them else.
    To no one but thyself would I entrust
    The secret of their value.

Enter Servant.

Serv. Sir Rudigere, the spearmen are without,
    Waiting your further orders, for the journey.

Rud. (*to servant*). I'll come to them anon.
                                    [*Exit servant.*

    Before I go, I'll speak to thee again.
                                    [*Exeunt severally.*

ACT III.

SCENE I

A forest with a half-ruined castle in the background, seen through the trees by moonlight. FRANKO *and several Outlaws are discovered sitting on the ground, round a fire, with flagons, &c. by them, as if they had been drinking.*

Song of several voices.

The chough and crow to roost are gone,
    The owl sits on the tree,
The hush'd wind wails with feeble moan,
    Like infant charity.
The wild-fire dances on the fen,
    The red star sheds its ray,
Uprouse ye, then, my merry men!
    It is our op'ning day.

Both child and nurse are fast asleep,
    And clos'd is every flower,
And winking tapers faintly peep
    High from my lady's bower;
Bewilder'd hinds with shorten'd ken
    Shrink on their murky way,
Uprouse, ye, then, my merry men!
    It is our op'ning day.

Nor board nor garner own we now,
    Nor roof nor latched door,
Nor kind mate, bound by holy vow
    To bless a good man's store;
Noon lulls us in a gloomy den,
    And night is grown our day,
Uprouse ye, then, my merry men!
    And use it as ye may.

Franko (to 1st out.). How lik'st thou this, Fernando?

1st out. Well sung i' faith! but serving ill our turn,
    Who would all trav'llers and benighted folks
    Scare from our precincts. Such sweet harmony
    Will rather tempt invasion.
Franko. Fear not, for mingled voices, heard afar,
    Through glade and glen and thicket, stealing on
    To distant list'ners, seem wild-goblin-sounds;
    At which the lonely trav'ller checks his steed,
    Pausing with long-drawn breath and keen-turn'd ear,
    And twilight pilferers cast down in haste
    Their ill-got burthens, while the homeward hind
    Turns from his path, full many a mile about,
    Through bog and mire to grope his blund'ring way.
    Such, to the startled ear of superstition,
    Were seraph's song, could we like seraphs sing.

Enter 2d outlaw, hastily.

2d out. Disperse ye diff'rent ways: we are undone.
Franko. How sayst thou, shrinking poltroon? we undone!
    Outlaw'd and ruin'd men, who live by daring!
2d out. A train of armed men, some noble dame
    Escorting (so their scatter'd words discover'd
    As, unperceiv'd, I hung upon their rear),
    Are close at hand, and mean to pass the night
    Within the castle.
Franko.   Some benighted travellers,
    Bold from their numbers, or who ne'er have heard
    The ghostly legend of this dreaded place.
1st out. Let us keep close within our vaulted haunts;
    The way to which is tangled and perplex'd,
    And cannot be discover'd: with the morn
    They will depart.
Franko. Nay, by the holy mass! within those walls
    Not for a night must trav'llers quietly rest,
    Or few or many. Would we live securely,
    We must uphold the terrors of the place:

Therefore, let us prepare our midnight rouse.
See, from the windows of the castle gleam

[*Lights seen from the castle.*

Quick passing lights, as though they moved within
In hurried preparation; and that bell,

[*Bell heard.*

Which from yon turret its shrill 'larum sends,
Betokens some unwonted stir. Come, hearts!
Be all prepared, before the midnight watch,
The fiend-like din of our infernal chace
Around the walls to raise.—Come; night advances.

[*Exeunt.*

SCENE II.

A Gothic room in the castle, with the stage darkened. Enter CATHRINA,
bearing a light, followed by ORRA.

Orra (*catching her by the robe and pulling her back*).
Advance no further: turn, I pray! This room
More dismal and more ghastly seems than that
Which we have left behind. Thy taper's light,
As thus aloft thou wav'st it to and fro,
The fretted ceiling gilds with feeble brightness;
While over-head its carved ribs glide past
Like edgy waves of a dark sea, returning
To an eclipsed moon its sullen sheen.
Cath. To me it seems less dismal than the other.
See, here are chairs around the table set,
As if its last inhabitants had left it
Scarcely an hour ago.

[*Setting the light upon the table.*

Orra. Alas! how many hours and years have past
Since human forms around this table sat,
Or lamp or taper on its surface gleam'd!
Methinks I hear the sound of time long past
Still murm'ring o'er us in the lofty void

Of those dark arches, like the ling'ring voices
Of those who long within their graves have slept.
It was their gloomy home; now it is mine.

[*Sits down, resting her arm upon the table, and covering her
eyes with her hand. Enter* RUDIGERE, *beckoning* CATHRINA
*to come to him; and speaks to her in a low voice at the corner
of the stage.*

Go and prepare thy lady's chamber; why
Dost thou for ever closely near her keep?

Cath. She charged me so to do.

Rud. I charge thee also
With paramount authority, to leave her:
I for awhile will take thy station here.
Thou art not mad? Thou dost not hesitate?

[*Fixing his eyes on her with a fierce threatening look, from
which she shrinks. Exit* CATH.

Orra. This was the home of bloody lawless power.
The very air rests thick and heavily
Where murder hath been done.
(*Sighing heavily.*) There is a strange oppression in my breast:
Dost thou not feel a close unwholesome vapour?

Rud. No; ev'ry air to me is light and healthful,
That with thy sweet and heavenly breath is mix'd.

Orra (*starting up*). Thou here! (*Looking round.*) Cathrina gone?

Rud. Does Orra fear to be alone with one,
Whose weal, whose being on her favour hangs?

Orra. Retire, Sir Knight. I choose to be alone.

Rud. And dost thou choose it, here, in such a place,
Wearing so near the midnight hour?—Alas!
How loath'd and irksome must my presence be!

Orra. Dost thou deride my weakness?

Rud. I deride it!
No, noble maid! say rather that from thee
I have a kindred weakness caught. In battle
My courage never shrank, as my arm'd heel
And crested helm do fairly testify:
But now when midnight comes, I feel by sympathy,

With thinking upon thee, fears rise within me
I never knew before.

Orra (*in a softened kindlier voice*). Ha! dost thou too
Such human weakness own?

Rud.   I plainly feel
We are all creatures, in the wakeful hour
Of ghastly midnight, form'd to cower together,
Forgetting all distinctions of the day,
Beneath its awful and mysterious power.
          [*Stealing closer to her as he speaks, and putting his arms
          round her.*

Orra (*breaking from him*). I pray thee hold thy parley further off:
Why dost thou press so near me?

Rud. And art thou so offended, lovely Orra?
Ah! wherefore am I thus presumptuous deem'd?
The blood that fills thy veins enriches mine;
From the same stock we spring; though by that glance
Of thy disdainful eye, too well I see
My birth erroneously thou countest base.

Orra. Erroneously!

Rud.   Yes, I will prove it so.
Longer I'll not endure a galling wrong
Which makes each word of tenderness that bursts
From a full heart, bold and presumptuous seem,
And severs us so far.

Orra.   No, subtile snake!
It is the baseness of thy selfish mind,
Full of all guile, and cunning, and deceit,
That severs us so far, and shall do ever.

Rud. Thou prov'st how far my passion will endure
Unjust reproaches from a mouth so dear.

Orra. Out on hypocrisy! who but thyself
Did Hughobert advise to send me hither?
And who the jailor's hateful office holds
To make my thraldom sure?

Rud. Upbraid me not for this: had I refused,
One less thy friend had ta'en th' ungracious task.
And, gentle Orra! dost thou know a man,

Who might in ward all that his soul holds dear
From danger keep, yet would the charge refuse,
For that strict right such wardship doth condemn?
O! still to be with thee; to look upon thee;
To hear thy voice, makes even this place of horrors,—
Where, as 'tis said, the spectre of a chief,
Slain by our common grandsire, haunts the night,
A paradise—a place where I could live
In penury and gloom, and be most bless'd.
Ah! Orra! if there's misery in thraldom,
Pity a wretch who breathes but in thy favour:
Who till he look'd upon that beauteous face,
Was free and happy.—Pity me or kill me!

                              [Kneeling and catching hold of her hand.

Orra. Off, fiend! let snakes and vipers cling to me
    So thou dost keep aloof.

Rud. (*rising indignantly*). And is my love with so much hatred met?
    Madam, beware lest scorn like this should change me
    E'en to the baleful thing your fears have fancied.

Orra. Dar'st thou to threaten me?

Rud. He, who is mad with love and gall'd with scorn,
    Dares any thing.—But O! forgive such words
    From one who rather, humbled at your feet,
    Would of that gentleness, that gen'rous pity,
    The native inmate of each female breast,
    Receive the grace on which his life depends.
    There was a time when thou didst look on me
    With other eyes.

Orra.   Thou dost amaze me much.
    Whilst I believ'd thou wert an honest man,
    Being no fool, and an adventurous soldier,
    I look'd upon thee with good-will; if more
    Thou didst discover in my looks than this,
    Thy wisdom with thine honesty, in truth,
    Was fairly match'd.

Rud. Madam, the proud derision of that smile
    Deceives me not. It is the lord of Falkenstein,
    Who better skill'd than I in tournay-war,

Though not in th' actual field more valiant found,
Engrosses now your partial thoughts. And yet
What may he boast which, in a lover's suit,
I may not urge? He's brave, and so am I.
In birth I am his equal; for my mother,
As I shall prove, was married to Count Albert,
My noble father, though for reasons tedious
Here to be stated, still their secret nuptials
Were unacknowledg'd, and on me hath fallen
A cruel stigma which degrades my fortunes.
But were I—O forgive th' aspiring thought!—
But were I Orra's lord, I should break forth
Like the unclouded sun, by all acknowledg'd
As ranking with the highest in the land.

Orra. Do what thou wilt when thou art Orra's lord;
But being as thou art, retire and leave me:
I choose to be alone. (*Very proudly.*)

Rud.   Then be it so.
Thy pleasure, mighty dame, I will not balk.
This night, to-morrow's night, and every night,
Shalt thou in solitude be left; if absence
Of human beings can secure it for thee.
          [*Pauses and looks on her, while she seems struck and
          disturbed.*
It wears already on the midnight hour;
Good night!
                              [*Pauses again, she still more disturbed.*
Perhaps I understood too hastily
Commands you may retract.

Orra (*recovering her state*). Leave me, I say; that part of my commands
          I never can retract.

Rud.   You are obey'd.
                                          [*Exit.*

Orra (*paces up and down hastily for some time, then stops short, and after
          remaining a little while in a thoughtful posture*).
Can spirit from the tomb, or fiend from hell,
More hateful, more malignant be than man—
Than villanous man? Although to look on such,

Yea, even the very thought of looking on them,
Makes natural blood to curdle in the veins,
And loosen'd limbs to shake,
There are who have endur'd the visitation
Of supernatural beings.—O forefend it!
I would close couch me to my deadliest foe
Rather than for a moment bear alone
The horrors of the sight.
Who's there? who's there?

                                        [*Looking round.*

Heard I not voices near? That door ajar
Sends forth a cheerful light. Perhaps my women,
Who now prepare my chamber. Grant it be!
            [*Exit, running hastily to a door from which a light is seen.*

SCENE III.

A chamber, with a small bed or couch in it.
Enter RUDIGERE *and* CATHRINA, *wrangling together.*

Rud. I say begone, and occupy the chamber
    I have appointed for thee: here I'm fix'd,
    And here I pass the night.
Cath.   Thou saidst my chamber
    Should be adjoining that which Orra holds?
    I know thy wicked thoughts: they meditate
    Some dev'lish scheme; but think not I'll abet it.
Rud. Thou wilt not!—angry, restive, simple fool!
    Dost thou stop short and say, "I'll go no further?"
    Thou, whom concealed shame hath bound so fast,—
    My tool,—my instrument?—Fulfil thy charge
    To the full bent of thy commission, else
    Thee, and thy bantling too, I'll from me cast
    To want and infamy.
Cath.   O, shameless man!
    Thou art the son of a degraded mother
    As low as I am, yet thou hast no pity.

Rud. Ay, and dost thou reproach my bastardy
　　　To make more base the man who conquer'd thee,
　　　With all thy virtue, rigid and demure?
　　　Who would have thought less than a sovereign prince
　　　Could e'er have compass'd such achievement? Mean
　　　As he may be, thou'st given thyself a master,
　　　And must obey him.—Dost thou yet resist?
　　　Thou know'st my meaning.

　　　　　　　　　　　[*Tearing open his vest in vehemence of action.*

Cath. Under thy vest a dagger!—Ah! too well,
　　　I know thy meaning, cruel, ruthless man!

Rud. Have I discovered it?—I thought not of it:
　　　The vehemence of gesture hath betray'd me.
　　　I keep it not for thee, but for myself;
　　　A refuge from disgrace. Here is another:
　　　He who with high, but dangerous fortune grapples,
　　　Should he be foil'd, looks but to friends like these.

　　　　　　　　　　　[*Pulling out two daggers from his vest.*

　　　This steel is strong to give a vig'rous thrust;
　　　The other on its venom'd point hath that
　　　Which, in the feeblest hand, gives death as certain,
　　　As though a giant smote the destin'd prey.

Cath. Thou desp'rate man! so arm'd against thyself!

Rud. Ay; and against myself with such resolves,
　　　Consider well how I shall deal with those
　　　Who may withstand my will or mar my purpose.
　　　Thinkst thou I'll feebly——

Cath.　　　　　　　　　　O be pacified.
　　　I will begone: I am a humbled wretch
　　　On whom thou tramplest with a tyrant's cruelty.

　　　　　　　　　　　　　　　　　　　[*Exit.*

Rud. (*looks after her with a malignant laugh, and then goes to the door of
　　　an adjoining chamber, to the lock of which he applies his ear*).
　　　All still within—I'm tired and heavy grown:
　　　I'll lay me down to rest. She is secure:
　　　No one can pass me here to gain her chamber.
　　　If she hold parley now with any thing,

It must in truth be ghost or sprite.—Heigh ho!
I'm tir'd, and will to bed.

> [*Lays himself on the couch and falls asleep.*

*The cry of hounds is then heard without at a distance, with the sound of
a horn; and presently* ORRA *enters, bursting from the door of the adjoining
chamber, in great alarm.*

Orra. Cathrina! sleepest thou? Awake! awake!

> [*Running up to the couch and starting back on seeing*
> RUDIGERE.

That hateful viper here!
Is this my nightly guard? Detested wretch!
I will steal back again.

> [*Walks softly on tiptoe to the door of her chamber, when
> the cry of hounds, &c. is again heard without, nearer than
> before.*

O no! I dare not.
Though sleeping, and most hateful when awake,
Still he is natural life and may be rous'd.

> [*Listening again.*

'Tis nearer now: that dismal thrilling blast!
I must awake him.

> [*Approaching the couch and shrinking back again.*

O no! no, no!
Upon his face he wears a horrid smile
That speaks bad thoughts.

> [RUD. *speaks in his sleep.*

He mutters too my name.—
I dare not do it.

> [*Listening again.*

The dreadful sound is now upon the wind,
Sullen and low, as if it wound its way
Into the cavern'd earth that swallow'd it.
I will abide in patient silence here;
Though hateful and asleep, I feel me still
Near something of my kind.

[*Crosses her arms, and leans in a cowering posture over the*
back of a chair at a distance from the couch; when presently the
horn is heard without, louder than before, and she starts up.

O it returns! as though the yawning earth
Had given it up again, near to the walls.
The horribly mingled din! 'tis nearer still:
'Tis close at hand: 'tis at the very gate!

[*Running up to the couch.*

Were he a murd'rer, clenching in his hands
The bloody knife, I must awake him.—No!
That face of dark and subtle wickedness!
I dare not do it. (*Listening again.*) Ay; 'tis at the gate—
Within the gate.—

              What rushing blast is that
Shaking the doors? Some awful visitation
Dread entrance makes! O mighty God of Heav'n!
A sound ascends the stairs.

                Ho, Rudigere!
Awake, awake! Ho! wake thee, Rudigere!

Rud. (*waking*). What cry is that so terribly strong?—Ha! Orra!
What is the matter?

Orra. It is within the walls. Didst thou not hear it?

Rud. What? The loud voice that called me?

Orra. No, it was mine.

Rud.   It sounded in my ears
With more than human strength.

Orra.   Did it so sound?
There is around us, in this midnight air,
A power surpassing nature. List, I pray:
Although more distant now, dost thou not hear
The yell of hounds; the spectre-huntsman's horn?

Rud. I hear, indeed, a strangely mingled sound:
The wind is howling round the battlements.
But rest secure where safety is, sweet Orra!
Within these arms, nor man nor fiend shall harm thee.

     [*Approaching her with a softened winning voice, while she*
     pushes him off with abhorrence.

Orra. Vile reptile! touch me not.

Rud. Ah! Orra! thou art warp'd by prejudice,
    And taught to think me base; but in my veins
    Lives noble blood, which I will justify.
Orra. But in thy heart, false traitor! what lives there?
Rud. Alas! thy angel-faultlessness conceives not
    The strong temptations of a soul impassion'd
    Beyond control of reason.—At thy feet—

                                                       [*Kneeling.*

    O spurn me not!

Enter several Servants, alarmed.

Rud. What, all these fools upon us! Staring knaves,
    What brings ye here at this untimely hour?
1st serv. We have all heard it—'twas the yell of hounds
    And clatt'ring steeds, and the shrill horn between.
Rud. Out on such folly!
2d serv. In very truth it pass'd close to the walls;
    Did not your honour hear it?
Rud. Ha! sayst thou so? thou art not wont to join
    In idle tales.—I'll to the battlements
    And watch it there: it may return again.
        [*Exeunt severally,* RUDIGERE *followed by servants, and*
        ORRA *into her own chamber.*

SCENE IV.

The Outlaws' cave. Enter THEOBALD.

Theo. (*looking round*). Here is a place in which some traces are
    Of late inhabitants. In yonder nook
    The embers faintly gleam, and on the walls
    Hang spears and ancient arms: I must be right
    A figure through the gloom moves towards me.
    Ho! there! Whoe'er you are: Holla! good friend!

Enter an Outlaw.

Out. A stranger! Who art thou, who art thus bold,
　　To hail us here unbidden?
Theo. That thou shalt shortly know. Thou art, I guess,
　　One of the outlaw'd band who haunt this forest.
Out. Be thy conjecture right or wrong, no more
　　Shalt thou return to tell where thou hast found us.
　　Now for thy life!

　　　　　　　　　　　　　　　　[Drawing his sword.
Theo.　　　　　　　　Hear me, I do entreat thee.
Out. Nay, nay! no foolish pleadings; for thy life
　　Is forfeit now; have at thee!

　　　　[Falls fiercely upon THEOBALD, *who also draws and defends*
　　　　himself bravely, when another outlaw enters and falls likewise
　　　　upon him. THEO. *then recedes fighting, till he gets his back to*
　　　　the wall of the cavern, and there defends himself stoutly.

　　　　　　　　　　Enter FRANKO.

Franko. Desist, I charge you! Fighting with a stranger,
　　Two swords to one—a solitary stranger!
1st out. We are discover'd; had he master'd me,
　　He had return'd to tell his mates above
　　What neighbours in these nether caves they have.
　　Let us despatch him.
Franko.　　　　　　　No, thou hateful butcher!
　　Despatch a man alone and in our power!
　　Who art thou, stranger, who dost use thy sword
　　With no mean skill; and in this perilous case
　　So bold an air and countenance maintainest?
　　What brought thee hither?
Theo. My name is Theobald of Falkenstein;
　　To find the valiant captain of these bands,
　　And crave assistance of his gen'rous arm:
　　This is my business here.
Franko (*struck and agitated, to his men*).
　　Go, join your comrades in the further cave.

　　　　　　　　　　　　　　　　[Exeunt outlaws.

And thou art Falkenstein? In truth thou art.

And who thinkst thou am I?

Theo. Franko, the gen'rous leader of those outlaws.

Franko. So am I call'd, and by that name alone

    They know me. Sporting on the mountain's side,

    Where Garva's wood waves green, in other days,

    Some fifteen years ago, they call'd me Albert.

Theo. (rushing into his arms). Albert; my playmate Albert! Woe the day!

    What cruel fortune drove thee to this state?

Franko. I'll tell thee all! but tell thou first to me

    What is the aid thou camest here to ask.

Theo. Ay, thou wert ever thus: still forward bent

    To serve, not to be serv'd.

                    But wave we this.

    Last night a lady to the castle came,

    In thraldom by a villain kept, whom I

    E'en with my life would rescue. Of armed force

    At present destitute, I come to thee

    Craving thy aid in counsel and in arms.

Franko. When didst thou learn that outlaws harbour here,

    For 'tis but lately we have held these haunts?

Theo. Not till within the precincts of the forest,

    Following the traces of that villain's course,

    One of your band I met, and recogniz'd

    As an old soldier, who, some few years back,

    Had under my command right bravely serv'd.

    Seeing himself discover'd, and encouraged

    By what I told him of my story, freely

    He offer'd to conduct me to his captain.

    But in a tangled path some space before me,

    Alarm'd at sight of spearmen through the brake,

    He started from his way, and so I miss'd him,

    Making my way alone to gain your cave.

Franko. Thou'rt welcome here: and gladly I'll assist thee,

    Though not by arms, the force within the castle

    So far out-numbering mine.

    But other means may serve thy purpose better.

Theo. What other means, I pray?

Franko. From these low caves, a passage under ground
    Leads to the castle—to the very tower
    Where, as I guess, the lady is confin'd.
    When sleep has still'd the house, we'll make our way.
Theo. Ay, by my faith it is a noble plan!
    Guarded or not, we well may overcome
    The few that may compose her midnight guard.
Franko. We shall not shrink from that.—But by my fay!
    To-morrow is St. Michael's eve: 'twere well
    To be the spectre-huntsman for a night,
    And bear her off, without pursuit or hindrance.
Theo. I comprehend thee not.
Franko.   Thou shalt ere long.
    But stand not here; an inner room I have,
    Where thou shalt rest and some refreshment take,
    And then we will more fully talk of this,
    Which, slightly mention'd, seems chimerical.
    Follow me.

                     [*Turning to him as they go out.*
    Hast thou still upon thine arm
    That mark which from mine arrow thou receiv'dst
    When sportively we shot? The wound was deep,
    And gall'd thee much, but thou mad'st light of it.
Theo. Yes, here it is.

          [*Pulling up his sleeve as they go out, and Exeunt.*

ACT IV.

SCENE I.

The ramparts of the castle. Enter ORRA *and* CATHRINA.

Cath. (*after a pause, in which* ORRA *walks once or twice across the stage,*
    thoughtfully). Go in, I pray; thou wand'rest here too long.
                           [*A pause again.*
    The air is cold; behind those further mountains
    The sun is set. I pray thee now go in.

Orra. Ha! sets the sun already? Is the day
    Indeed drawn to its close?
Cath.   Yes, night approaches.
    See, many a gather'd flock of cawing rooks
    Are to their nests returning.
Orra (*solemnly*).   Night approaches!—
    This awful night which living beings shrink from;
    All now of every kind scour to their haunts,
    While darkness, peopled with its hosts unknown,
    Awful dominion holds. Mysterious night!
    What things unutterable thy dark hours
    May lap!—What from thy teeming darkness burst
    Of horrid visitations, ere that sun
    Again shall rise on the enlighten'd earth!

                                     [*A pause.*

Cath. Why dost thou gaze intently on the sky?
    Seest thou aught wonderful?
Orra. Look there, behold that strange gigantic form
    Which yon grim cloud assumes; rearing aloft
    The semblance of a warrior's plumed head,
    While from its half-shaped arm a streamy dart
    Shoots angrily! Behind him too, far stretch'd,
    Seems there not, verily, a serried line
    Of fainter misty forms?
Cath.   I see, indeed,
    A vasty cloud, of many clouds composed,
    Towering above the rest; and that behind
    In misty faintness seen, which hath some likeness
    To a long line of rocks with pine-wood crown'd:
    Or, if indeed the fancy so incline,
    A file of spearmen, seen through drifted smoke.
Orra. Nay, look how perfect now the form becomes:
    Dost thou not see?—Ay, and more perfect still.
    O thou gigantic lord, whose robed limbs
    Beneath their stride span half the heavens! art thou
    Of lifeless vapour formed? Art thou not rather
    Some air-clad spirit—some portentous thing—

Some mission'd being—Such a sky as this
Ne'er usher'd in a night of nature's rest.
Cath. Nay, many such I've seen; regard it not.
That form, already changing, will ere long
Dissolve to nothing. Tarry here no longer.
Go in, I pray.
Orra.   No; while one gleam remains
Of the sun's blessed light, I will not go.
Cath. Then let me fetch a cloak to keep thee warm,
For chilly blows the breeze.
Orra.   Do as thou wilt.

                                        [*Exit* Cath.

Enter an Outlaw, stealing softly behind her.

Out. (*in a low voice*). Lady!—the Lady Orra!
Orra (*starting*).   Heaven protect me!
Sounds it beneath my feet, in earth or air?

                                   [*He comes forward.*

Welcome is aught that wears a human face.
Didst thou not hear a sound?
Out. What sound, an't please you?
Orra. A voice which call'd me now: it spoke, methought,
In a low, hollow tone, suppress'd and low,
Unlike a human voice.
Out.   It was my own.
Orra. What wouldst thou have?
Out.   Here is a letter, lady.
Orra. Who sent thee hither?
Out. It will tell thee all.

                                        [*Gives a letter.*

I must begone, your chieftain is at hand.

                                             [*Exit.*

Orra. Comes it from Falkenstein? It is his seal.
I may not read it here. I'll to my chamber.

          [*Exit hastily, not perceiving* Rudigere, *who enters by the
          opposite side, before she has time to go off.*

Rud. A letter in her hand, and in such haste!
    Some secret agent here from Falkenstein?
    It must be so.

                [*Hastening after her, Exit.*

SCENE II.

The Outlaws cave. Enter THEOBALD *and* FRANKO *by opposite sides.*

Theo. How now, good captain; draws it near the time?
    Are those the keys?
Franko.   They are: this doth unlock
    The entrance to the staircase, known alone
    To Gomez, ancient keeper of the castle,
    Who is my friend in secret, and deters
    The neighb'ring peasantry with dreadful tales
    From visiting by night our wide domains.
    The other doth unlock a secret door,
    That leads us to the chamber where she sleeps.
Theo. Thanks, gen'rous friend! thou art my better genius.
    Didst thou not say, until the midnight horn
    Hath sounded thrice, we must remain conceal'd?
Franko. Even so. And now I hear my men without
    Telling the second watch.
Theo.   How looks the night?
Franko. As we could wish: the stars do faintly twinkle
    Through sever'd clouds, and shed but light sufficient
    To show each nearer object closing on you
    In dim unshapely blackness. Aught that moves
    Across your path, or sheep or straggling goat,
    Is now a pawing steed or grizzly bull,
    Large and terrific; every air-mov'd bush
    Or jutting crag, some strange gigantic thing.
Theo. Is all still in the castle?
Franko. There is an owl sits hooting on the tower,
    That answer from a distant mate receives,
    Like the faint echo of his dismal cry;

While a poor houseless dog by dreary fits
Sits howling at the gate. All else is still.
Theo. Each petty circumstance is in our favour,
That makes the night more dismal.
Franko. Ay, all goes well; as I approach'd the walls,
I heard two sentinels—for now, I ween,
The boldest spearman will not watch alone—
Together talk in the deep hollow voice
Of those who speak at midnight, under awe
Of the dead stillness round them.
Theo. Then let us put ourselves in readiness,
And heaven's good favour guide us!

                                                [*Exeunt.*

SCENE III.

A gloomy apartment. Enter ORRA *and* RUDIGERE.

Orra (aside). The room is darken'd: yesternight a lamp
Did shed its light around on roof and walls,
And made the dreary space appear less dismal.
Rud. (overhearing her, and calling to a servant without).
    Ho! more lights here!

                  [*Servant enters with a light and exit.*
                  Thou art obey'd: in aught
But in the company of human kind,
Thou shalt be gratified. Thy lofty mind
For higher superhuman fellowship,
If such there be, may now prepare its strength.
Orra. Thou ruthless tyrant! They who have in battle
Fought valiantly, shrink like a helpless child
From any intercourse with things unearthly.
Art thou a man? And bearst thou in thy breast
The feelings of a man? It cannot be!
Rud. Yes, madam; in my breast I bear too keenly
The feelings of a man—a man most wretched:
A scorn'd, rejected man.—Make me less miserable;

Nay rather should I say, make me most blest;
And then—

> [*Attempting to take her hand, while she steps back from him,
> drawing herself up with an air stately and determined, and
> looking steadfastly in his face.*

I too am firm. Thou knowst my fix'd resolve:
Give me thy solemn promise to be mine.
This is the price, thou haughty, scornful maid,
That will redeem thee from the hour of terror!
This is the price—

Orra.   Which never shall be paid.

> [*Walks from him to the further end of the apartment.*

Rud. (*after a pause*). Thou art determin'd, then.
    Be not so rash:
Bethink thee well what flesh and blood can bear:
The hour is near at hand.

> [*She, turning round, waves him with her hand to leave her.*

Thou deignst no answer.
Well; reap the fruits of thine unconquer'd pride.

> [*Exit.*

Manet ORRA.

Orra. I am alone: that closing door divides me
From every being owning nature's life.—
And shall I be constrain'd to hold communion
With that which owns it not?

> [*After pacing to and fro for a little while.*

O that my mind
Could raise its thoughts in strong and steady fervour
To HIM, the Lord of all existing things,
Who lives, and is where'er existence is;
Grasping its hold upon HIS skirted robe,
Beneath whose mighty rule angels and spirits,
Demons and nether powers, all living things,
Hosts of the earth, with the departed dead
In their dark state of mystery, alike
Subjected are!—And I will strongly do it.—

Ah! would I could! Some hidden powerful hindrance
Doth hold me back, and mars all thought.—

> [*After a pause, in which she stands fixed with her arms crossed on her breast.*

Dread intercourse!
O! if it look on me with its dead eyes!
If it should move its lock'd and earthy lips,
And utt'rance give to the grave's hollow sounds!
If it stretch forth its cold and bony grasp—
O horror, horror!

> [*Sinking lower at every successive idea, as she repeats these four last lines, till she is quite upon her knees on the ground.*

Would that beneath these planks of senseless matter
I could, until the dreadful hour is past,
As senseless be!

> [*Striking the floor with her hands.*

O open and receive me,
Ye happy things of still and lifeless being,
That to the awful steps which tread upon ye
Unconscious are!

> *Enter* CATHRINA *behind her.*

Who's there? Is't any thing?
Cath. 'Tis I, my dearest lady; 'tis Cathrina.
Orra (*embracing her*).

How kind! such blessed kindness keep thee by me;
I'll hold thee fast; an angel brought thee hither.
I needs must weep to think thou art so kind
In mine extremity.—Where wert thou hid?
Cath. In that small closet, since the supper hour,
I've been conceal'd. For searching round the chamber,
I found its door and enter'd. Fear not now,
I will not leave thee till the break of day.
Orra. Heaven bless thee for it! Till the break of day!
The very thought of daybreak gives me life.
If but this night were past, I have good hope

That noble Theobald will soon be here
For my deliv'rance.

Cath. Wherefore thinkst thou so?

Orra. A stranger, when thou leftst me on the ramparts,
Gave me a letter, which I quickly open'd,
As soon as I, methought, had gain'd my room
In privacy; but close behind me came
That demon, Rudigere, and, snatching at it,
Forced me to cast it to the flames, from which,
I struggling with him still, he could not save it.

Cath. You have not read it then?

Orra.   No; but the seal
Was Theobald's, and I could swear ere long
He will be here to free me from this thraldom.

Cath. God grant he may!

Orra. If but this night were past! How goes the time?
Has it not enter'd on the midnight watch?

Cath. (*pointing to a small slab at the corner of the stage on which is
placed a sand-glass*). That glass I've set to measure it. As soon
As all the sand is run, you are secure;
The midnight watch is past.

Orra (*running to the glass, and looking at it eagerly*).
There is not much to run; O an't were finish'd!
But it so slowly runs!

Cath.   Yes; watching it,
It seemeth slow. But heed it not; the while,
I'll tell thee some old tale, and ere I've finish'd,
The midnight watch is gone. Sit down, I pray.
                    [*They sit,* ORRA *drawing her chair close to* CATHRINA.
What story shall I tell thee?

Orra. Something, my friend, which thou thyself hast known,
Touching the awful intercourse which spirits
With mortal men have held at this dread hour.
Didst thou thyself e'er meet with one whose eyes
Had look'd upon the spectred dead—had seen
Forms from another world?

Cath.   Never but once.

Orra (*eagerly*). Once then thou didst. O tell it! tell it me!

Cath. Well, since I needs must tell it, once I knew
 A melancholy man, who did aver,
 That journeying on a time o'er a wild waste,
 By a fell storm o'erta'en, he was compell'd
 To pass the night in a deserted tower,
 Where a poor hind, the sole inhabitant
 Of the sad place, prepared for him a bed:
 And, as he told his tale, at dead of night,
 By the pale lamp that in his chamber burn'd
 As it might be an arm's-length from his bed—
Orra. So close upon him?
Cath.   Yes.
Orra.   Go on; what saw he?
Cath. An upright form, wound in a clotted shroud—
 Clotted and stiff, like one swath'd up in haste
 After a bloody death.
Orra.   O horrible!
Cath. He started from his bed and gazed upon it.
Orra. And did he speak to it?
Cath.   He could not speak.
 Its visage was uncover'd, and at first
 Seem'd fix'd and shrunk, like one in coffin'd sleep;
 But, as he gaz'd, there came, he wist not how,
 Into its beamless eyes a horrid glare,
 And turning towards him, for it did move—
 Why dost thou grasp me thus?
Orra. Go on, go on!
Cath. Nay, heaven forefend! Thy shrunk and sharpen'd features
 Are of the corse's colour, and thine eyes
 Are full of tears. How's this?
Orra.   I know not how.
 A horrid sympathy jarr'd on my heart,
 And forced into mine eyes these icy tears.
 A fearful kindredship there is between
 The living and the dead—an awful bond!
 Woe's me! that we do shudder at ourselves—

At that which we must be!—A dismal thought!
Where dost thou run? thy story is not told.

> [*Seeing* CATH. *go towards the sand-glass.*

Cath. (*showing the glass*). A better story I will tell thee now;
    The midnight watch is past.
Orra. Ha! let me see.
Cath.   There's not one sand to run.
Orra. But it is barely past.
Cath.   'Tis more than past.
    For I did set it later than the hour,
    To be assur'dly sure.
Orra. Then it is gone indeed. O heaven be praised!
    The fearful gloom gone by!

> [*Holding up her hands in gratitude to heaven, and then
> looking round her with cheerful animation.*

                In truth, already
    I feel as if I breath'd the morning air;
    I'm marvellously lighten'd.
Cath.   Ne'ertheless,
    Thou art forespent; I'll run to my apartment,
    And fetch some cordial drops that will revive thee.
Orra. Thou needst not go; I've ta'en thy drops already;
    I'm bold and buoyant grown.

> [*Bounding lightly from the floor.*

Cath.   I'll soon return;
    Thou art not fearful now?
Orra.   No; I breathe lightly;
    Valour within me grows most powerfully,
    Wouldst thou but stay to see it, gentle Cathrine!
Cath. I will return to see it, ere thou canst
    Three times repeat the letters of thy name.

> [*Exit hastily by the concealed door.*

Orra. (*alone*). This burst of courage shrinks most shamefully.
    I'll follow her.—

> [*Striving to open the door.*

        'Tis fast; it will not open.
    I'll count my footsteps as I pace the floor
    Till she return again.

[*Paces up and down, muttering to herself, when a horn is
heard without, pausing and sounding three times, each time
louder than before.*

[ORRA *runs again to the door.*

Despair will give me strength; where is the door?
Mine eyes are dark, I cannot find it now.
O God! protect me in this awful pass!

[*After a pause, in which she stands with her body bent in
a cowering posture, with her hands locked together, and
trembling violently, she starts up and looks wildly round
her.*

There's nothing, yet I felt a chilly hand
Upon my shoulder press'd. With open'd eyes
And ears intent I'll stand. Better it is
Thus to abide the awful visitation,
Than cower in blinded horror, strain'd intensely
With ev'ry beating of my goaded heart.

[*Looking round her with a steady sternness, but shrinking
again almost immediately.*

I cannot do it: on this spot I'll hold me
In awful stillness.

[*Bending her body as before; then, after a momentary pause,
pressing both her hands upon her head.*

The icy scalp of fear is on my head;
The life stirs in my hair; it is a sense
That tells the nearing of unearthly steps,
Albeit my ringing ears no sounds distinguish.

[*Looking round, as if by irresistible impulse, to a great door
at the bottom of the stage, which bursts open, and the form
of a huntsman, clothed in black, with a horn in his hand,
enters and advances towards her. She utters a loud shriek,
and falls senseless on the ground.*

Theo. (*running up to her, and raising her from the ground*).
No semblance, but real agony of fear.
Orra, oh, Orra! knowst thou not my voice?
Thy knight, thy champion, the devoted Theobald?
Open thine eyes and look upon my face:

[*Unmasking.*

I am no fearful waker from the grave.
Dost thou not feel? 'Tis the warm touch of life.
Look up, and fear will vanish.—Words are vain!
What a pale countenance of ghastly strength
By horror chang'd! O idiot that I was
To hazard this—The villain hath deceiv'd me:
My letter she has ne'er receiv'd. O fool!
That I should trust to this!

> [*Beating his head distractedly.*

Enter FRANKO, *by the same door.*

Franko. What is the matter? what strange turn is this?
Theo. O cursed sanguine fool! could I not think—
    She moves, she moves!—rouse thee, my gentle Orra!
    'Tis no strange voice that calls thee; 'tis thy friend.
Franko. She opens now her eyes.
Theo.   But, oh, that look!
Franko. She knows thee not, but gives a stifled groan,
    And sinks again in stupor.
    Make no more fruitless lamentation here,
    But bear her hence: the cool and open air
    May soon restore her. Let us, while we may,
    Occasion seize, lest we should be surprised.

> [*Exeunt:* ORRA *borne off in a state of insensibility.*

ACT V.

SCENE I.

The great hall of the castle.
Enter RUDIGERE, CATHRINA, *and Attendants, by different doors.*

Rud. (*to attend.*) Return'd again! Is any thing discover'd?
    Or door or passage, garment dropt in haste,
    Or footstep's track, or any mark of flight?

1st att. No, by my faith! though we have search'd the castle
　　From its high turret to its deepest vault.
Cath. 'Tis vain to trace the marks of trackless feet.
　　If that in truth it hath convey'd her hence,
　　The yawning earth has yielded them a passage,
　　Or else, through rifted roofs, the buoyant air.
Rud. Fools! search again. I'll raze the very walls
　　From their foundations, but I will discover
　　If door or pass there be to us unknown.
　　Ho! Gomez, there!
　　　　　　　　　　　　　　　　[Calling off the stage.
　　　　　　　He keeps himself aloof:
　　Nor aids the search with true and hearty will.
　　I am betray'd—Ho! Gomez, there, I say!
　　He shrinks away: go, drag the villain hither,
　　And let the torture wring confession from him.
　　　　　　　　　　　　[A loud knocking heard at the gate.
　　Ha! who seeks entrance at this early hour
　　In such a desert place?
Cath. 　　　　　　　　　　Some hind, perhaps,
　　Who brings intelligence. Heaven grant it be!

　　　　　　　　Enter an armed vassal.

Rud. Ha! one from Aldenberg! what brings thee hither?
Vass. (seizing Rud.)
　　Thou art my prisoner. (To attendants.) Upon your peril,
　　Assist me to secure him.
Rud. Audacious hind! by what authority
　　Speakst thou such bold commands? Produce thy warrant.
Vass. 'Tis at the gate, and such as thou must yield to:
　　Count Hughobert himself, with armed men,
　　A goodly band, his pleasure to enforce.
　　　　　　　　　　　　　　　　　　[Secures him.
Rud. What sudden freak is this? am I suspected
　　Of aught but true and honourable faith?
Vass. Ay, by our holy saints! more than suspected.
　　Thy creature Maurice, whom thou thought'st to bribe

With things of seeming value, hath discover'd
The cunning fraud; on which his tender conscience,
Good soul! did o' the sudden so upbraid him,
That to his lord forthwith he made confession
Of all the plots against the Lady Orra,
In which thy wicked arts had tempted him
To take a wicked part. All is discover'd.

Cath. (*aside*). All is discover'd! Where then shall I hide me?
    (*Aloud to vass.*) What is discover'd?

Vass.   Ha! most virtuous lady!
Art thou alarm'd? Fear not: the world well knows
How good thou art; and to the countess shortly,
Who with her lord is near, thou wilt no doubt
Give good account of all that thou hast done.

Cath. (*aside, as she retires in agitation*).
    O heaven forbid! What hole o' th' earth will hide me!
                                [*Exit.*

Enter by the opposite side, HUGHOBERT, ELEANORA, ALICE, GLOTTENBAL,
    URSTON, MAURICE, *and* ATTENDANTS.

Hugh. (*speaking as he enters*). Is he secured?

Vass.   He is, my lord; behold!
                      [*Pointing to* RUD.

Hugh. (*to* RUD.) Black, artful traitor! Of a sacred trust,
    Blindly reposed in thee, the base betrayer
    For wicked ends; full well upon the ground
    Mayst thou decline those darkly frowning eyes,
    And gnaw thy lip in shame.

Rud. And rests no shame with him, whose easy faith
    Entrusts a man unproved; or, having proved him,
    Lets a poor hireling's unsupported testimony
    Shake the firm confidence of many years?

Hugh. Here the accuser stands; confront him boldly,
    And spare him not.
                 [*Bringing forward* MAURICE.

Maur. (*to* RUD.) Deny it if thou canst. Thy brazen front,
    All brazen as it is, denies it not.

Rud. (*to* MAUR.) Fool! that of prying curiosity
    And av'rice art compounded! I in truth
    Did give to thee a counterfeited treasure
    To bribe thee to a counterfeited trust;
    Meet recompense! Ha, ha! Maintain thy tale,
    For I deny it not.

                                  [*With careless derision.*

Maur.   O, subtle traitor!
    Dost thou so varnish it with seeming mirth?
Hugh. Sir Rudigere, thou dost, I must confess,
    Outface him well. But call the Lady Orra;
    If towards her thou hast thyself comported
    In honesty, she will declare it freely.
(*To attendant.*) Bring Orra hither.
1st att. Would that we could; last night i' the midnight watch
    She disappear'd; but whether man or devil
    Hath borne her hence, in truth we cannot tell.
Hugh. O both! Both man and devil together join'd.
(*To* RUD. *furiously.*) Fiend, villain, murderer! Produce her instantly.
    Dead or alive, produce thy hapless charge.
Rud. Restrain your rage, my lord; I would right gladly
    Obey you, were it possible: the place,
    And the mysterious means of her retreat,
    Are both to me unknown.
Hugh.   Thou liest! thou liest!
Glot. (*coming forward*).
    Thou liest, beast, villain, traitor! thinkst thou still
    To fool us thus? Thou shalt be forced to speak.
    (*To* HUGH.) Why lose we time in words when other means
    Will quickly work? Straight to those pillars bind him,
    And let each sturdy varlet of your train
    Inflict correction on him.
Maur. Ay, this alone will move him.
Hugh.   Thou sayst well:
    By heaven it shall be done!
Rud. And will Count Hughobert degrade in me
    The blood of Aldenberg to shame himself?

Hugh. That plea avails thee not; thy spurious birth
    Gives us full warrant, as thy conduct varies,
    To reckon thee or noble or debased.
    (*To att.*) Straight bind the traitor to the place of shame.
              [*As they are struggling to bind* RUD. *he gets one of his hands*
              free, and, pulling out a dagger from under his clothes, stabs
              himself.
Rud. Now, take your will of me, and drag my corse
    Through mire and dust; your shameless fury now
    Can do me no disgrace.
Urston (advancing).
    Rash, daring, thoughtless wretch! dost thou so close
    A wicked life in hardy desperation?
Rud. Priest, spare thy words: I add not to my sins
    That of presumption, in pretending now
    To offer up to heaven the forced repentance
    Of some short moments for a life of crimes.
Urst. My son, thou dost mistake me: let thy heart
    Confession make—
Glot. (*interrupting* URST.) Yes, dog! Confession make
    Of what thou'st done with Orra; else I'll spurn thee,
    And cast thy hateful carcass to the kites.
Hugh. (*pulling back* GLOT. *as he is going to spurn* RUD. *with his foot,*
    who is now fallen upon the ground).
    Nay, nay, forbear; such outrage is unmanly.
            [ELEANORA, *who with* ALICE *had retired from the shocking*
            sight of RUDIGERE, *new comes forward to him.*
El. Oh, Rudigere! thou art a dying man,
    And we will speak to thee without upbraiding.
    Confess, I do entreat thee, ere thou goest
    To thy most awful change, and leave us not
    In this our horrible uncertainty.
    Is Orra here conceal'd?
Al.   Thou hast not slain her?
    Confession make, and heaven have mercy on thee!
Rud. Yes, ladies; with these words of gentle meekness
    My heart is changed; and that you may perceive
    How greatly changed, let Glottenbal approach me;

Spent am I now, and can but faintly speak—
E'en unto him in token of forgiveness
I'll tell what ye desire.

El. Thank heaven, thou art so changed!

Hugh. (*to* GLOT.) Go to him, boy.

> [GLOTTENBAL *goes to* RUDIGERE, *and stooping over him to
> hear what he has to say,* RUDIGERE, *taking a small dagger
> from his bosom, strikes* GLOTTENBAL *on the neck.*

Glot. Oh, he has wounded me!—Detested traitor!
Take that and that; would thou hadst still a life
For every thrust.

> [*Killing him.*

Hugh. (*alarmed*). Ha! has he wounded thee. my son?

Glot. A scratch;
'Tis nothing more. He aim'd it at my throat,
But had not strength to thrust.

Hugh. Thank God, he had not!

> [*A trumpet sounds without.*

Hark! martial notice of some high approach!
(*To attendants.*) Go to the gate.

> [*Exeunt attendants.*

El. Who may it be? This castle is remote
From every route which armed leaders take.

Enter a Servant.

Serv. The Banneret of Basle is at the gate.

Hugh. Is he in force?

Serv. Yes, through the trees his distant bands are seen
Some hundreds strong, I guess; though with himself
Two followers only come.

Enter HARTMAN attended.

Hugh. Forgive me, banneret, if I receive thee
With more surprise than courtesy. How is it?
Com'st thou in peace?

Hart. To you, my lord, I frankly will declare
The purpose of my coming: having heard it,

It is for you to say if I am come,
As much I wish, in peace.
(*To* EL.) Countess, your presence much emboldens me
To think it so shall be.

Hugh. (*impatiently*).   Proceed, I beg.
When burghers gentle courtesy affect,
It chafes me more than all their sturdy boasting.

Hart. Then with a burgher's plainness, Hughobert,
I'll try my tale to tell,—nice task I fear!
So that it may not gall a baron's pride.
Brave Theobald, the lord of Falkenstein,
Co-burgher also of our ancient city,
Whose cause of course is ours, declares himself
The suitor of thy ward, the Lady Orra;
And learning that within these walls she is,
By thine authority, in durance kept,
In his behalf I come to set her free;
As an oppressed dame, such service claiming
From ev'ry gen'rous knight. What is thy answer?
Say, am I come in peace? Wilt thou release her?

Hugh. Ah, would I could! In faith thou gall'st me shrewdly.

Hart. I've been inform'd of all that now disturbs you,
By one who held me waiting at the gate.
Until the maid be found, if 'tis your pleasure,
Cease enmity.

Hugh. Then let it cease. A traitor has deceived me,
And there he lies.
                              [*Pointing to the body of* RUD.

Hart. (*looking at the body*). A ghastly smile of fell malignity
On his distorted face death has arrested.
                              [*Turning again to* HUGH.
And has he died, and no confession made?
All means that may discover Orra's fate
Shut from us?

Hugh. Ah! the fiend hath utter'd nothing
That could betray his secret. If she lives—

El. Alas, alas! think you he murder'd her?

Al. Merciful heaven forefend!

Enter a Soldier in haste.

Sold. O, I have heard a voice, a dismal voice!
Omnes. What hast thou heard?
El.   What voice?
Sold.   The Lady Orra's.
El. Where? Lead us to the place.
Hugh. Where didst thou heart it, soldier?
Sold. In a deep-tangled thicket of the wood,
    Close to a ruin'd wall, o'ergrown with ivy,
    That marks the ancient outworks of the castle.
Hugh. Haste; lead the way.
            [*Exeunt all eagerly, without order, following the soldier,*
            GLOTTENBAL *and one attendant excepted.*
Att. You do not go, my lord?
Glot. I'm sick, and strangely dizzy grows my head,
    And pains shoot from my wound. It is a scratch,
    But from a devil's fang.—There's mischief in it.
    Give me thine arm, and lead me to a couch:
    I'm very faint.
Att. This way, my lord; there is a chamber near.
                    [*Exit* GLOTTENBAL, *supported by the attendant.*

SCENE II.

*The forest near the castle; in front a rocky bank crowned with a ruined
wall overgrown with ivy, and the mouth of a cavern shaded with bushes.
Enter* FRANKO, *conducting* HUGHOBERT, HARTMAN, ELEANORA, ALICE,
and URSTON, *the soldier following them.*

Franko (to HUGH.). This is the entry to our secret haunts.
    And now, my lord, having inform'd you truly
    Of the device, well meant, but most unhappy,
    By which the Lady Orra from her prison
    By Falkenstein was ta'en, myself, my outlaws,
    Unhappy men—who better days have seen,

Driv'n to this lawless life by hard necessity,
Are on your mercy cast.

Hugh. Which shall not fail you, valiant Franko. Much
  Am I indebted to thee: hadst thou not
  Of thine own free good will become our guide,
  As wand'ring here thou foundst us, we had ne'er
  The spot discover'd; for this honest soldier,
  A stranger to the forest, sought in vain
  To thread the tangled path.

El. (*to* FRANKO). She is not well, thou sayst, and from her swoon
  Imperfectly recover'd.

Franko. When I left her,
  She so appear'd.—But enter not, I pray,
  Till I give notice.—Holla, you within!
  Come forth and fear no ill.

                              [*A shriek heard from the cave.*

Omnes. What dismal shriek is that?

Al.   'Tis Orra's voice.

El. No, no! it cannot be! It is some wretch,
  In maniac's fetters bound.

Hart. The horrid thought that bursts into my mind!
  Forbid it, righteous Heaven!

          [*Running into the cave, he is prevented by* THEOBALD, *who
          rushes out upon him.*

Theo. Hold, hold! no entry here but o'er my corse,
  When ye have master'd me.

Hart.   My Theobald,
  Dost thou not know thy friends?

Theo. Ha! thou, my Hartman! Art thou come to me?

Hart. Yes, I am come. What means that look of anguish?
  She is not dead!

Theo. Oh, no! it is not death!

Hart. What meanst thou? Is she well?

Theo.   Her body is.

Hart. And not her mind?—Oh! direst wreck of all!
  That noble mind!—But 'tis some passing seizure,
  Some powerful movement of a transient nature;
  It is not madness?

Theo. (shrinking from him, and bursting into tears).
    'Tis heaven's infliction; let us call it so;
    Give it no other name.

                                            [*Covering his face.*
El. (to THEO.) Nay, do not thus despair: when she beholds us,
    She'll know her friends, and, by our kindly soothing,
    Be gradually restored.
Al. Let me go to her.
Theo.   Nay, forbear, I pray thee;
    I will myself with thee, my worthy Hartman,
    Go in and lead her forth.

            [THEOBALD *and* HARTMAN *go into the cavern, while those*
            without wait in deep silence, which is only broken once or
            twice by a scream from the cavern and the sound of THEO-
            BALD's *voice speaking soothingly, till they return, leading*
            forth ORRA, *with her hair and dress disordered, and the ap-*
            pearance of wild distraction in her gait and countenance.
Orra (shrinking back as she comes from under the shade of the trees, &c.
    and dragging THEOBALD *and* HARTMAN *back with her).*
    Come back, come back! The fierce and fiery light!
Theo. Shrink not, dear love! it is the light of day.
Orra. Have cocks crow'd yet?
Theo.   Yes; twice I've heard already
    Their matin sound. Look up to the blue sky;
    Is it not daylight there? And these green boughs
    Are fresh and fragrant round thee: every sense
    Tells thee it is the cheerful early day.
Orra. Ay, so it is; day takes his daily turn,
    Rising between the gulfy dells of night
    Like whiten'd billows on a gloomy sea;
    Till glow-worms gleam, and stars peep through the dark,
    And will-o'-the-wisp his dancing taper light,
    They will not come again.

                              [*Bending her ear to the ground.*
                Hark, hark! Ay, hark!
    They are all there: I hear their hollow sound
    Full many a fathom down.

Theo. Be still, poor troubled soul! they'll ne'er return:
    They are for ever gone. Be well assured
    Thou shalt from henceforth have a cheerful home
    With crackling faggots on thy midnight fire,
    Blazing like day around thee; and thy friends—
    Thy living, loving friends still by thy side,
    To speak to thee and cheer thee.—See, my Orra!
    They are beside thee now; dost thou not know them? (*Pointing
    to Eleanora and Alice.*)
Orra (*gazing at them with her hand held up to shade her eyes*).
    No, no! athwart the wav'ring garish light,
    Things move and seem to be, and yet are nothing.
El. (*going near her*). My gentle Orra! hast thou then forgot me?
    Dost thou not know my voice?
Orra. 'Tis like an old tune to my ear return'd.
    For there be those, who sit in cheerful halls,
    And breathe sweet air, and speak with pleasant sounds;
    And once I liv'd with such; some years gone by;
    I wot not now how long.
Hugh. Keen words that rend my heart!—Thou hadst a home,
    And one whose faith was pledged for thy protection.
Urst. Be more composed, my lord, some faint remembrance
    Returns upon her with the well-known sound
    Of voices once familiar to her ear.
    Let Alice sing to her some fav'rite tune,
    That may lost thoughts recall.
        [ALICE *sings an old tune, and* ORRA, *who listens eagerly
        and gazes on her while she sings, afterwards bursts into a
        wild laugh.*
Orra. Ha, ha! the witched air sings for thee bravely.
    Hoot owls through mantling fog for matin birds?
    It lures not me.—I know thee well enough:
    The bones of murder'd men thy measure beat,
    And fleshless heads nod to thee.—Off, I say!
    Why are ye here?—That is the blessed sun.
El. Ah, Orra! do not look upon us thus!
    These are the voices of thy loving friends

That speak to thee: this is a friendly hand
That presses thine so kindly.
> [*Putting her hand upon* ORRA's, *who gives a loud shriek,
> and shrinks from her with horror.*

Hart. O grievous state. (*Going up to her.*) What terror seizes thee?
Orra. Take it away! It was the swathed dead!
I know its clammy, chill, and bony touch.
> [*Fixing her eyes fiercely on* ELEANORA.

Come not again; I'm strong and terrible now:
Mine eyes have look'd upon all dreadful things;
And when the earth yawns, and the hell-blast sounds,
I'll 'bide the trooping of unearthly steps
With stiff-clench'd, terrible strength.
> [*Holding her clenched hands over her head with an air of
> grandeur and defiance.*

Hugh. (*beating his breast*). A murd'rer is a guiltless wretch to me.
Hart. Be patient; 'tis a momentary pitch;
Let me encounter it.
> [*Goes up to* ORRA, *and fixes his eyes upon her, which she,
> after a moment, shrinks from and seeks to avoid, yet still, as
> if involuntarily, looks at him again.*

Orra. Take off from me thy strangely-fasten'd eye:
I may not look upon thee, yet I must.
> [*Still turning from him, and still snatching a hasty look at
> him as before.*

Unfix thy baleful glance: art thou a snake?
Something of horrid power within thee dwells.
Still, still that powerful eye doth such me in
Like a dark eddy to its wheeling core.
Spare me! O spare me, being of strange power,
And at thy feet my subject head I'll lay!
> [*Kneeling to* HARTMAN *and bending her head submissively.*

El. Alas the piteous sight! to see her thus;
The noble generous, playful, stately Orra!
Theo. (*running to* HARTMAN, *and pushing him away with indignation*).
Out on thy hateful and ungenerous guile!
Thinkst thou I'll suffer o'er her wretched state
The slightest shadow of a base control?

[*Raising* ORRA *from the ground.*

No, rise thou stately flower with rude blasts rent:
As honour'd art thou with thy broken stem,
And leaflets strew'd, as in thy summer's pride.
I've seen thee worshipp'd like a regal dame
With every studied form of mark'd devotion,
Whilst I in distant silence, scarcely proffer'd
E'en a plain soldier's courtesy; but now,
No liege-man to his crowned mistress sworn,
Bound and devoted is, as I to thee;
And he who offers to thy alter'd state
The slightest seeming of diminish'd reverence,
Must in my blood—(*To* HARTMAN.) O pardon me, my friend!
Thou'st wrung my heart.

Hart. Nay, do thou pardon me: I am to blame:
Thy nobler heart shall not again be wrung.
But what can now be done? O'er such wild ravings
There must be some control.

Theo. O none! none, none! but gentle sympathy
And watchfulness of love.
                              My noble Orra!
Wander where'er thou wilt; thy vagrant steps
Shall follow'd be by one, who shall not weary,
Nor e'er detach him from his hopeless task;
Bound to thee now as fairest, gentlest beauty
Could ne'er have bound him.

Al. See how she gazes on him with a look,
Subsiding gradually to softer sadness.
Half saying that she knows him.

El. There is a kindness in her changing eye.
Yes, Orra, 'tis the valiant Theobald,
Thy knight and champion, whom thou gazest on.

Orra. The brave are like the brave; so should it be.
He was a goodly man—a noble knight.
(*To* THEOBALD.) What is thy name, young soldier?—Woe is me!
For prayers of grace are said o'er dying men,
Yet they have laid thy clay in unblest earth—
Shame! shame! not with the still'd and holy dead.

This shall be rectified; I'll find it out;
And masses shall be said for thy repose;
Thou shalt not troop with these.

El. 'Tis not the dead, 'tis Theobald himself,
Alive and well, who standeth by thy side.

Orra (looking wildly round).
Where, where? All dreadful things are near me. round me,
Beneath my feet and in the loaded air.
Let him begone! The place is horrible!
Baneful to flesh and blood.—The dreadful blast!
Their hounds now yell below i' the centre gulph;
They may not rise again till solemn bells
Have giv'n the stroke that severs night from morn.

El. O rave not thus! Dost thou not know us, Orra?

Orra (hastily). Ay, well enough I know ye.

Urst. Ha! think ye that she does?

El. It is a terrible smile of recognition,
If such it be.

Hart. Nay, do not thus your restless eye-balls move,
But look upon us steadily, sweet Orra.

Orra. Away! your faces waver to and fro;
I'll know you better in your winding-sheets,
When the moon shines upon you.

Theo. Give o'er, my friends; you see it is in vain;
Her mind within itself holds a dark world
Of dismal phantasies and horrid forms!
Contend with her no more.

Enter an attendant in an abrupt disturbed manner.

Att. (to ELEANORA, *aside).* Lady, I bring to you most dismal news:
Too grievous for my lord, so suddenly
And unprepar'd to hear.

El. (aside).   What is it? Speak.

Att. (aside to EL.) His son is dead, all swell'd and rack'd with pain;
And on the dagger's point, which the sly traitor
Still in his stiffen'd grasp retains, foul stains,

Like those of limed poison, show full well
The wicked cause of his untimely death.

Hugh. (*overhearing them*).

 Who speaks of death? What didst thou whisper there?
 How is my son?—What look is that thou wearst?
 He is not dead?—Thou dost not speak! O God!
 I have no son.

[After a pause.

      I am bereft!—But this!
 But only him!—Heaven's vengeance deals the stroke.

Urst. Heaven oft in mercy smites, e'en when the blow
 Is most severe.

Hugh.   I had no other hope.
 Fell is the stroke, if mercy in it be!
 Could this—could this alone atone my crime?

Urst. Submit thy soul to Heaven's all-wise decree.
 Perhaps his life had blasted more thy hopes
 Than e'en his grievous end.

Hugh. He was not all a father's heart could wish;
 But, oh! he was my son!—my only son:
 My child—the thing that from his cradle grew,
 And was before me still.—Oh, oh! Oh, oh!

[Beating his breast and groaning deeply.

Orra (*running up to him*).

 Ha! dost thou groan, old man? art thou in trouble?
 Out on it! though they lay him in the mould,
 He's near thee still.—I'll tell thee how it is:
 A hideous burst hath been: the damn'd and holy,
 The living and the dead, together are
 In horrid neighbourship—'Tis but thin vapour,
 Floating around thee, makes the wav'ring bound.
 Pooh! blow it off, and see th' uncurtain'd reach.
 See! from all points they come; earth casts them up!
 In grave-clothes swath'd are those but new in death;
 And there be some half bone, half cased in shreds
 Of that which flesh hath been; and there be some
 With wicker'd ribs, through which the darkness scowls.
 Back, back!—They close upon us.—Oh! the void

Of hollow unball'd sockets staring grimly,
And lipless jaws that move and clatter round us
In mockery of speech!—Back, back, I say!
Back, back!

> [*Catching hold of* HUGHOBERT *and* THEOBALD, *and
> dragging them back with her in all the wild strength of
> frantic horror, whilst the curtain drops.*

THE DREAM:

A TRAGEDY,

IN PROSE,

IN THREE ACTS.

PERSONS OF THE DRAMA.

MEN.

OSTERLOO, *an imperial general.*
Prior of the monastery.
BENEDICT,
JEROME, } *monks.*
PAUL,
MORAND,
WOVELREID, } *officers in the service of the prior.*
The imperial ambassador.
Officers serving under OSTERLOO.

Sexton, monks, soldiers, peasants, &c.

WOMEN.

LEONORA.
AGNES.

Scene: the monastery of St. Maurice in Switzerland; a castle near it.

Time, the middle of the 14th century.

ACT I.

SCENE I.

A court within the monastery, with a grated iron gate opening into an outer court, through which are seen several peasants waiting; JEROME *is discovered on the front of the stage, walking backwards and forwards in a disturbed manner, then stopping and speaking to himself.*

Jer. Twice in one night the same awful vision repeated! And Paul also terrified with a similar visitation! This is no common accidental mimicry of sleep: the shreds and remnants of our day-thoughts, put together at night in some fantastic incongruous form, as the drifting clouds of a broken-up storm piece themselves again into uncertain shapes of rocks and animals. No, no! there must be some great and momentous meaning in this.

Enter BENEDICT *behind him.*

Ben. Some great and momentous meaning in this! What art thou musing upon?

Jer. Be satisfied! be satisfied! It is not always fitting that the mind should lay open the things it is busy withal, though an articulate sound may sometimes escape it to set curiosity on the rack. Where is brother Paul? Is he still at his devotions?

Ben. I believe so. But look where the poor peasants are waiting without: it is the hour when they expect our benefactions. Go, and speak to them: thou hast always been their favourite confessor, and they want consolation.

[*Beckoning the peasants, who thereupon advance through the gate, while* JEROME *stretches out his hand to prevent them.*

Jer. Stop there! Come not within the gates! I charge you advance no farther. (*To* BENEDICT *angrily*) here is death and contagion in every one of them, and yet thou would'st admit them so near us. Dost thou indeed expect a miracle to be wrought in our behalf? Are we not flesh and blood? and does not the grave yawn for us as well as other men? (*To the Peasants still more vehemently*) Turn, I charge you, and retire without the gate.

1st peas. Oh! be not so stern with us, good father! There are ten new corpses in the village since yesterday, and scarcely ten men left in it with strength enough to bury them. The best half of the village are now under ground, who, but three weeks gone by, were all alive and well. O do not chide us away!

2d peas. God knows if any of us shall ever enter these gates again; and it revives us to come once a day to receive your blessings, good Fathers.

Jer. Well, and you shall have our blessing, my children; but come not so near us; we are mortal men like yourselves, and there is contagion about you.

1st peas. Ah! no, no! Saint Maurice will take care of his own; there is no fear of you, Fathers.

Jer. I hope he will; but it is presumptuous to tempt danger. Retire, I beseech you, and you shall have relief given to you without the gates. If you have any love for us, retire.

[*The Peasants retire.*

Ben. Well, I feel a strong faith within me, that our saint, or some other good spirit, will take care of us. How is it that thou art so alarmed and so vehement with those good people? It is not thy usual temper.

Jer. Be satisfied, I pray thee: I cannot tell thee now. Leave me to myself a little while.—Would to God brother Paul were come to me! Ha! here he is.

Enter PAUL; *and* JEROME, *after waiting impatiently till* BENEDICT *retires, advances to him eagerly.*

Was it to a spot near the black monument in the stranger's burying vault, that it pointed?

Paul. Yes, to the very spot described by thee yesterday morning, when thou first told'st me thy dream: and, indeed, every circumstance of my last night's vision strongly resembled thine; or rather, I should say, was the same. The fixed frown of its ghastly face—

Jer. Ay, and the majestic motion of its limbs. Did it not wear a mantle over its right shoulder, as if for concealment rather than grace?

Paul. I know not; I did not mark that: but it strode before me as distinctly as ever mortal man did before my waking sight; and yet as no mortal man ever did before the waking sight.

Jer. But it appeared to thee only once.

Paul. Only once; for I waked under such a deep horror, that I durst not go to sleep again.

Jer. When it first appeared to me, as I told thee, the night before last, the form, though distinctly, was but faintly imaged forth; and methought it rose more powerfully to my imagination as I told it to thee, than in the dream itself. But last night, when it returned, it was far more vivid than before. I waked indeed as thou did'st, impressed with a deep horror, yet irresistible sleep seized upon me again; and O how it appeared to me the third time, like a palpable, horrid reality! (*After a pause*) What is to be done?

Paul. What can be done? We can stop no division of the Imperial army till one shall really march by this pass.

Jer. And this is not likely; for I received a letter from a friend two days ago, by an express messenger, who says, he had delayed sending it, hoping to have it conveyed to me by one of Count Osterloo's soldiers, who, with his division, should have marched through our pass, but was now, he believed, to conduct them by a different route.

Paul. What noise and commotion is that near the gate? (*Calling to those without*) Ho there! What is the matter?

1st peas. (*without*) Nothing, father; but we hear a trumpet at a distance, and they say, there is an army marching amongst the mountains.

Jer. By all our holy saints, if it be so— (*Calling again to the 1st peas.*) Are ye sure it is trumpets you hear?

1st peas. As sure as we ever heard any sound, and here is a lad too, who saw from the top-most crag, with his own eyes, their banners waving at a distance.

Jer. (*to* PAUL) What think'st thou of it?

Paul. We must go to the prior, and reveal the whole to him directly. Our own lives and those of the whole brotherhood depend upon it; there can be no hesitation now.

Jer. Come then; lose no time. We have a solemn duty imposed upon us.

[*Exeunt.*

SCENE II.

An open space by the gate of the monastery, with a view of the building on one side, while rocks and mountains, wildly grand, appear in every other direction, and a narrow pass through the mountains opening to the bottom of the stage. Several peasants, both men and women, are discovered, waiting as if to see some sight; a trumpet and warlike music heard at a little distance.

1st *peas.* Hear how it echoes amongst the rocks: it is your true warlike sound, that makes a man's heart stir within him, and his feet beat the ground to its measure.

2d *peas.* Ah! what have our hearts to do with it now, miserable as we are!

1st *peas.* What have we to do with it! Speak for thyself. Were I to be laid in the grave this very night, it would rouse me to hear those sounds which remind me of the battle of Laupen.

2d *peas.* Well; look not so proudly at me: though I have not yet fought for my country, I am of a good stock nevertheless: my father lost his life at Morgarten. (*Calling up to* MORAND, *who now appears scrambling down the sides of the rocks.*) Are they near us, lieutenant?

Mor. They'll be here in a trice. I know their ensigns already: they are those brave fellows under the command of Count Osterloo, who did such good service to the emperor in his last battle.

3d *peas.* (*Woman.*) Ay; they be goodly men no doubt, and bravely accoutred I warrant ye.

4th *peas.* (*Old Woman.*) Ay, there be many a brave man amongst them I trow, returning to his mother again. My Hubert never returned.

2d *peas.* (*to* MOR.) Count Osterloo! Who is he?

Mor. Did'st thou never hear of him? He has been in as many battles as thou hast been in harvest fields.

2d *peas.* And won them too?

Mor. Nay, some of them he has won, and some he has lost; but whether his own side were fighting or flying, he always kept his ground, or retreated like a man. The enemy never saw his back.

1st *peas.* True, lieutenant; I once knew an old soldier of Osterloo's who boasted much of his general: for his men are proud of him, and would go through flood and flame for his sake.

Mor. Yes, he is affable and indulgent to them, although passionate and unreasonable when provoked; and has been known to punish even his greatest favourites severely for a slight offence. I remember well, the officer I first served under, being a man of this kidney, and—

1st *peas.* Hist, hist! the gates are thrown open, and yonder come the monks in procession with the prior at their head.

Enter Prior and monks from the monastery, and range themselves on one side of the stage.

Prior (to the peasants). Retire, my children, and don't come so near us. Don't stand near the soldiers as they pass neither, but go to your houses.

1st *Woman.* O bless St. Maurice and your holy reverence! We see nothing now but coffins and burials, and hear nothing but the ticking of the death-watch, and the tolling of bells: do let us stand here and look at the brave sight. Lord knows if any of us may be above ground to see such another, an' it were to pass this way but a week hence.

Prior. Be it so then, daughter, but keep at a distance on the rocks, where you may see every thing without communicating infection.

> [*The peasants retire, climbing amongst the rocks: then enter by the narrow pass at the bottom of the stage, soldiers marching to martial music, with officers and* OSTERLOO.

Prior (advancing, and lifting up his hands with solemnity.) Soldiers and officers, and the noble chief commanding this band! in the name of our patron St. Maurice, once like yourselves a valiant soldier upon earth, now a holy, powerful saint in heaven, I conjure you to halt.

1st off. (*in the foremost rank*) Say you so, reverend prior, to men pressing forward as we do, to shelter our heads for the night, and that cold wintry sun going down so fast upon us?

1st sold. By my faith! if we pass the night here amongst the mountains, it will take something besides prayers and benedictions to keep us alive.

2d sold. Spend the night here amongst chamois and eagles! Some miracle no doubt will be wrought for our accommodation.

1st off. Murmur not, my friends: here comes your general, who is always careful of you.

Ost. (*advancing from the rear.*) What is the matter?

Prior. (*to* Ost.) You are the commander in chief?

Ost. Yes, reverend father: and, with all respect and deference, let me say, the night advances fast upon us, Martigny is still at a good distance, and we must not be detained. With many thanks, then, for your intended civilities, we beg your prayers, holy prior, with those of your pious monks, and crave leave to pass on our way.

Prior (*lifting his hands as before.*) If there be any piety in brave men, I conjure you in the name of St. Maurice to halt! The lives of our whole community depend upon it: men, who for your lives have offered to heaven many prayers.

Ost. How may this be, my lord? Who will attack your sacred walls, that you should want any defence?

Prior. We want not, general, the service of your arms: my own troops, with the brave captain who commands them, are sufficient to defend us from mortal foes.

Soldiers. (*murmuring*). Must we fight with devils then?

Ost. Be quiet, my good Comrades. (*To Prior*). Well, my Lord, proceed.

Prior. A fatal pestilence rages in this neighbourhood; and by command of a vision, which has appeared three times to the Senior of our order, and also to another of our brotherhood, threatening in case of disobedience, that the whole community shall fall victims to the dreadful disease, we are compelled to conjure you to halt.

Ost. And for what purpose?

Prior. That we may choose by lot from the first division of the imperial army which marches through this pass, (so did the vision precisely direct us,) a man, who shall spend one night within the walls of our monastery; there to undergo certain penances for the expiation of long-concealed guilt.

Ost. This is very strange. By lot did you say? It will be tedious. There are a hundred of my men who will volunteer the service.— What say ye, soldiers?

1st sold. Willingly, general, if you desire it. Yet I marvel what greater virtue there can be in beleaguering the war-worn hide of a poor soldier, than the fat sides of a well-fed monk.

Ost. Wilt thou do it, then?

1st sold. Ay; and more than that, willingly, for my general. It is not the first time a cat-o'-nine-tails has been across my back for other men's misdeeds. Promise me a good flask of brandy when I'm done with it, and I warrant ye I'll never winch. As to the saying of Pater-nosters, if there be any thing of that kind tacked to it, I let you to wit my dexterity is but small.

Ost. Then be it as thou wilt, my good friend; yet I had as lief my own skin should smart for it as thine, thou art such a valiant fellow.

Prior. No, noble general, this must not be; we must have our man chosen by lot. The lives of the whole community depending upon it; we must strictly obey the vision.

Ost. It will detain us long.

Prior. Nay, my Lord; the lots are already prepared. In the first place, six men only shall draw; four representing the soldiers, and two the officers. If the soldiers are taken, they shall draw by companies, and the company that is taken shall draw individually; but if the lot falls to the officers, each of them shall draw for himself.

Ost. Let it be so; you have arranged it well. Produce the lots.

> [*The Prior giving the sign, a monk advances, bearing a stand, on which are placed three vases, and sets it near the front of the stage.*

Prior. Now, brave soldiers, let four from your body advance.

> [OST. *points to four men, who advance from the ranks.*

Ost. And two from the officers, my lord?

Prior. Even so, noble Count.

[OST. *then points to two officers, who, with the four soldiers, draw lots from the smallest vase directed by the prior.*)

1st sold. (*speaking to his comrades as the others are drawing.*) This is strange mummery i' faith! but it would have been no joke, I suppose, to have offended St. Maurice.

Prior (*after examining the lots.*) Soldiers, ye are free; it is your officers who are taken.

1st sold. (*as before*). Ha! the vision is dainty it seems; it is not vulgar blood like ours, that will serve to stain the ends of his holy lash. (*A monk having removed two of the vases, the prior beckons the officers to draw from the remaining one.*)

Prior. Stand not on order; let him who is nearest put in his hand first.

1st sold. (*aside to the others as the officers are drawing.*) Now by these arms! I would give a month's pay that the lot should fall on our prim, pompous lieutenant. It would be well worth the money to look in at one of their narrow windows, and see his dignified back-bone winching under the hands of a good brawny friar.

Ost. (*aside, unrolling his lot*). Mighty heaven! Is fate or chance in this?

1st off. (*aside to* Ost.) Have you got it, general? Change it for mine if you have.

Ost. No no, my noble Albert; let us be honest; but thanks to thy generous friendship!

Prior. Now shew the lots.

[*All the officers shew their lots, excepting* OSTERLOO, *who continues gloomy and thoughtful.*

Has no one drawn the sable scroll of election? (*To* OSTERLOO). You are silent, my Lord; of what colour is your lot?

Ost. (*holding out his scroll.*) Black as midnight.

[*Soldiers quit their ranks and crowd round* OSTERLOO, *tumultuously.*

1st sold. Has it fallen upon our general; 'tis a damned lot—an unfair lot.

2d sold. We will not leave him behind us, though a hundred St. Maurices commanded it.

3d sold. Get within your walls again, ye cunning friars.

1st sold. An' we should lie i' the open air all night, we will not leave brave Osterloo behind us.

Prior. (*to* OST.) Count, you seem gloomy and irresolute: have the goodness to silence these clamours. I am in truth as sorry as any of your soldiers can be, that the lot has fallen upon you.

1st off. (*aside to* OST.) Nay, my noble friend, let me fulfil this penance in your stead. It is not now a time for scruples: the soldiers will be mutinous.

Ost. Mutinous! Soldiers, return to your ranks. (*Looking at them sternly as they seem unwillingly to obey.*) Will you brave me so far that I must repeat my command? (*They retire.*) I thank thee, dear Albert. (*To 1st off.*) Thou shalt do something in my stead; but it shall not be the service thou thinkest of. (*To prior*) Reverend father, I am indeed somewhat struck at being marked out by fate from so many men; but, as to how I shall act thereupon, no wise irresolute. (*To the sold.*) Continue your march. The brave Albert shall conduct you to Martigny; and there you will remain under his command, till I join you again.

1st sold. God preserve you then, my noble general! and if you do not join us again by tomorrow evening, safe and sound, we will not leave one stone of that building standing on another.

Many soldiers at once. So swear we all! So swear, &c.

Ost. (*assuming a cheerful look.*) Go to, foolish fellows! Were you to leave me in a den of lions, you could not be more apprehensive. Will watching all night by some holy shrine, or walking barefoot through their midnight aisles, be such a hardship to one, who has passed so many nights with you all on the cold field of battle? Continue your march without delay; else these good fathers will count you no better than a band of new raised city troops, with some jolly tankard-chief for your leader. A good march to you, my friends, with kind hostesses and warm firesides where you are going.

1st sold. Ah! What good will our fire-sides do us, when we think how our general is lodged?

Ost. Farewell! March on as quickly as you may: you shall all drink my health to-morrow evening in a good hogshead of rhenish.

1st sold. (*with others*) God grant we may! (*1st to Prior*) Look to it, reverend prior: if our general be not with us by to-morrow's sunset, St. Maurice will neither have monastery nor monks on this mountain.

Ost. No more! (*Embracing first officer, and shaking hands with others.*) Farewell! Farewell!

> [*The soldiers, after giving him a loud cheer, march off with their officers to martial music, and exeunt* OSTERLOO, *Prior, and monks into the monastery, while the peasants disappear amongst the rocks. Manent* MORAND *and* AGNES, *who has for some time appeared, looking over a crag.*

Agn. Morand, Morand!

Mor. Ha! art thou there? I might have guessed indeed, that so brave a sight would not escape thee. What made thee perch thyself like an eagle upon such a crag as that?

Agn. Chide not, good Morand, but help me down, lest I pay a dearer price for my sight than thou, with all thy grumbling, would'st wish.

> [*He helps her down.*

Mor. And now thou art going no doubt to tell the Lady Leonora, what a band of gallant fellows thou hast seen.

Agn. Assuredly, if I can find in my heart to speak of any but their noble leader.—What is his name? What meaning had all that drawing of lots in it? What will the monks do with him? Walk with me a little way towards the castle, brave Morand, and tell me what thou knowest.

Mor. I should walk to the castle and miles beyond it too, ere I could answer so many questions, and I have duty in the monastery, besides.

Agn. Come with me a little way, at least.

Mor. Ah, witch! thou knowest too well that I must always do what thou bidest me.

> [*Exeunt.*

SCENE III.

The refectory of the monastery, with a small table, on which are placed refreshments, discovered in one corner.

Enter OSTERLOO, *Prior,* BENEDICT, JEROME, *and* PAUL, *&c.*

Prior. Noble Osterloo, let me welcome you here, as one appointed by
heaven to purchase our deliverance from this dreadful malady;
and I hope the price to be paid for it will not be a heavy one.
Yet ere we proceed further in this matter, be entreated, I pray,
to take some refreshment after your long march. (*The table is
placed near the front of the stage.*)

Ost. I thank you, my lord; this is a gentle beginning to my penance: I
will, then, by your leave. (*Sitting down at the table.*) I have fasted
long, and am indeed somewhat exhausted. (*After taking some
refreshment.*) Ah! My poor soldiers! You must still endure two
hours' weary march, before you find such indulgence. Your
wine is good, reverend father.

Prior. I am glad you find it so; it is old.

Ost. (*cheerfully*). And your viands are good too; and your bread is
delicious. (*Drinking another cup.*) I shall have vigour now for any
thing.—Pray tell me something more of this wonderful vision:
was it a saint or an angel that appeared to the senior brother?

Prior (*pointing to* JEROME). He will answer for himself, and (*pointing to*
PAUL) this man saw it also.

Jer. It was neither angel nor saint, noble count, but a mortal form
wonderfully noble.

Ost. And it appeared to you in the usual manner of a dream?

Jer. It did; at least I know no sensible distinction. A wavy envelope-
ment of darkness preceded it, from which appearances seemed
dimly to wake into form, till all was presented before me in the
full strength of reality.

Paul. Nay, Brother, it broke upon me at once; a vivid distinct
apparition.

Ost. Well, be that as it may; what did appear to you? A mortal man,
and very noble?

Jer. Yes, general. Methought I was returning from mass, through the
cloisters that lead from the chapel, when a figure, as I have said,
appeared to me, and beckoned me to follow it. I did follow it;
for at first I was neither afraid, nor even surprised; but so won-
derfully it rose in stature and dignity as it strode before me,
that, ere it reached the door of the stranger's burying vault, I
was struck with unaccountable awe.

Ost. The stranger's burying vault!

Prior. Does any sudden thought strike you, count?

Ost. No, no! here's your health, fathers! (*Drinking.*) Your wine is excellent.

Prior. But that is water you have just now swallowed: this is the wine.

Ost. Ha! is it? No matter, no matter! it is very good too.

> [*A long pause;* OSTERLOO *with his eyes fixed thoughtfully on the ground.*

Prior. Shall not our brother proceed with his story, general?

Ost. Most certainly: I have been listening for it.

Jer. Well then, as I have said, at the door of the stranger's burying vault it stopped, and beckoned me again. It entered, and I followed it. There, through the damp mouldering tombs, it strode still before me, till it came to the farther extremity, as nearly as I could guess, two yards westward from the black marble monument; and then stopping and turning on me its fixed and ghastly eyes, it stretched out its hands—

Ost. Its hands! Did you say, its hands?

Jer. It stretched out one of them; the other was covered with its mantle; and in a voice that sounded—I know not how it sounded—

Paul. Ay, brother; it was something like a voice, at least it conveyed words to the mind, though it was not like a voice neither.

Jer. Be that as you please: these words it solemnly uttered,—"Command the brothers of this monastery, on pain of falling victims to the pestilence now devastating the country, to stop on its way the first division of the imperial army that shall march through your mountain pass; and choose from it, by lot, a man who shall abide one night within these walls, to make expiation for long concealed guilt. Let the suffering be such as the nature of the crime and the connection of the expiator therewith shall dictate. This spot of earth shall reveal——" It said no more, but bent its eyes stedfastly upon me with a stern threatening frown, which became, as it looked, keener than the looks of any mortal being, and vanished from my sight.

Paul. Ay, that look; that last terrible look! it awoke me with terror, and I know not how it vanished.

Jer. This has been repeated to me three times; last night twice in the course of the night, while brother Paul here was at the same time terrified with a similar apparition.

Prior. This, you will acknowledge, Count, was no common visitation, and could not but trouble us.

Ost. You say well.—Yet it was but a dream.

Prior. True; it was but a dream, and as such these pious men strove to consider it; when the march of your troops across our mountains, a thing so unlikely to happen, compelled them to reveal to me, without loss of time, what had appeared to them.

Ost. A tall figure, you say, and of a noble aspect?

Jer. Like that of a king, though habited more in the garb of a foreign soldier of fortune than of a state so dignified.

[OSTERLOO *rises from table agitated.*

Prior. What is the matter, general? Will you not finish your repast?

Ost. I thank you; I have had enough. The night grows cold; I would rather walk than sit.

[*Going hastily to the bottom of the stage, and pacing to and fro.*

Jer. (*aside to* PAUL *and the prior.*) What think ye of this?

Prior (*aside to* JEROME.) His countenance changed several times as he listened to you: there is something here different from common surprise on hearing a wonderful thing.

Enter a peasant by the bottom of the stage, bearing a torch.

Peas. (*eagerly, as he enters.*) We have found it.

Ost. (*stopping short in his walk.*) What hast thou found?

Peas. What the prior desired us to dig for.

Ost. What is that?

Peas. A grave.

[OSTERLOO *turns from him suddenly, and paces up and down very rapidly.*

Prior. (*to peas.*) Thou hast found it?

Peas. Ay, please you, and in the very spot, near the black monument, where your reverence desired us to dig. And it is well you sent for my kinsman and I to do it, for there is not a lay-brother in

the monastery strong enough to raise up the great stones that
covered it.

Prior. In the very spot, sayest thou?

Peas. In the very spot.

Prior. Bear thy torch before us, and we'll follow thee.

Omnes. (*eagerly,* OSTERLOO *excepted.*) Let us go immediately.

Prior (*to* OSTERLOO, *who stands fixed to the spot.*) Will not Count
Osterloo go also? It is fitting that he should.

Ost. (*rousing himself.*) O, most assuredly: I am perfectly ready to
follow you.

[*Exeunt.*

ACT II.

SCENE I.

*A burying vault, almost totally dark; the monuments and grave-stones
being seen very dimly by the light of a single torch, stuck by the side of
a deep open grave, in which a sexton is discovered, standing leaning on
his mattock, and* MORAND, *above ground, turning up, with his sheathed
sword, the loose earth about the mouth of the grave.*

Mor. There is neither skull nor bone amongst this earth: the ground
must have been newly broken up, when that coffin was let
down into it.

Sex. So one should think; but the earth here has the quality of
consuming whatever is put into it in a marvellous short time.

Mor. Ay; the flesh and more consumable parts of a body; but hath
it grinders in its jaws, like your carnivorous animal, to craunch
up bones and all? I have seen bones on an old field of battle,
some hundred years after the action, lying whitened and hard
in the sun.

Sex. Well, an't be new ground, I'll warrant ye somebody has paid
money enough for such a good tenement as this: I could not
wish my own father a better.

Mor. (*looking down*). The coffin is of an uncommon size: there must
be a leaden one within it, I should think.

Sex. I doubt that: it is only a clumsy shell that has been put together in haste; and I'll be hanged if he who made it ever made another before it. Now it would pine me with vexation to think I should be laid in such a bungled piece of workmanship as this.

Mor. Ay; it is well for those who shall bury thee, sexton, that thou wilt not be a looker on at thine own funeral.—Put together in haste, sayest thou! How long may it be since this coffin was laid in the ground?

Sex. By my say, now, I cannot tell; though many a grave I have dug in this vault, instead of the lay-brothers, who are mighty apt to take a cholic or shortness of breath, or the like, when any thing of hard labour falls to their share. (*After pausing.*) Ha, now! I have it. When I went over the mountain some ten years ago to visit my father-in-law, Baldwick, the stranger, who died the other day, after living so long as a hermit amongst the rocks, came here; and it was shrewdly suspected he had leave from our late prior, for a good sum of money, to bury a body privately in this vault. I was a fool not to think of it before. This, I'll be sworn for it, is the place.

Enter the Prior, OSTERLOO, JEROME, PAUL, BENEDICT, *and other monks, with the peasant carrying light before them. They enter by an arched door at the bottom of the stage, and walk on to the front, when every one, but* OSTERLOO, *crowds eagerly to the grave, looking down into it.*

Prior (to sexton). What hast thou found, friend?

Sex. A coffin an't please you, and of a size, too, that might almost contain a giant.

Omnes. (OSTERLOO *excepted.*) The inscription—is there an inscription on it?

Sex. No, no! They who put these planks together had no time for inscriptions.

Omnes. (*as before*). Break it open:—break it open. (*They crowd more eagerly about the grave, when, after a pause, the sexton is heard wrenching open the lid of the coffin.*)

Omnes. (*as before*). What is there in it? What hast thou found, sexton?

Sex. An entire skeleton, and of no common size.

Ost. (*in a quick hollow voice*). Is it entire?

Sex. (*after a pause*) No, the right hand is wanting, and there is not a loose bone in the coffin. (OST. *shudders and steps back.*)

Jer. (*to Prior, after a pause*). Will you not speak to him, father? His countenance is changed, and his whole frame seems moved by some sudden convulsion. (*The prior remains silent*). How is this? You are also changed, reverend father. Shall I speak to him?

Prior. Speak thou to him.

Jer. (*to* OSTERLOO). What is the matter with you, general? Has some sudden malady seized you?

Ost. (*to* JEROME). Let me be alone with you, holy prior; let me be alone with you instantly.

Jer. (*pointing*). This is the prior.—He would be alone with you, father: he would make his confession to you.

Prior. I dare not hear him alone: there must be witnesses. Let him come with me to my apartment.

Jer. (*to* OSTERLOO, *as they leave the grave*). Let me conduct you, count. (*After walking from it some paces*) Come on, my lord, why do you stop short?

Ost. Not this way—not this way, I pray you.

Jer. What is it you would avoid?

Ost. Turn aside, I pray you; I cannot cross over this.

Jer. Is it the grave you mean? We have left it behind us.

Ost. Is it not there? It yawns across our path, directly before us.

Jer. Indeed, my Lord, it is some paces behind.

Ost. There is delusion in my sight then; lead me as thou wilt.

[*Exeunt.*

SCENE II.

The private apartment of the prior. Enter BENEDICT, *looking round as he enters.*

Ben. Not yet come; aye, penitence is not very swift of foot. (*Speaking to himself as he walks up and down.*) Miserable man!—brave, goodly creature!—but alas, alas! most subdued; most miserable; and, I fear, most guilty!

Enter JEROME.

Jerome here!—Dost thou know, brother, that the prior is coming here immediately to confess the penitent?

Jer. Yes, brother; but I am no intruder; for he has summoned me to attend the confession as well as thyself.

Ben. Methinks some other person of our order, unconcerned with the dreaming part of this business, would have been a less suspicious witness.

Jer. Suspicious! Am I more concerned in this than any other member of our community? Heaven appoints its own agents as it listeth: the stones of these walls might have declared its awful will as well as the dreams of a poor friar.

Ben. True, brother Jerome; could they listen to confessions as he does, and hold reveries upon them afterwards.

Jer. What dost thou mean with thy reveries and confessions? Did not Paul see the terrible vision as well as I?

Ben. If thou hadst not revealed thy dream to him, he would have slept sound enough, or, at worst, have but flown over the pinnacles with his old mate the horned serpent, as usual: and had the hermit Baldwick never made his deathbed confession to thee, thou wouldst never have had such a dream to reveal.

Jer. Thinkest thou so? Then what brought Osterloo and his troops so unexpectedly by this route? With all thy heretical dislike to miraculous interposition, how wilt thou account for this?

Ben. If thou hadst no secret intelligence of Osterloo's route, to set thy fancy a working on the story the hermit confessed to thee, I never wore cowl on my head.

Jer. Those, indeed, who hear thee speak so lightly of mysterious and holy things, will scarcely believe thou ever didst.—But hush! the prior comes with his penitent; let us have no altercation now.

Enter Prior and OSTERLOO.

Prior (after a pause, in which he seems agitated.) Now, Count Osterloo, we are ready to hear your confession. To myself and these pious monks; men appointed by our holy religion to search into the crimes of the penitent, unburthen your heart of its terrible secret; and God grant you afterwards, if it be his righteous will, repentance and mercy.

Ost. (*making a sign, as if unable to speak, then uttering rapidly.*) Presently, presently.

Jer. Don't hurry him, reverend father; he cannot speak.

Ben. Take breath awhile, noble Osterloo, and speak to us when you can.

Ost. I thank you.

Ben. He is much agitated. (*To* OSTERLOO). Lean upon me, my lord.

Prior (*to* BENEDICT). Nay, you exceed in this. (*To* OSTERLOO). Recollect yourself, general, and try to be more composed. You seem better now; endeavour to unburden your mind of its fatal secret; to have it labouring within your breast is protracting a state of misery.

Ost. (*feebly*) I have voice now.

Jer. (*to* OSTERLOO). Give to Heaven then, as you ought—

Ben. Hush, brother Jerome! no exhortations now! let him speak it as he can. (*To* OSTERLOO). We attend to you most anxiously.

Ost. (*after struggling for utterance.*) I slew him.

Prior. The man whose bones have now been discovered?

Ost. The same: I slew him.

Jer. In the field, count?

Ost. No, no! many a man's blood has been on my hands there:—this is on my heart.

Prior. It is then premeditated murder you have committed.

Ost. (*hastily*) Call it so, call it so.

Jer. (*to* OSTERLOO, *after a pause.*) And is this all? Will you not proceed to tell us the circumstances attending it?

Ost. Oh! they were terrible!—But they are all in my mind as the indistinct horrors of a frenzied imagination. (*After a short pause.*) I did it in a narrow pass on St. Gothard, in the stormy twilight of a winter day.

Prior. You murdered him there?

Ost. I felt him dead under my grasp; but I looked at him no more after the last desperate thrust that I gave him. I hurried to a distance from the spot: when a servant, who was with me, seized with a sudden remorse, begged leave to return and remove the body, that, if possible, he might bury it in consecrated ground, as an atonement for the part he had taken in the terrible deed.—I gave him leave, with means to procure his desire:—I waited for him three days, concealed in the mountains;—but I neither saw him, nor heard of him again.

Ben. But what tempted a brave man like Osterloo to commit such a horrible act?

Ost. The torments of jealousy stung me to it, (*Hiding his face with his hands and then uncovering it*) I loved her, and was beloved:—He came,—a noble stranger—

Jer. Ay, if he was in his mortal state, as I in my dream beheld him, he was indeed most noble.

Ost. (*waving his hand impatiently.*) Well, well! he did come, then, and she loved me no more.—With arts and enchantments he besotted her.—Even from her own lips I received— (*Tossing up his arms violently, and then covering his face as before*) But what is all this to you? Maimed as he was, having lost his right arm in a battle with the Turks, I could not defy him to the field.—— After passing two nights in all the tossing agony of a damned spirit, I followed him on his journey 'cross the mountains.—On the twilight of the second day, I laid wait for him in a narrow pass; and as soon as his gigantic form darkened the path before me—I have told you all.

Prior. (*eagerly*) You have not told his name.

Ost. Did I not say Montera? He was a noble Hungarian.

Prior. (*much agitated*) He was so!—He was so. He was noble and beloved.

Jer. (*aside to Prior*). What is the matter with you, reverend father? Was he your friend?

Prior (*aside to Jerome*). Speak not to me now, but question the murderer as ye will.

Ben. (*overhearing the prior.*) He is indeed a murderer, reverend father, but he is our penitent.

Prior. Go to! what are names?—Ask him what questions you will, and finish the confession quickly.

Ben. (*to* OSTERLOO). But have you never till now confessed this crime; nor in the course of so many years reflected on its dreadful turpitude?

Ost. The active and adventurous life of a soldier is most adverse
to reflection: but often, in the stillness of midnight, the
remembrance of this terrible deed has come powerfully upon
me; till morning returned, and the noise of the camp began,
and the fortunes of the day were before me.

Prior (in a severe voice). Thou hast indeed been too long permitted to
remain in this hardened state. But heaven, sooner or later, will
visit the man of blood with its terrors. Sooner or later, he shall
feel that he stands upon an awful brink; and short is the step
which engulphs him in that world, where the murdered and
the murderer meet again, in the tremendous presence of him,
who is the Lord and giver of life.

Ost. You believe then in such severe retribution?

Prior. I believe in it as in my own existence.

Ost. (turning to JEROME *and* BENEDICT). And you, good fathers, you
believe in this?

Ben. Nature teaches this as well as revelation: we must believe it.

Jer. Some presumptuous minds, dazzled with the sunshine of
prosperity, have dared to doubt; but to us, in the sober shade of
life; visited too, as we have now been, by visions preternatural
and awful, it is a thing of certainty, rather than of faith.

Ost. That such things are!—It makes the brain confused and giddy.—
These are tremendous thoughts.

> [*Leans his back against the wall, and gazes fixedly on the
> ground.*

Prior. Let us leave him to the bitterness of his thoughts. We now must
deliberate with the brethren on what is to be done. There must
be no delay: the night advances fast. Conduct him to another
apartment: I must assemble a council of the whole order.

Jer. (to OSTERLOO). We must lead you to another apartment, count,
while we consider what is to be done.

Ost. (roused). Ay, the expiation you mean: let it be severe; if atonement
in this world may be made. (*Turning to Prior as* JEROME *leads him
off.*) Let your expiation be severe, holy father: a slight penance
matches not with such a crime as mine.

Prior. Be well assured it shall be what it ought.

Ost. (turning again and catching hold of the prior's robe.) I regard not
bodily pain. In battle once, with the head of a broken arrow in

my thigh, I led on the charge, and sustained all the exertions of a well-fought field, till night closed upon our victory. Let your penance be severe, my reverend father; I have been long acquainted with pain.

[*Exeunt* OSTERLOO *and* JEROME.

Ben. You seem greatly moved, father; but it is not with pity for the wretched. You would not destroy such a man as this, though his crime is the crime of blood?

Prior. He shall die: ere another sun dawn on these walls, he shall die.

Ben. Oh, say not so! Think of some other expiation.

Prior. I would think of another, were there any other more dreadful to him than death.

Ben. He is your penitent.

Prior. He is the murderer of my brother.

Ben. Then Heaven have mercy on him, if he must find none here!— Montero was your brother?

Prior. My only brother. It were tedious to tell thee now, how I was separated from him after the happy days of our youth.—I saw him no more; yet he was still the dearest object of my thoughts. After escaping death in many a battle, he was slain, as it was conjectured, by banditti, in travelling across the mountains. His body was never discovered. Ah! little did I think it was lying so near me!

Ben. It is indeed piteous; and you must needs feel it as a brother: but consider the danger we run, should we lay violent hands on an Imperial general, with his enraged soldiers, within a few hours' march of our walls.

Prior. I can think of nothing but revenge. Speak to me no more. I must assemble the whole order immediately.

[*Exeunt.*

SCENE III.

Another apartment. Enter OSTERLOO *as from a small recess at the bottom of the stage, pacing backwards and forwards several times in an agitated manner; then advancing slowly to the front, where he stands musing and muttering to himself for some moments, before he speaks aloud.*

Ost. That this smothered horror should burst upon me at last! And there be really such things as the darkened fancy imageth to itself, when the busy day is stilled.—An unseen world surrounds us: spirits and powers, and the invisible dead hover near us; while we in unconscious security—Oh! I have slept upon a fearful brink! Every sword that threatened my head in battle, had power in its edge to send me to a terrible account.—I have slept upon a fearful brink.—Am I truly awake? (*Rubbing his eyes, then grasping several parts of his body, first with one hand and then with the other.*) Yes, yes! it is so!—I am keenly and terribly awake. (*Paces rapidly up and down, and then stopping short.*) Can there be virtue in penances suffered by the body to do away offences of the soul? If there be—O if there be! let them runnel my body with stripes; and swaith me round in one continued girth of wounds! Any thing, that can be endured here, is mercy compared to the dreadful abiding of what may be hereafter.

Enter WOVELREID, *behind followed by soldiers, who range themselves at the bottom of the stage.* OSTERLOO *turning round, runs up to him eagerly.*

Ha! my dear Albert, returned to me again, with all my noble fellows at thy back!——Pardon me; I mistook you for one of my captains.
Wov. I am the prior's captain.
Ost. And those men too?
Wov. They are the prior's soldiers, who have been ordered from distant quarters to repair to the monastery immediately.
Ost. In such haste?
Wov. Ay, in truth! We received our orders after sun-set, and have marched two good leagues since.
Ost. What may this mean?

Wov. Faith I know not. My duty is to obey the prior, and pray to our good saint; and whether I am commanded to surprise the strong hold of an enemy, or protect an execution, it is the same thing to me.

Ost. An execution! can ought of this nature be intended?

Wov. You turn pale, sir: wearing the garb of a soldier, you have surely seen blood ere now.

Ost. I have seen too much blood.

Enter Prior, JEROME, PAUL, *and monks, walking in order; the prior holding a paper in his hand.*

Prior (with solemnity). Count Osterloo, lieutenant-general of our liege lord the emperor; authorized by this deed, which is subscribed by all the brethren of our holy order here present, I pronounce to you our solemn decision, that the crime of murder, as, by the mysterious voice of heaven, and your own confession, your crime is proved to be, can only be expiated by death: you are therefore warned to prepare yourself to die this night. Before day-break, you must be with the inhabitants of another world; where may the great Maker of us all deal with you in mercy!

[*Osterloo staggers back from the spot where he stood, and remains silent.*

Prior. It is a sentence, count, pronounced against you from necessity, to save the lives of our whole community, which you yourself have promised to submit to; have you any thing to say in reply to it?

Ost. Nothing: my thoughts are gone from me in the darkness of astonishment.

Prior. We are compelled to be thus hasty and severe: ere day-break, you must die.

Ost. Ere day-break! not even the light of another sun, to one so ill prepared for the awful and tremendous state into which you would thrust him! this is inhuman! it is horrible!

Prior. He was as ill prepared for it, who, with still shorter warning, was thrust into that awful state in the narrow pass of St. Gothard.

Ost. The guilt of murder was not on his soul.—Nay, nay, holy prior! consider this horrible extremity: let the pain of the executioner's

stroke be twenty fold upon me; but thrust me not forth to that
state from which my soul recoils with unutterable horror.——
Never but once, to save the life of a friend, did I bend the knee
to mortal man in humble supplication. I am a soldier; in many
battles I have bled for the service of my country; I am a noble
soldier, and I was a proud one; yet do I thus—Contemn not my
extremity! my knee is on the ground.

Prior. Urge me no further. It must not be; no respite can be granted.

Ost. (*starting up furiously from the ground, and drawing his sword.*) Then
subdue as you may, stern priest, the strength of a desperate
man.

> [*Wovelreid and soldiers rush forward, getting behind him,
> and surrounding him on every side, and after a violent
> struggle disarm him.*

Wov. What a noble fellow this would be to defend a narrow breach,
though he shrinks with such abhorrence from a scaffold. It is a
piteous thing to see him so beset.

Prior (*to* WOVELREID). What sayest thou, fool!

Wov. Nay it is no business of mine, my lord, I confess. Shall we
conduct him to the prison chamber?

Prior. Do so; and see that he retain no concealed arms about him.

Wov. I obey, my lord: every thing shall be made secure.

> [*Exit* OSTERLOO, *guarded by* WOVELREID *and soldiers, and,
> at the same time, enter Benedict, by the opposite side, who
> stands looking after him piteously.*

Prior (*sternly to* BENEDICT). What brings thee here? Dost thou repent
having refused to concur with us in an act that preserves the
community?

Ben. Say rather, reverend father, an act that revenges your brother's
death, which the laws of the empire should revenge.

Prior. A supernatural visitation of heaven hath commanded us to
punish it.—What; dost thou shake thy head? Thou art of a
doubting and dangerous spirit; and beware lest, sooner or
later, the tempter do not lure thee into heresy. If reason cannot
subdue thee, authority shall.—Return again to thy cell; let me
hear of this no more.

Ben. I will, reverend father. But for the love of our holy saint, bethink
you, ere it be too late, that though we may be saved from the

pestilence by this bloody sacrifice, what will rescue our throats from the swords of Osterloo's soldiers, when they shall return, as they have threatened, to demand from us their general?

Prior. Give thyself no concern about this. My own bands are already called in, and a messenger has been dispatched to the abbess Matilda; her troops, in defence of the church, will face the best soldiers of the empire.—But why lose we time in unprofitable contentions? Go, my sons, (*speaking to other monks*) the night advances fast, and we have much to do ere morning. (*Knocking heard without.*) Ha! who knocks at this untimely hour? Can the soldiers be indeed returned upon us?—Run to the gate; but open it to none.

[*Exeunt several monks in haste, and presently re-enter with a lay-brother.*

Lay-B. Please ye, reverend father; the marchioness has sent a messenger from the castle, beseeching you to send a confessor immediately to confess one of her women, who was taken ill yesterday, and is now at the point of death.

Prior. I'm glad it is only this.—What is the matter with the penitent?

Lay-B. I know not, please you: the messenger only said, she was taken ill yesterday.

Prior (*shaking his head*). Ay, this malady has got there also.—I cannot send one of the brothers to bring infection immediately amongst us.—What is to be done? Leonora is a most noble lady; and the family have been great benefactors to our order.—I must send somebody to her. But he must stop well his nostrils with spicery, and leave his upper garment behind him, when he quits the infected apartment. Jerome, wilt thou go? Thou art the favorite confessor with all the women at the castle.

Jer. Nay, father; I must attend on our prisoner here, who has most need of ghostly assistance.

Prior (*to another monk*). Go thou, Anselmo; thou hast given comfort to many a dying penitent.

Monk. I thank you, father, for the preference; but Paul is the best of us all for administering comfort to the dying; and there is a sickness come over my heart, o'the sudden, that makes me unfit for the office.

Prior (*to* PAUL). Thou wilt go then, my good son.

Paul. I beseech you, don't send me, reverend father; I ne'er escaped contagion in my life, where malady or fever were to be had.

Prior. Who will go then?

[*A deep silence.*

Ben. What; has no one faith enough in the protection of St. Maurice, even purchased, as it is about to be, by the shedding of human blood, to venture upon this dangerous duty? I will go then, father, though I am sometimes of a doubting spirit.

Prior. Go, and St. Maurice protect thee!

[*Exit* BEN.

Let him go; it is well that we get rid of him for the night, should they happily detain him so long at the castle.—He is a troublesome, close-searching, self-willed fellow. He hath no zeal for the order. Were a miser to bequeath his possessions to our monastery, he would assist the disappointed heir himself to find out a flaw in the deed.—But retire to your cells, my Sons; and employ yourselves in prayer and devotion, till the great bell warn you to attend the execution.

[*Exeunt.*

SCENE III.

An apartment in the castle.
Enter LEONORA *and* AGNES, *speaking as they enter.*

Ag. But she is asleep now; and is so much and so suddenly better, that the confessor, when he comes, will be dissatisfied, I fear, that we have called him from his cell at such an unreasonable hour.

Leo. Let him come, nevertheless; don't send to prevent him.

Ag. He will be unwilling to be detained, for they are engaged in no common matters tonight at the monastery. Count Osterloo, as I told you before, is doing voluntary penance at the shrine of St. Maurice to stop the progress of this terrible malady.

Leo. I remember thou did'st.

Ag. Ah, Marchioness! you would not say so thus faintly, had you seen him march through the pass with his soldiers. He is the bravest and most graceful man, though somewhat advanced in years, that I ever beheld.—Ah, had you but seen him!

Leo. I have seen him, Agnes.

Ag. And I spoke of him all the while, yet you did not tell me this before! Ah, my noble mistress and friend! the complexion of your cheek is altered; you have indeed seen him, and you have not seen him with indifference.

Leo. Think as thou wilt about this. He was the friend and fellow-soldier of my lord, when we first married; though before my marriage I had never seen him.

Ag. Friend! Your lord was then in the decline of life; there must have been great disparity in their friendship.

Leo. They were friends, however; for the marquis liked society younger than himself; and I, who had been hurried into an unequal marriage, before I could judge for myself, was sometimes foolish enough to compare them together.

Ag. Ay, that was natural enough. (*Eagerly*). And what happened then?

Leo. (*offended.*) What happened then! (*Drawing herself up proudly.*) Nothing happened then, but subduing the foolish fancy of a girl, which was afterwards amply repaid by the self-approbation and dignity of a woman.

Ag. Pardon me, madam; I ought to have supposed all this. But you have been long a widow, and Osterloo is still unmarried; what prevented you when free.

Leo. I was ignorant what the real state of his sentiments had been in regard to me. But had this been otherwise; received, as I was, into the family of my lord, the undowried daughter of a petty nobleman; and left as I now am, by his confiding love, the sole guardian of his children and their fortunes; I could never think of supporting a second lord on the wealth entrusted to me by the first, to the injury of his children. As nothing, therefore, has ever happened in consequence of this weakness of my youth, nothing ever shall.

Ag. This is noble.

Leo. It is right.—But here comes the father confessor.

Enter BENEDICT.

You are welcome, good father! yet I am almost ashamed to see you; for our sick person has become suddenly well again, and is now in a deep sleep. I fear I shall appear to you capricious and inconsiderate in calling you up at so late an hour.

Ben. Be not uneasy, lady, upon this account: I am glad to have an occasion for being absent from the monastery for some hours, if you will permit me to remain here so long.

Leo. What mean you, father Benedict? Your countenance is solemn and sorrowful: what is going on at the monastery? (*He shakes his head.*) Ha! will they be severe with him in a voluntary penance, submitted to for the good of the order?—What is the nature of the penance? It is to continue, I am told, but one night.

Ben. It will, indeed, soon be over.

Leo. And will he be gone on the morrow?

Ben. His spirit will, but his body remains with us for ever.

Leo. (*uttering a shriek*). Death, dost thou mean?—O horror! horror! Is this the expiation? Oh most horrible, most unjust!

Ben. Indeed I consider it as such. Though guilty, by his own confession, of murder, committed, many year's since, under the frenzy of passion; it belongs not to us to inflict the punishment of death upon a guilty soul, taken so suddenly and unprepared for its doom.

Leo. Murder! didst thou say murder? Oh Osterloo, Osterloo! hast thou been so barbarous? and art thou in this terrible state?—Must thou thus end thy days, and so near me too!

Ben. You seem greatly moved, noble Leonora: would you could do something more for him than lament.

Leo. (*catching hold of him eagerly*). Can I do any thing? Speak, father: O tell me how! I will do any thing and every thing.—Alas, alas! my vassals are but few, and cannot be assembled immediately.

Ben. Force were useless. Your vassals, if they were assembled, would not be persuaded to attack the sacred walls of a monastery.

Leo. I did indeed rave foolishly: but what else can be done?—Take these jewels and every thing of value in the castle, if they will bribe those who guard him, to let him escape.—Think of it.— O think well of it, good Benedict!

Ag. I have heard that there is a secret passage, leading from the prison-chamber of the monastery under its walls, and opening to the free country at the bottom of the rocks.

Ben. By every holy saint, so there is! and the most sordid of our brothers is entrusted with the key of it. But who will be his conductor? None but a monk of the order may pass the soldiers who guard him; and the monk who should do it, must fly from his country for ever, and break his sacred vows. I can oppose the weak fears and injustice of my brethren, for misfortunes and disgust of the world, not superstitious veneration for monastic sanctity, has covered my head with a cowl; but this I cannot do.

Ag. There is the dress of a monk of your order in the old wardrobe of the castle, if some person were disguised in it.

Leo. Thanks to thee! thanks to thee, my happy Agnes! I will be that person.—I will put on the disguise.—Good father! your face gives consent to this.

Ben. If there be time; but I left them preparing for the execution.

Leo. There is, there is!—Come with me to the wardrobe, and we'll set out for the monastery forthwith.—Come, come! a few moments will carry us there.

       [Exit, hastily, followed by Ag. and Ben.

SCENE IV.

A wood near the castle; the stage quite dark. Enter two servants with torches.

1st ser. This must surely be the entry to the path, where my lady ordered us to wait for those same monks.

2d ser. Yes; I know it well, for yonder is the postern. It is the nearest path to the monastery, but narrow and difficult. The night is cold: I hope they will not keep us long waiting.

1st ser. I heard the sound of travellers coming up the eastern avenue, and they may linger belike; for monks are marvellously fond of great people and of strangers; at least the good fathers of our monastery are.

2d ser. Ay, in their late prior's time they lived like lords themselves; and they are not very humble at present.—But there's light from the postern: here they come.

> [Enter BENEDICT, LEONORA *disguised like a monk, and* AGNES *with a peasant's cloak thrown over her.*

Leo. (*speaking as she enters.*) It is well thought of, good Benedict. Go thou before me to gain brother Baldwin, in the first place; and I'll wait without on the spot we have agreed upon, until I hear the signal.

Ben. Thou comprehendest me completely, brother; so God speed us both! (*To 1st ser.*) Torch-man, go thou with me. This is the right path, I trust?

1st ser. Fear not, father; I know it well.

> [*Exit* BEN. *and 1st ser.*

Leo. (*to* AGNES, *while she waves her hand to 2d servant to retire to a greater distance.*) After I am admitted to the monastery, fail not to wait for me at the mouth of the secret passage.

Ag. Fear not: Benedict has described it so minutely, I cannot fail to discover it.

Leo. What steps are those behind us? Somebody following us from the castle?

Enter 3d servant in haste.

3d ser. There are travellers arrived at the gate, and desire to be admitted for the night.

Leo. In an evil hour they come. Return, dear Agnes, and receive them. Benighted strangers, no doubt. Excuse my absence any how: go quickly.

Ag. And leave you to proceed alone?

Leo. Care not for me: there is an energy within me now, that bids defiance to fear.

> [*Beckons to 2d servant who goes out before her with the torch, and Exit.*

Ag. (*muttering to herself, as she turns to the castle.*) The evil spirit hath brought travellers to us at this moment: but I'll send them to their chambers right quickly, and join her at the secret passage, notwithstanding.

> [*Exeunt.*

ACT III.

SCENE I.

The prison-chamber of the monastery: OSTERLOO *is discovered, sitting in a bending posture, with his clenched hands pressed upon his knees and his eyes fixed on the ground,* JEROME *standing by him.*

Jer. Nay, sink not thus, my son; the mercy of Heaven is infinite. Let other thoughts enter thy soul: let penitence and devotion subdue it.

Ost. Nothing but one short moment of division between this state of humanity and that which is to follow! The executioner lets fall his axe, and the dark veil is rent; the gulf is uncovered; the regions of anguish are before me.

Jer. My son, my son! this must not be; thine imagination overpowers thy devotion.

Ost. The dead are there; and what welcome shall the murderer receive from that assembled host? Oh the terrible form that stalks forth to meet me! the stretching out of that hand! the greeting of that horrible smile! And it is thou, who must lead me before the tremendous majesty of my offended Maker! Incomprehensible and dreadful! What thoughts can give an image of that which overpowers all thought! (*Clasping his hands tightly over his head, and bending himself almost to the ground.*)

Jer. (*after a pause*). Art thou entranced? art thou asleep? art thou still in those inward agonies of imagination? (*Touching him softly.*) Speak to me.

Ost. (*starting up*). Are they come for me? They shall not yet: I'll strangle the first man that lays hold of me. (*Grasping* JEROME *by the throat.*)

Jer. Let go your hold, my lord; I did but touch you gently to rouse you from your stupor.

[OSTERLOO *lets go his hold, and* JEROME *shrinks to a distance.*

Ost. I have grasped thee, then, too roughly. But shrink not from me thus. Strong men have fallen by my arm, but a child might contend with me now. (*Throwing himself back again into his chair, and bursting into tears.*)

Jer. Forgive me, my son, there was a wildness in your eyes that made me afraid.

Ost. Thou need'st not be afraid: thou art a good man, and hast days of life still before thee; thou need'st not be afraid.—But, as thou art a good man, speak to me, I conjure thee, as a man, not as a monk: answer me as the true sense and reason of a man doth convince thee.

Jer. I will, my son.

Ost. Dost thou in truth believe, that the very instant after life has left the body, we are forthwith awake and conscious in the world of spirits? No intermediate state of slumbering insensibility between?

Jer. It is indeed my belief. Death is but a short though awful pass; as it were a winking of the eyes for a moment. We shut them in this world and open them in the next: and there we open them with such increased vividness of existence, that this life, in comparison, will appear but as a state of slumber and of dreams.—But wherefore dost thou cross thine arms so closely on thy breast, and coil thyself together so wretchedly? What is the matter, my son? Art thou in bodily anguish?

Ost. The chilly night shoots icy coldness through me.

Jer. O regard not the poor feelings of a fleshly frame, which thou so soon must part withal: a little time will now put an end to every thing that nature can endure.

Ost. (*raising his head quickly*). Ha! how soon? Has the bell struck again since I listened to it last?

Jer. No; but it will soon strike, and daybreak is at hand. Rouse ye then, and occupy the few minutes that remain in acts of devotion becoming thine unhappy state. O, my son, pour out thy soul in penitent prayers to an offended but merciful God. We, too, will pray for thee. Months, nay years after thy death, masses shall be said for the repose of thy soul, that it may at last be received into bliss. O my unhappy son! pour forth thy spirit to God; and let thy prayers also ascend to our blessed saint and martyr, who will intercede for thee.

Ost. I cannot: I have not thoughts for prayer.—The gulf yawns before me—the unknown, the unbounded, the unfathomable!— Prayers! prayers! what prayers hath despair?

Jer. Hold, hold, refractory spirit! This obstinacy is destruction.—I
must call in brother Bernard to assist me: I cannot be answerable
alone, in a service of such infinite moment.

> [*Exit; and after a pause, in which* OSTERLOO *seems absorbed
> in the stupor of despair, enter* LEONORA *disguised.*

Leo. (*coming eagerly forward, and then stopping short to look at him.*)
There is some mistake in this: it is not Osterloo.—It is, it is! but
Oh, how changed! Thy hand, great God! has been upon him.
(*Going closer to him.*) Osterloo! Osterloo!

Ost. I hear thee, father.

Leo. (*throwing aside her disguise*). O no! it is no father. Lift up thine
eyes and see an old friend before thee, with deliverance in her
hand. (*Holding out a key.*)

Ost. (*looking up wildly*). Is it a sound in my ears, or did any one say
deliverance? (*Gazing on her.*) What thing art thou? A form of
magic or delusion?

Leo. Neither, Count Osterloo; but an old friend, bringing this key
in her hand for thy deliverance. Yet much I fear thou hast not
strength enough to rise and follow me.

Ost. (*bounding from his seat*). I have strength for any thing if there
be deliverance in it.—Where go we? They will be upon us
immediately.

Leo. (*lifting a small lamp from a table, and holding it to examine the
opposite wall*). The door, as he described it, is to the right of a
small projection of the wall.—Here—here it is!

> [*Opens a small door, and beckons* OSTERLOO *to follow her.*

Ost. Yes, blessed being! I will follow thee.—Ha! they are coming!

> [*Strides hastily to the door, while Leonora holds up the lamp
> to light him in to it, and then going in herself, shuts the door
> softly behind her.*

SCENE II.

An old ruinous vault, with a strong grated door on one side, through which the moon-beams are gleaming: on the other side, an old winding staircase, leading from the upper regions of the monastery, from which a feeble light is seen, increasing by degrees; and presently LEONORA *appears, descending the stairs with a lamp in her hand, followed by* OSTERLOO. *As she enters, something on the wall catches her robe, and she turns round to disentangle it, bending her face close to the light.*

Ost. (stopping to assist her, and then gazing on her). Thou art something I have known and loved somewhere, though it has passed away from my mind with all my better thoughts.—Great power of Heaven! art thou Leonora?

Leo. (smiling). Dost thou know me now?

Ost. I do, I do! My heart knew thee before, but my memory did not. *(Kneeling and kissing both her hands.)* And so it is to thee—thou whom I first loved—Pardon me, pardon me!—thou whom I loved and dared not love;—thou from whom I fled to be virtuous—thou art my deliverer. Oh! had I never loved another after thee, it had been well.—Knowest thou it is a murderer thou art saving?

Leo. Say no more of this: I know thy story, and I came—

Ost. O! thou camest like a blessed spirit to deliver me from many horrors. I was terribly beset: thou hast snatched me from a tremendous brink.

Leo. I hope so, if this key prove to be the right one.

Ost. (alarmed). Dost thou doubt it?

Leo. It seems to me smaller than it ought to be, when I consider that massive door.

Ost. Give it me.

> [*Snatches the key from her, and runs to the door; then turns the key in the lock, and finding it too small, stamps with his feet, throws it from him, and holds up his clenched hands in despair.*

Leo. Oh, cross fate! But I'll return again for the right one. Baldwin cannot be so wicked as to deceive me, and Benedict is still on

the watch, near the door of the prison-chamber. Stay here till
I return.

> [*She ascends the stairs, whilst* OSTERLOO *leans his back
> to the wall, frequently moving his body up and down with
> impatient agitation: a bell tolls;* OSTERLOO *starts from his
> place, and* LEONORA *descends again, re-entering in great
> alarm.*

Leo. Oh! I cannot go now: that bell tolls to warn them to the great
hall: I shall meet them on their way. What is to be done? The
strength of three men could not force that heavy door, and
thou art feeble and spent.

Ost. (*running furiously to the door*). Despair has strength for any
thing.

> [*Seizes hold of the door, and, making two or three terrible
> efforts, bursts it open with a loud jar.*

Leo. Supernatural strength has assisted thee: now thou art free.

> [*As* OSTERLOO *and* LEONORA *are about to pass on through
> the door,* WOVELREID *and three armed soldiers appear in
> the porch beyond it, and oppose their passage.*

Wov. Hold! we are the prior's soldiers, and will suffer no prisoner to
escape.

Ost. Those who dare prevent me!

> [*Wrests a sword from one of the soldiers, and, fighting
> furiously, forces his way past them all, they not daring to
> pursue him; when* WOVELREID *seizing on* LEONORA *to
> prevent her from following him, she calls out.*

Leo. O let me pass! and I'll reward you nobly.

Ost. (*returning to rescue* LEO.) Let go thine unhallowed grasp.

Leo. For Heaven's sake care not for me! Save thyself—save thyself!
I am in no danger. Turn not again to fight, when such terrible
odds are against thee.

Ost. I have arms in my hand now, and my foes are before me!

> [*Fights fiercely again, till* MORAND, *with a strong band of
> soldiers, entering the porch behind him, he is overpowered
> and secured;* LEONORA *sinks down by the wall in a swoon.*

Wov. Give me a rope. We must bind him securely; for the devil has
put the strength of ten men into him, though, but half an hour

ago, his face was as pale as a moon-light icicle, and he could
scarcely walk without being supported.

Mor. Alas, alas! his face has returned to its former colour; his head
sinks on his breast, and his limbs are again feeble and listless. I
would rather see him fighting like a fiend than see him thus.

Wov. Let us move him hence; would'st thou stop to lament over
him?

Mor. It was base work in Baldwin to betray their plot to the prior, for
he took their money first I'll be sworn.

Wov. He had betrayed the prior then, and all the community
besides.

Mor. Well, let us move him hence: this is no business of ours.

[*Exeunt* MORAND, WOVELREID *and soldiers, leading out* OSTERLOO.

Enter AGNES *by the grated door, and discovers* LEONORA *on the ground.*

Ag. O holy virgin! On the ground, fainting and ill! Have the barbar-
ians left her thus? (*Chafing her temples and hand.*) She begins to
revive. It is me, my dearest lady: look up and see me: those men
are all gone.

Leo. And Osterloo with them?

Ag. Alas, he is.

Leo. It is fated so. Let me lie where I am: I cannot move yet, my good
Agnes.

Ag. Nay, do not yet despair of saving the count.

Leo. (*starting up and catching hold of her eagerly.*) How so? Is it
possible?

Ag. The travellers, arrived at the castle, are the imperial ambassador
and his train. Night overtook them on the mountains, and they
are now making merry in the hall.

Leo. Thank Heaven for this! Providence has sent him hither. I'll go to
him instantly, and conjure him to interpose his authority to save
the life of Osterloo. Representing his liege lord, the emperor,
the prior dare not disobey his commands, and the gates of the
monastery will be opened at his call. Who comes here? Let us
go.

Re-enter MORAND.

Mor. (*to* LEONORA). You are revived again: I am glad to see it. Pardon me, lady, that I forgot you in your extremity, and let me conduct you safely to the castle.

Leo. I thank you; but my servants are without. Let me go. Don't follow me, I pray you.

Mor. Let me support you through the porch, and I'll leave you to their care, since you desire it.

[*Exeunt,* LEONORA *supported by* MORAND *and* AGNES.

SCENE III.

A grand hall, prepared for the execution; soldiers are discovered drawn up on each side of the scaffold, with BENEDICT *and several of the monks on the front of the stage. A bell tolls at measured intervals, with a deep pause between; after which enter* MORAND, *hanging his head sorrowfully.*

Ben. (*to* MOR.) Is he come forth?

1st monk. Hast thou seen him?

Mor. They are leading him hither, but they move slowly.

1st monk. Thou hast seen him then; how does he look now?

Mor. I cannot tell thee. These few hours have done on him the work of many years: he seems broken and haggarded with age, and his quenched eyes are fixed in their sockets, like one who walks in sleep.

Ben. Alas, alas! how changed in little time the bold and gallant Osterloo!

1st monk. Have I not told thee, Morand, that fear will sometimes couch under the brazen helmet as well as the woollen cowl?

Mor. Fear, dost thou call it! Set him this moment in the field of battle, with death threatening him from a hundred points at once, and he would brave it most valiantly.

Ben. (*preventing 1st monk from answering.*) Hush, brother! Be not so warm, good lieutenant; we believe what thou sayest most perfectly. The bravest mind is capable of fear, though it fears no mortal man. A brave man fears not man; and an innocent and brave man united, fears nothing.

Mor. Ay, now you speak reason: call it fear then if you will.—But the prior comes; let us go to our places. (*They arrange themselves; and then enter the prior, with a train of monks, who likewise arrange themselves: a pause, in which the bell tolls as before, and enter* OSTERLOO, *supported by* JEROME *and* PAUL, WOVELREID, *and soldiers following.*)

Prior (*meeting him with solemnity*). Count Osterloo, in obedience to the will of Heaven, for our own preservation, and the just punishment of guilt, I am compelled with the monks of this monastery over whom I preside, to see duly executed within the time prescribed, this dismal act of retribution.—You have, I trust, with the help of these holy men, as well as a few short moments would allow, closed your mortal account with Heaven: if there be aught that rests upon your mind, regarding worldly concerns which you leave behind you unsettled, let me know your last will, and it shall be obeyed. (*To* JEROME, *after pausing for an answer.*) Dost thou think he understands me?

Jer. (*to* OSTERLOO) Did you hear, my son, what the prior has been saying to you?

Ost. I heard words through a multitude of sounds.

Jer. It was the prior, desiring to know if you have any wishes to fulfil, regarding worldly affairs, left behind you unsettled.—Perhaps to your soldiers you may.

Ost. (*interrupting him eagerly and looking wildly round.*) My soldiers! are they here?

Jer. Ah, no! they are not here; they are housed for the night in their distant quarters: they will not be here till the setting of to-morrow's sun.

Ost. (*groaning deeply*). To-morrow's sun!

Jer. Is there any wish you would have conveyed to them? Are there any of your officers to whom you would send a message or token of remembrance?

Ost. Ye speak again imperfectly, through many ringing sounds.

         [JER. *repeats the question in a slow distinct voice.*

Ost. Ay there is: these, these—— (*Endeavouring to tear off his cincture and some military ornaments from his dress*) I cannot hit upon these fastenings.

Jer. We'll assist you, my son.

[*Undoing his cincture or girdle, &c.*

Ost. (*still endeavouring to do it himself.*) My sword too, and my daggers.—My last remembrance to them both.

Jer. To whom, my lord?

Ost. Both—all of them.

Ben. (*who has kept sorrowfully at some distance, now approaching eagerly.*) Urge him no more: his officers will themselves know what names he would have uttered. (*Turning to* OST. *with an altered voice.*) Yes, noble count; they shall be given as you desire with your farewell affection to all your brave followers.

Ost. I thank ye.

Jer. And this is all?

Ost. Nay, nay!

Ben. What is there besides?

Prior (*angrily*). There is too much of this: and some sudden rescue may prevent us.

Ben. Nay, reverend father, there is no fear of this: you would not cut short the last words of a dying man?

Prior. And must I be guided by thy admonitions? Beware; though Baldwin has not named thee, I know it is thou who art the traitor.

Ben. There is but one object at present to be thought of, and with your leave, reverend father, I will not be deterred from it. (*To* OST. *again in a voice of tenderness.*) What is there besides, noble Osterloo, that you would wish us to do?

Ost. There is something.

Ben. What is it, my lord?

Ost. I wot not.

Ben. Then let it rest.

Ost. Nay, nay! This—this—— (*Pulling a ring from his finger which falls on the ground.*) My hands will hold nothing.

Ben. I have found it; and what shall I do with it?

Ost. (*in a faint hurried voice.*) Leonora—Leonora.

Ben. I understand you, my lord.

Prior. I am under the necessity, Count Osterloo, of saying, your time is run to its utmost limit: let us call upon you now for your last exertion of nature. These good brothers must conduct you to the scaffold.

> [JER. *and* PAUL *support him towards the scaffold, while* BENEDICT *retires to a distance, and turns his back to it.*

Jer. Rest upon me, my son, you have but a few paces to go.

Ost. The ground sinks under me; my feet tread upon nothing.

Jer. We are now at the foot of the scaffold, and there are two steps to mount: lean upon us more firmly.

Ost. (*stumbling*). It is dark; I cannot see.

Jer. Alas, my son! there is a blaze of torches round you. (*After they are on the scaffold.*) Now, in token of thy faith in heaven, and forgiveness of all men, raise up thy clasped hands. (*Seeing* OST. *make a feeble effort, he raises them for him in a posture of devotion.*) And now to heaven's mercy we commit thee.

> [JEROME *and* PAUL *retire, and two executioners prepare him for the block, and assist him to kneel. He then lays down his head, and they hold his hands while a third executioner stands with the raised axe.*

1st ex. (*speaking close into his ear.*) Press my hand when you are ready for the stroke. (*A long pause.*) He gives no sign.

2d ex. Stop, he will immediately. (*A second pause.*) Does he not?

1st ex. No.

Prior. Then give the stroke without it. (*3d ex. prepares to give the stroke, when the imperial ambassador rushes into the hall, followed by* LEONORA *and* AGNES, *and a numerous train.*)

Ambass. Stop the execution! In the name of your liege lord the emperor, I command you to stop upon your peril. My lord prior, this is a treacherous and clandestine use of your seignorial power. This noble servant of our imperial master (*pointing to* OSTERLOO) I take under my protection; and you must first deprive an imperial ambassador of life, ere one hair of his head fall to the ground.

Ben. (*running to the scaffold.*) Up, noble Osterloo! Raise up thy head: thou art rescued: thou art free.

Leo. Rise, noble Osterloo! dost thou not know the voice that calls thee?

Ben. He moves not; he is in a swoon.

[*Raises* OSTERLOO *from the block whilst* LEONORA *bends
over him with anxious tenderness.*

Leo. He is ghastly pale: yet it surely can be but a swoon. Chafe his
hands, good Benedict, while I bathe his temples. (*After trying to
restore him.*) Oh, no, no! no change takes place. What thinkest
thou of it? Is there any life here?

Ben. In truth I know not: this seems to me the fixed ghastly visage of
complete death.

Leo. On, no, no! he will be restored. No stroke has fallen upon him:
it cannot be death. Ha! is not that something? Did not his lips
move?

Ben. No, Lady; you but deceive yourself: they moved not: they are
closed for ever.

Leo. (*wringing her hands.*) Oh it is so! it is so!—after all thy struggles
and exertions of despair, this is thy miserable end!—Alas, alas!
thou who didst bear thy crest so proudly in many a well-fought
field; this is thy miserable end! (*Turning away, and hiding her face
in the bosom of* AGNES.)

Ambass. (*examining the body more closely.*) I think in very truth he is
dead.

1st gentleman of his train. Yes; the face never looks thus, till every
spark of life is extinguished.

Ambass. (*turning fiercely to the prior.*) How is this, prior? What sorcery
has been here, that your block alone should destroy its victim,
when the stroke of the axe has been wanting? What account
shall I carry to my master of the death of his gallant general?

Prior. No sorcery hath been practised on the deceased: his own mind
has dealt with him alone, and produced the effects you behold.
And, when you return to Lewis of Bavaria your master, tell him
that his noble general, free from personal injury of any kind,
died, within the walls of this monastery, of fear.

Ambass. Nay, nay, my good prior; put the fool's cap on thine own
head, and tell him this tale thyself.—Fear! Osterloo and fear
coupled together! when the lion and the fawn are found couch-
ing in the same lair, we will believe this.

Prior. All the brothers of the order will attest it.

Ambass. Away with the testimony of your cowled witnesses!
(*Beckoning* MORAND *to come near*) Morand, thou art a brave

fellow; I have known thee of old. Thou art the prior's officer indeed; but thou art now under my protection, and shalt be received into the emperor's service with encreased rank: Speak the truth then, boldly; how died Count Osterloo?

Mor. In very truth then, my lord, according to my simple thoughts, he died even as the prior has told you.

Ambass. Out upon thy hireling's tongue! art thou not ashamed, thyself wearing a soldier's garb, to blast a soldier's fame? There is no earthly thing the brave Osterloo was ever known to fear.

Mor. You say true, my lord; and on my sword's point I'll maintain it against any man as stoutly as yourself. But here is a pious monk (*pointing to* JEROME) who will explain to you what I should speak of but lamely.

Jer. With the prior's permission, my lord, if you will retire with me a little while, I'll inform you of this mysterious event, even simply as it happened. And perhaps you will then confess, that, called upon suddenly, under circumstances impressing powerfully the imagination, to put off this mortal frame, and stand forth in that tremendous presence, before which this globe, with all its mighty empires, hangs but as a crisped rain-drop, shivering on the threaded gossamer; the bravest mind may, if a guilty one, feel that within which is too powerful for human nature to sustain.

Ambass. Explain it as thou wilt; I shall listen to thee: but think not to cheat our imperial master of his revenge for the loss of his gallant general. I shall not fail, my lord prior, to report to him the meek spirit of your christian authority, which has made the general weal of the community subservient to your private revenge; and another month, I trust, shall not pass over our heads, till a worthier man (*pointing to* BENEDICT) shall possess this power which you have so greatly abused.——Let the body be removed, and laid in solemn state, till it be delivered into the hands of those brave troops, who shall inter it with the honours of a soldier!

THE FAMILY LEGEND:

A TRAGEDY,

IN FIVE ACTS.

TO WALTER SCOTT, ESQ.,

WHOSE FRIENDLY ZEAL ENCOURAGED ME TO OFFER IT TO THE NOTICE OF
MY INDULGENT COUNTRYMEN, I INSCRIBE THIS PLAY

PERSONS OF THE DRAMA

MEN.

MACLEAN, *chief of the clan of that name.*

EARL OF ARGYLL.

JOHN OF LORNE, *son to* ARGYLL.

SIR HUBERT DE GREY, *friend to Lorne.*

BENLORA,
LOCHTARISH, } *the kinsmen and chief vassals of* MACLEAN.
GLENFADDEN,
MORTON.
DUGALD.

Piper, fishermen, vassals, &c.

WOMEN.

HELEN, *daughter of* ARGYLL, *and wife of* MACLEAN.

ROSA.

Fisherman's wife.

Scene in the Island of Mull, *and the opposite coast, &c.,
and afterwards in* ARGYLL'*s castle.*

ACT I.

SCENE I.

Before the gate of MACLEAN'*s castle, in the Isle of Mull: several Highlanders discovered crossing the stage, carrying loads of fuel; whilst* BENLORA *is seen on one side, in the background, pacing to and fro, and frequently stopping and muttering to himself.*

1st high. This heavy load, I hope, will be the last:
 My back is almost broken.
2d high.   Sure am I,
 Were all the beeves in Mull slain for the feast,
 Fuel enough already has been stow'd
 To roast them all: and must we still with burdens
 Our weary shoulders gall?

Enter MORTON.

Mor.   Ye lazy lubbards!
 Grumble ye thus?—Ye would prefer, I trow,
 To sun your easy sides, like household curs,
 Each on his dung-hill stretch'd, in drowsy sloth.
 Fy on't! to grumble on a day like this,
 When to the clan a rousing feast is giv'n,
 In honour of an heir born to the chief—
 A brave Maclean, still to maintain the honours
 Of this your ancient race!
1st high. A brave Maclean indeed!—vile mongrel hound!
 Come from the south, where all strange mixtures be
 Of base and feeble! sprung of varlet's blood!
 What is our race to thee?
2d high. (*to* MORTON).   Thou'lt chew, I doubt not,
 Thy morsel in the hall with right good relish,
 Whether Maclean or Campbell be our lord.
Mor. Ungracious surly lubbards! in, I say,
 And bring your burdens quicker. And, besides,

Where are the heath and hare-bells, from the glen,
To deck my lady's chamber?
2d high. To deck my lady's chamber!
Mor.   Heartless hounds!
Is she not kind and gentle? spares she aught
Her gen'rous stores afford, when you or yours
Are sick, or lack relief? Hoards she in chests,
When shipwreck'd strangers shiver on our coast,
Or robe or costly mantle?—All comes forth!
And when the piercing shriek of drowning mariners
Breaks through the night, up-starting from her couch,
To snatch, with eager haste, the flaming torch,
And from the tower give notice of relief,
Who comes so swiftly as her noble self?
And yet ye grumble.
1st high.   Ay, we needs must own,
That, were she not a Campbell, fit she were
To be a queen, or e'en the thing she is—
Our very chieftain's dame. But, in these towers,
The daughter of Argyll to be our lady!
Mor. Out! mountain savages! is this your spite?
Go to!
2d high.   Speakst thou to us? thou Lowland loon!
Thou wand'ring pedlar's son, or base mechanic!
Com'st thou to lord it here o'er brave Macleans?
We'll carry loads at leisure, or forbear,
As suits our fancy best, nor wait thy bidding.
            [*Exeunt highlanders grumbling, and followed by* MORTON.
            [*Manet* BENLORA, *who now comes forward, and after
            remaining some time on the front of the stage, wrapt in
            thought, not observing* LOCHTARISH, *who enters behind
            him.*
        Heigh ho! heigh ho, the day!
Loch. How so? What makes Benlora sigh so deeply?
Ben. (*turning round*). And does Lochtarish ask? Full well thou knowst,
        The battles of our clan I've boldly fought,
        And well maintain'd its honour.
Loch.   Yes, we know it.

Ben. Who dared, unpunish'd, a Maclean to injure?
    Yea; he who dared but with a scornful lip
    Our name insult, I thought it feeble vengeance
    If steed or beast within his walls were left,
    Or of his holds one tower unruin'd stood.
Loch. Ay; who dared then to brave us?
Ben. Thus dealt Benlora e'en with common foes;
    But in the warfare of our deadly feud,
    When rang the earth beneath our bloody strife,
    And brave Macleans brave Campbells boldly fronted,
    (Fiends as they are, I still must call them brave,)
    What sword more deeply drank the hated blood
    Than this which now I grasp—but idly grasp!
Loch. There's ne'er a man of us that knows it not,
    That swears not by thy valour.
Ben. Until that fatal day, by ambush ta'en,
    And in a dungeon kept, where, two long years,
    Nor light of day, nor human voice e'er cheer'd
    My loneliness, when did I ever yield,
    To e'en the bravest of that hateful name,
    One step of ground upon the embattled field—
    One step of honour in the banner'd hall?
Loch. Indeed thou hast our noble champion been;
    Deserving well the trust our chief deceased,
    This chieftain's father, did to thee consign.
    But when thou wast a captive, none to head us,
    But he, our youthful lord, yet green in arms,
    We fought not like Macleans; or else our foe,
    By fiends assisted, fought with fiend-like power,
    Far—far beyond the Campbells' wonted pitch.
    E'en so it did befal:—we lost the day:—
    That fatal day!—Then came this shameful peace.
Ben. Ay, and this wedding; when, in form of honour
    Conferr'd upon us, Helen of Argyll
    Our sov'reign dame was made,—a bosom worm,
    Nursed in that viper's nest, to infuse its venom
    Through all our after race.
                  This is my welcome!

From dungeons freed, to find my once-loved home
With such vile change disgraced; to me more hateful
Than thraldom's murkiest den. But to be loosen'd
From captive's chains to find my hands thus bound!

Loch. It is, indeed, a vile and irksome peace.

Ben. Peace, say they! who will bonds of friendship sign
Between the teeming ocean's finny broods,
And say, "Sport these upon the hither waves,
And leave to those that farther billowy reach?"
A Campbell here to queen it o'er our heads,
The potent dame o'er quell'd and beaten men,
Rousing or soothing us, as proud Argyll
Shall send her secret counsel!—hold, my heart!
This, base degen'rate men!—this, call ye peace?
Forgive my weakness: with dry eyes I laid
My mother in her grave, but now my cheeks
Are, like a child's, with scalding drops disgraced.

Loch. What I shall look upon, ere in the dust
My weary head be laid to rest, heav'n knows,
Since I have lived to see Benlora weep.

Ben. One thing, at least, thou ne'er shalt live to see—
Benlora crouching, where he has commanded.
Go ye, who will, and crowd the chieftain's hall,
And deal the feast, and nod your grizzled heads
To martial pibrochs, play'd, in better days,
To those who conquer'd, not who woo'd their foes;
My soul abhors it. On the sea-beaten rock,
Remov'd from ev'ry form and sound of man;
In proud communion with the fitful winds
Which speak, with many tongues, the fancied words
Of those who long in silent dust have slept;
While eagles scream, and sullen surges roar—
The boding sounds of ill;—I'll hold my feast,—
My moody revelry.

Loch.   Nay, why so fierce?
Thinkst thou we are a tame and mongrel pack?
Dogs of true breed we are, though for a time
Our master-hound forsakes us. Rouse him forth

The noble chace to lead: his deep-toned yell
Full well we know; and for the opening sport
Pant keenly.
Ben.   Ha! is there amongst you still
Spirit enough for this?
Loch. Yes, when good opportunity shall favour.
Of this, my friend, I'll speak to thee more fully
When time shall better serve.
                  Maclean, thou knowst,
Is of a soft, unsteady, yielding nature;
And this, too well, the crafty Campbell knew,
When to our isle he sent this wily witch
To mould, and govern, and besot his wits,
As suits his crafty ends. I know the youth:
This dame or we must hold his will in thraldom:
Which of the two,—But softly: steps approach.
Of this again.
Ben.   As early as thou wilt.
Loch. Then be it so: some staunch determined spirits
This night in Irka's rocky cavern meet;
There must thou join us. Wear thou here the while
A brow less cloudy, suited to the times.

Enter GLENFADDEN.

See, here comes one who wears a merry face;
Yet, ne'ertheless, a clan's-man staunch he is,
Who hates a Campbell, worse than Ilcom's monks
The horned fiend.
Ben.   Ha! does he so?
                [*Turning graciously to* GLENFADDEN.
                Glenfadden!
How goes it with thee?—Joyous days are these—
These days of peace.
Glen.   These days of foul disgrace!
Com'st thou to cheer the piper in our hall,
And goblets quaff to the young chieftain's health,
From proud Argyll descended?

Ben. (smiling grimly).   Yes, Glenfadden,
     If ye will have it so; not else.
Glen.   Thy hand—
     Thy noble hand!—thou art Benlora still.
             [*Shaking* BENLORA *warmly by the hand, and then turning
               to* LOCHTARISH.
     Know ye that banish'd Allen is return'd—
     Allen of Dura?
Loch.   No; I knew it not.
     But in good time he comes. A daring knave!
     He will be useful.
                               [*After considering.*
                     Of Maclean we'll crave
     His banishment to cancel; marking well
     How he receives it. This will serve to show
     The present bent and bearing of his mind.
                          [*After considering again.*
     Were it not also well, that to our council
     He were invited, at a later hour,
     When of our purpose we shall be assured?
Glen. Methinks it were.
Loch.   In, then; now is our time.
Ben. I'll follow thee when I awhile have paced
     Yon lonely path, and thought upon thy counsel.
             [*Exeunt* LOCHTARISH *and* GLENFADDEN *into the castle, and*
               BENLORA *by the opposite side.*

SCENE II.

An apartment in the castle.
Enter MORTON *and* ROSA, *speaking as they enter.*

Rosa. Speak with my lady privately?
Mor.   Ay, please you:
     Something I have to say, regards her nearly.
     And though I doubt not, madam, your attachment—

Rosa. Good Morton, no apology: thy caution
 Is prudent; trust me not till thou hast proved me.
 But oh! watch o'er thy lady with an eye
 Of keen and guarded zeal! she is surrounded—
          [*Looking round the room.*
 Does no one hear us?—O those baleful looks
 That, from beneath dark surly brows, by stealth,
 Are darted on her by those stern Macleans!
 Ay; and the gestures of those fearful men,
 As on the shore in savage groups they meet,
 Sending their loosen'd tartans to the wind,
 And tossing high their brawny arms where oft
 In vehement discourse, I have, of late,
 At distance mark'd them. Yes; thou shakest thy head:
 Thou hast observed them too.
Mor. I have observed them oft. That calm Lochtarish,
 Calm as he is, the growing rancour fosters:
 For, fail the offspring of their chief, his sons
 Next in succession are. He hath his ends,
 For which he stirs their ancient hatred up;
 And all too well his dev'lish pains succeed.
Rosa. Too well indeed! The very bed-rid crones
 To whom my lady sends, with kindly care,
 Her cheering cordials,—couldst thou have believed it?
 Do mutter spells to fence from things unholy,
 And grumble, in a hollow smother'd voice,
 The name of Campbell, as unwillingly
 They stretch their wither'd hands to take her bounty.
 The wizards are in pay to rouse their fears
 With dismal tales of future ills foreseen,
 From Campbell and Maclean together join'd,
 In hateful union.—E'en the very children,
 Sporting the heath among, when they discover
 A loathsome toad or adder on their path,
 Crush it with stones, and, grinding wickedly
 Their teeth, in puny spite, call it a Campbell.
 Benlora, too, that savage gloomy man—

Mort. Ay, evil is the day that brings him back,
      Unjustly by a Campbell hath he been,
      The peaceful treaty of the clans unheeded,
      In thraldom kept; from which but now escaped,
      He like a furious tiger is enchafed,
      And thinks Argyll was privy to the wrong
      His vassal put upon him. Well I know
      His bloody vengeful nature: and Maclean,
      Weak and unsteady, moved by ev'ry counsel,
      Brave in the field, but still in purpose timid,
      Ofttimes the instrument in wicked hands
      Of wrongs he would abhor,—alas, I fear,
      Will ill defend the lovely spouse he swore
      To love and cherish.
Rosa.   Heavy steps approach:
      Hush! see who comes upon us!—sly Lochtarish,
      And his dark colleagues.—Wherefore come they hither?
            [MORTON *retires to the bottom of the stage, and enter*
            LOCHTARISH, BENLORA, *and* GLENFADDEN.
Loch. We thought, fair maid, to find the chieftain here.
Rosa. He is in these apartments.
Loch.   Would it greatly
      Annoy your gentleness to tell his honour,
      We wait to speak with him upon affairs
      Of much concernment?
Rosa. My service is not wanted; to your wish,
      See, there he comes unwarn'd, and with him too
      His noble lady.
                        [*Retiring to the bottom of the stage.*
Loch. Ha! there they come! see how he hangs upon her
      With boyish fondness!
Glen.   Ah, the goodly creature!
      How fair she is! how winning!—See that form;
      Those limbs beneath their foldy vestments moving,
      As though in mountain clouds they robed were,
      And music of the air their motion measured.
Loch. Ay, shrewd and crafty earl! 'tis not for nought
      Thou hither sent'st this jewel of thy race.

A host of Campbells, each a chosen man,
Could not enthral us, as, too soon I fear,
This single Campbell will. Shrewd crafty foe!
Ben. Hell lend me aid, if heaven deny its grace,
But I will thwart him, crafty though he be!
Loch. But now for your petition: see we now
How he receives your suit.

Enter MACLEAN *and* HELEN.

Ben. (*eyeing her attentively as she enters*).
A potent foe it is: ay, by my faith,
A fair and goodly creature!
Mac. Again, good morrow to you, gallant kinsmen:
Come ye to say I can with any favour
The right good liking prove, and high regard
I bear to you, who are my chiefest strength,—
The pillars of my clan?
Ben. Yes, we are come, Maclean, a boon to beg.
Loch. A boon that, granted, will yourself enrich.
Mac. Myself enrich?
Loch.　　　　　　Yes; thereby wilt thou be
One gallant man the richer. Hear us out.
Allen of Dura, from his banishment—
Mac. False reiver! name him not.—Is he return'd?
Dares he again set foot upon this isle?
Ben. Yes, chief; upon this isle set foot he hath:
And on nor isle nor mainland doth there step
A braver man than he.—Lady, forgive me:
The boldest Campbell never saw his back.
Helen. Nay, good Benlora, ask not my forgiveness:
I love to hear thee praise, with honest warmth,
The valiant of thy name, which now is mine.
Ben. (*aside*). Ha! good Benlora!—this is queenly pride.
(*Aloud.*) Madam, you honour us.
Helen. If so, small thanks be to my courtesy,
Sharing myself with pride the honest fame
Of every brave Maclean.—I'll henceforth keep

A proud account of all my gallant friends:
And every valiant Campbell therein noted,
On the opposing leaf, in letters fair,
Shall with a brave Maclean be proudly match'd.

> [BENLORA *and* GLENFADDEN *bow in silence.*

Loch. Madam, our grateful duty waits upon you.
    (*Aside to* BENLORA.) What thinkst thou of her, friend?
Ben. (*aside to* LOCHTARISH). What think I of her?
    Incomparable hypocrite!
Loch. (*aloud*). But to our suit: for words of courtesy
    It must not be forgotten.—Chief, vouchsafe:
    Benlora here, who from his loathly prison,
    Which for your sake two years he hath endured,
    Begs earnestly this grace for him we mention'd,
    Allen of Dura.

> [*Aside to* BENLORA.
> Kneel, man; be more pressing.

Ben. (*aside to* LOCHTARISH).
    Nay, by my fay! if crouching pleases thee,
    Do it thyself.

> [*Going up proudly to* MACLEAN.

    Maclean; thy father put into these hands
    The government and guidance of thy nonage.
    How I the trust fulfill'd, this castle strengthen'd
    With walls and added towers, and stored, besides,
    With arms and trophies in rough warfare won
    From even the bravest of our western clans,
    Will testify. What I in recompense
    Have for my service earn'd, these galled wrists

> [*Pushing up the sleeve from his arm.*

    Do also testify.—Such as I am,
    For an old friend I plainly beg this grace:
    Say if my boon be granted or denied.
Mac. The man for whom thou pleadst is most unworthy;
    Yet let him safely from my shores depart:
    I harm him not.
Ben. (*turning from him indignantly*). My suit is then denied.

> [*To* LOCHTARISH *and* GLENFADDEN.

Go ye to Dura's Allen; near the shore
He harbours in his aged mother's cot;
Bid him upon the ocean drift again
His shatter'd boat, and be a wanderer still.

Helen (*coming forward eagerly*). His aged mother!
 (*To* MACLEAN.) Oh! and shall he go?
 No, no, he shall not! On this day of joy,
 Wilt thou to me refuse it?

> [*Hanging upon him with looks of entreaty, till, seeing him relent, she then turns joyfully to* BENLORA.

 Bid your wanderer
 Safe with his aged mother still remain,—
 A banish'd man no more.

Mac. This is not well: but be it as thou wilt;
 Thou hast prevail'd, my Helen.

Loch. and *Glen.* (*bowing low*). We thank thee, lady.

> [BENLORA *bows slightly, in sullen silence.*

Mac. (*to* BENLORA). Then let thy friend remain; he has my pardon.

> [BENLORA *bows again in silence.*

 Clear up thy brow, Benlora; he is pardon'd.

> [*Pauses, but* BENLORA *is still silent.*

 We trust to meet you shortly in the hall;
 And there, my friends, shall think our happy feast
 More happy for your presence.

> [*Going up again, with anxious courtesy, to* BENLORA.

 Thy past services,
 Which great and many are, my brave Benlora,
 Shall be remember'd well. Thou hast my honour,
 And high regard.

Helen. And mine to boot, good kinsman, if the value
 You put upon them makes them worth the having.

Ben. (*bows sullenly and retires; then muttering aside to himself as he goes out*). Good kinsman! good Benlora! gracious words
 From this most high and potent dame, vouchsafed
 To one so poor and humble as myself.

> [*Exit.*

Loch. (*aside to* GLENFADDEN). But thou forgettest—

Glen. (*aside to* LOCHTARISH). No; I'll stay behind,
And move Maclean to join our nightly meeting.
Midnight the hour when you desire his presence?
Loch. Yes, even so; then will we be prepared.

[*Exit.*

Glen. (*returning to* MACLEAN).
Chieftain, I would some words of privacy
Speak with you, should your leisure now permit.
Mac. Come to my closet, then, I'll hear thee gladly.

[*Exeunt* MACLEAN *and* GLENFADDEN.

Helen (*to* ROSA, *who now comes forward*).
Where hast thou been, my Rosa, with my boy,
Have they with wild flowers deck'd his cradle round?
And peeps he through them like a little nestling—
A little heath-cock broken from its shell,
That through the bloom puts forth its tender beak,
As steals some rustling footstep on its nest?
Come, let me go and look upon him. Soon,
Ere two months more go by, he'll look again
In answer to my looks, as though he knew
The wistful face that looks so oft upon him,
And smiles so dearly, is his mother's.
Thinkst thou
He'll soon give heed and notice to my love?
Rosa. I doubt it not: he is a lively infant,
And moves his little limbs with vigour, spreading
His fingers forth, as if in time they would
A good claymore clench bravely.
Helen. A good claymore clench bravely!—O! to see him
A man!—a valiant youth!—a noble chieftain!
And laying on his plaided shoulder, thus,
A mother's hand, say proudly, "This is mine!"
I shall not then a lonely stranger be
'Mid those who bless me not: I shall not then—
But silent be my tongue.

[*Weeps.*

Rosa. Dear madam, still in hope look forward cheerly.

[MORTON *comes from the bottom of the stage.*

And here is Morton, with some tidings for you:
God grant they comfort you!—I must withdraw:
His wary faithfulness mistrusts my love,
But I am not offended.

                                    [*Offering to retire.*

Helen. Nay, remain.

                                    [*Beckoning her back.*

Say what thou hast to say, my worthy Morton,
For Rosa is as faithful as thyself.

Mor. This morning, lady, 'mongst the farther cliffs,
Dress'd like a fisher peasant, did I see
The Lord of Lorne, your brother.

Helen.   Ha! sayst thou,
The Lord of Lorne, my brother?—Thou'rt deceived.

Mor. No, no: in vain his sordid garb conceal'd him!
His noble form and stately step I knew
Before he spoke.

Helen.   He spoke to thee?

Mor.   He did.

Helen. Was he alone?

Mor.   He was; but, near at hand,
Another stranger, noble as himself,
And in like garb disguised, amongst the rocks
I mark'd, though he advanced not.

Helen. Alas, alas, my brother! why is this?
He spoke to thee, thou sayst—I mean my brother:
What did he say?

Mor.   He earnestly entreats
To see you privately; and bids you say
When this may be. Meantime he lies conceal'd
Where I may call him forth at your command.

Helen. O, why disguised?—Thinkst thou he is not safe?

Mor. Safe in his hiding-place he is: but yet
The sooner he shall leave this coast, the better.

Helen. To see him thus! O, how I am beset!
Tell him at twilight, in my nurse's chamber,
I will receive him. But be sure thou add,
Himself alone will I receive—alone—

With no companion must he come. Forget not
    To say, that I entreat it earnestly.
Mor. I will remember this.
Helen. Go to him quickly then: and, till the hour,
    Still do thou hover near him. Watch his haunt,
    Lest some rude fisherman or surly hind
    Surprise him. Go thou quickly. O, be prudent!
    And be not for a moment off the watch.
Mor. Madam, I will obey you: trust me well.

[Exit.

Helen (*much disturbed*). My brother on the coast; and with him too,
    As well I guess, the man I must not see!
Rosa. Mean you the brave Sir Hubert?
Helen. Yes, my Rosa.
    My noble brother in his powerful self
    So strong in virtue stands, he thinks full surely
    The daughter of his sire no weakness hath;
    And wists not how a simple heart must struggle
    To be what it would be—what it must be—
    Ay, and so aid me, heaven! what it shall be.
Rosa. And heaven will aid you, madam, doubt it not.
    Though on this subject still you have repress'd
    All communing, yet, ne'ertheless, I well
    Have mark'd your noble striving, and revered
    Your silent inward warfare, bravely held;
    In this more pressing combat firm and valiant,
    As is your noble brother in the field.
Helen. I thank thee, gentle Rosa; thou art kind—
    I should be franker with thee; but I know not—
    Something restrains me here.

[Laying her hand on her heart.

    I love and trust thee;
    And on thy breast I'll weep when I am sad;
    But ask not why I weep.

[Exeunt.

ACT II.

SCENE I.

An apartment in twilight, almost dark; the door of an inner chamber,
standing a little ajar, at the bottom of the stage. Enter JOHN OF LORNE *and*
SIR HUBERT DE GREY, *disguised as peasants.*

De Grey. Nay, stop, I pray; advance we not too far?
Lorne. Morton hath bid us in this place to wait.
    The nurse's chamber is adjoining to it;
    And, till her light within give notice, here
    Thou mayst remain; when I am call'd, thou'lt leave me.
De Grey. Till thou art call'd! and may I stay to hear
    The sweetness of her voice—her footstep's sound;
    Perhaps snatch in the torch's hasty light
    One momentary vision of that form—
    The form that hath to me of earthly make
    No fellow? May it be without transgression?
Lorne. Why shouldst thou not? De Grey, thou art too fearful;
    Here art thou come with no dishonest will;
    And well she knows thine honour. Her commands,
    Though we must yield to them, capricious seem;
    Seeing thou art with me, too nicely scrupulous;
    And therefore need no farther be obey'd
    Than needs must be. She puts thee not on honour.
    Were I so used——
De Grey.   'Spite of thy pride, wouldst thou
    Revere her still the more.—O, no, brave Lorne,
    I blame her not. When she, a willing victim,
    To spare the blood of two contending clans,
    Against my faithful love her suffrage gave,
    I bless'd her; and the deep, but chasten'd sorrow
    With which she bade me—Oh! that word! farewell,
    Is treasured in my bosom as its share
    Of all that earthly love hath power to give.
    It came from Helen, and, from her received,
    Shall not be worn with thankless dull repining.

Lorne. A noble heart thou hast: such manly meekness
Becomes thy gen'rous nature. But for me,
More fierce and wilful, sorely was I chafed
To see thy faithful heart robb'd of its hope,
All for the propping up a hollow peace
Between two warlike clans, who will, as long
As bagpipes sound, and blades flash to the sun,
Delighting in the noble sport of war,
Some fierce opponents find. What doth it boot,
If men in fields must fight, and blood be shed,
What clans are in the ceaseless strife opposed?
De Grey. Ah, John of Lorne! too keenly is thy soul
To war inclined—to wasteful, ruthless war.
Lorne. The warlike minstrel's rousing lay thou lov'st:
Shall bards i' the hall sing of our fathers' deeds
To lull their sons to sleep? Vain simple wish!
I love to hear the sound of holy bell,
And peaceful men their praises lift to heaven:
I love to see around their blazing fire
The peasant and his cheerful family set,
Eating their fearless meal. But, when the roar
Of battle rises, and the closing clans,
Dark'ning the sun-gleam'd heath, in dread affray
Are mingled; blade with blade, and limb with limb,
Nerve-strain'd, in terrible strength; yea, soul with soul
Nobly contending; who would raise aloft
The interdicting hand, and say, "Be still'd?"
If this in me be sin, may heaven forgive me!
That being am not I.
De Grey.   In very deed
This is thy sin; and of thy manly nature
The only blemish worthy of that name.
More peaceful be, and thou wilt be more noble.
Lorne. Well, here we will not wrangle for the point.
None in th'embattled field who have beheld
Hubert de Grey in mailed hauberk fight,
Will guess how much that knight in peace delights.

Still burns my heart that such a man as thou
Wast for this weak, unsteady, poor Maclean—
De Grey. Nay, with contempt, I pray thee, name him not.
  Her husband, and despised! O, no, no, no!
  All that pertains to her, e'en from that hour,
  Honour'd and sacred is.
Lorne. Thou gen'rous heart! more noble than myself!
  I will not grieve thee.—I'll to Helen go,
  With every look and word that might betray
  Indignant thoughts, or wound her gentle spirit,
  Strictly suppress'd: and to her ear will give
  Thy gen'rous greetings, and thy manly words
  Of cheering comfort;—all most faithfully
  Shall be remember'd.
De Grey.   Ay, and my request.
Lorne. To see the child?
De Grey.   E'en so: to look upon it;—
  Upon the thing that is of her; this bud—
  This seedling of a flower so exquisite.
                    [*Light is seen in the inner chamber.*
  Ha! light is in the chamber! moves the door?
  Some one approaches. O! but for a moment
  Let me behind thy friendly tartans be,
  And snatch one glance of what that light will give.
            [*Conceals himself behind* LORNE, *who steps some paces
            back, setting his hand to his side, and tilting his plaid over
            his arms to favour him; while the door of the inner chamber
            opens, and* HELEN *appears, bearing a lamp, which she
            afterwards sets upon a stone slab as she advances.*
  Her form—her motion—yea, that mantled arm,
  Press'd closely to her breast, as she was wont
  When chilly winds assail'd.—The face—O, woe is me!
  It was not then so pale.
Lorne (*to him, in a low voice*). Begone: begone.
De Grey. Blest vision, I have seen thee! Fare thee well!
                    [*Exit in haste.*

Helen (coming forward, alarmed).
> What sound is that of steps that hasten from us?
> Is Morton on the watch.

Lorne. Fear nothing; faithful Morton is at hand:
> The steps thou heardst were friendly.

Helen (embracing LORNE*).*
> My brother! meet we thus,—disguised, by stealth?
> Is this like peace? How is my noble father?
> Hath any ill befallen?

Lorne. Argyll is well;
> And nothing ill, my sister, hath befallen,
> If thou art well and happy.

Helen. Speakst thou truly?
> Why art thou come? Why thus upon our coast?
> O take it not unkindly that I say,
> "Why art thou come?"

Lorne. Near to the opposite shore,
> With no design, but on a lengthen'd chase,
> A lusty deer pursuing from the hills
> Of Morven, where Sir Hubert and myself
> Guests of the social lord two days had been,
> We found us; when a sudden strong desire
> To look upon the castle of Maclean,
> Seen from the coast, our eager fancy seized,
> And that indulged, forthwith we did agree
> The frith to cross, and to its chief and dame
> A hasty visit make. But as our boat
> Lay waiting to receive us, warn'd by one
> Whom well I knew (the vassal of a friend
> Whose word I could not doubt), that jealous rancour,
> Stirr'd up amongst the vassals of Maclean,
> Who, in their savage fury, had been heard
> To utter threats against thy innocent self,
> Made it unsafe in open guise to venture,
> Here in this garb we are to learn in secret
> The state in which thou art.—How is it then?
> Morton's report has added to my fears:
> All is not well with thee.

Helen.   No, all is well.

Lorne. A cold constrained voice that answer gave:
    All is not well.—Maclean—dares he neglect thee?

Helen. Nay, wrong him not; kind and affectionate
    He still remains.

Lorne. But it is said, his vassals with vile names
    Have dared to name thee, even in open clan:
    And have remain'd unpunish'd. Is it so?

                        [Pauses for an answer, but she is silent.
    All is not well.

Helen. Have I not said it is?

Lorne. Ah! dost thou thus return a brother's love
    With cold reserve?—O speak to me, my Helen!
    Speak as a sister should.—Have they insulted thee?
    Has any wrong—my heart within me burns
    If I but think upon it.—Answer truly.

Helen. What, am I question'd then? Thinkst thou to find me
    Like the spoil'd heiress of some Lowland lord,
    Peevish and dainty; who, with scorn regarding
    The ruder home she is by marriage placed in,
    Still holds herself an alien from its interest,
    With poor repining, losing every sense
    Of what she is, in what she has been? No.—
    I love thee, Lorne; I love my father's house:
    The meanest cur that round his threshold barks
    Is in my memory as some kindred thing:
    Yet take it not unkindly when I say,
    The lady of Maclean no grievance hath
    To tell the Lord of Lorne.

Lorne.   And has the vow,
    Constrain'd, unblest, and joyless as it was,
    Which gave thee to a lord unworthy of thee,
    Placed thee beyond the reach of kindred ties—
    The warmth of blood to blood—the sure affection
    That nature gives to all—a brother's love?
    No, by all sacred things! here is thy hold:
    Here is thy true, unshaken, native stay:
    One that shall fail thee never, though the while,

A faithless, wavering, intervening band
Seems to divide thee from it.
          [*Grasping her hand vehemently, as if he would lead her away.*
Helen. What dost thou mean? What violent grasp is this?
          Com'st thou to lead me from my husband's house,
          Beneath the shade of night, with culprit stealth?
Lorne. No, daughter of Argyll; when John of Lorne
          Shall come to lead thee from these hated walls
          Back to thy native home,—with culprit stealth,
          Beneath the shades of night, it shall not be.
          With half our western warriors at his back,
          He'll proudly come. Thy listening timid chief
          Shall hear our martial steps upon his heath,
          With heavy measured fall, send, beat by beat,
          From the far-smitten earth, a sullen sound,
          Like deep-dell'd forests groaning to the strokes
          Of lusty woodmen. On the watch-tower's height,
          His straining eye shall mark our sheathless swords
          From rank to rank their lengthen'd blaze emit,
          Like streams of shiv'ring light, in hasty change,
          Upon the northern firmament.—By stealth!
          No! not by stealth!—believe me, not by stealth
          Shalt thou these portals pass.
Helen.   Them have I enter'd,
          The pledge of peace: and here my place I'll hold
          As dame and mistress of the warlike clan
          Who yield obedience to their chief, my lord;
          And whatsoe'er their will to me may bear,
          Of good or ill, so will I hold me ever.
          Yea, did the Lord of Lorne, dear as he is,
          With all the warlike Campbells at his back
          Here hostile entrance threaten; on these walls,
          Failing the strength that might defend them better,
          I would myself, while by my side in arms
          One valiant clan's-man stood, against his powers,
          To the last push, with desp'rate opposition,
          This castle hold.

Lorne. And wouldst thou so? so firm and valiant art thou?
Forgive me, noble creature!—Oh! the fate—
The wayward fate that binds thy gen'rous soul
To poor unsteady weakness!
Helen.   Speakst thou thus?
Thus pressing still upon the galled spot?
Thou dealst unkindly with me. Yes, my brother,
Unkindly and unwisely. Wherefore hast thou
Brought to this coast the man thou knowest well
I ought not in mysterious guise to see?
And he himself—seeks he again to move
The hapless weakness I have striv'n to conquer?
I thought him generous.
Lorne.   So think him still.
His wishes tend not to disturb thy peace:
Far other are his thoughts.—He bids me tell thee
To cheer thy gentle heart, nor think of him,
As one who will in vain and stubborn grief
His ruin'd bliss lament,—he bids me say
That he will even strive, if it be possible,
Amongst the maidens of his land to seek
Some faint resemblance of the good he lost,
That thou mayst hear of him with less regret,
As one by holy bands link'd to his kind.
He bids me say, should ever child of his
And child of thine—but here his quivering lip
And starting tears spoke what he could not speak.
Helen. O noble, gen'rous heart; and does he offer
Such cheering manly comfort? Heaven protect,
And guide, and bless him! On his noble head
Such prosp'rous bliss be pour'd, that hearing of it
Shall, through the gloom of my untoward state,
Like gleams of sunshine break, that from afar
Look o'er the dull dun heath.
Lorne.   But one request—
Helen. Ha! makes he one?
Lorne.   It is to see thy child.

Helen. To see my child! Will he indeed regard it?
    Shall it be bless'd by him?

                    Enter MORTON *in haste.*

Mor. Conceal yourself, my lord, or by this passage
                            [*Pointing off the stage.*
    The nearest postern gain: I hear the sound
    Of heavy steps at hand, and voices stern.
Helen. O fly, my brother! Morton will conduct thee.
    (*To* MORTON.) Where is Sir Hubert?
Mor. Safe he is without.
Helen. Heaven keep him so!
    (*To* LORNE.) O leave me! I, the while,
    Will in, and, with mine infant in mine arms,
    Meet thee again, ere thou depart.—Fly! fly!
        [*Exeunt;* HELEN *into the inner chamber, putting out the lamp
        as she goes, and* LORNE *and* MORTON *by a side passage.*

                    SCENE II.

*A cave, lighted by flaming brands fixed aloft on its rugged sides, and
shedding a fierce glaring light down upon the objects below.* LOCHTARISH,
BENLORA, GLENFADDEN, *with several of the chief vassals of* MACLEAN,
*are discovered in a recess, formed by projecting rocks, at the bottom of the
stage, engaged in earnest discourse, from which they move forward slowly,
speaking as they advance.*

Loch. And thus ye see, by strong necessity,
    We are compell'd to this.
1st vas.   Perhaps thou'rt right.
Loch. Sayst thou *perhaps?* Dost thou not plainly see
    That ne'er a man amongst us can securely
    His lands possess, or say, "My house is mine,"
    While, under tutorage of proud Argyll,
    This beauteous sorceress our besotted chief
    By soft enchantment holds?

[*Laying his hand on the 1st vassal.*

My brave Glenore,
What are thy good deserts, that may uphold thee
In favour with a Campbell?—Duncan's blood,
Slain in his boat, with all its dashing oars
Skirting our shore, while that his vaunting piper
The Campbell's triumph play'd? Will this speak for thee?

[*Turning to 2d vassal.*

And, Thona, what good merit pleadest thou?
The coal-black steed of Clone, thy moonlight plunder,
Ta'en from the spiteful laird, will he, good sooth!
Neigh favour on thee?

[*To 3d vassal.*

And my valiant Fallen,
Bethink thee well if fair-hair'd Flora's cries
Whom from her native bower by force thou tookst,
Will plead for thee.—And say ye still perhaps—
Perhaps there is necessity?

1st vas. Strong should it be, Lochtarish; for the act
Is fell and cruel thou wouldst push us to.

Glen. (to 1st vas.) Ha, man of mercy! are thy lily hands
From bloody taint unstain'd? What sights were those
Thou look'dst upon in Brunock's burning tower,
When infants through the flames their wailings sent,
And yet unaided perish'd?

Loch. (soothingly).   Tush, Glenfadden!
Too hasty art thou.
(*To the vassals.*) Ye will say, belike,
"Our safety—our existence did demand
Utter extinction of that hold of foes."
And well ye may.—A like necessity
Compels us now, and yet ye hesitate.

Glen. Our sighted seers the fun'ral lights have seen,
Not moving onward in the wonted path
On which by friends the peaceful dead are borne,
But hov'ring o'er the heath like countless stars,
Spent and extinguish'd on the very spot
Where first they twinkled. This too well foreshows

  Interment of the slain, whose bloody graves
  Of the same mould are made on which they fell.

2d vas. Ha! so indeed! some awful tempest gathers.

1st vas. What sighted man hath seen it?

Glen.   He whose eye
  Can see on northern waves the found'ring bark,
  With all her shrieking crew, sink to the deep,
  While yet, with gentle winds, on dimpling surge
  She sails from port in all her gallant trim:
  John of the Isle hath seen it.

Omnes (starting back). Then hangs some evil over us.

Glen.   Know ye not
  The mermaid hath been heard upon our rocks?

Omnes (still more alarmed). Ha! when?

Glen. Last night, upon the rugged crag
  That lifts its dark head through the cloudy smoke
  Of dashing billows, near the western cliff.
  Sweetly, but sadly, o'er the stilly deep
  The passing sound was borne. I need not say
  How fatal to our clan that boding sound
  Hath ever been.

3d vas. In faith thou makest me quake.

2d vas. Some fearful thing hangs o'er us.

1st vas. If 'tis fated
  Our clan before our ancient foe shall fall,
  Can we heav'n's will prevent? Why should we then
  The Campbells' wrath provoke?

Ben. (stepping up fiercely to 1st vassal).
  Heav'n's will prevent—the Campbells' ire provoke!
  Is such base tameness utter'd by the son
  Of one, who would into the fiery pit
  Of damned fiends have leapt, so that his grasp
  Might pull a Campbell with him?

              Bastard blood!
  Thy father spoke not thus.

Loch. (soothingly).   Nay, brave Benlora,
  He means not as thou thinkst.

Ben.							If heaven decree
Slaughter and ruin for us, come it then!
But let our enemies, close grappled to us,
In deadly strife, their ruin join with ours.
Let corse to corse, upon the bloody heath,
Maclean and Campbell, stiff'ning side by side,
With all the gnashing ecstasy of hate
Upon their ghastly visages impress'd,
Lie horribly!—For ev'ry widow's tear
Shed in our clan, let matron Campbells howl!

Loch. Indeed, my friends, although too much in ire,
Benlora wisely speaks.—Shall we in truth
Wait for our ruin from a crafty foe,
Who here maintains this keenly watchful spy
In gentle kindness masked?

Glen.						Nor need we fear,
As good Lochtarish hath already urged,
Her death will rouse Argyll. It will be deem'd,
As we shall grace it with all good respect
Of funeral pomp, a natural visitation.

Loch. Ay, and besides, we'll swear upon the book,
And truly swear, if we are call'd upon,
We have not shed her blood.

Ben.						I like not this.
If ye her life will take, in open day
Let her a public sacrifice be made.
Let the loud trumpet far and near proclaim
Our bloody feast, and at the rousing sound,
Let every clans-man of the hated name
His vengeful weapon clench.—
I like it not, Lochtarish. What we do,
Let it be boldly done.—Why should we slay her?
Let her in shame be from the castle sent;
Which, to her haughty sire, will do, I ween,
Far more despite than taking of her life.—
A feeble woman's life!—I like it not.

			[*Turning on his heel angrily, and striding to the bottom of
			the stage.*

Loch. (*aside to* GLEN.) Go to him, friend, and soothe him to our
purpose.
    The fiery fool! how madly wild he is!
           [GLENFADDEN *goes to the bottom of the stage, and is*
           seen remonstrating, in dumb-show, with BENLORA, *while*
           LOCHTARISH *speaks to the vassals on the front.*
Loch. My friends, why on each other look ye thus
    In gloomy silence? freely speak your thoughts.
    Mine have I freely spoken: that advising
    Which for the good—nay, I must say existence,
    Of this our ancient clan most needful is.
    When did Lochtarish ever for himself
    A separate 'vantage seek, in which the clan
    At large partook not? Am I doubted now?
2d vas. No, nothing do we doubt thy public zeal.
Loch. Then is my long experience o' the sudden
    To childish folly turn'd?
                Thinkst thou, good Thona,
    We should beneath this artful mistress live,
    Hush'd in deceitful peace, till John of Lorne,
    For whom the office of a treacherous spy
    She doth right slily manage, with his powers
    Shall come upon us? Once ye would have spurn'd
    At thoughts so base; but now, when forth I stand
    To do what vengeance, safety, nay, existence,
    All loudly call for; even as though already
    The enemy's baleful influence hung o'er you,
    Like quell'd and passive men ye silent stand.
1st vas. (*roused*). Nay, cease, Loctarish! quell'd and passive men
    Thou knowst we are not.
Loch.   Yet a woman's life,
    And that a treacherous woman, moves you thus.
    Bold as your threats of dark revenge have been,
    A strong decisive deed appals you now.
    Our chieftain's feeble undetermined spirit
    Infects you all: ye dare not stand by me.
Omnes. We dare not, sayst thou?

Loch.   Dare not, will I say!
Well spoke the jeering Camerons, I trow,
As past their fishing boats our vessel steer'd,
When with push'd lip, and finger pointing thus,
They call'd our crew the Campbell-cow'd Macleans.
Omnes (roused fiercely). The Campbell-cow'd Macleans!
2d vas.   Infernal devils!
Dare they to call us so?
Loch.   Ay, by my truth!
Nor think that from the Camerons alone
Ye will such greeting have, if back ye shrink,
And stand not by me now.
Omnes (eagerly). We'll stand!—We'll stand!
2d vas. Tempt us not more. There's ne'er a man of us
That will not back thee boldly.
Loch.   Ay, indeed?
Now are ye men! Give me your hands to this.
                              [*They all give him their hands.*
Now am I satisfied.
                              [*Looking off the stage.*
The chief approaches.
Ye know full well the spirit of the man
That we must deal withal; therefore be bold.
Omnes. Mistrust us not.

Enter MACLEAN, *who advances to the middle of the stage, while*
LOCHTARISH, BENLORA, GLENFADDEN, *and all the other vassals gather
round him with stern determined looks. A pause;* MACLEAN *eyeing them all
round with inquisitive anxiety.*

Mac. A goodly meeting at this hour convened.
                              [*A sullen pause.*
Benlora; Thona; Allen of Glenore;
And all of you, our first and bravest kinsmen;
What mystery in this sullen silence is?
Hangs any threaten'd evil o'er the clan?

Ben. Yes, chieftain; evil, that doth make the blood
    Within your grey-hair'd warriors' veins to burn,
    And their brogued feet to spurn the ground that bears them.
Loch. Evil, that soon will wrap your tower in flames,
    Your ditches fill with blood, and carrion birds
    Glut with the butcher'd corses of your slain.
Glen. Ay; evil, that doth make the hoary locks
    Of sighted men around their age-worn scalps
    Like quicken'd points of crackling flame to rise;
    Their teeth to grind, and strained eye-balls roll
    In fitful frenzy, at the horrid things,
    In terrible array before them raised.
1st vas. The mermaid hath been heard upon our rocks:
    The fatal song of waves.
Glen.   The northern deep
    Is heard with distant moanings from our coast,
    Uttering the dismal bodeful sounds of death.
2d vas. The funeral lights have shone upon our heath,
    Marking in countless groups the graves of thousands.
Ben. Yea, chief; and sounds like to thy father's voice
    Have from the sacred mould wherein he lies,
    At dead of night, by wakeful men been heard
    Three times distinctly.
                                [*Turning to* GLENFADDEN.
    Saidst thou not thrice?
Glen. Yes; three times heard distinctly.
Mac. Ye much amaze me, friends.—Such things have been?
Loch. Yea, chief; and thinkst thou we may lightly deem
    Of coming ills, by signs like these forewarn'd?
Mac. Then an it be, high heav'n have mercy on us!
Loch. (*in a loud solemn voice*). Thyself have mercy on us!
Mac.   How is this?
    Your words confuse and stun me.—Have I power
    To ward this evil off?
Omnes.   Thou hast! thou hast!
Mac. Then God to me show mercy in my need,
    As I will do for you and for my clan
    Whate'er my slender power enables me.

Omnes. Amen! and swear to it.

Mac. (starting back). What words are these,
　　With such wild fierceness utter'd? name the thing
　　That ye would have me do.

Ben. (stepping out from the rest). Ay, we will name it.
　　Helen the Campbell, foster'd in your bosom,
　　A serpent is, who wears a hidden sting
　　For thee and all thy name; the oath-bound spy
　　Of dark Argyll, our foe; the baleful plague
　　To which ill-omen'd sounds and warnings point,
　　As that on which existence or extinction—
　　The name and being of our clan depend;—
　　A witch of deep seduction.—Cast her forth.
　　The strange, unnatural union of two bloods,
　　Adverse and hostile, most abhorred is.
　　The heart of every warrior of your name
　　Rises against it. Yea, the grave calls out,
　　And says it may not be.—Nay, shrink not, chief,
　　When I again repeat it,—cast her off.

Mac. Art thou a man? and bidst me cast her off,
　　Bound as I am by sacred holy ties?

Loch. Bound as thou art by that which thou regardest
　　As sacred holy ties; what tie so sacred
　　As those that to his name and kindred vassals
　　The noble chieftain bind? If ties there be
　　To these opposed, although a saint from heav'n
　　Had bless'd them o'er the cross'd and holy things,
　　They are annull'd and broken.

Ben. Ay, Lochtarish;
　　Sound doctrine hast thou utter'd. Such the creed
　　Of ancient warriors was, and such the creed
　　That we their sons will with our swords maintain.

　　　　　[Drawing his sword fiercely, whilst the rest follow his example.

Mac. Ye much confound me with your violent words.
　　I can in battle strive, as well ye know:
　　But how to strive with you, ye violent men,
　　My spirit knows not.

Loch. Decide—decide, Maclean: the choice is thine
    To be our chieftain, leading forth thy bands,
    As heretofore thy valiant father did,
    Against our ancient foe, or be the husband,
    Despised, forsaken, cursed, of her thou prizest
    More than thy clan and kindred.
Glen.   Make thy choice.
    Benlora, wont in better times to lead us
    Against the Campbells, with a chieftain's power,
    Shall, with the first blast of his warlike horn,
    If so he will it, round his standard gather
    Thy roused and valiant vassals to a man.
Mac. (*greatly startled*). Ha! go your thoughts to this? Desert me so?
    My vassals so desert me?
Loch. Ay, by my faith, our very women too:
    And in your hall remain, to serve your state,
    Nor child nor aged crone.
Mac. (*after great agitation*).
    Decide, and cast her off!—How far the thoughts
    To which these words ye yoke may go, I guess not.
    (*Eagerly.*) They reach not to her life?
                [*Pauses and looks at them anxiously, but they are silent.*
    Oh, oh! oh, oh! that stern and dreadful silence!
Loch. We will not shed her blood.
Mac. Then ye will spare her?
Loch. Commit her to our keeping: ask us not
    How we shall deal with her.
Mac. Some fearful mystery is in your words,
    Which covers cruel things. O woe the day,
    That I on this astounding ridge am poised!
    On every side a fearful ruin yawns.
                [*A voice heard without, uttering wild incoherent words,
                mixed with shrieks of horror.*
    What frenzied voice is that?

                Enter 4th vassal, as if terribly frightened.

Loch. (*to 4th vas.*) What brings thee hither?

4th vas. He fixes wildly on the gloomy void
    His starting eyeballs, bent on fearful sights,
    That make the sinews of his aged limbs
    In agony to quiver.
Loch.   Who didst thou say?
4th vas. John of the Isle, the sighted awful man.
    Go, see yourselves: i' the outer cave he is.
    Entranced he stands; arrested on his way
    By horrid visions, as he hurried hither
    Enquiring for the chief.
                  [*Voice heard without, as before.*
Loch. Hark! hark, again! dread powers are dealing with him.
    Come, chieftain—come and see the awful man.
    If heaven or hell hath power to move thy will,
    Thou canst not now withstand us.
    (*Pausing for him to go.*) Hearst thou not?
    And motionless?
Mac.   I am beset and stunn'd,
    And every sense bewilder'd. Violent men!
    If ye unto this fearful pitch are bent,—
    When such necessity is press'd upon me,
    What doth avail resistance? Woe the day!
    Even lead me where ye will.
           [*Exit* MACLEAN, *exhausted and trembling, leaning on*
           Lochtarish, *and followed by* BENLORA *and* GLENFADDEN
           and vassals; two inferior vassals alone left upon the stage.
1st vas. (*looking after* MACLEAN).
    Ay, there he goes; so spent, and scared, and feeble!
    Without a prophet's skill, we may foretell,
    John of the Isle, by sly Lochtarish taught,
    Will work him soon to be an oath-bound wretch
    To this their fell design.—Are all things ready?
2d vas. All is in readiness.
1st vas.   When ebbs the tide?
2d vas. At early dawn, when in the narrow creek
    Near to the castle, with our trusty mates,
    Our boat must be in waiting to receive her.

1st *vas.* The time so soon! alas, so young and fair!
That slow and dismal death! To be at once
Plunged in the closing deep many have suffer'd,
But to sit waiting on a lonely rock
For the approaching tide to throttle her—
But that she is a Campbell, I could weep.
2d *vas.* Weep, fool! think soon how we'll to war again
With our old enemy; and, in the field,
Our good claymores die with their hated blood:
Think upon this, and change thy tears to joy.

            [*Exeunt.*

SCENE III.

The bed-chamber of MACLEAN. *Enter* MACLEAN, *followed by* HELEN.

Helen. Ah! wherefore art thou so disturb'd? the night
Is almost spent: the morn will break ere long,
And rest hast thou had none. Go to thy bed:
I pray thee, go.
Mac.   I cannot: urge me not.
Helen. Nay, try to rest: I'll sit and watch by thee.
Mac. Thou'lt sit and watch! O woe betide the hour!
And who will watch for thee?
Helen.   And why for me?
Can any harm approach? When thou art near,
Or sleeping or awake, I am secure.
Mac. (*pacing to and fro distractedly*). O God! O God!
Helen. Those exclamations!

    [*Going up to him, while he avoids her.*
      Turnst thou from me thus?
Have I offended? dost thou doubt my faith?
Hath any jealous thought—I freely own
Love did not make me thine: but, being thine,
To no love-wedded dame, bound in the ties
Of dearest sympathy, will I in duty—
In steady, willing, cheerful duty yield.
Yea, and though here no thrilling rapture be,

I look to spend with thee, by habit foster'd,
The evening of my days in true affection.
Mac. The evening of thy days! alas, alas!
Would heaven had so decreed it!

> [*Pulling away his hand from hers.*

Grasp me not!
It is a fiend thou clingst to.

> [*A knock at the door.*

Power of heaven!
Are they already at the chamber door!
Helen. Are those who knock without unwelcome?—hush!
Withdraw thyself, and I will open to them.

> [*Goes to the door.*

Mac. O go not! go not!

> [*Runs after her to draw her back, when a vassal, rushing
> from behind the bed, lays hold of him.*

Vas. Art thou not sworn to us? Where is thy faith?
Mac. I know, I know! the bands of hell have bound me.
O fiends! ye've made of me—what words can speak
The hateful wretch I am!

> Hark! hark! she cries!

She shrieks and calls on me!

> [HELEN's *cries heard without, first near and distinct,
> afterwards more and more distant as they bear her away;
> while the vassal leads* MACLEAN *forcibly off the stage by the
> opposite side, he breaks from him, and hastens towards that
> by which* HELEN *went out.*

Vas. Thou art too strong for me. Do as thou wilt;
But if thou bringst her back, even from that moment
Benlora is our leader, and thyself,
The Campbell's husband, chieftain and Maclean
No more shalt be. We've sworn as well as thou.

> [MACLEAN *stops irresolutely, and then suffers the vassal to
> lead him off by the opposite side.*

ACT III.

SCENE I.

A small island, composed of a rugged craggy rock, on the front of the stage, and the sea in the background.

Enter two vassals dragging in HELEN, *as if just come out of their boat.*

Helen. O why is this? Speak, gloomy, ruthless men!
    Our voyage ends not here?
1st vas.   It does: and now,
    Helen the Campbell, fare thee—fare thee well!
2d vas. Helen the Campbell, thy last greeting take
    From mortal thing.
Helen.   What! leave me on this rock,
    This sea-girt rock, to solitude and famine?
1st vas. Next rising tide will bring a sure relief
    To all the ills we leave thee.
Helen (starting). I understand you.
                  [*Raising her clasped hands to heaven.*
                Lord of heaven and earth;
    Of storms and tempests, and th' unfathom'd deep;
    Is this thy righteous will?
               [*Grasping the hands of the men imploringly*
                Ye cannot mean it!
    Ye cannot leave a human creature thus
    To perish by a slow approaching end,
    So awful and so terrible! Instant death
    Were merciful to this.
1st vas. If thou prefer it, we can shorten well
    Thy term of pain and terror: from this crag,
    Full fourteen fathom deep thou mayst be plunged.
    In shorter time than three strokes of an oar
    Thy pains will cease.
2d vas.   Come, that were better for thee.
       [*Both of them take her hands, and are going to hurry her to the brink of the rock, when she shrinks back.*

Helen. O no! the soul recoils from swift destruction!
  Pause ye awhile.

  [*Considering for a moment.*
  The downward terrible plunge!
The coil of whelming waves!—O fearful nature!

  [*Catching hold of a part of the rock near her.*
To the rough rock I'll cling: it still is something
Of firm and desp'rate hold—Depart and leave me.

  [*Waving her hand for the vassals to go, whilst she keeps close
  hold of the rock with the other.*

1st vas. Thou still mayst live within a prison pent,
  If life be dear to thee.

Helen (*eagerly*). If life be dear!—Alas, it is not dear!
  Although the passing fearful act of death
  So very fearful is.—Say how, even in a prison,
  I still may wait my quiet natural end.

1st vas. Whate'er thou art, such has thy conduct been,
  Thy wedded faith, e'en with thy fellest foes,
  Sure and undoubted stands:—Sign thou this scroll,
  Owning the child, thy son, of bastard birth;
  And this made sure, Lochtarish bade me say
  Thy life shall yet be spared.

Helen (*pushing him away with indignation as he offers her the scroll*).
  Off, off, vile agent of a wretch so devilish!
  Now do I see from whence my ruin comes:
  I and my infant foil his wicked hopes.
  O harmless babe! will heav'n abandon thee?
  It will not!—No; it will not!

  [*Assuming firmness and dignity.*
  Depart and leave me. In my rising breast
  I feel returning strength. Heav'n aids my weakness:
  I'll meet its awful will.

  [*Waving them off with her hand.*
1st vas. Well, in its keeping rest thee: fare thee well,
  Helen the Campbell!

2d vas.   Be thy suff'rings short!

(*Aside to the other.*) Come, quickly let us go, nor look behind.
Fell is the service we are put upon:
Would we had never ta'en that cruel oath!

[*Exeunt vassals.*

Helen (*alone, after standing some time gazing round her, paces backwards
and forwards with agitated steps, then, stopping suddenly, bends her
ear to the ground as if she listened earnestly to something*).
It is the sound; the heaving hollow swell
That notes the turning tide.—Tremendous agent!
Mine executioner, that, step by step,
Advances to the awful work of death.—
Onward it wears: a little space removed
The dreadful conflict is.

[*Raising her eyes to heaven, and moving her lips, as in the
act of devotion, before she again speaks aloud.*

Thou art i' the blue coped sky—th' expanse immeasurable;
I' the dark roll'd clouds, the thunder's awful home:
Thou art i' the wide-shored earth,—the pathless desert;
And in the dread immensity of waters,—
I' the fathomless deep Thou art.
Awful but excellent! beneath Thy hand,
With trembling confidence, I bow me low,
And wait Thy will in peace.

[*Sits down on a crag of the rock, with her arms crossed over
her breast in silent resignation; then, after a pause of some
length, raises her head hastily.*

Is it a sound of voices in the wind?
The breeze is on the rock: a gleam of sunshine
Breaks through those farther clouds. It is like hope
Upon a hopeless state.

[*Starting up, and gazing eagerly around her.*

I'll to that highest crag and take my stand:
Some little speck upon the distant wave
May to my eager gaze a vessel grow—
Some onward wearing thing,—some boat—some raft—
Some drifted plank.—O hope! thou quitt'st us never!

[*Exit, disappearing amongst the rugged divisions of the rock.*

SCENE II.

A small island, from which the former is seen in the distance, like a little pointed rock standing out of the sea.

Enter SIR HUBERT DE GREY, *followed by two fishermen.*

De Grey. This little swarded spot, that o'er the waves,
 Cloth'd in its green light, seem'd to beckon to us,
 Right pleasant is: until our comrades join,
 Here will we rest. I marvel much they stand
 So far behind. In truth, such lusty rowers
 Put shame upon their skill.
1st fish. A cross-set current bore them from the track,
 But see, they now bear on us rapidly.
 (*Voices without.*)   Holla!
2d fish. They call to us.—Holla! holla!
 How fast they wear! they are at hand already.
De Grey. Right glad I am: the Lord of Lorne, I fear,
 Will wait impatiently: he has already
 With rapid oars the nearer mainland gain'd,
 Where he appointed us to join him.—Ho!
           [*Calling off the stage.*
 Make to that point, my lads.
 (*To those near him.*) Here, for a little while, upon the turf
 We'll snatch a hasty meal, and, so refresh'd,
 Take to our boats again.

Enter three other Fishermen, as from their boat,
on the other side of the stage.

 Well met, my friends! I'm glad you're here at last.
 How was it that you took that distant track?
3d fish. The current bore us wide of what we wist;
 And, were it not your honour is impatient
 Mainland to make, we had not come so soon.
De Grey. What had detain'd you?
3d fish. As near you rock we bore, that o'er the waves
 Just shows its jetty point, and will, ere long,

Beneath the tide be hidd'n, we heard the sound
Of feeble lamentation.

De Grey.   A human voice?

3d fish. I cannot think it was;
For on that rock, sea-girt, and at high tide
Sea-cover'd, human thing there cannot be;
Though, at the first, it sounded in our ears
Like a faint woman's voice.

De Grey.   Perceived ye aught?

3d fish. Yes; something white that moved, and, as we think,
Some wounded bird that there hath dropp'd its wing,
And cannot make its way.

4th fish.   Perhaps some dog,
Whose master, at low water, there hath been,
And left him.

3d fish.   Something 'tis in woeful case,
Whate'er it be. Right fain I would have gone
To bear it off.

De Grey (eagerly). And wherefore didst thou not?
Return and save it. Be it what it may;
Something it is, lone and in jeopardy,
Which hath a feeling of its desperate state,
And therefore doth to woe-worn, fearful man,
A kindred nature bear.—Return, good friend:—
Quickly return and save it, ere the tide
Shall wash it from its hold. I to the coast
Will steer the while, and wait your coming there.

3d fish. Right gladly, noble sir.

4th fish.   We'll gladly go:
For, by my faith! at night I had not slept
For thinking of that sound.

De Grey. Heaven speed you then! whate'er ye bring to me
Of living kind, I will reward you for it.
Our different tracks we hold; nor longer here
Will I remain. Soon may we meet:
God speed you!

                              [*Exeunt severally.*

SCENE III.

A fisherman's house on the mainland.

Enter JOHN OF LORNE *and* SIR HUBERT DE GREY.

Lorne. Then wait thou for thy boat; I and my men
    Will onward to the town, where, as I hope,
    My trusty vassals and our steeds are station'd.
    But lose not time.
De Grey.   Fear not; I'll follow quickly.
Lorne. I must unto the castle of Argyll
    Without delay proceed; therefore, whate'er
    Of living kind, bird, beast, or creeping thing,
    This boat of thine produces, bring it with thee;
    And, were it eaglet fierce, or wolf, or fox,
    On with us shall it travel, mounted bravely,
    Our homeward cavalcade to grace. Farewell!
De Grey. Farewell, my friend! I shall not long delay
    Thy homeward journey.
Lorne (*calling off the stage*). But ho! good host and hostess! (*To* DE
    GREY.) Ere I go
    I must take leave of honest Duncan here,
    And of his rosy wife.—Ay, here they come.

Enter the host and his wife.

(*To host, &c.*) Farewell, my friends, and thanks be to you both!
    Good cheer, and kindly given, of you we've had.
    Thy hand, good host. May all the fish o' th' ocean
    Come crowding to thy nets!—And healthy brats,
    Fair dame, have thou! with such round rosy cheeks
    As brats of thine befit: and, by your leave,

                                    [*Kissing her.*

    So be they kiss'd by all kind comers too!
    Good luck betide you both!
Host. And, sir, to you the same. Whoe'er you be,
    A brave man art thou, that I will be sworn.

Wife. Come you this way again, I hope, good sir,
    You will not pass our door.

Lorne. Fear not, good hostess;
    It is a pleasant, sunny, open door,
    And bids me enter of its own accord;
    I cannot pass it by.—Good luck betide you!
                  [Exit, followed to the door by SIR HUBERT.

Host. I will be sworn it is some noble chieftain,
    Though homely be his garb.

Wife. Ay, so will I: the Lord of Lorne himself
    Could not more courteous be.

Host.   Hush! hush! be quiet!
    We live not now amongst the Campbells, wife.
    Should some Maclean o'erhear thee—hush, I say.
             [Eyeing DE GREY, *who returns from the door.*
    And this man, too; right noble is his mien;
    He is no common rambler.
    (*To* DE GREY.)   By your leave,
    If I may be so bold without offending,
    Your speech, methinks, smacks of a southern race;
    I guess at least of Lowland kin ye be.
    But think no shame of this; we'll ne'ertheless
    Regard thee: thieves and cowards be not all
    Who from the Lowlands come.

Wife. No; no, in sooth! I knew a Lowlander,
    Some years gone by, who was as true and honest—
    Ay, and I do believe well nigh as brave,
    As though, with brogued feet, he never else
    Had all his days than muir or mountain trodd'n.

De Grey. Thanks for your gentle thoughts!—It has indeed
    Been my misluck to draw my earliest breath
    Where meadows flower, and corn fields wave i' th' sun.
    But let us still be friends! Heaven gives us not
    To choose our birth-place, else these wilds, no doubt,
    Would be more thickly peopled.

Host. Ay, true it is, indeed.

Wife.   And hard it were
    To quarrel with him too for his misfortune.

[Noise heard without.

De Grey. Ha! 'tis my boat return'd.

Enter 1st Fisherman.

1st *fish.*   Ay, here we are.
De Grey. And aught saved from the rock?
1st *fish.* Yes, by my faith! but neither bird nor beast.
   Look there, my master.

[Pointing to the door.

Enter HELEN, *extremely exhausted, and almost senseless, wrapped closely
   up in one of their plaids, and supported by the other two Fishermen.*

De Grey. A woman! Heaven in mercy! was it then
   A human creature there exposed to perish?
1st *fish.* (*opening the plaid to show her face*). Ay, look; and such a
   creature!
De Grey (*starting back*). Helen of Argyll!
   O God! was this the feeble wailing voice?

*[Clasping his arms about her knees, as she stands almost
   senseless, supported by the fishermen, and bursting into
   tears.*

   Could heart of man so leave thee? thou, of all
   That lovely is, most lovely.—Woe is me!
   Some aid, I pray you.

[To host and his wife.

                    Bear her softly in,
   And wrap warm garments round her. Breathes she freely?
   Her eyes half open are, but life, alas!
   Is almost spent, and holds within her breast
   A weak uncertain seat.

[Helen moves her hand.

                    She moves her hand:—
   She knows my voice.—O heaven, in mercy save her!
   Bear her more gently, pray you:—Softly, softly!
   How weak and spent she is!

1st fish. No marvel she is weak: we reach'd her not
 Until the swelling waters laved her girdle.
 And then to see her——
De Grey.   Cease, I pray thee, friend,
 And tell me not——
2d fish.   Nay, faith, he tells you true:
 She stood above the water, with stretched arms
 Clung to the dripping rock, like the white pinions—
De Grey. Peace, peace, I say! thy words are agony:—
 Give to my mind no image of the thing!
     [*Exeunt, bearing* HELEN *into an inner part of the house.*

ACT IV.

SCENE I.

A small Gothic hall, or ante-room, in ARGYLL's *castle, a door at the bottom of the stage, leading to the apartment of the earl, before which is discovered the piper pacing backwards and forwards, playing on his bagpipe.*

Enter DUGALD.

Dugald. Now, pray thee, piper, cease! That stunning din
 Might do good service by the ears to set
 Two angry clans; but for a morning's rouse,
 Here at an old man's door, it does, good sooth,
 Exceed all reasonable use. The Earl
 Has pass'd a sleepless night: I pray thee now
 Give o'er, and spare thy pains.
Piper. And spare my pains, sayst thou? I'll do mine office,
 As long as breath within my body is.
Dugald. Then mercy on us all! if wind thou meanst,
 There is within that sturdy trunk of thine,
 Old as it is, a still exhaustless store.
 A Lapland witch's bag could scarcely match it.
 Thou couldst, I doubt not, belly out the sails
 Of a three-masted vessel with thy mouth:

But be thy mercy equal to thy might!
I pray thee now give o'er: in faith the earl
Has pass'd a sleepless night.
Piper. Thinkst thou I am a Lowland, day-hired minstrel,
To play or stop at bidding? Is Argyll
The lord and chieftain of our ancient clan,
More certainly, than I to him, as such,
The high hereditary piper am?
A sleepless night, forsooth! He's slept full oft
On the hard heath, with fifty harness'd steeds
Champing their fodder round him;—soundly too.
I'll do mine office, loon, chafe as thou wilt.
          [*Continuing to pace up and down, and play as before.*
Dugald. Nay, thou the chafer art, red-crested cock!
The Lord of Lorne has spoilt thee with indulging
Thy wilful humours. Cease thy cursed din!
See; here the earl himself comes forth to chide thee.
                             [*Exit.*

      Enter ARGYLL, *attended, from the chamber.*

Arg. Good morrow, piper! thou hast roused me bravely:
A younger man might gird his tartans on
With lightsome heart to martial sounds like these,
But I am old.
Piper.   O no, my noble chieftain!
It is not age subdues you.
Arg.   No; what else?
Piper. Alack! the flower and blossom of your house
The wind hath blown away to other towers.
When she was here, and gladsome faces brighten'd
With looking on her, and around your board
Sweet lays were sung, and gallants in the hall
Footed it trimly to our varied measures,
There might, indeed, be found beneath your roof
Those who might reckon years fourscore and odds,
But of old folks, I warrant, ne'er a soul.
No; we were all young then.

Arg. (sighing deeply).   'Tis true, indeed,
     It was even as thou sayst. Our earthly joys
     Fly like the blossoms scatter'd by the wind.

Enter a Servant.

Serv. Please you, my lord,
     Some score of vassals in the hall attend
     To bid good morrow to you, and the hour
     Wears late: the chamberlain hath bid me say
     He will dismiss them, if it please your honour.
Arg. Nay, many a mile have some of them, I know,
     With suit or purpose lurking in their minds,
     Ridd'n o'er rough paths to see me; disappointed
     Shall none of them return. I'm better now.
     I have been rather weary than unwell.
     Say, I will see them presently.

                                        [*Exit servant.*

Re-enter DUGALD *in haste.*

(*To* DUGALD.) Thou comest with a busy face: what tidings?
Dugald. The Lord of Lorne's arrived, an' please your honour:
     Sir Hubert too, and all their jolly train;
     And with them have they brought a lady, closely
     In hood and mantle muffled: ne'er a glimpse
     May of her face be seen.
Arg.   A lady, sayst thou?
Dugald. Yes; closely muffled up.
Arg. (*pacing up and down, somewhat disturbed*).
     I like not this.——It cannot surely be——
                    [*Stopping short, and looking hard at* DUGALD.
     Whence comes he?
Dugald.   He a-hunting went, I know,
     To Cromack's ancient laird, whose youthful dame
     So famed for beauty is; but whence he comes,
     I cannot tell, my lord.
Arg. (*pacing up and down, as he speaks to himself in broken sentences,
     very much disturbed*).

To Cromack's ancient laird!—If that indeed—
Beshrew me, if it be!—I'd rather lose
Half of my lands, than son of mine such wrong,
Such shameful wrong, should do. This sword I've drawn
Like robbery to revenge, ne'er to abet it:
And shall I now with hoary locks—No, no!—
My noble Lorne! he cannot be so base.

Enter LORNE, *going up to* ARGYLL *with agitation.*

Arg. (*eyeing him suspiciously*).
　　Well, John, how is it? Welcome art thou home,
　　If thou returnst, as well I would believe,
　　Deserving of a welcome.
Lorne.　　　　　　　　　　　Doubts my lord
　　That I am so return'd?
　　　　　　　[*Aside to* ARGYLL, *endeavouring to draw him apart from his*
　　　　　　　attendants.
　　Your ear, my father.
　　Let these withdraw: I have a thing to tell you.
Arg. (*looking still more suspiciously upon* LORNE, *from seeing the*
　　eagerness and agitation with which he speaks, and turning from him
　　indignantly).
　　No, by this honest blade! if wrong thou'st done,
　　Thou hast no shelter here. In open day,
　　Before th' assembled vassals shalt thou tell it;
　　And he whom thou hast injured be redress'd,
　　While I have power to bid my Campbells fight
　　I' the fair and honour'd cause.
Lorne.　　　　　　　　　　　I pray, my lord——
　　Will you vouchsafe to hear me?
Arg.　　　　　　　　　　　Thoughtless boy!
　　How far unlike the noble Lorne I thought thee!—
　　Proud as I am, far rather would I see thee
　　Join'd to the daughter of my meanest vassal,
　　Than see thy manly, noble worth engaged
　　In such foul raid as this.

Lorne.   Nay, nay! be pacified!
I'd rather take, in faith, the tawny hand
Of homeliest maid, that doth, o' holidays,
Her sun-burnt locks with worsted ribbon bind,
Fairly and freely won, than brightest dame
That e'er in stately bower or regal hall
In graceful beauty shone, gain'd by such wrong—
By such base treachery as you have glanced at.
These are plain words: then treat me like a man,
Who hath been wont the manly truth to speak.

Arg. Ha! now thy countenance and tone again
Are John of Lorne's. That look, and whispering voice,
So strange appear'd, in truth I liked it not.
Give me thy hand.—Where is the stranger dame?
If she in trouble be——

Lorne (aside).   Make these withdraw,
And I will lead her hither.

> [*Exit, while the earl waves his hand, and* DUGALD *and
> attendants, &c. go out: presently re-enter* LORNE, *leading in*
> HELEN, *covered closely up in a mantle.*

Lorne. This is the dame, who, houseless and deserted,
Seeks shelter here, nor fears to be rejected.

Helen (sinking down, and clasping ARGYLL's *knees).* My father!

Arg. That voice!—O God!—unveil—unveil, for mercy!

> [*Tearing off the mantle that conceals her.*

My child! my Helen!

> [*Clasping her to his heart, and holding her there for some
> time, unable to speak.*

My child! my dearest child!—my soul! my pride!
Deserted!—houseless!—com'st thou to me thus?
Here is thy house—thy home: this aged bosom
Thy shelter is, which thou shalt quit no more.
My child! my child!

> [*Embracing her again;* HELEN *and he weeping upon one
> another's necks.*

Houseless! deserted—'neath the cope of heaven
Breathes there a wretch who could desert thee?—Speak,
If he hath so abused his precious trust,

If he—it makes me tear these hoary locks
To think what I have done!—Oh thoughtless father!
Thoughtless and selfish too!
  [*Tearing his hair, beating his forehead with all the violent*
  gestures of rage and grief.
Helen. Oh, oh! forbear! It was not you, my father;
I gave myself away: I did it willingly:
We acted both for good; and now your love
Repays me richly—stands to me instead
Of many blessings.—Noble Lorne, besides—
O, he hath been to me so kind—so tender!
  [*Taking her brother's hand, and pressing it to her breast;*
  then joining her father's to it, and pressing them both
  ardently to her lips.
Say not I am deserted: heaven hath chid me—
Hath chid me sorely: but hath bless'd me too,—
O, dearly bless'd me!
Arg. Hath chid thee sorely!—how I burn to hear it!
What hast thou suffer'd?
Lorne. We will not tell thee now. Go to thy chamber,
And be awhile composed. We have, my father,
A tale to tell that will demand of thee
Recruited strength to hear.—We'll follow thee.

 [*Exeunt;* LORNE *supporting his father and* HELEN *into the chamber.*

SCENE II.

The garden of the castle.

Enter ARGYLL, LORNE, *and* SIR HUBERT DE GREY, *speaking as they enter.*

Lorne. A month!—A week or two!—No, not an hour
Would I suspend our vengeance. Such atrocity
Makes e'en the little term between our summons,
And the dark crowding round our martial pipes
Of plumed bonnets nodding to the wind,

> Most tedious seem; yea, makes the impatient foot
> To smite the very earth beneath its tread,
> For being fix'd and inert.

Arg. Be less impatient, John: thou canst not doubt
> A father's keen resentment of such wrong:
> But let us still be wise; this short delay
> Will make revenge the surer; to its aim
> A just direction give.

De Grey.   The earl is right:
> We shall but work in the dark, impatient Lorne,
> If we too soon begin.

Arg.   How far Maclean
> Hath to this horrible attempt consented,
> Or privy been, we may be certified,
> By waiting silently to learn the tale
> That he will tell us of his lady's loss,
> When he shall send to give us notice of it,
> As doubtless soon he will.

De Grey. If he, beset and threaten'd, to those fiends,
> Unknowing of their purpose, hath unwillingly
> Committed her, he will himself, belike,
> If pride prevent him not, your aid solicit
> To set him free from his disgraceful thraldom.

Lorne. And if he should, shrunk be this sinew'd arm,
> If it unsheath a weapon in his cause!
> Let ev'ry ragged stripling on his lands
> In wanton mock'ry mouth him with contempt;
> Benlora head his vassals; and Lochtarish—
> That serpent, full of ev'ry devilish wile,
> His prison-keeper and his master be!

De Grey. Ay; and the keeper also of his son,
> The infant heir.

Lorne (starting). I did not think of this.

Arg. Then let thy headstrong fury pause upon it.
> Thanks to Sir Hubert's prudence! thou as yet
> Before thy followers hast restrained been;
> And who this lady is, whom to the castle,
> Like a mysterious stranger, ye have brought,

From them remains conceal'd.—My brave De Grey!
This thy considerate foresight, join'd to all
Thy other service in this woeful matter,
Hath made us much thy debtor.

De Grey. I have indeed, my lord, consider'd only
What I believed would Helen's wishes be,
Ere she herself could utter them; if this
Hath proved equivalent to wiser foresight,
Let it direct us still; let Helen's wishes
Your measures guide.

Arg. Ah, brave De Grey! would they had ever done so!
I had not now—

> [Taking *Sir Hubert's* hand with emotion.

> Forgive me, noble youth!

Alas, alas! the father's tenderness
Before the chieftain's policy gave way,
And all this wreck hath been.

Lorne.   'Tis even so.
That cursed peace; that coward's shadeless face
Of smiles and promises, to all things yielding
With weak, unmanly pliancy, so gain'd you—
Even you, the wise Argyll!—it made me mad!
Who hath no point that he maintains against you,
No firmness hath to hold him of your side:
Who cannot sturdily against me stand,
And say, "Encroach no farther," friend of mine
Shall never be.

De Grey. Nay, Lorne, forbear!—forbear!
Thine own impetuous wilfulness did make
The other's pliant mind more specious seem;
And thou thyself didst to that luckless union,
Although unwittingly, assistance lend.
Make now amends for it, and curb thy spirit,
While that the Earl with calmer judgment waits
His time for action.

Lorne. Beshrew me, but thy counsel strangely smacks
Of cautious timid age! In faith, De Grey,

But that I know thy noble nature well,
I could believe thee—

Arg.   Peace, unruly spirit!
Bold as thou art, methinks, with locks like these,
Thy father still may say to thee, "Be silent!"

Lorne (checking himself, and bowing very low to ARGYLL).
And be obey'd devoutly.—O forgive me!
Those locks are to your brows a kingly fillet
Of strong authority, to which my heart
No rebel is, though rude may be my words.
          [*Taking* SIR HUBERT's *hand with an assured countenance.*
I ask not thee, De Grey, to pardon me.
Resistance here with gentleness is join'd:
Therefore I've loved thee, and have laid upon thee
The hand of sure possession! claiming still
A friend's endurance of my froward temper,
Which, froward as it is, from thee hath borne
What never human being but thyself
Had dared to goad it with.

De Grey.   It is indeed
Thy well-earn'd right thou askest, noble Lorne,
And it is yielded to thee cheerfully.

Arg. My aged limbs are tired with pacing here;
Some one approaches: within that grove
We'll find a shady seat, and there conclude
This well-debated point.

                              [*Exeunt.*

SCENE III.

A court within the castle, surrounded with buildings.

Enter DUGALD *and a Vassal, two servants at the same time crossing the
stage, with covered dishes in their hands.*

Vas. I'll wait until the Earl shall be at leisure;
My business presses not. Where do they carry

Those cover'd meats? Have ye within the castle
Some noble prisoner?

Dugald. Would so it were! but these are days of peace.
They bear them to the stranger dame's apartment,
Whom they have told thee of. There, at her door,
An ancient faithful handmaid of the house,
Whate'er they bring receives; for none beside
Of all the household is admitted.

Vas. Now, by my fay! my purse and dirk I'd give
To know who this may be.—Some chieftain's lady
Whom John of Lorne—

Dugald.   Nay, there, I must believe,
Thou guessest erringly.—I grant, indeed,
He doffs his bonnet to each tacks-man's wife,
And is with every coif amongst them all,
Both young and old, in such high favour held,
Nor maiden, wife, nor beldame of the clan
But to the Earl doth her petition bring
Through intercession of the Lord of Lorne;
But never yet did husband, sire, or brother,
Of wrong from him complain.

Vas.   I know it well.

Dugald. But be she who she may,
This stranger here; I doubt not, friend, ere long,
We shall have bickering for her in the field
With some fierce foe or other.

Vas.   So I trust:
And by my honest faith! this peace of ours
Right long and tiresome is—I thought, ere now,
Some of our restless neighbours would have trespass'd
And inroads made: but no; Argyll and Lorne
Have grown a terror to them: all is quiet;
And we ourselves must the aggressors be,
Or still this dull and slothful life endure,
Which makes our men of three-score years and ten
To fret and murmur.

Enter ROSA, *with a servant conducting her.*

Serv. (*to* DUGALD). A lady here, would see my Lord of Lorne.

Dugald. Yes, still to him they come.

> [*Looking at* ROSA.
>
> Ha! see I rightly?

Rosa from Mull?

Rosa.   Yes, Dugald; here thou seest
A woeful bearer of unwelcome tidings.

Dugald. What, hath thy lady sent thee?

Rosa. Alas, alas! I have no lady now.

Dugald. Ha! is she dead? not many days ago
She was alive and well.—Hast thou so soon
The castle quitted—left thy lady's corse?

Rosa. Thinkst thou I would have left her?—On the night
When, as they say, she died, I from the castle
By force was ta'en, and to mainland convey'd;
Where in confinement I remain'd, till chance
Gave me the means of breaking from my prison;
And hither am I come, in woeful plight,
The dismal tale to tell.

Dugald.   A tale, indeed,
Most dismal, strange, and sudden.

Rosa.   How she died
God knows; but much I fear foul play she had.
Where is the Lord of Lorne? for first to him
I wish to speak.

Dugald. Come, I will lead thee to him.—Had foul play!

Vas. Fell fiends they are could shed her blood! If this
Indeed hath been, 'twill make good cause, I wot;
The warlike pipe will sound our summons soon.

> [*Exeunt* DUGALD *and* ROSA, *&c., as* ARGYLL *and* SIR
> HUBERT *enter by the opposite side.*

Arg. And wilt thou leave us then, my noble friend?
May we not still for some few days retain thee?

De Grey. Where'er I go, I carry in my heart
A warm remembrance of the friendly home
That still within these hospitable walls
I've found; but longer urge me not to stay.
In Helen's presence now, constrain'd and strange,

With painful caution, chasing from my lips
The ready thought, half-quiver'd into utterance,
For cold corrected words, expressive only
Of culprit consciousness,—I sit; nor e'en
May look upon her face but as a thing
On which I may not look; so painful now
The mingled feeling is, since dark despair
With one faint ray of hope hath temper'd been.
I can no more endure it. She herself
Perceives it, and it pains her.—Let me then
Bid you farewell, my lord. When evening comes,
I'll, under favour of the rising moon,
Set forth.
Arg.   Indeed! so soon? and must it be?
De Grey. Yes; to Northumberland without delay
I fain would take my road. My aged father
Looks now impatiently for my return.
Arg. Then I'll no longer urge thee. To thy father,
The noble baron, once, in better days,
My camp-mate and my friend, I must resign thee.
Bear to him every kind and cordial wish
An ancient friend can send, and—
                              [*A horn heard without.*
                    Hark! that horn!
Some messenger of moment is arrived.—
We'll speak of this again.—The moon to-night
Is near the full, and at an early hour—

          Enter a Messenger, bearing a letter.

Whose messenger art thou, who in thy hand
That letter bearst with broad and sable seal,
Which seems to bring to me some dismal tidings?
Mess. From Mull, my lord, I come; and the Maclean,
Our chief, commission'd me to give you this,
Which is indeed with dismal tidings fraught.
          [ARGYLL *opens the letter, and reads it with affected surprise
          and sorrow.*

Arg. Heavy, indeed, and sudden is the loss—
    The sad calamity that hath befallen.
    The will of heaven be done!

> [*Putting a handkerchief to his eyes, and leaning, as if for
> support, upon* SIR HUBERT; *then, after a pause, turning to
> the messenger.*

    How didst thou leave the chieftain? He, I hope,
    Permits not too much sorrow to o'er come
    His manhood. Doth he bear his grief composedly?
Mess. O no, it is most violent! At the funeral,
    Had not the good Lochtarish, by his side,
    Supported him, he had with very grief
    Sunk to the earth.—And good Lochtarish too
    Was in right great affliction.
Arg.   Ay, good man;
    I doubt it not.—Ye've had a splendid funeral?
Mess. O yes, my lord! that have we had. Good truth!
    A grand and stately burial has it been.
    Three busy days and nights through all the isle
    Have bagpipes play'd, and sparkling beakers flow'd;
    And never corse, I trow, i' th' earth was laid
    With louder lamentations.
Arg.   Ay, I doubt not,
    Their grief was loud enough.—Pray pass ye in.
    (*To attendants at a distance.*) Conduct him there; and see that
    he be treated,
    After his tedious journey, as befits
    A way-tired stranger.

> [*Exeunt all but* ARGYLL *and* SIR HUBERT.

    This doth all hope and all belief exceed.
    Maclean will shortly follow this his notice,

> [*Giving* SIR HUBERT *the letter.*

    To make me here a visit of condolence;
    And thus within our power they put themselves
    With most assured blindness.
De Grey (after reading it).   'Tis Lochtarish,
    In all the arts of dark hypocrisy

So deeply skill'd, who doth o'ershoot his mark,
As such full often do.
Arg.   And let him come!
At his own arts we trust to match him well.—
Their force, I guess, is not in readiness;
Therefore, meantime, to stifle all suspicion,
This specious mummery he hath devised;
And his most wretched chief, led by his will,
Most wretchedly submits.—Well, let us go
And tell to Lorne the news, lest too unguardedly
He should receive it.

[*Exeunt.*

SCENE IV.

An apartment in the castle. Enter Sir Hubert de Grey, *beckoning to*
Rosa, *who appears on the opposite side.*

De Grey. Rosa; I pray thee, spare me of thy leisure
Some precious moments: something would I say:
Wilt thou now favour me?
Rosa.   Most willingly.
De Grey. As yet thy mistress knows not of the letter
Sent by Maclean, announcing his design
Of paying to the earl this sudden visit—
This mockery of condolence?
Rosa.   No; the earl
Forbade me to inform her.
De Grey.   This is well;
Her mind must be prepared. Meantime I go,
And thou art here to comfort and attend her:
O do it gently, Rosa! do it wisely!
Rosa. You need not doubt my will.—Go ye so soon;
And to Northumberland?
De Grey.   So I intended.
And so Argyll and John of Lorne believe:
But since this messenger from Mull arrived,
Another thought has struck me.—Saidst thou not

The child—thy lady's child, ta'en from the castle,
Is to the keeping of Lochtarish' mother
Committed, whose lone house is on the shore?
Rosa. Yes, whilst in prison pent, so did I hear
My keeper say, and much it troubled me.
De Grey. Canst thou to some good islander commend me,
Within whose house I might upon the watch
Conceal'd remain?—It is to Mull I go,
And not to England. While Maclean is here,
Attended by his vassals, the occasion
I'll seize to save the infant.
Rosa.   Bless thee for it!
Heaven bless thee for the thought!—I know a man—
An aged fisherman, who will receive you;
Uncle to Morton: and if he himself
Still in the island be, there will you find him,
Most willing to assist you.
De Grey.   Hush, I pray
I hear thy lady's steps.
Rosa. Near to the castle gate, ere you depart,
I'll be in waiting to inform you farther
Of what may aid your purpose.
De Grey. Do, good Rosa,
And make me much thy debtor. But be secret.
Rosa. You need not doubt me.

Enter HELEN, *and* DE GREY *goes up to her as if he would speak, but the
words falter on his lips, and he is silent.*

Helen. Alas! I see it is thy parting visit;
Thou com'st to say "farewell!"
De Grey. Yes, Helen: I am come to leave with thee
A friend's dear benison—a parting wish—
A last—rest ev'ry blessing on thy head!
Be this permitted to me:
                              [*Kissing her hand with profound respect.*
                              Fare thee well!
Heaven aid and comfort thee! Farewell! farewell!

[Is about to retire hastily, whilst HELEN *follows to prevent him.*

Helen. O go not from me with that mournful look!
　　Alas! thy gen'rous heart, depress'd and sunk,
　　Looks on my state too sadly.—
　　I am not, as thou thinkst, a thing so lost
　　In woe and wretchedness.—Believe not so!
　　All whom misfortune with her rudest blasts
　　Hath buffeted, to gloomy wretchedness
　　Are not therefore abandon'd. Many souls
　　From cloister'd cells, from hermits' caves, from holds
　　Of lonely banishment, and from the dark
　　And dreary prison-house, do raise their thoughts
　　With humble cheerfulness to heaven, and feel
　　A hallow'd quiet, almost akin to joy;
　　And may not I, by heaven's kind mercy aided,
　　Weak as I am, with some good courage bear
　　What is appointed for me?—O be cheer'd!
　　And let not sad and mournful thoughts of me
　　Depress thee thus.—When thou art far away,
　　Thou'lt hear, the while, that in my father's house
　　I spend my peaceful days, and let it cheer thee.
　　I too shall ev'ry southern stranger question,
　　Whom chance may to these regions bring, and learn
　　Thy fame and prosperous state.
De Grey. My fame and prosperous state, while thou art thus!
　　If thou in calm retirement liv'st contented,
　　Lifting thy soul to heaven, what lack I more?
　　My sword and spear, changed to a pilgrim's staff,
　　Will be a prosperous state; and for my fame,—
　　A feeble sound that after death remains,
　　The echo of an unrepeated stroke
　　That fades away to silence,—surely this
　　Thou dost not covet for me.
Helen.　　　　　　　　　　　　Ah, I do!
　　Yet, granting here I err, didst thou not promise
　　To seek in wedded love and active duties
　　Thy share of cheerful weal?—and dost thou now
　　Shrink from thy gen'rous promise?—No, thou shalt not.

I hold thee bound—I claim it of thee boldly.
It is my right. If thou, in sad seclusion,
A lonely wanderer art, thou dost extinguish
The ray that should have cheer'd my gloom: thou makest
What else had been a calm and temper'd sorrow,
A state of wretchedness.—O no! thou wilt not!
Take to thy gen'rous heart some virtuous maid,
And doubt not thou a kindred heart wilt find.
The cheerful tenderness of woman's nature
To thine is suited, and when join'd to thee,
Will grow in virtue:—Take thou then this ring,
If thou wilt honour so my humble gift,
And put it on her hand; and be assured
She who shall wear it,—she whose happy fate
Is link'd with thine, will prove a noble mate.
De Grey. O there I am assured! she whose fate
Is link'd with mine, if fix'd be such decree,
Most rich in every soft and noble trait
Of female virtue is: in this full well
Assured I am.—I would—I thought—forgive—
I speak but raving words:—a hasty spark,
Blown and extinguish'd, makes me waver thus.
Permit me then again.

                                      [Kissing her hand.
               High heaven protect thee!
Farewell!
Helen. Farewell! and heaven's good charge be thou!

       [They part, and both turn away to opposite sides of the
       stage, when SIR HUBERT, *looking round just as he is about to*
       go off, and seeing HELEN *also looking after him sorrowfully,*
       eagerly returns.
De Grey. Ah! are those looks—

       [Going to kneel at her feet, but immediately checking himself
       with much embarrassment.
Alas! why come I back?
Something there was—thou gavest me a ring;
I have not dropp'd it?
Rosa (coming forward).   No, 'tis on your finger.

De Grey. Ay, true, good Rosa; but my wits are wilder'd;
   I knew not what I sought.—
                                    Farewell! farewell!
   [*Exit* DE GREY *hastily, while* HELEN *and* ROSA *go off by
   the opposite side.*

ACT V.

SCENE I.

ARGYLL's *castle, the vestibule, or grand entrance; a noise of bustle and
voices heard without, and servants seen crossing the stage, as the scene
opens.*

Enter DUGALD, *meeting* 1st *servant.*

Dugald. They are arrived, Maclean and all his train;
   Run quickly, man, and give our chieftains notice.
1st *serv.* They know already: from the tower we spied
   The mournful cavalcade: the Earl and Lorne
   Are down the staircase hasting to receive them.
Dugald. I've seen them light, a sooty-coated train,
   With lank and woeful faces, and their eyes
   Bent to the ground, as though our castle gate
   Had been the scutcheon'd portal of a tomb,
   Set open to receive them.
2d *serv.* Ay, on the pavement fall their heavy steps
   Measured and slow, as if her palled coffin
   They follow'd still.
Dugald.   Hush, man! Here comes the Earl,
   With face composed and stern; but look behind him
   How John of Lorne doth gnaw his nether lip,
   And beat his clenched hand against his thigh,
   Like one who tampers with half-bridled ire!
2d *serv.* Has any one offended him?
Dugald.   Be silent,
   For they will overhear thee.—Yonder too

> [*Pointing to the opposite side of the stage.*

Come the Macleans: let us our stations keep,
And see them meet.

> [*Retiring with the other to the bottom of the stage. Enter* ARGYLL *and* LORNE, *attended, and in deep mourning; while, at the same time, by the opposite side of the stage, enter* MACLEAN, BENLORA, LOCHTARISH, *and* GLENFADDEN, *with attendants, also in deep mourning:* ARGYLL *and* MACLEAN *go up to one another, and formally embrace.*

Arg. Welcome! if such a cheerful word as this
May with our deep affliction suited be.
Lochtarish too, and brave Benlora, ay,
And good Glenfadden also,—be ye all
With due respect received, as claims your worth.

> [*Taking them severally by the hand as he names them.* MACLEAN *then advances to embrace* LORNE, *who shrinks back from him, but immediately correcting himself, bends his body another way, as if suddenly seized with some violent pain.*

Arg. (*to* MACLEAN). Regard him not: he hath imprudently
A recent wound exposed to chilling air,
And oft the pain with sudden pang attacks him.

Loch. Ay, what is shrewder? we have felt the like,
And know it well, my lord.

Arg. (*bowing to* LOCHTARISH, *but continuing to speak to* MACLEAN).
Yet, ne'ertheless, good son-in-law and chieftain,
Believe thou well that with a brother's feelings,
Proportion'd to the dire and dismal case
That hath befallen, he now receives you; also
Receiving these your friends with equal favour.
This is indeed to us a woeful meeting,
Chieftain of Mull.

> [*Looking keenly in his face, while the other shuns his eye.*

I see full well the change
Which violent grief upon that harrow'd visage
So deeply hath impress'd.

Mac. (still embarrassed, and shrinking from ARGYLL'*s observation).*
    Ah! ah! the woeful day!—I cannot speak.
    Alas, alas!
Arg.   Alas, in truth,
    Too much the woeful widower's alter'd looks,
    Upon thy face I see.
Loch. (to ARGYLL*).* You see, my lord, his eyes with too much
    weeping
    Are weak, and shun the light. Nor should we marvel:
    What must to him the sudden loss have been,
    When even to us, who were more distantly
    Connected with her rare and matchless virtue,
    It brought such keen affliction?
Arg. Yes, good Lochtarish, I did give her to you—
    To your right worthy chief, a noble creature,
    With every kindly virtue—every grace
    That might become a noble chieftain's wife:
    And that ye have so well esteem'd—so well
    Regarded, cherish'd, and respected her,
    As your excessive sorrow now declares,
    Receive from me a grateful father's thanks.
    Lochtarish, most of all to thy good love
    I am beholden.
Loch.   Ah! small was the merit
    Such goodness to respect.
Arg.   And thou, Benlora;
    A woman, and a stranger, on the brave
    Still potent claims maintain; and little doubt I
    They were by thee regarded.
        [BENLORA *steps back, frowning sternly, and remains silent.*
                    And, Glenfadden,
    Be not thy merits overlook'd.
Glen.   Alas!
    You overrate, my lord, such slender service.
Arg. Wrong not, I pray, thy modest worth.—But here,
                [*Turning again to* MACLEAN.
    Here most of all, from whom her gentle virtues,

(And so indeed it right and fitting was,)
Their best and dearest recompense received,
To thee, most generous chieftain, let me pay
The thanks that are thy due.

Mac.   Oh, oh! alas!

Arg. Ay, in good sooth! I see thy grief-worn eyes
Do shun the light.
But grief is ever sparing of its words.
In brief, I thank you all: and for the love
Ye have so dearly shown to me and mine,
I trust, before we part, to recompense you
As suits your merit and my gratitude.

Lorne (aside to ARGYLL).
Ay, father; now ye speak to them shrewd words;
And now I'm in the mood to back you well.

Arg. (aside to LORNE). 'Tis well thou art; but check those eager
looks;
Lochtarish eyes thee keenly.

[*Directing a hasty glance to* LOCHTARISH, *who is whispering
to* GLENFADDEN, *and looking suspiciously at* LORNE.

Lorne (stepping forward to MACLEAN, &c.).
Chieftain, and honour'd gentlemen, I pray
The sullen, stern necessity excuse
Which pain imposed upon me, and receive,
Join'd with my noble father's, such poor thanks
As I may offer to your loving worth.

Arg. Pass on, I pray you; till the feast be ready,
Rest ye above, where all things are prepared
For your refreshment.

[*Exeunt.*

SCENE II.

A narrow arched room or closet, adjoining to a gallery.

Enter LOCHTARISH *and* GLENFADDEN.

Loch. How likest thou this, Glenfadden? Doth the face
    Argyll assumes, of studied courtesy,
    Raise no suspicion?
Glen.   Faith, I know not well!—
    The speech, indeed, with which he welcomed us,
    Too wordy, and too artificial seem'd
    To be the native growth of what he felt.
Loch. It so to me appear'd: and John of Lorne,
    First shrinking from Maclean, with sudden pain,
    As he pretended, struck; then stern and silent;
    Till presently assuming, like his father,
    A courtesy minute and over-studied,
    He glozed us with his thanks:—
    Didst thou not mark his keenly flashing eye,
    When spoke Argyll of recompensing us
    Before we part?
Glen.   I did indeed observe it.
Loch. This hath a meaning.
Glen.   Faith, I do suspect
    Some rumour must have reach'd their ear; and yet
    Our agents faithful are; it cannot be.
Loch. Or can, or can it not, beneath this roof
    A night I will not sleep. When evening comes
    Meet we again. If at this banquet, aught
    Shall happen to confirm our fears, forthwith
    Let us our safety seek in speedy flight.
Glen. And leave Maclean behind us?
Loch. Ay, and Benlora too. Affairs the better
    At Mull will thrive, when we have rid our hands
    Of both these hind'rances, who in our way
    Much longer may not be.
                              [*Listening.*

We're interrupted.
Let us into the gallery return,
And join the company with careless face,
Like those who have from curiosity
But stepp'd aside to view the house.—Make haste!
It is Argyll and *Lorne*.

> [*Exeunt, looking at the opposite side, alarmed, at which
> enter* ARGYLL *and* LORNE.

Lorne. Are you not now convinced? his conscious guilt
Is in his downcast and embarrass'd looks,
And careful shunning of all private converse
Whene'er aside you've drawn him from his train,
Too plainly seen: you cannot now, my lord,
Doubt of his share in this atrocious deed.
Arg. Yet, Lorne, I would, ere further we proceed,
Prove it more fully still. The dinner hour
Is now at hand.

> [*Listening*.

What steps are those,
That in the gallery, close to this door,
Like some lone straggler from the company
Withdrawn, sound quickly pacing to and fro?
Look out and see.
Lorne (*going to the door, and calling back to* ARGYLL *in a low voice*).
It is Maclean himself.
Arg. Beckon him hither then.—Thank heaven for this!
Now opportunity is fairly given,
If that constrainedly he cloaks their guilt,
To free him from their toils.

Enter MACLEAN, *conducted by* LORNE.

Arg. (*to* MACLEAN). My son, still in restraint before our vassals
Have we conversed; but now in privacy—
Start not, I pray thee:—sit thee down, Maclean:
I would have close and private words of thee:
Sit down, I pray; my aged limbs are tired.

[ARGYLL *and* MACLEAN *sit down, whilst* LORNE *stands
behind them, with his ear bent eagerly to listen, and his eyes
fixed with a side-glance on* MACLEAN.

Chieftain, I need not say to thee, who deeply
Lament'st with us our sad untimely loss,
How keenly I have felt it.—
And now indulge a father in his sorrow,
And say how died my child.—Was her disease
Painful as it was sudden?

Mac. It was—alas! I know not how it was.
A fell disease!—Her end was so appointed.

Lorne (*behind*). Ay, that I doubt not.

Mac. A fearful malady! though it received
All good assistance.

Lorne (*behind*). That I doubt not either.

Mac. A cruel ill!—but how it dealt with her,
My grief o'erwhelm'd me so, I could not tell.

Arg. Say—wast thou present? didst thou see her die?

Mac. Oh, oh! the woeful sight, that I should see it!

Arg. Thou didst not see it then?

Mac. Alack! alack!
O would that I had seen—O woe is me!
Her pain—her agony was short to mine!

Lorne (*behind, impatiently*).
Is this an answer, chieftain, to the question
Argyll hath plainly ask'd thee—wast thou present
When Helen died? didst thou behold her death?

Mac. O yes; indeed I caught your meaning lamely;
I meant—I thought—I know not certainly
The very time and moment of her death,
Although within my arms she breathed her last.

Lorne (*rushing forward eagerly*). Now are we answered.

[ARGYLL, *covering his face with his hands, throws himself
back in his chair for some time without speaking.*

Mac. (*to* ARGYLL). I fear, my lord, too much I have distress'd you.

Arg. Somewhat you have indeed.—And further now
I will not press your keen and recent sorrow
With questions that so much renew its anguish.

Mac. You did, belike, doubt of my tenderness.

Arg. O no! I have no doubts. Within your arms
    She breathed her last?

Mac.   Within my arms she died.

Arg. (*looking hard at* MACLEAN, *and then turning away*).
    His father was a brave and honest chief!

Mac. What says my lord?

Arg.   A foolish exclamation,
    Of no determined meaning.

                              [*Bell sounds without.*

              Dry our tears:
    The hall-bell warns us to the ready feast;
    And through the gallery I hear the sound
    Of many footsteps hastening to the call.
    Chieftain, I follow thee.

                  [*Exeunt* ARGYLL *and* MACLEAN.

Lorne (*alone, stopping to listen*).
    The castle, throng'd throughout with moving life,
    From every winding stair, and arched aisle,
    A mingled echo sends.
    Ay; light of foot, I hear their sounding steps
    A-trooping to the feast, who never more
    At feast shall sit, or social meal partake.
    O wretch! O fiend of vile hypocrisy!
    How fiercely burns my blood within my veins
    Till I am match'd with thee!

                                  [*Exit.*

SCENE III.

The great hall of the castle, with a feast set out, and the company already placed at table, with servants and attendants in waiting, who fill the stage in every part: ARGYLL *is seated at the head of the table, with* MACLEAN *on his left hand, and a chair left empty on his right.*

Arg. (*to* MACLEAN, *&c.*)
    Most worthy chief, and honour'd guests and kinsmen,
    I crave your pardon for this short delay:

One of our company is wanting still,
For whom we have reserved this empty place;
Nor will the chief of Mull unkindly take it,
That on our better hand this chair of honour
Is for a lady kept.

Omnes.   A lady!

> [*A general murmur of surprise is heard through the hall.*

Arg.   Yes;
Who henceforth of this house the mistress is;
And were it palace of our Scottish king,
Would so deserve to be.

Omnes. We give you joy, my lord.

> [*A confused murmur heard again.*

Mac. We give you joy, my lord: your age is bless'd.
We little thought, in these our funeral weeds,
A bridal feast to darken.

Lorne.   No, belike.
Many who don their coat at break of day,
Know not what shall befal them, therein girt,
Ere evening close.

> [*Assuming a gay tone.*

The Earl hath set a step-dame o'er my head
To cow my pride—What think you, brave Maclean?
This world so fleeting is and full of change,
Some lose their wives, I trow, and others find them.
Bridegrooms and widowers do, side by side,
Their beakers quaff; and which of them at heart
Most glad or sorry is, the subtle fiend,
Who in men's hollow hearts his council holds,
He wotteth best, though each good man will swear,
His, lost or found, all other dames excell'd.

Arg. Curb, Lorne, thy saucy tongue: Maclean himself
Shall judge if she—the lady I have found,
Equal in beauty her whom he hath lost.
In worth I'm sure she does. But hush! she comes.

> [*A great commotion through the hall amongst the attendants, &c.*

Omnes. It is the lady.

Arg. (rising from his seat, and making signs to the attendants nearest the door). Ho there! make room, and let the lady pass.

> [*The servants, &c. stand apart, ranging themselves on every side to let the lady pass; and enter* HELEN, *magnificently dressed, with a deep white veil over her face; while Lorne, going forward to meet her, conducts her to her chair on* ARGYLL'*s right hand.*

Arg. (to the CAMPBELLS). Now, fill a cup of welcome to our friends!

Loch. (to MACLEAN). Chieftain, forgettest thou to greet the lady?

Mac. (turning to ARGYLL).

Nay, rather give, my lord, might I presume,
Our firstling cup to this fair lady's health,
The noble dame of this right princely house.
And though close veil'd she be, her beauty's lustre
I little question.

> [*Fills up a goblet, while* LOCHTARISH, BENLORA, &c. *follow his example, and standing up, bow to the lady.*

Your health, most noble dame!

> [HELEN, *rising also, bows to him, and throws back her veil: the cup falls from his hands; all the company start up from table; screams and exclamations of surprise are heard from all corners of the hall, and confused commotion seen every where.* MACLEAN, LOCHTARISH, *and* GLENFADDEN, *stand appalled and motionless; but* BENLORA, *looking fiercely round him, draws his sword.*

Ben. What! are we here like deer bay'd in a nook?
And think ye so to slay us, crafty foe?
No, by my faith! like such we will not fall,
Arms in our hands, though by a thousand foes
Encompass'd. Cruel, murderous, ruthless men,
Too good a warrant have you now to think us,
But cowards never!

                    Rouse ye, base Macleans!
And thou, whose subtlety around us thus
With wreckful skill these cursed toils hast wound,
Sinks thy base spirit now?

> [*To* LOCHTARISH.

Arg. (*holding up his hand*). Be silence in the hall!
    Macleans, ye are my guests; but if the feast
    Delight you not, free leave ye have to quit it.
    Lorne, see them all, with right due courtesy,
    Safely protected to the castle gate.

                    [*Turning to* MACLEAN.
    Here, other name than chieftain or Maclean
    He may not give thee; but, without our walls,
    If he should call thee murderer, traitor, coward,
    Weapon to weapon, let your fierce contention
    Be fairly held, and he, who first shall yield,
    The liar be.——

                Campbells! I charge you there,
    Free passage for the chieftain and his train.

        [MACLEAN *and* LOCHTARISH, *&c., without speaking, quit*
        the hall through the crowd of attendants, who divide, and
        form a line to let them pass. HELEN, *who had sunk down*
        almost senseless upon her seat, seeing the hall cleared of the
        crowd, who go out after the MACLEANS, *now starts up, and*
        catches hold of ARGYLL *with an imploring look of strong*
        distress.

Helen. O father! well I know foul are his crimes,
    But what—O what, am I, that for my sake
    This bloody strife should be?—O think, my lord!
    He gave consent and sanction to my death,
    But thereon could not look: and at your gate—
    E'en on your threshold, must his life be ta'en?
    For well I know the wrath of Lorne is deadly.
    And gallant Lorne himself, if scath should be,—
    O pity! pity!—O for pity stay them!
Arg. Let go thy hold, weak woman: pity now!
    Rosa, support her hence.

        [*Committing her to* ROSA, *who now comes forward, and*
        tearing himself away.
Helen (*endeavouring to run after him, and catch hold of him again*).
    O be not stern! beneath the ocean rather

Would I had sunk to rest, than been the cause
Of horrid strife like this! O pity! pity!

> [*Exeunt, she running out after him distractedly.*

SCENE IV.

Before the gate of the castle: a confused noise of an approaching crowd heard within, and presently enter, from the gate, MACLEAN, BENLORA, LOCHTARISH, *and* GLENFADDEN, *with their attendants, conducted by* LORNE, *and followed by a crowd of Campbells, who range themselves on both sides of the stage.*

Lorne (to MACLEAN).

    Now, chieftain, we the gate have pass'd,—the bound
    That did restrain us. Host and guest no more,
    But deadly foes we stand, who from this spot
    Shall never both with life depart. Now, turn,
    And boldly say to him, if so thou darest,
    Who calls thee villain, murd'rer, traitor, coward,
    That he belies thee. Turn then, chief of Mull!
    Here, man to man, my single arm to thine,
    I give thee battle; or, refusing this,
    Our captive here retain thee to be tried
    Before the summon'd vassals of our clans,
    As suits thy rank and thine atrocious deeds.
    Take thou thy choice.

Mac.   Yes, John of Lorne, I turn.
    This turf on which we tread my death-bed is;
    This hour my latest term; this sky of light
    The last that I shall look on. Draw thy sword:
    The guilt of many crimes o'erwhelms my spirit
    But never will I shame my brave Macleans,
    By dying, as their chief, a coward's death.

Ben. What! shalt thou fight alone, and we stand by
    Idly to look upon it?

> [*Going up fiercely to* LORNE.

          Turn me out
The boldest, brawniest Campbell of your bands;
Ay, more than one, as many as you will;
And I the while, albeit these locks be grey,
Leaning my aged back against this tree,
Will show your youngsters how, in other days,
Macleans did fight, when baited round with foes.

Lorne. Be still, Benlora; other sword than these,
    Thy chief's and mine, shall not this day be drawn.
    If I prevail against him, here with us
    Our captives you remain. If I be conquer'd,
    Upon the faith and honour of a chieftain,
    Ye shall again to Mull in safety go.

Ben. Spoken like a noble chieftain!

Lorne. Ye shall, I say, to Mull in safety go.
    But there prepare ye to defend your coast
    Against a host of many thousand Campbells.
    In which, be well assured, swords as good
    As John of Lorne's, to better fortune join'd,
    Shall of your crimes a noble vengeance take.

        [LORNE *and* MACLEAN *fight; and, after a combat of some*
        length, MACLEAN *is mortally wounded, and the* CAMPBELLS
        give a loud shout.

Mac. It is enough, brave Lorne; this wound is death:
    And better deed thou couldst not do upon me,
    Than rid me of a life disgraced and wretched.
    But guilty though I be, thou seest full well,
    That to the brave opposed, arms in hand,
    I am no coward.—Oh! could I as bravely,
    In home-raised broils, with violent men have striv'n,
    It had been well: but there, alas! I proved
    A poor, irresolute, and nerveless wretch.

        [*After a pause, and struggling for breath.*
    To live, alas! in good men's memories
    Detested and contemn'd:—to be with her
    For whom I thought to be—Come, gloomy grave!
    Thou coverest all!

[*After another painful struggle, every one standing in
deep silence round him, and* LORNE *bending over him
compassionately.*

                        Pardon of man I ask not,
And merit not.—Brave Lorne, I ask it not;
Though in thy piteous eye a look I see
That might embolden me.—There is above
One who doth know the weakness of our nature,—
Our thoughts and conflicts:—all that e'er have breathed,
The bann'd and bless'd must pass to Him:—my soul
Into His hands, in humble penitence,
I do commit.

                                         [*Dies.*

Lorne. And may Heaven pardon thee, unhappy man!

      Enter ARGYLL, *and* HELEN *following him, attended by* ROSA.

Lorne (to attendants). Alas, prevent her!

                        [*Endeavouring to keep her back.*
                Helen, come not hither:
This is no sight for thee.
Helen (pressing forward, and seeing the body).
          Oh! oh! and hast thou dealt with him so quickly,
Thou fell and ruthless Lorne?—No time allow'd?

                           [*Kneeling by the body.*
O that within that form sense still were lodged!
To hear my voice,—to know that in my heart
No thought of thee—Let others scan thy deeds,
Pitied and pardon'd art thou here.

                          [*Her hand on her breast.*
                  Alas!
So quickly fell on thee th' avenging stroke,
No sound of peace came to thy dying ear,
No look of pity to thy closing eyes!
Pitied and pardon'd art thou in this breast,
But canst not know it now.—Alas! alas!

Arg. (to attendants). Prepare ye speedily to move the body.
 Mean time, our prisoners within the castle
 Secure ye well.

> [*To other attendants, who lay hold of* LOCHTARISH *and*
> GLENFADDEN, *while* BENLORA, *drawing his sword, attacks
> furiously those who attempt to seize and disarm him, and
> they, closing round and endeavouring to overpower him, he
> is mortally wounded in the scuffle.*

Ben. Ay, bear me now within your prison walls;
 Alive indeed, thought ye to bind me? No.
 Two years within your dungeons have I lived,
 But lived for vengeance: closed that hope, the earth
 Close o'er me too!—Alive to bind Benlora!

> [*Falls.*

Lorne (running up to him).
 Ha! have ye slain him?—Fierce and warlike spirit!
 I'm glad that thou hast had a soldier's death,
 Arms in thy hands, all savage as thou art.

> [*Turning to* LOCHTARISH *and* GLENFADDEN.

 But thou, the artful, base, contriving villain,
 Who hast of an atrocious, devilish act
 The mover been, and this thy vile associate,
 Prepare ye for the villains' shameful end,
 Ye have so dearly earn'd.

> [*Waving his hand for the attendants to lead them off.*

Loch. Be not so hasty, Lorne.—Thinkst thou indeed
 Ye have us here within your grasp, and nought
 Of hostage or security retain'd
 For our protection?
Lorne.   What dost thou mean?
Loch. Deal with us as ye will:
 But if within a week, return'd to Mull,
 In safety I appear not, with his blood,
 The helpless heir, thy sister's infant son,
 Who in my mother's house our pledge is kept,
 Must pay the forfeit.

Helen (starting up from the body in an agony of alarm).
    O horrible! ye will not murder him?
    Murder a harmless infant!
Loch. My aged mother, lady, loves her son
    As thou dost thine; and she has sworn to do it.
Helen. Has sworn to do it! Oh! her ruthless nature
    Too well I know.
    (*To* LORNE *eagerly.*) Loose them, and let them go!
Lorne. Let fiends like these escape?
Arg. (*to* HELEN).   He does but threaten
    To move our fears: they dare not slay the child.
Helen. They dare! they will!—O if thou art my father!
    If Nature's hand e'er twined me to thy heart
    As this poor child to mine, have pity on me!
    Loose them and let them go!—Nay, do it quickly.
    O what is vengeance? Spare my infant's life!
    Unpitying Lorne!—art thou a brother too?
    The hapless father's blood is on thy sword,
    And wilt thou slay the child? O spare him! spare him!

        [*Kneeling to* ARGYLL *and* LORNE, *who stand irresolute,
        when enter* SIR HUBERT DE GREY, *carrying something in
        his arms, wrapped up in a mantle, and followed by* MORTON.
        On seeing* SIR HUBERT, *she springs from the ground, and
        rushes forward to him.*

    Ha! art thou here? in blessed hour return'd
    To join thy prayers with mine,—to move their hearts—
    Their flinty hearts;—to bid them spare my child!
De Grey (lifting up the mantle, and showing a sleeping child).
    The prayer is heard already: look thou here
    Beneath this mantle where he soundly sleeps.

        [HELEN *utters a cry of joy, and holds out her arms for the
        child, but at the same time sinks to the ground, embracing
        the knees of* SIR HUBERT. ARGYLL *and* LORNE *run up to
        him, and all their vassals, &c., crowding round close them
        about on every side, while a general murmur of exultation is
        heard through the whole.* LOCHTARISH *and* GLENFADDEN,
        remaining on the side of the stage with those who guard
        them, are struck with astonishment and consternation.*

Arg. (to those who guard LOCHTARISH, *&c. stepping forward from the*
    crowd). Lead to the grated keep your prisoners,
    There to abide their doom. Upon the guilty
    Our vengeance falls, and only on the guilty.
    To all their clan beside, in which I know
    Full many a gallant heart included is,
    I still extend a hand of amity.
    If they reject it, fair and open war
    Between us be: and trust we still to find them
    The noble, brave Macleans, the valiant foes,
    That, ere the dark ambition of a villain,
    For wicked ends, their gallant minds had warp'd,
    We heretofore had found them.
                        O that men
    In blood so near, in country, and in valour,
    Should spend in petty broils their manly strength,
    That might, united for the public weal,
    On foreign foes such noble service do!
    O that the day were come when gazing southron,
    Whilst these our mountain warriors, marshall'd forth
    To meet in foreign climes their country's foes,
    Along their crowded cities slowly march,
    To sound of warlike pipe, their plaided bands,
    Shall say, with eager fingers pointing thus,
    "Behold those men!—their sunn'd but thoughtful brows:
    Their sinewy limbs; their broad and portly chests,
    Lapp'd in their native vestments, rude but graceful!—
    Those be our hardy brothers of the north;—
    The bold and gen'rous race, who have, beneath
    The frozen circle and the burning line,
    The rights and freedom of our native land
    Undauntedly maintain'd."
                      That day will come,
    When in the grave this hoary head of mine,
    And many after heads, in death are laid;
    And happier men, our sons, shall live to see it.
    O may they prize it too with grateful hearts;
    And, looking back on these our stormy days

Of other years, pity, admire, and pardon
The fierce, contentious, ill-directed valour
Of gallant fathers, born in darker times!

                                    [*The curtain drops.*

THE PHANTOM:

A MUSICAL DRAMA,

IN TWO ACTS.

PERSONS OF THE DRAMA.

MEN.

DUNARDEN, *Highland chief.*
MALCOLM, *his son.*
THE PROVOST OF GLASGOW.
CLAUDE, *his son.*
CRAWFORD, *friend of Claude.*
GRAHAM.
ALLEN, CULLOCH, *and other Highlanders.*
      Sexton, servants, and other inhabitants of Glasgow.

ALICE, *daughter of the* Provost of Glasgow.
MARIAN, *daughter of* DUNARDEN.
JESSIE, ATTENDING ON *Marian.*
      Bride, bridemaids, housekeeper, &c.

Scene, in the Western Highlands of Scotland,
and afterwards in the city of Glasgow.

ACT I.

SCENE I.

*A green lawn, surrounded with rocks, and mountains seen in the distance.
An assembly of Highlanders are discovered, holding bridal revelry: bagpipes
playing, and a noise of voices heard, as the curtain draws up.*

Enter ALLEN.

1st *high.* Welcome, brave Allen! we began to fear
 The water-kelpy, with her swathing arms,
 Had drown'd thee at the ford.
2d *high.* Faith did we, man! thee and thy shelty too.
Allen. Am I so late? There's time enough, I hope,
 To foot a measure with the bonnie bride,
 And maidens too.—'Tis well I'm come at all:
 I met the ill-eyed carline on my way.
1st *high.* And suffer'd scath by her?
Allen.   Ay, scath enough:
 My shelty, in the twinkling of an eye,
 Became so restive, neither switch nor heel
 Could move him one step further.
2d *high.* And so you were obliged to come on foot.
Allen. What could I do? It was not with the beast
 I held contention, but the evil spell
 Of that untoward witch.—Ay, but for that,
 I would defy the wildest four-legg'd thing
 In all Lochaber so to master me!
1st *high.* Well, well; the pipes are playing merrily,—
 Make up lost time as fleetly as thou canst.
Allen. And so I will; for here are rosy partners,
 Ribbon'd and cockernonied, by my faith!
 Like very queens. They make, here as I stand,
 Each garter'd leg to thrill, and toes to tickle.
    [*Seizing one of a group of girls, advancing from the dancers
    at the bottom of the stage.*

Come, winsome Jean! I'll have a reel with thee.
Look not so coy: where did I meet thee last?
We have not had a merry-making here
Since Duncan Mory's latewake.
Jean. Say nought of latewakes here, I warn you well:
Wot ye who is the bridesmaid?
Allen. Some gentle dame, belike.
Jean.   Some gentle dame!
Dumbarton Mary, with her Lowland airs.
Allen. Ay! she that look'd so stern, and said it was
A savage thing, or some such word as that,
To dance at old Glenlyon's funeral.—
But, could the laird himself have raised his head,
He with his ivory stick had rapp'd her pate
For marring with her mincing gentleness
The decent bravery of his last rouse.—
Come, let us have a merry reel together.
> [*They mix with dancers, who now advance to the front,
> where a bumpkin, or dance of many interwoven reels, is
> performed; after which the bride is led to a seat, and some of
> her maidens sit by her.*

Bridegroom. Now, while the bride and bonnie maidens all
Take needful rest, we'll pass the cheering cup.
And, Rory of Glenoruch, clear thy throat,
And sing some merry song, meet for a wedding,
Where all are boon and gay.
Bride. O, never mind for that! give us the song
Which thou wast wont on Clachen braes to sing,
And we to praise. Thou knowst the song I mean.
Rory. On bridal day the bride must be obey'd:
But 'tis a song devised for gentle-folks,
Made by the youthful laird of Ballamorin,
And not for common clansfolk like ourselves.
Bride. But let us have it ne'ertheless, good Rory;
It shows how sweetly thwarted lovers meet
O' moonlight nights, and talk of happy times
Which fortune has in store for faithful hearts:
The silliest moorland herd can follow that.

Rory. Then be it as you please: I'll do my best.

SONG.

I've seen the moon gleam through the cave,
    And minute drops like diamonds glancing;
I've seen, upon a heaving wave,
    The tressy-headed mermaid dancing:
But ne'er was seen, in summer night,
    Beneath the moon, in brightness riding,
A moving thing, to charm the sight,
    Like Flora to her Malcolm gliding.

I've heard a pibroch, through the wind,
    As absent chief his home was nearing;
A half-stripp'd infant, sweetly kind,
    With mimic words its mother cheering:
But ne'er were evening sounds so sweet,
    As, near the spot of promise stealing,
The quick, soft tread of Flora's feet,
    Then whisper'd words, herself revealing.

My boat I've fastened to the stake,
    And on the shelly beach am pacing,
While she is passing moor and brake,
    On heather braes her shadow tracing;
And here we'll pass a happy hour,
    For hours and years of bliss preparing,
When we shall grace our girdled tower,
    Lands, life, and love, together sharing.

Enter CULLOCH.

Allen. Ha! our young chief must be return'd, for here
    Comes Culloch, with his staring freckled face.
Omnes (gathering round CULLOCH).
    Well, man, what are thy news? where hast thou been?
Cul. We've been at Glasgow.

1st high.   Glasgow! Save us all!

Allen (half aside to 1st high.). I doubt it not: his master, I hear say,
    Goes oftener there than his good father wots of;
    Ay, or his sister either. I suspect
    There is some dainty lady—

1st high.   Hush! say nothing.

Allen. And so, brave Culloch, thou hast travell'd far:
    And what is Glasgow like?

Cul. Like all Drumleary craigs set up in rows,
    And chimneys smoking on the top of them.
    It is an awful sight!

1st high. And what sawst thou besides the craigs and chimneys?

Cul. There be six kirks,—I told them on my fingers;
    And, rising from the slates of every kirk,
    There is a tower, where great bells ring so loud,
    That you might hear them, standing on this sward,
    Were they on great Benlawers.

1st high. Tut! tut! thy ears are better than thy wits.

Bride. And sawst thou any silken ladies there,
    With all their bravery on?

Cul. Ay, ladies, gentlemen, and red-coat soldiers,
    And plaided drovers, standing at the cross,
    As close as heather stalks on Hurroch moss.
    Ah! well I trow it is an awful place!

Allen (aside as before). And well I trow the chief has business there
    He wishes no observer to discover,
    When he, of all the idle household loons,
    Took such an oaf as Culloch to attend him.
    But I'll e'en go, before he join the dance,
    And have a private word of him, to favour
    My poor old mother in her ruin'd cot.
    I know full well he will not say me nay,
    Though the old laird himself be cold and close.

1st high. Go, then, and speed thee well!

                           [*Exit* ALLEN.

Bridegroom. Hear, bonnie lassies! the young laird himself
    Will soon be here, and foot it with you featly.

Old woman. O, bless his comely face! among you all
  There is not one that foots the floor like him,—
  With such a merry glee and manly grace!
Bridegroom. We'll have no further dancing till he come.
  Meantime, good Rory, sing another song;
  Both bride and maidens like thy chanting well:
  And those who list may join the chorus rhyme.

SONG.

Upon her saddle's quilted seat,
  High sat the bonnie Lowland bride;
Squires rode before, and maidens sweet
  Were gently ambling by her side.
What makes her look so pale and wan?—
She's parted from her Highlandman.
    What makes her look, &c.

Where'er they pass'd, at every door
  Stood maids and wives the sight to see;
Curs bark'd, and bairnies by the score
  Ran bawling loud and merrily,
But still the bride looks dull and wan;
She's thinking of her Highlandman.
    But still the bride, &c.

The Lowland laird, in bridegroom's gear,
  Prick'd forth to meet the fair array;
His eye was bright, his voice was clear,
  And every word was boon and gay.
Ah! little did he reckon then
Of bold and burly Highlandmen.
    Ah! little did he reckon, &c.

The bride she raised her drooping brow,
  And red as crimson turn'd her cheek.—
What sound is that? The war-pipe now
  Descending from yon broomy peak.
It sounds like marching of a clan;

O can it be her Highlandman?
   It sounds like, &c.

Their bonnets deck'd with heather green,
   Their shoulders broad with tartans bound,
Their checker'd hose were plainly seen
   Right fleetly moving to the sound.
Quick beat her heart, within a ken,
To see the valiant Highlandmen.
    Quick beat her heart, &c.

Now challenge-shout is heard, and soon
   The bare claymores are flashing bright;
And off scour'd many a Lowland loon,
   Who ill could brook the fearful sight.
"The fiend," quoth they, "from cave and glen
Has pour'd those stalwart Highlandmen.
    "The fiend," quoth they, &c.

Then pistols from their holsters sprang,
   Then wax'd the skirmish fierce and hot,
Blades clashing fell, and harness rang,
   And loudly bluster'd fire and shot;
For, sooth to say, the bridegroom then
Full bravely met the Highlandmen.
    For, sooth to say, &c.

And so did all his near o' kin,
   As Lowland race such stour may bide:
But sank, at last, the mingled din,
   And where was then the bonnie bride?
Ay, ask at those who answer can;
Ask at the cunning Highlandman.
    Ay, ask at those, &c.

The bridegroom, in a woeful plight,
   Back to his furnish'd hall has gone,
Where spread on boards so gaily dight,

Cold has the wedding banquet grown.
How changed since break of morning, when
He thought not of the Highlandmen!
    How changed since, &c.

And who, upon Benledi's side,
    Beneath his shieling blest and gay,
Is sitting by that bonnie bride,
    While round them moves the light strathspey?
It is the flower of all his clan,—
It is her gallant Highlandman.
    It is the flower, &c.

Re-enter ALLEN, *snapping his fingers, and footing the ground, as he speaks.*

Allen. I've seen him, sirs; I have had words of him.
1st high. Had words of whom?
Allen.   Of the young laird himself.
Omnes. Hast thou? and is he coming to the green?
Allen. He bade me say he'll join you in the evening.
Omnes. And not till then?
Allen.   Some strangers have arrived.
    And I have seen them too: the lady's mounted
    Upon a milk-white nag; and o'er her saddle
    A scarlet cloth is spread, both deep and wide,
    With bobs and fringes deck'd right gallantly;
    And in her riding gear she sits with grace
    That might become the daughter of a chief,
    Ay, or the king himself.
1st high. Perhaps it is the Glasgow provost's daughter,
    Who is, as they have said, the very match
    That our old laird is planning for his son.
Allen. Ay, he may plan, but love will have its way,—
    Free, fitful love thinks scorn of prudent planning.
    No, young Dunarden went not to the town
    With simple Culloch for his sole attendant,
    To see the provost's daughter.
Bride (to ALLEN*).* And so he will not join us till the evening?

Allen. No, damsels; but here are ribands for the bride,
  And for you all, which he has sent by me.
  Now they who have the nimblest hands among you,
  Will catch their favourite colours as they fly.

> [*Pulls out ribands from his pouch, and dances about in a
> whirling figure to the bottom of the stage, strewing about
> pieces of ribands, while the girls follow, to catch them as
> they fall.*

> [*Exeunt.*

SCENE II.

The hall in the tower of DUNARDEN. *Enter* DUNARDEN *and Marian.*

Dun. (*speaking as they enter*).
  In sooth, she well may grace a noble mansion,
  Or chieftain's hall, or palace of a prince,
  Albeit her veins swell not with ancient blood.
  If so much grace and sweetness cannot please him,
  He must be ill to win. And by my faith!
  Perhaps she is this same mysterious lady,
  To whom, as thou suspectest, his late visits,
  So frequent and so long, have been devoted.
Marian. Ah, no! I fear another has his heart,—
  His constant heart, whom he, at least, will think
  Fairer than this sweet maid, or all besides.
Dun. And if it should be so, will nothing please him
  But the top-flower of beauty and perfection?
  The second best, methinks, ay, or the third,
  Where fortune gilds the prize, might suit him well.
  Why dost thou shake thy head?
Marian. What might be, and what is, stand far apart,
  When age and youth on the same objects look.
Dun. Was I not young, when, of thy grandsire's daughters,
  I chose the fairest, and was plainly told
  Her heart and hand were promised to another?
  But did I then perversely mope and pine?

No, I trow not: I clear'd my cloudy brow,
And woo'd the second fairest, thy poor mother.
Marian. So will not he.
Dun.   Why so: belike he will not,
If thou abet his folly, as, methinks,
Thou art inclined to do.
Marian. No, father; not inclined: I shall regret
As much as you, if any prepossession
Prevent him from approving this fair maid,
Who is, indeed, most gentle and engaging.
Dun. Out on thy prepossessions! Younger sons,
Who may be soldiers, sailors, drovers, ay,
Or tinkers if they will, may choose a mate
With whom, o'er sea or land, through burgh or city,
To scour the world. But for the elder born,
Who must uphold the honours of the race,—
His ancient race,—he is not thus at liberty
To please a youthful fancy.
Marian. But yet, dear sir, you may be ignorant—
Dun. What! am I ignorant? Do I not know
The world sufficiently to guide and counsel
Those through whose body my own blood is flowing?
Not many men have had more opportunity
To know men and their ways, and I have turn'd it
To some account; at least I fain would think so.
I have been thrice in Edinburgh, as thou knowest,
In London once, in Glasgow many times;
And I, forsooth, am ignorant!
Marian.   Dear father!
You would not hear me out: I did not mean
That you were ignorant of aught belonging
To worldly wisdom; but his secret heart,
As I have said before, his prepossessions—
Dun. And what has he to do with prepossessions?
He is, of all men, bound to wed for wealth,
Since he, with his unceasing liberalities,
Would bare me to the quick. No tacksman dies,
But he must have appointed for his widow

A house, with right of browsing for her goats,
And pasture for a cow, all free of charge.
The bedrid carlines, too, and orphan brats,
Come all on me, through his petitioning;
And I, God help me! have been weak enough
To grant such suits too often.

Marian. You will not say so on your dying day.

Dun. For that, indeed, it may be well enough;
But for our living days, I needs must say,
It doth not suit at all.—If he were frugal,
And would with care lay up what is our own,
Having some hoarded store, he might more reasonably
Indulge his prepossessions, as you phrase it.

Marian. Nay, be not angry with him.

Dun.   Angry with him!
Such want of reason would provoke a saint!
Is he to spend the rents with open hand,
Stretch'd out to all who need, or all who ask;
And please himself besides, by an alliance
With some slight May, who brings but smiles and bloom
To pay the yearly charges of her state?

Marian. We do not know her yet, and cannot say
That she is poor.

Dun.   But we may shrewdly guess.
Else why those stealthy visits,—this concealment?
Oh, 'tis provoking! This, our Provost's daughter,
Is just the match that would have suited us,—
That would support our house, and clear our lands,
And he, forsooth!—I'll cast him from my favour!

Marian. I know you will not.

Dun.   Lady Achinmore,
If he persist, I'll say and do it too.
His prepossessions truly! mighty plea!
Supported, too, by Lady Achinmore.
                          [*Walking in wrath to the other end of the hall.*

Marian (aside). I'll hold my tongue, and let the storm subside;
For when he calls me Lady Achinmore,
Reply is worse than useless.

Dun. (*returning*). Methinks the lady tarries in her chamber.

Marian. To lay aside her travelling attire,
　　And put her robe or fashion'd mantua on,
　　Requires some time.

Dun. And where is Malcolm? Surely he should be
　　In readiness, for very decency,
　　To bid a stranger lady welcome here.

Marian. He will appear ere long, and is, perhaps,
　　Attending on her brother.

Dun.　　　　　　　　　No, he is not.
　　I saw young Denison walk forth alone,
　　As if to look for him.

Marian.　　　　　　　Here comes the lady.

Enter Alice.

Dun. Ah, gentle lady! were I half the man
　　That once I was (how many years gone by
　　We shall not say), you should to this poor hold,—
　　To these old walls which your fair presence brightens,
　　A rousing welcome have. But times are changed,
　　And fashion now makes all things dull and spiritless.

Alice. My welcome, as it is, gives me such pleasure,
　　I will not think of what it might have been.
　　Your daughter has received me with a kindness
　　That has already freed me from restraint,
　　And given me courage to express my pleasure.

Marian (*to her*). Thanks to thee, gentle friend! so may I call thee,
　　Knowing so well thy worth. Might we retain thee
　　Some weeks beneath our roof, then we might boast
　　That our poor welcome had not miss'd its aim.

Dun. Some weeks! We'll try to turn those weeks to months,
　　And then, who knows but that our mountain soil
　　May e'en prove warm enough for Lowland flow'r
　　Therein to flourish sweetly.

Alice. Thanks, noble sir; but we must go tomorrow.

Dun. So soon! the daughter of my early friend
　　Beneath my roof, seen like a Will o' th' wisp,

Glancing and vanishing! It must not be.
Were I but half the man that once I was,
I'd fight thy stubborn brother hand to hand,
And glaive to glaive, but he should tarry longer,
Or leave his charge behind him.

Alice. Nay, blame him not: it was his own good will
That made him from our nearest homeward route,
Though press'd for time, start these long miles aside,
To pay his father's friend a passing visit;
For Malcolm, he believed, was still in Glasgow,
So rumour said.

Dun. I thank his courtesy;
But, if my name be Fergus of Dunarden,
Neither the morrow, nor next morrow's morrow
Shall see thee quit my tow'r. I'll go and find him,
And tell him thou thyself art captive here,
Though others be in thraldom of thy beauty,
And shalt not be released.

[*Exit.*

Marian. Thou seest how gallantly old hearts will warm
At sight of winning youth. He almost woos thee:
And yet I would not pay a stepdame's duty,
Where I would rather yield a sister's love.

Alice. These words of kindness! Oh, you will undo me
With so much kindness!

[*Bursts into tears.*

Marian. Dear, gentle creature! Have I given thee pain?
I have unwittingly—

Alice. Done nought amiss.
I have a silly weakness in my nature:
I can bear frowning coldness or neglect,
But kindness makes me weep.

Marian. And can it be that coldness or neglect
Should e'er be thine to bear?

Alice. Better than I have borne it.

Marian. Better than thou! In all your stately city,
Is there a lady fairer than thyself?

Alice. Yes, Lady Achinmore, there is a creature
    Whose beauty changes every other face
    To an unnoticed blank; whose native grace
    Turns dames of courtly guise to household damsels;
    Whose voice of winning sweetness makes the tones
    Of every other voice intruding harshness.
Marian. And if there be, conceit will mar it all;
    For too much homage, like the mid-day sun,
    Withers the flower it brightens.
Alice. It may be so with others, not with her.
Marian. Thou lovest her, then?
Alice.   O, yes! I love her dearly;
    And if I did not, I should hate myself.
    Heed not these tears, nor think, because I weep
    In saying that I love her, aught lurks here,
    Begrudging her felicity. O, no!
Marian (*taking her hands affectionately*). Sweet Alice! why so moved?
Alice. 'Tis my infirmity: I am a fool,
    And should not go from home, so to expose
    A mind bereft of all becoming firmness.
Marian (*embracing her*). Come to my bosom; thou hast but exposed
    That which the more endears thee to my heart;
    And, wert thou firmer, I should love thee less.
    But, hush! let me kiss off those falling tears
    From thy soft cheek. I hear thy brother coming.
Alice. Thy brother?
Marian. No; thine own,—thy brother *Claude.*
    Ha! Malcolm, too, is with him! this is well.

Enter MALCOLM *and* CLAUDE, *whilst* ALICE *composes herself, and endeavours to look cheerful.*

Mal. Fair Alice, welcome to our Highland mountains!
    Which, as your brother tells me, you admire,
    In spite of all their lone and silent barrenness.
Alice. He tells you true: our fertile Lowland dales,
    With all their crofts and woodlands richly chequer'd,
    Have less variety than their bare sides.

Mal. Yes, when fleet shadows of the summer clouds,
    Like stag-hounds on the chase, each other follow
    Along their purple slopes; or when soft haze
    Spreads o'er them its light veil of pearly grey,
    Through the slight rents of which the sunshine steals,
    Showing bright colour'd moss and mottled stones,
    Like spots of polish'd beauty,—they appear
    Objects of varied vision most attractive.

Alice. Then, to behold them in their winter guise,
    As I have never done!

Mal. You might then see their forms enlarged and dark,
    Through the dim drapery of drifted rain,
    Like grim gigantic chieftains in array,
    Bidding defiance to approaching host;
    Or lifting their black shoulders o'er the mass
    Of volumed vapour gather'd round their base,
    Which seem like islands raised above the earth
    In purer regions of the firmament.

Alice. And then how sweet the bushy glens between them,
    Where waterfalls shoot from the rocks, and streams
    Course on their wimpled way with brawling din!

Mal. Where low-roof'd cots, with curling smoke are seen,
    Each with its little stack of winter fuel,
    And scanty lot of furrow'd corn-land near;
    And groups of hardy imps, who range at will,
    Or paddle in the brook, while bearded goats
    Browse on the rocky knolls, and kids are sporting
    Among the yellow broom.

Claude. Pray thee have done, good Malcolm; thou wilt fill
    This girl's fancy with romantic visions,
    Which may, perhaps, make the rich, fertile fields
    Of her own country seem insipid things.

Marian (to CLAUDE). One thing, you would observe, he has omitted
    In the description of his bonnie glen,—
    The cottage matron, with her cumbrous spade,
    Digging the stubborn soil; and lazy husband
    Stretch'd on the ground, or seated by the door,
    Or on his bagpipe droning some dull dirge.

Mal. Well, freely I confess our mountain matrons
    In useful virtues do excel their mates;
    And in what earthly region is it otherwise?
Claude. I dare not contradict thee, and be deem'd
    Ungallant for my pains.

Enter a Servant, who delivers a packet to CLAUDE.

Alice.   Is it from Glasgow?
    Is there within the cover aught for me?
Claude. There is a letter with thy name upon it.
            [MALCOLM *withdraws some paces from her.*
Alice. Which, ne'ertheless, thou keepest to thyself,
    With eyes intently fix'd upon the writing.
    Is it a stranger's hand to thee unknown?
Claude (*giving the letter*). No, not unknown.
Alice. It is from Emma Graham (*to* MARIAN), and with your leave,
    I'll read it by this window.
        [*Turns round, and starts upon finding* MALCOLM *close to her.*
Marian. Why do you start?
Alice.   I knew not he was near me.
Mal. (*in confusion*). I crave your pardon: 'twas unwittingly;
    I scarcely know myself why I return'd.
        [ALICE *opens the letter, whilst* CLAUDE *and* MALCOLM *stand
        gazing anxiously on her as she reads it to herself.*
Mal. (*to* ALICE, *who seems to have come to the conclusion*).
    Your friends are well, I hope; all's well in Glasgow?
Alice. She says a deadly fever rages there,
    And nought is seen along their dismal streets
    But funeral processions; nothing heard
    But death-bells tolling, and the hammer's sound
    Nailing in haste the corse's narrow house.
Mal. (*agitated*). And she herself amidst this wreck of life!
Alice. She is, ere this, removed from the contagion;
    For these concluding lines inform me plainly,
    That she and all her family were prepared
    To leave the town upon the following day
    To that on which her letter has its date.

Mal. (*eagerly*). I thank thee, Alice.

Claude (*peevishly*). Wherefore dost thou thank her?

Mal. (*haughtily*). Whate'er thou hast a right to ask of me
Shall have its answer.

Marian (*to* CLAUDE).
When Highland pride is touch'd, some lack of courtesy
Must be excused. You have not from this window
Admired the falling of our mountain stream.
[*Leads him to the bottom of the hall, and detains him there
in apparent conversation.*

Mal. (*in a softened voice*). So, gentle Alice, thou'rt in friendship knit
With Emma Graham! and meet companions are ye!
[*Looking closer to the letter, which she still holds open in
her hand.*

Forgive me; Lowland ladies far surpass,
As fair and ready scribes, our mountain maids:
I ne'er before saw lines by her indited.

Alice (*putting it up hastily; then hesitating, then recovering herself.*)
No; why should I withhold it from thine eye;
For still the sweet expressions from her pen
Excel the beauty of its characters.
[*Gives it to him.*

Peruse it then (*aside, as she turns from him*) while I peruse myself.

Mal. (*returning the letter, after having read it*).
Thou art in tears, sweet Alice; has thy mind
Some boding apprehensions for her safety?

Alice. No, God forbid! I have a feeble body,
The worn-out case of a more feeble mind,
And oft will weep for nothing. Heed me not

Mal. No, say not so: thy mind and body both
Are lovely yoke-fellows, and will together—
God grant it be so!—hold their prosp'rous course
For many years. (*Seeing her endeavours to speak.*)
Strive not to answer me;
This wish, though most sincere, deserves no thanks.

Enter DUNARDEN, *followed by Servants, carrying dishes of meat, &c.*

Dun. Come, honour'd guests, the first dish of our meal,
    Poor though it be, is passing to the board;
    Shall we not follow it? Although, in verity,
    I am ashamed that such a poor reception
    Is offer'd to such friends.
Marian. Dear sir, they will forgive what things are lacking,
    The heart's kind cheer not being of the number.
Dun. (*to* ALICE). Had I had timely notice of your coming,
    I had sent messengers for thirty miles,
    Cross moor and mountain, to invite our neighbours;
    And tables had been cover'd in this hall,
    Round which we should have held a merry feast.
    And this same wedding, too, detains the clan:
    So that our wings are clipt on every side.
Alice. Your courtesy is great: but surely, sir,
    A merry wedding well may make amends
    For a lost feast, e'en in Dunarden hall.
Dun. And so it shall, fair Alice.—Pardon me
    That I should be so bold to name you thus!
    At fall of eve we'll join their merriment;
    And thou shalt be my partner in the dance.

                        [*Taking her hand gallantly.*

    I'll have thee all and solely to myself;
    Unless, perhaps, if these old legs should fail,
    Thou wilt accept of this young Highlander

                        [*Pointing to Malcolm.*

    To be my substitute.—Come, gentles all!
    By this soft lily hand let me conduct
    The daughter of my old and honour'd friend;
    My trysted partner too. Aha! aha!

        [*Leading off Alice gaily with a strathspey step.*
                            [*Exeunt.*

SCENE III.

A lobby or entrance-room, with fire-arms, swords, and fishing-tackle hung on the walls. Servants are seen passing to and fro with plaids and bundles of heath in their hands.

Enter Housekeeper.

House. Make all the speed ye may: in the long chamber
　　　There must be twenty bed-frames quickly set,
　　　And stuff'd with heather for the tacksmen; ay,
　　　And for their women, in the further room,
　　　Fourteen besides, with plaidings for them all.
　　　The wedding folks have broken up their sport,
　　　And will be here before we are prepared.

Enter the Butler.

Butler. And what are twenty beds, when all the drovers,
　　　And all the shieling herdsmen from Bengorach,
　　　Must have a lair provided for the night.
House. And who says so?
Butler. 　　　　　　　　E'en the young laird himself.
House. 'Tis always so; Dunarden's courtesy,
　　　With all his honied words, costs far less trouble
　　　Than young Dunarden's thoughtless kindness doth.
　　　The foul fiend take them all! Have we got plaids
　　　For loons like them!
Butler. Faith, we at least must try to find them bedding.
House. Let each of them find on the green hill sward
　　　The breadth of his own back, and that, I trow,
　　　Is bed enough for them. Herdsmen, indeed!
　　　　　　　　　　　[*Several servants coming all about together.*
　　　More plaids! more plaids! we have not yet enow.
Another servant. An Elspy says the gentlefolks must have
　　　Pillows and other gear.

House. Out on you! clamouring round me with your wants,
　　Like daws about the ruin'd turret! think ye
　　That I—I am distracted with you all!
Butler (aside). And with some cups of good Ferntosh besides.
House. Howe'er the shieling herdsmen may be lodged,
　　I have provided for the Lowland strangers
　　Right handsomely.
Butler. The bed of state, no doubt, is for the lady,
　　And for the gentleman the arras chamber.
House. Thou art all wrong: the arras is so ragged,
　　And bat holes in the cornice are so rife,
　　That Lady Achinmore bade me prepare
　　His lodging in the north side of the tower,
　　Beside Dunarden's chamber.
Butler. They leave the house to-morrow, waiting only
　　To take a social breakfast. My best wine
　　And good Ferntosh must be upon the table,
　　To which the beef, and fish, and old ewe cheese
　　Will give a relish. And your pretty playthings
　　Of china saucers, with their fairy cups,
　　In which a wren could scarcely lay her egg,—
　　Your tea-pot, pouring from its slender beak
　　Hot water, as it were some precious drug,
　　Must be, for fashion's sake, set in array
　　To please the Lowland lady.
House. Mind thy concerns, and I will look to mine.
　　My pretty playthings are in daily use,
　　As I hear say, in the great town of Edinburgh;
　　And 'tis a delicate and wholesome beverage
　　Which they are filled withal. I like, myself,
　　To sip a little of it.
Butler.　　　　　　　Dainty dear!
　　No doubt thou dost; aught stronger would offend thee.
　　Thou wouldst, I think, call rue or wormwood sweet,
　　Were it the fashion in your town of Edinburgh.
　　But, hark! the bridal folks are at the door;
　　We must not parley longer.

　　　　　　　　　　　　　　　　[Music without.

I hear their piper playing the "Good-night."

Enter ALLEN.

Butler. They are at hand, I hear: and have ye had
    A merry evening, Allen?
Allen.   That we have.
    Dunarden danced with that sweet Lowland lady,
    As though it made him twenty years the younger.
House. Dunarden! Danced she not with young Dunarden,
    Who is, so says report, her destined husband?
Allen. Yes; at the end, for one dull reel or two
    They footed it together. But, believe me,
    If this rich Provost's daughter be not satisfied
    With being woo'd by substitute, which homage
    The old laird offers her abundantly,
    She'll ne'er be lady of this mansion; no,
    Nor of her many, many thousand marks,
    One golden piece enrich Dunarden's house.
House. Woe's me! our Malcolm is a wilful youth!
    And Lady Achinmore would dance with Claude?
Allen. She danced with him, and with the bridegroom also.
House. That, too, would be a match of furtherance
    To the prosperity of our old house.
Butler. But that she is a widow, and, I reckon,
    Some years his elder, it might likely be.
House. And why should that be such a mighty hindrance?
Allen. Fie, butler! dost thou utter, in such presence,
    Disqualifying words of age and widowhood?
House. You are mislearn'd and saucy, both of you.—
    But now they are at hand.

SONG *without, of several voices.*

The sun is down, and time gone by,
The stars are twinkling in the sky,
Nor torch nor taper longer may
Eke out a blithe but stinted day;

The hours have pass'd with stealthy flight,
We needs must part: good night, good night!

The bride unto her bower is sent,
And ribald song and jesting spent;
The lover's whisper'd words and few
Have bid the bashful maid adieu;
The dancing floor is silent quite,
No foot bounds there: good night, good night!

The lady in her curtain'd bed,
The herdsman in his wattled shed,
The clansmen in the heather'd hall,
Sweet sleep be with you, one and all!
We part in hopes of days as bright
As this gone by: good night, good night!

Sweet sleep be with us, one and all!
And if upon its stillness fall
The visions of a busy brain,
We'll have our pleasure o'er again,
To warm the heart, to charm the sight,
Gay dreams to all! good night, good night!

House. We've listened here too long: go all of you
    And get the rooms prepared! My head's distracted!
                                    [*Exeunt all, different ways.*

SCENE IV.

A bed-chamber. Enter ALICE *and* MARIAN, *with a Servant before them,
carrying lights.*

Marian. You must be tired with all this noisy merriment
    So closely following a lengthen'd journey.
Alice. To be among the happy and the kind
    Keeps weariness at bay; and yet I own
    I shall be glad to rest.

Marian. And may you find it, sound and undisturb'd!
　　There is among our household damsels here,
　　A humble friend of yours, the child of one
　　Who was your father's servant.
Alice. Ha! little Jessie, once my playfellow,
　　And since well known to me, as the attendant
　　Of a relation, in whose house I found her,
　　Some two years past: a gentle, faithful creature.
Marian. The same, she will attend upon you gladly,
　　And do what you require. See, here she is.

Enter JESSIE.

Alice. Jessie, my old acquaintance! I am glad
　　To find thee thus, domesticated happily
　　In such a home. I hope thou hast been well,
　　Since I last met with thee.
Jessie.　　　　　　　　　　I thank you, madam;
　　I am right well; and, were I otherwise,
　　To see you here would make me well again,
Marian (*to* ALICE). The greatest kindness I can show thee now
　　Is to retire, and leave thee to prepare
　　For what thou needst so much.
　　　　　　　　　　　　　　　　　　[*Kissing her.*
　　May sweet sound sleep refresh thee! Oh! it grieves me
　　To think that we must part with thee so soon;
　　And that ye are determined to return
　　To that infected city.
Alice. Be not afraid for us. We shall pass through it,
　　And only tarry for an hour or two.
　　Good night, and thanks for all your gentle kindness!
　　Thanks, in few words, but from my inmost heart!
　　　　　　　　　　　　　　　　　　[*Exit Marian.*
　　And thou art here, good JESSIE. I am glad,—
　　Right glad to see thee; but I'm tired and spent,
　　And (take it not unkindly) cannot speak
　　As I was wont to do.

[*Throws herself into a chair, whilst* JESSIE *begins to uncoil
her hair, and take out the ornaments.*

Jessie. I will prepare you for your bed, dear madam,
    As quickly as I can. To-morrow morning
    Your strength and spirits too will be restored.
Alice. Thou'rt a good creature. Dost thou still remember
    The pretty songs thou used to sing so sweetly?

SONG.

Jessie (singing gaily).

My heart is light, my limbs are light,
    My purse is light, my dear;
Yet follow me, my maiden bright,
    In faith! thou needst not fear.

The wallet on a rover's back
    Is scanty dower for thee,
But we shall have what lordies lack
    For all their golden fee.

The plume upon my bonnet bound,
    And broadsword by my side,
We'll follow to the war-pipe's sound,
    With fortune for our guide.

Light are my limbs, my purse, my heart,
    Yet follow me, my dear;
Bid Care good-bye, with kinsfolk part;
    In faith! thou needst not fear.

Alice. I thank thee: that was once a favourite song.
    I know not how it was; I liked it then
    For the gay reckless spirit of the tune.
    But there is one which I remember well,
    One my poor aunt was wont to bid thee sing;
    Let me have that, I pray thee.

SONG.

They who may tell love's wistful tale,
  Of half its cares are lighten'd;
Their bark is tacking to the gale,
  The sever'd cloud is brighten'd.

Love like the silent stream is found
  Beneath the willows lurking,
The deeper, that it hath no sound
  To tell its ceaseless working.

Submit, my heart; thy lot is cast,
  I feel its inward token;
I feel this mis'ry will not last,
  Yet last till thou art broken.

Alice. Thou singest sweetly, ay, and sadly too,
  Even as it should be sung. I thank thee, Jessie.
Jessie (*after having entirely undone her hair, and taken the fastenings from
  other parts of her dress*). Now, madam, let me fetch your gown
  and coif.
Alice. I want no further service, my good Jessie,
  I'll do the rest myself: and so, good night;
  I shall be soon in bed. Good night, and thanks.
Jessie. Not yet good night; I will return again,
  And take away the light.
Alice. Well; as thou wilt: but leave me for a while.

  [*Exit* Jessie.

    This day, with all its trials, is at length
    Come to an end. My wrung and wrestling heart!
    How is it with thee now? Thy fond delusions
    Lie strew'd and broken round thee, like the wrecks
    Of western clouds when the bright sun is set.
    We look upon them glowing in his blaze,
    And sloping wood, and purple promontory,
    And castled rock distinctly charm the eye:

What now remains but a few streaky fragments
Of melting vapour, cold and colourless?

[After a thoughtful pause.

There's rest when hope is gone—there should be rest.
And when I think of her who is the cause,
Should I complain? To be preferr'd to her!
Preferr'd to Emma Graham, whom I myself
Cannot behold but with an admiration
That sinks into the heart, and in the fancy
Goes hand in hand with every gentle virtue
That woman may possess or man desire!—
The thought was childish imbecility.
Away, away! I will not weep for this.
Heaven granting me the grace for which I'll pray
Humbly and earnestly, I shall recover
From this sad state of weakness. If she love him,
She'll make him happier far than I could do;
And if she love him not, there is good cause
That I should pity him; not selfishly
On my own misery dwell.—Ay, this should be;
But will it be?—Oh, these rebellious tears!

*[Covering her face with her hands, and throwing herself
back in her chair, in a state of abandonment. Enter, by the
other end of the chamber, the phantom of a beautiful young
woman, which advances a few paces, and then remains still.*

Alice (raising her face). Who's there?—Is there true vision in mine
eyes?

*[Rising quickly, and going with open arms towards the
phantom.*

Dear Emma! dear, dear Emma! how is this,
That thou art here, unlook'd for at this hour,
So many miles from home? Alas! that face
Of ghastly paleness, and that alter'd look
Of sad solemnity!—Speak to me quickly;
I dare approach no nearer, till I hear
Words of thy natural voice. Art thou alive?

Phantom. A term, short as the passing of a thought,
  Hath brought me from the chamber where my friends
  Are now lamenting round my lifeless body.
Alice. And 'tis thy spirit which before mine eyes
  Thy body's semblance wears: and thou art nothing
  That mortal hands may touch or arms encircle!
  O look not on me with that fixed look!
  Thou lovest me still, else thou hadst not been here,
  And yet I fear thee.
Phantom.   Fear me not, dear Alice!
  I yearn'd to look upon thee ere I pass
  That gulf which parts the living from the dead:
  And I have words to utter which thine ear
  Must listen to, thy mind retain distinctly.
Alice. Say what thou wilt; thou art a blessed spirit.
  And canst not do me harm.—
  I know it well: but let thy words be few;
  The fears of nature are increasing on me.
        [*Bending one knee to the ground.*
  O God! Lord of all beings, dead and living!
  Strengthen and keep me in this awful hour!
Phantom. And to thy fervent prayer I say, Amen.
  Let this assure thee, that, though diff'rent natures
  Invest us now, we are the children still
  Of one great Parent; thou in mortal weeds
  Of flesh and blood; I in a state inexplicable
  To human comprehension.—Hear my words.
Alice. I listen most intently.
Phantom. The room in which I died, hath a recess
  Conceal'd behind the arras, long disused
  And now forgotten; in it stands a casket,
  The clam shell of our house is traced upon it;
  Open, and read the paper therein lodged.
  When my poor body is to earth committed,
  Do this without delay. And now, farewell!
  I must depart.

Alice. Ah! whither, dearest Emma? Will a moment
  Transport thee to heaven's court of blessedness,
  To ecstasy and glory?
Phantom. These are presumptuous words. My place, appointed
  In mercy to a weak and sinful creature,
  I soon shall know. Farewell, till we shall meet,
  From sin, and fear, and doubt, released for ever!

  [*Exit.*

  [ALICE *stands trembling and gazing, as the phantom
  disappears, and then falls on the ground in a swoon.
  Presently re-enter* JESSIE.

Jessie. Mercy upon us! lying on the ground!
  Life is not gone; God grant it be not so!
  Lady, dear lady! No; she does not hear.

  [*Endeavours in vain to raise her, then runs off in great
  alarm, and is heard without, knocking and calling at the
  door of another chamber.*

(*Without.*) Open the door! Rise, Lady Achinmore.
Marian (*without*). I am not yet undress'd: what is the matter?
Jessie (*without*). Come to the lady's chamber: follow me.
Mal. (*without, opening the door of his apartment*). What has befallen?
  Is any one unwell?

Re-enter JESSIE, *followed by* MARIAN, *who both run to* ALICE, *raising her
from the floor, and one supporting her head, while the other chafes her
temples and the palms of her hands, &c.*

Marian. Support her drooping head, while from my closet
  I fetch some water, and restoring drugs,
  Whose potent smell revives suspended life.
Mal. (*looking in upon them from the door*). O leave her not! I'll find
  whate'er is wanting.

  [*Exit.*

Marian. There is a little motion of her lip;
  Her bosom heaves: thank God! life is not fled.
  How long hadst thou been absent from the room?
Jessie. Some little time; and thought, on my return,
  To find her gone to bed.

Marian. How was she when thou leftst her?
Jessie. She was well then.
Marian.   It hath been very sudden.

Re-enter MALCOLM, *with phials, &c.*

Mal. (*applying herbs to her nostrils, while* MARIAN *pours out essence from the phial, and rubs her temples and hands*).
Life is returning; she is laid uneasily;
Let me support her on a stronger arm.
                    [*Taking her from* MARIAN, *and supporting her.*
There's motion on her lips, and on her eyelids.
Her eyes begin, through their soft raven lashes,
To peer like dew-drops from the harebell's core,
As the warm air of day by slow degrees
The closed leaves gently severs.—Yes; she moves.
How art thou now, sweet Alice?
Marian. See, she looks up, and gazes on us too;
But, oh, how strangely!
Mal. Why do her eyes thus wander round the chamber?
(*To* ALICE.) Whom dost thou seek for, Alice?
Alice. She's gone; I need not look; a mortal eye
Shall never, never look on her again.
                    [*A peal of thunder heard.*
Hear ye that sound? She is upon her way.
Marian. What does she mean? It was a sultry night,
And threaten'd storm and lightning.
Mal. (*to* ALICE). Thou'st been asleep, and scarcely yet art waking,
Thy fancy is still busied with its dream.
Alice (*raising herself more, and looking towards the place where the phantom disappeared*). It was no dream: upon that spot it stood;
I saw it,—saw it for a lengthen'd time,—
Saw it distinctively.
Mal.   Whom didst thou see?
No living creature could have enter'd here.
Alice. O would that it had been a living creature!
Her beauty was the beauty of a corse

Newly composed in death; yet her dark eyes
Were open, gazing wistfully upon me.

Mal. (*hastily withdrawing his arms from her, and clasping his hands
together in agony*). Thou hast seen Emma Graham!

Alice (*rousing herself*). Is Malcolm here? I am confused,—bewilder'd;
I know not what I've seen, or what I've said:
Perhaps it was a dream.

Mal.   It was no dream;
Or if it was, 'twas one of sad import.
Oh, if it be!—there is distraction in it.

                              [*Tossing his arms, &c.*

Marian. Dear brother! such wild gestures of despair
For the mere shapings of a sleepy brain!

Mal. It was not sleep from which we have revived her.

Marian. And grant it were not, swooning, I've been told,
Will sometimes have its dream as well as sleep.

Alice. I was not well; I have been long unwell;
Weakness and wretchedness disturb the brain;
Perhaps it was the vision of a swoon.
Be not so miserable, gentle Malcolm!
O that this vision did foretell my death,
If she were well and happy!

Mal. Forgive me, dearest Alice! O, forgive me!
When paining thee, I'm hateful to myself.

          [*Taking both her hands, which he presses to his lips.*

Marian. Leave us, dear brother! go to thine apartment.

Mal. I'll go where yearning nature urges me.

          [*Going, then returning again to* ALICE.

And didst thou hear her voice?

                    Enter CLAUDE.

Claude. Is Alice well? I heard a busy noise.
How art thou, sister?

Alice.   I have had a swoon,
But am recover'd from it. Go to rest.

                    [*Aside to* MARIAN *and* MALCOLM.

Say nothing of the vision. O, be silent!

Mal. (*aside to himself, as he goes off*).
    Is he so much concern'd? No, no, he is not:
    He does not,—cannot feel what tortures me.
Claude. Dost thou avoid me, Malcolm? Dost thou think
    That kindness to my sister can offend me?
Mal. I've other thoughts, which do no wrong to thee,
    And owe thee no account.
                                  [*Exit.*

Claude (*aside*). He is offended. (*Aloud to* MARIAN.)
    Thanks to you, dear madam!
    For your kind care of Alice. Rest, I hope,
    Will perfectly restore her. The fatigue
    Of her long journey, and the evening pastime
    Has been too much for one so delicate.
    (*To* ALICE.) Undress and go to bed, poor harass'd creature!
    I trust to-morrow thou wilt wake refresh'd.
Alice. I hope so too, dear Claude; and so good night.
    Remain no longer here. (*Exit* CLAUDE.) I'm glad he's gone.
                      [*A peal of thunder as before.*
    That awful sound again! she's on her way:
    But storm or thunderbolt can do no harm
    To disembodied spirits.
Marian. I may not leave thee here, my gentle friend;
    In my apartment thou shalt pass the night.
    Come then with me: I dare not leave thee here,
    Where, sleeping or awake, thou hast received
    Some painful shock—Rise: lean upon my arm.
                            [*Exeunt.*

SCENE V.

A rudely paved court, with a low building in front. The stage perfectly dark, and thunder heard at a distance. Enter MALCOLM, *who goes to the door of the building, and knocks.*

Mal. Ho! Culloch! art thou waking? Rouse thee, Culloch!
    I hear him snoring in his heavy sleep,
    Press'd with the glutton feasting of the day.
                               [Knocking louder than before.
    Canst thou not hear? Holla! ho! rouse thee, Culloch!
    The heavy sluggard! Ha! he's stirring now.
                             [Laying his ear close to the door.
Cul. (*within*). Who's there?
Mal.   It is thy master.
Cul.   What is wanted?
    It is not morning yet.
Mal.   That drawling voice!
    He is not yet awake. (*Very loud.*) Rise, man, immediately:
    Open the door, and do what I desire thee.
                     [To himself, after a short pause.
    Six hours upon my gallant steed will end
    This agony of doubt.—I'll know my fate—
    Joy or despair.—He is asleep again.
                          [Knocking as before.
    Make haste, make haste, I say! inert and sluggish!
    O that, like spirits, on the tempest borne,
    The transit could be made! Alas! alas!
    If what I fear hath happen'd, speed or stillness,
    Or day or midnight,—every circumstance
    Of mortal being will to me be nothing.
    Not ready yet!—Ha! now I see the light.
                      [Light seen from the window.
    Six hours of my brave steed, and if my fears
    Are then confirm'd—forgive me, noble creature!
    We'll lay our burdens down and die together.

Enter CULLOCH *slowly from the building, rubbing his eyes with one hand,*
and holding a candle in the other.

Haste, tardy creature! art thou sleeping still?
Cul. What is your honour's will? O hone! O hone!
It is a murky night.
Mal.   I know it is.
Unlock the stable door, and saddle quickly
My gallant Oscar.

[*Thunder again.*

Cul.   Does your honour hear it?
Mal. Hear what?
Cul.   The thunder growling o'er Benmore:
And that was lightning too that flared so fleetly:
The welkin's black as pitch.
Mal. And let it growl; and be the welkin pall'd
In sackcloth! To the spot where I am going
We'll find the way by instinct.—Linger not:
Do what I have desired thee instantly.
Cul. Ay, ay! the saddle upon Oscar's back.
The bran new saddle would your honour have?
Mal. Yes, fool, and set about it instantly.

[*Exit* CULLOCH.

These dark and heavy bodings of my mind
Come from no natural bent of apprehension.
It must be so. Yet, be it dream or vision,
Unmeaning chance, or preternatural notice,
As oft hath been vouchsafed, if living seers
Or old tradition lie not,—this uncertainty
Ere morning dawn would drive my brain distracted,
Were I inactively to wait for day;
Therefore, to horse!

[*Thunder louder than before.*

That sound is in accordance with the storm
In this perturbed breast. Is it not ominous
Of that which soon shall strike me to the dust,
A blasted lonely remnant?—
Methinks he should ere this—time flies apace;

The listless sluggard must be urged to hasten
His so unwilling task.

[*Exit hastily.*

ACT II.

SCENE I.

The cross of Glasgow. A great crowd of people are discovered, and bells heard tolling occasionally from the neighbouring churches.

1st *crowd.* Ah! woe is me! so bonnie and so young!
        Of all that death hath ta'en in this fell ravage,
        None hath he ta'en that seem'd so ill to suit
        The coffin and the mould. Ah! woe is me!
2d *crowd.* Ay, neighbour, she was one mark'd from them all.
        Though we have many fair and gracious ladies,
        We had not one who could be pair'd with her:
        The bonniest lass in all the west of Scotland.
1st *crowd.* Ay, thou mayst say, the bonniest and the best.
3d *crowd.* Nay, softly, David! for the point of goodness,
        That is a matter, on her burial day,
        We may not question; yet, if it be true—
1st *crowd.* If it be true! It is not: nought is true
        That can throw speck or spot upon her virtue.
1st *crowd woman* (*to* 1st *crowd*).
        Be not so angry, man; my husband means
        Against her maiden virtue no reproach,
        E'en if her faith was papishly inclined.
1st *crowd.* She was no Papish; I'll take oath upon it.
        The cloven foot of Satan in my shoe
        Is at this point of time as surely buckled,
        As that she was aught but a pure believer—
        A good and godly lady.
1st *crowd woman.* That gentleman, so brave and soldierly,
        Who lately has return'd from foreign wars,
        Is a rank Romanist, and has been oft

Received by her. But, Lord preserve us all!
We, by God's grace, may sit by Satan's side,—
Ay, on the self-same settle, yet the while,
Be ne'er one whit the worse.

3d crowd. And I should guess—

2d crowd.   Hist, hist! the funeral's coming:
I hear the heavy wheels, and o'er the top
Of all those cluster'd heads I see the feathers,—
The snow-white feathers of the high-coped hearse
Move slowly. Woe the day! oh, woe the day!
How changed her state! She was on milk-white steed
Mounted right gallantly, with cap and plume,
When I beheld her last.

Voice (without). Make way, good folks, and let the ladies pass.

2d crowd (to him without). None can pass here on horseback.

Voice (without). It is the Provost's family: make way.

2d crowd (as before). An 'twere the king's, they must dismount, I trow,
Or wait till the procession be gone by.

Enter ALICE, MARIAN, *and* CLAUDE.

Claude (to crowd). What makes so great a concourse; and those bells
To toll so dismally? Whose funeral
Are ye convened to see?

1st crowd. Ah, sir! the fairest lady of the place.
I warrant you have seen her many a time;
They call'd her Emma Graham.

Claude. It cannot be! What didst thou call her? Speak;
Repeat her name.

1st crowd. Her name is Emma Graham; her father is—

Claude. No more! no more! too well I comprehend it.
And death hath dealt his blow on what was life's
Completest, dearest, best.

                         [*Covers his face with his cloak.*

Marian (turning to ALICE, *and supporting her).*
Dear Alice, thou art pale, and faint, and ill;
Lean upon me, my friend.

Alice. Think not of me: poor Claude! my heart-struck brother!
    His wound is deep and sudden: for this stroke
    I was prepared.
Voices (without). Stand back; stand closer: it is now at hand.
            [*A funeral procession crosses the stage: the mourners
            following the hearse on foot.*
1st crowd. Ah! never corse was follow'd to the grave
    With deeper sorrow!
1st crowd woman. Ay, tears are following tears down manly cheeks,
    As gouts fall in Saint Mungo's dripping aisle,
    Near which the grave is dug that shall receive her.
1st crowd. That is her grey-hair'd father, so bow'd down;
    And those her brothers walking by his side.
2d crowd. Then all the kindred walking, two and two.
3d crowd. But who is he that follows after all,
    In mourner's cloak so muffled to the eyes?
    He walks alone, not mated like the rest;
    And yet, methinks, his gait and motion say
    The greatest weight of grief falls to his share.
Claude. God knows who hath the greatest share! Not he.
                 [*Pushing eagerly through the crowd.*
Alice. Where goest thou, Claude?
                 [*Endeavouring to hold him.*
Claude. Prevent me not. Shall mourning weeds alone
    Have privilege, and sorrow be debarr'd.
            [*Exit hastily after the funeral, and the crowd disperses
            different ways,* ALICE, MARIAN, *and their servants alone
            occupying the front of the stage.*
Marian. Dear Alice! how thou tremblest every limb,
    As in an ague fit!
Alice.   It was no dream;
    It was no strong delusion of the fancy.
Marian. This is indeed an awful confirmation.
    But stay no longer here: go to thy home;
    Thou hast great need of rest.
Alice.   I have more need,
    Within my closet, on my bended knees,
    To pray for mercy on my sinful self,

And those to me most dear,—poor sinners all.
This is a sad and awful visitation.
Marian. But didst thou not expect to find it so?
I thought thou wast prepared.
Alice.   I thought so too;
But certainty makes previous expectation
Seem, by comparison, a state of hope.
Marian. We now are free to hold upon our way.
Let us proceed: come on with me, dear Alice!

[*Exeunt.*

SCENE II.

The house of the provost, and the apartment of CLAUDE, *who enters, followed by* CRAWFORD, *and throws himself back into a chair with the action of deep distress.*

Claude. Follow me not, my friend; it is in vain
That friendly soothing would assuage my grief.
Craw. Grieve not for that which is, indeed, most grievous,
Beyond all measure.
Claude.   Can we measure grief,
And say, so much of it shall be my portion,
And only this? A prudent, lesson'd sorrow,
Usurps the name it bears.—She was the light
That brighten'd every object; made this world
A place worth living in. This beauteous flame
Hath in the socket sunk: I am in darkness,
And no returning ray shall cheer my sight.
This earth, and every thing that it contains,
Is a dull blank around me.
Craw.   Say not so!
It grieves my heart to hear thee. Say not so.
Claude. I will not grieve thee then; I'll hold my tongue;
But shall I feel the less?—Oh, had she lived!

Craw. Perhaps she had but caused thee greater sorrow;
    For how wouldst thou have brook'd to see her hand,
    Had it so been, bestow'd upon another?
Claude. Why should I entertain a thought so painful?
                  [*Raising his head proudly, after a thoughtful pause.*
    Yes, I can entertain it, and believe
    That, even as another's, it were happiness
    To see her yet alive; to see her still
    Looking as never eyes but hers did look;
    Speaking such words as she alone could speak,
    Whose soften'd sounds thrill'd through the nerves, and dwelt,
    When heard no more, on the delighted fancy,
    Like chanted sweetness!—All is now extinct!—
    Like some base thing, unmeet for mortal eye,
    The sod hath cover'd all.
                      [*After a thoughtful pause.*
    Hath cover'd all!
Craw. Dear Claude! why wilt thou dwell on things so dismal?
    Let me read to thee from some pious book;
    Wilt thou permit me?
                [*He remains silent and thoughtful.*
    Dost thou hear me, Claude?
Claude (*muttering to himself, without attending to* CRAWFORD).
    The sexton has the key; and if he had not,
    The wall may yet be clear'd.—
    The banded mourners scatter to their homes,
    Where kinsfolk meet, and social hearths blaze bright,
    And leave the grave in midnight loneliness!
    But should it be?
Craw. (*listening to him*). I understand these words.
    But if he go, he shall not go alone.

Enter a Servant.

Claude (*impatiently*). What brings thee here?
Serv. A gentleman desires to see you, sir.

Claude. Tell him I am gone forth.—Such ill-timed visits!
 Is the sore heart a sear'd and harden'd thing
 For every fool to handle?

[Exit.

Craw. I'll follow him: he should not be alone.

[Exeunt.

SCENE III.

A large room, with rich furniture, and the walls hung with pictures.
Enter the Provost and MARIAN, *by different doors.*

Provost. How is poor Alice?
Marian. She is more composed;
 For tears have flow'd uncheck'd, and have relieved her.
 I have persuaded her to take an hour
 Of needful rest upon her bed; and Jessie,
 That kindly creature, watches her the while.
Provost. Ay, that is right. And now, my right good lady,
 Let me in plain but grateful words repeat,
 That your great kindness, leaving thus your home,
 And taking such a journey for the comfort
 Of my poor child, is felt by me most truly,
 As it deserves. May God reward you for it!
Marian. I will not, sir, receive such thanks unqualified;
 They are not due to me. Regard for Alice,—
 And who that knows her feels not such regard,—
 Was closely blended with another motive,
 When I determined on this sudden journey.
Provost. Another motive!
Marian.   Has not Claude inform'd you
 That Malcolm left Dunarden secretly,
 The night before we did ourselves set forth?
Provost. He has not. Ha! and wot you where he went?
Marian. I wot not, but I guess: and it was he,
 As I am almost confident, who walk'd

The last of all the mourners, by himself,
In this day's sad procession.

Provost (*pulling a letter hastily from his pocket*).

Madam, sit down; I'll cast mine eyes again
O'er this your father's letter. Pray sit down!
I may not see you thus.

> [*Setting a chair with much courtesy, and obliging her to sit,
> whilst he goes aside and reads a letter earnestly. He then
> returns to her.*

My friend has many words of courtesy;
It is his habit; but subtracting from them
The plain unvarnish'd sense, and thereto adding
What, from this secret journey of your brother,
May be inferr'd,—the real truth is this—
At least it so appears to my poor reason—

> [*Preventing her as she rises from her seat.*

Nay, sit, I pray you, Lady Achinmore;
We'll talk this matter over thoroughly,
And leave no bashful doubts hid in a corner,
For lack of honest courage to produce them.

> [*Sits down by her.*

Marian. Proceed, good sir, I listen earnestly.

Provost. As it appears to me, the truth is this,
That Malcolm, whom your father doth admit,
Albeit a great admirer of my daughter,
To be at present somewhat disinclined
To give up youthful liberty so early,
As he from more acquaintance with her virtues
Ere long will of his own accord desire,—
(*Pointing to the letter*)—so he expresses it.

Marian. And with sincerity.

Provost.   Well, grant it, lady!
The truth doth ne'ertheless appear to be,
That this young gallant, Malcolm of Dunarden,
With all her virtues, loves not Alice Denison,
And loves another.

Marian.   Rather say, *hath* loved.

Provost. I'll not unsay my words. His heart is with her,
 Low as she lies: and she who won his heart
 From such a maid as Alice Denison,
 Will keep it too, e'en in her shroud. No, no!
 We've spread our vaunting sails against the wind,
 And cannot reach our port but with such peril
 As will o'ermatch the vantage.
Marian.   Say not so.
 Time will make all things as we wish to have them.
Provost. Time works rare changes, which they may abide
 Who are intent upon them. Shall I carry
 My vessel where her cargo is not wanted?—
 Tobacco to th' Antipodes, and wait
 Till they have learn'd to use and relish it?—
 Shall I do this, when other marts are near
 With open harbours ready to receive her?
Marian. Dear sir, you must not think I will assent
 To what would mar the long and cherish'd wish
 Of me and mine. And we had fondly hoped
 That you had been desirous of this union
 Between our families.
Provost. Your father won my friendship years ago,
 When with his goodly mien and belted plaid,
 His merry courtesy and stately step,
 He moved amongst our burghers at the Cross,
 As though he had been chieftain o'er us all;
 And I have since enjoy'd his hospitality,
 In his proud mountain hold.
Marian. I recollect it: proud and glad he was
 Of such a guest.
Provost.   Dost thou? Ay, then it was,
 That, seeing his fair stripling by his side—
 A graceful creature, full of honest sense
 And manly courage—I did like the notion,
 That Alice, then a little skipping child,
 With years before her still to play about me,
 Should in some future time become the lady
 Of that young Highland chief. But years bring thoughts

Of a more sober and domestic hue.
Why should I covet distant vanities,
And banish from my sight its dearest object?
(*Rising from his chair.*) Have you observed those pictures?
Marian (*rising also*). I have. They are the portraits of your parents:
    Their features bear resemblance to your own.
Provost. My mother's do: and look at her, dear madam!
    With all the bravery of that satin dress
    Clasp'd up with jewels, and those roses stuck
    Amongst her braided hair, she was the daughter
    And sober heiress of a saving burgher,
    Whose hoarded pelf in my brave father's hands
    Raised such industrious stir in this good city,
    As changed her from a haunt of listless sluggards
    To the fair town she is. What need have I
    To eke my consequence with foreign matches?
    Alice shall wed, I hope, some prosperous merchant,
    And live contentedly, my next door neighbour,
    With all her imps about her.
Marian. Wed whom she may, I hope she will be happy.
Provost. I do believe that is your hearty wish:
    And having plainly told you what I think
    Of this projected match, as it concerns
    My daughter and myself,—I will proceed
    To that which may concern my ancient friend.
    Should any mortgage press on his estate,
    Or any purchase of adjoining lands
    Make money a desired object with him,
    He need but speak the word; at easy int'rest
    He shall receive what sums he may require,
    And need not fear that I shall e'er distress him
    With hard ill-timed demands. In faith, he need not!
Marian. Dear sir, he knows full well your gen'rous heart
    Hath for its minister a liberal hand:
    In truth, he would not fear to be your debtor.
Provost. Not all the rum and sugar of Jamaica,
    In one huge warehouse stored, should make me press him,
    Though apt occasion offer'd e'er so temptingly.

Then why should Malcolm bend his youthful neck
To wedlock's yoke for sordid purposes?
The boy shall be my friend; and when his mind
Is free to think upon another love,
I'll guide him to a very comely lady—
Yea, more than one, that he may have a choice—
Who may prove both a match of love and profit;
But hear you plainly, not to Alice Denison.
Marian. Oh, you are kind and noble! but my father—
Provost. Say nought for him; he'll answer for himself:
And through his maze of friendly compliments,
I'll trace at last his veritable thoughts.

                                        [*Taking her hand kindly.*

Now, having thus so plainly told my mind,
Look on me as a man to whom again
You may as freely speak.
Marian.   And so I will:
The happiness of one, dear to us both,
Requires that I should do it.
Provost (surprised). How so? is it of Alice you would speak?
Marian. Yes, but another time; for here comes Jessie.

                    Enter JESSIE.

(*To* JESSIE.) How is she now? I hope she is asleep.
Jessie. She has not slept, but lies composed and easy,
And wishes now to see you.

                                       [*Exit* MARIAN.

Provost. How art thou, Jessie?
Jessie.   Well, an' please your honour.
Provost. I hear thou hast become a Highland lass;
But, if thou really like the Lowlands better,
Thy native country, tell me honestly:
I'll make thy husband, whomsoe'er thou choose,
A freeman of this town. If he have brains,
And some few marks beside, he'll thrive upon it.
Jessie. I thank you, sir: his marks are few indeed.

Provost. Well, never mind; let us but have the brains,
  And we will make the best of it.—Poor Jessie!
  I well remember thee a barefoot girl,
  With all thy yellow hair bound in a snood:
  Thy father too.
Jessie.   Do you remember him?
Provost. Yes, Saunders Fairlie. Better man than Saunders
  In factory or warehouse never bustled.

     Enter Servant.

Provost. What is the matter, Archy? On thy face
  Thou wearst a curious grin: what is the matter?
Serv. The baillie bid me to inform your honour,
  The country hucksters and the market wives
  Have quarrell'd, and are now at deadly strife,
  With all the brats and schoolboys of the town
  Shouting and bawling round them.
Provost. Good sooth! whene'er those wives with hands and tongue
  Join in the fray, the matter must be look'd to.
  I will be with them soon.

          [Exit servant.

  To think now of those creatures!
  E'en at the time when death is in the city
  Doing his awful work, and our sad streets
  Blacken'd with funerals, that they must quarrel
  About their worldly fractions! Woe is me!
  For all our preachings and our Sabbath worship,
  We are, I fear, but an ungodly race.

    Enter another Servant.

  And what has brought thee, too?
Serv. There is a woman come from Anderston,
  Whose neighbour, on pretence of some false debt,
  Has pounded her milch cow,—her only cow.
Provost. Is that a case to occupy my time?
  Let her go with it to the younger baillie.

Serv. I told her so, your honour, but she weeps,
  And says the younger baillie is so proud,
  She dare not speak to him.
Provost. Poor simpleton! Well, then, I needs must see her.

Re-enter 1st Servant.

  Tut! here again! What is the matter now?
1st serv. A servant all cross'd o'er wi' livery lace,
  As proud and grand as any trumpeter,
  Is straight from Blantyre come, and says, my lord
  Would greatly be obliged, if that your honour
  Would put off hearing of that suit to-morrow,
  As he must go to Edinburgh.
Provost.   Tell the messenger
  To give my humble service to his lordship,
  And say, I could not, but with great injustice
  To the complaining party, grant delay,
  Who, being poor, should not be further burden'd
  With more attendance; I will therefore hear
  The cause to-morrow, at the hour appointed.

Exit 1st, and re-enter 2d Servant.

  Still more demands! For what foul sin of mine
  Was I promoted to this dignity?
  From morn till eve, there is no peace for me.
          [*Exit Provost, speaking to the servants as they go out.*

SCENE IV.

*Before the walls of a churchyard, a narrow iron gate at the bottom of the
stage, behind which the gleaming of a torch is faintly seen; the front of the
stage entirely dark. Solemn music is heard, as the scene opens.*

Enter a Sexton, with keys, followed by CLAUDE *and* CRAWFORD.

Claude. Music! and from the spot! what may it be?

Sexton. Leave was requested that a solemn dirge
  Should be this night sung by some grave; but whose,
  Or e'en by whom requested, I am ignorant.
  Some Papist, like enough: but what of that?
Craw. (*to sexton*). How many graves thou'st made in one short week!
  Thou hast been busy in thy sad vocation.
Sexton. I have, good sooth, and knew it would be so,
  A month before the fell disease began.
Craw. How knew it?
Sexton. He, the sighted man from Skye,
  Was in the town; and, at the crowded cross,
  Fell into strong convulsions, at the sight
  Which there appear'd to him.
Craw.   What did he see?
Sexton. Merchants, and lairds, and deacons, making bargains,
  And setting trystes, and joking carelessly,
  Swathed in their shrouds; some to the very chin,
  Some breast-high, others only to the loins.
  It was a dismal, an appalling sight;
  And when I heard of it, I knew right well
  My busy time was coming.
Claude (*to sexton, impatiently*). Didst thou say
  That leave has been requested for a dirge
  To be this night sung by some Papist's grave?
Sexton. Papist or not I cannot surely say,
  I ask'd no questions.
Craw.   Having cause, no doubt,
  To be well satisfied no harm would ensue.
Sexton. No harm. In this retired nook it cannot
  Annoy the living; and for the departed,
  Nought can disturb their rest.
Craw. Hast thou not heard of restless souls returning?
  Perhaps thou'st seen it, during thirty years
  In which thou hast been sexton of this parish.
Sexton. In all that time I ne'er could say with certainty
  That aught of such a nature pass'd before me;
  But I have seen uncertain shadows move

As 'twere confusedly, and heard strange sounds,—
Stranger than wind or natural cause could utter.
Craw. And thou wast sure they were unnatural sounds?
And hast thou heard them often?
Sexton.   Many times:
But that was in the first years of mine office.
I am not now alarm'd: use makes me feel
As if no harm could e'er befall the sexton:
And e'en my wife will in dark winter nights
Enter the church alone and toll the bell.
Craw. And ne'er has been alarm'd by any sight
Of apparition or unearthly thing?
Sexton. Yes; she was once alarm'd.
Craw. (*eagerly*).   And what appear'd?
Sexton. It was, as nearly as I can remember,
Upon a Friday night——
Craw. (*quickly*). Ne'er mind the night: what was it that she saw?
Sexton. Nay, she herself saw nothing; but the dog
That follow'd her bark'd briskly, then stopp'd short,
And, with a kind of stifled choking howl,
Look'd in her face, then cower'd by her side,
Trembling for fear; and then right well she knew
Some elrich thing was near her, though its form
Was only visible to the poor brute.
Craw. You think the dog saw something.
Sexton.   Certes did he!
And had he not been dumb, he could, no doubt,
Have told a tale to set our hair on end.
Claude (*who, during their discourse, has been pacing to and fro
impatiently, to sexton*). You know not who it was?
Sexton. The Lord preserve us, sir! for she saw nothing.
Claude. What dost thou mean? Couldst thou not guess, at least,
Who 'twas who made request to chant the dirge?
Sexton. Ay, ay! the dirge. In truth I cannot say.
It was a man I never saw before.
Claude (*eagerly*). Stately, and of a stature somewhat taller
Than middle size, of countenance somewhat younger
Than middle age?

Sexton. No; short, and grave, and ancient, like a priest
    From foreign parts.

                                    [*Music sounds again.*

Craw.   Be still and hear the dirge.

          DIRGE, *sung by several voices without.*

    Dear spirit! freed from earthy cell,
      From mortal thraldom freed;
    The blessed Virgin keep thee well,
      And thy dread passage speed!

    Quick be thy progress, gentle soul!
      Through purifying pain,
    To the saved Christian's happy goal,
      Thy Father's bright domain!

    Beloved on earth! by love redeem'd,
      Which earthly love transcends,
    Earth's show,—the dream that thou hast dream'd,
      In waking transport ends.

    Then, bathed in fountains of delight,
      Mayst thou God's mercy prove,
    His glory open'd to thy sight,
      And to thy heart His love!

    There may thy blessed dwelling be,
      For ever to endure
    With those who were on earth like thee,
      The guileless and the pure!

    Dear spirit! from thy earthy cell,
      From mortal thraldom freed, &c. &c.

Claude (*seeing the light disappear*). They are all gone at last: unlock
    the gate.

[*The sexton applies the key, but in vain.*

Canst thou not open it? what is the matter?

Sexton. I've brought a key made for another gate;
    Woe worth my stupid head!

Claude. I'll climb the wall.

Sexton. Be not so very hasty, please your honour.
    This key unlocks the southern gate: I pray you
    To follow me, and you will soon have entrance.
    Woe worth my stupid head!

[*Exeunt.*

SCENE V.

The churchyard, near the walls of St. Mungo's church, which occupies the bottom of the stage. A newly covered grave is dimly seen near the front; the stage darkened, but not entirely so; a degree of light, as from a new-risen moon in a cloudy night, showing objects imperfectly. Enter MALCOLM, *who bends over the grave for some time in silence.*

Mal. And here beneath this trampled sod she lies,
    Stiffen'd and cold, and swathed in coffin-weeds,
    Who, short while since, moved like a gleam of brightness,
    Lighting each face, and cheering every heart.
    Oh, Emma, Emma Graham, is this thy place?
    Dearer than thou a lover's soul ne'er worshipp'd;
    Fairer than thou a virgin's robe ne'er wrapt;
    Better than thou a parent's tongue ne'er bless'd.
    Oh, Emma Graham, the dearest, fairest, best!
    Pair'd with thee in the dance, this hand in thine,
    I've led thee through the whirl of mazy transport,
    And o'er thy chair have hung with wistful ear,
    Catching thy words like strains of melody,
    To be with fancy's treasures stored for ever.
    I've waited near thy portal many an hour,
    To see thy hasty transit from its steps
    To the grim gaping coach, that seem'd to swallow,
    Like a leviathan, its beauteous prey.
    And now alas! I come to seek thee here!

I come to seek thee here, but not to find.
This heart, which yearns through its ribb'd fence to break
Into the darken'd cell where thou art laid
In Nature's thraldom, is from thee divided
As by a gulf impassable. Oh, oh!
So short a time! such fearful, sad transition!
My day is turn'd to night; my youth to age;
May life to death be the next welcome change!

> [*Throws himself on the grave in a burst of sorrow.*

Sweet love, who sleepst beneath, canst thou not hear me?
Oh, if thou couldst! Alas! alas! thou canst not!

> [*After a pause, and half-raising himself from the grave.*

But is it well, and is it holy, thus,
On such a sacred spot, to mourn the dead,
As lost and perish'd treasure? God forgive me!
The silver lamp, with all its rich embossments
Of beauteous workmanship, is struck and broken,
But is the flame extinguish'd? God forgive me!
Forgive a wretched and distracted man,
And grant me better thoughts!—The unclothed spirit
In blessed purity hath still existence.
Perhaps, in its high state is not unconscious
Of what remains behind; perhaps, beholds
The very spot. Oh, if she does! her pity—
Her pity, yea, her love now rests upon me.
Her spirit, from the body newly freed,
Was in my father's house, ere it departed
To its celestial home; was it not sympathy?
O! Emma, Emma! could I surely know
That I was dear to thee, a word,—a token
Had been to me a cherish'd, rich possession,
Outvaluing all that martial chiefs contend for
On their embattled fields.—Ha! who approaches?

Enter CLAUDE.

Come not, I warn thee, near this sacred spot.

> [*Springing up from the ground.*

Claude. A sacred spot, indeed! but yet to all
    Who loved in life the dead whom it contains,
    Free as the house of God.
Mal.   I say it is not.
    In this, her first night of the grave, the man
    Who loved her best when living, claims a right
    To watch the new-closed tomb, and none beside.
Claude. Then yield to me that right, for it is mine;
    For I have loved her longest,—long ere thou
    Hadst look'd upon her face, or heard her name.
Mal. 'Tis not the date, but potency of love
    Which bears account: I say, approach no nearer.
Claude. Must I endure such passion? Frantic man!
    Are we not both in grief smitten to the earth?
    May we not both weep o'er this sacred spot,
    Partners in wretchedness?
Mal. Away, away! I own no partnership;
    He who hath spok'n such word hath thereby proved
    The poorness of his love. Approach no nearer.
    I'll yield my heart's blood rather than resign
    This my sad eminence in widow'd sorrow.
Claude. Dar'st thou to hinder me?
Mal.   I dare and will.

                            [*They grapple fiercely.*
              Enter CRAWFORD.

Craw. (*separating them.*) For shame! for shame! to hold contention here!
    Mutual affliction should make friends of foes,
    Not foes of friends. The grave of one beloved
    Should be respected e'en as holy ground,—
    Should have a charm to smother all resentment.
Mal. And so it should, and shall.—Forgive me, Claude;
    I have been froward in my wretchedness.
Claude. And I, dear Malcolm, was to blame, so suddenly
    To break upon thy sorrow.
Craw. The provost hath despatch'd a messenger
    Upon our track, who found me out e'en now,

Requesting both of you to give your presence
On an occasion solemn and important.
Claude. What may it be?
Craw. Within the late apartment of the dead,
　　Your sister has a duty to perform,
　　Enjoin'd her by the dead. And 'tis her wish
　　That ye should both be present.
Claude and Mal. (together). We will obey her shortly. Go before us.
　　　　　[*Exeunt* CRAWFORD *and* MALCOLM; *and* CLAUDE, *after bending*
　　　　　in silence for a few moments over the grave, follows them.

SCENE VI.

An apartment, the walls of which are lined with oak, and partly hung with
arras. Enter a Maid Servant, carrying a lamp and a basket, &c.

Maid (speaking as she enters).
　　I trow, when we have burnt this second parcel,
　　The sickly air must needs be purified.
　　But what does all this fuming signify,
　　Since we must die at our appointed time?
　　What dost thou think—(*looking round and seeming alarmed*)—
　　She has not follow'd me.
　　I thought she was behind me. Lord preserve us!
　　Here in this ghastly chamber all alone!
　　　　　　　　　[*Going to the door and calling.*
　　Art thou not coming. Marjory? Where art thou?
　　I say, where art thou? I have need of thee.

Enter a 2d Maid.

2d maid. Why didst thou call so loud? What is the matter?
1st maid. I thought thou wast behind me: mercy on us!
　　A kind of qualm came o'er me, when I look'd
　　On all within this silent dismal room,
　　And to that corner where the death-bed stood,—
　　A sudden qualm came o'er me.

2d maid. Let us be busy—there's no time to lose;
    The provost and his daughter will be here
    Ere we have done our work.

        [*They take gums and dried herbs from the basket, which they
        set fire to by the lamp, and fumigate the chamber, speaking
        the while occasionally.*

1st maid. The Lord preserve us! 'tis an awful thing.
2d maid. It was a sudden call: so young,—so good!
1st maid. Ay, many a sore heart thinks of her this night.
2d maid. And he, the most of all, that noble gentleman:
    Lord pardon him for being what he is!
1st maid. And what is that?
2d maid.   A rank and Roman papist.
1st maid. The Lord forgive him that, if it be so!—
    And quickly, too; for this same deadly fever,
    As I hear say, has seized upon him also.

               Enter Provost.

Provost. That's well, good damsels; you have done your task
    Right thoroughly: a wholesome, fragrant smell
    Is floating all about. Where is your master?
1st maid. In his own chamber. When he knows your honour
    Is in the house, he will attend you presently.
2d maid. And it will do him good to see your honour.
Provost. I fear, my joe, the good that I can do him,
    Or e'en the minister, if he were here,
    Would be but little. Grief must have its time.
    Some opiate drug would be to him, I reckon,
    Worth all my company, and something more.
    Howbeit, I'll go to him. My good old friend!
    My heart bleeds for him.—Ye have done enough;
    The ladies are at hand.

                     [*Exit by the opposite side.*
           Enter ALICE *and* MARIAN.

Marian. Take hold of me; thy summon'd strength, I fear,
    Forsakes thee now.

[She supports ALICE, *and they walk slowly to the middle of
the room.*

Ay, thou lookst round, as if in search of something?

Alice. They have removed it.

Marian.   What have they removed?

Alice. The bed on which she lay. Oh, woe is me!
The last time I was in this chamber, Marian,
Becoming suddenly, from some slight cause,
A passing sufferer, she laid my head
On her own pillow, and her own soft hand
Press'd me so gently; I was then the patient,
And she the tender nurse. I little thought
So short a time—Alas! my dear, dear friend!

Marian. Short time indeed for such a dismal change:
I may not chide thy tears.

Alice. Here are the virginals on which she play'd;
And here's her music, too.

[Taking up a book from the virginals, and opening it.
Ah, woe is me!
The very tune which last she play'd to me
Has open'd to my hand, and 'twixt the leaves
The little flower lies press'd which then I gave her!

Marian. 'Tis sweet to find it so.

Alice.   But, oh! how sad!
She was—she was——

[Bursting into tears.
Well may I weep for her!

Marian. Be comforted, dear Alice! she is gone
Where neither pain nor woe can touch her more.

Alice. I know—I know it well: but she is gone!
She who was fair, and gifted, and beloved:
And so beloved!—Had it been heaven's blest will
To take me in her stead, tears had been shed,
But what had been their woe, compared to this?

Marian. Whose woe, dear Alice?

Alice. His woe—their woe; poor Claude's, and Malcolm's too.
Death seizes on the dearest and the best!

Marian (*embracing her*). I will not hear thee say so, gentle Alice.
    A dearer and a better than thyself
    'Twere hard to find. No; nor do I believe
    That she whom thou lamentest did surpass thee.
Alice. Hush! say it not!—I pray thee, say not so:
    In pitying me thou must not rob the dead.
    That he preferr'd a creature of such excellence,
    Took from the wound its sting and bitterness.
    Thou mayst not wrong the dead!
Marian.   I will not, then.
Alice (*looking round*). There is the arras that conceals the place:
    Her awful words are sounding in my ears,
    Which bade me search. I feel a secret awe!
    But that her spirit from the earth has ta'en—
    As I am well assured—its final leave,
    I could believe that she is near me still,
    To see the very act!
                    [*Looking round her fearfully.*
Marian. Nay, check thy ardent fancy: 'tis not good
    To let such dismal notions haunt thee so—
    Thy father comes, with his afflicted friend.

        Enter Provost, leading GRAHAM *by the hand.*

        [ALICE *advances affectionately to* GRAHAM, *who opens his
        arms to receive her, and she weeps upon his neck, without
        speaking. She then leads him to a chair, and seats herself
        upon a stool at his feet, taking his hand in hers, and bending
        over it, while the Provost and Marian remain in the front.*

Provost (*looking at them*). That poor old man! he utters not a word
    Of sorrow or complaint; and all the more
    I grieve for him. God help him! in whose hands
    The hearts of men are kept.
Marian. And he is help'd, for he is weeping now.
Provost. He did not weep when we for him were weeping,
    And he will weep when all our tears are dried.
    —Our two young men, methinks, are long of coming.

Marian. But are you sure your messenger hath found them?

Provost. I scarcely doubt it. I have those in pay,
  But little better than the prey they follow,
  Who are expert in dogging stealthy rogues;
  And it were strange indeed if artless men
  Should foil their skill.—
  And I am right—I hear their coming steps!

Enter MALCOLM *and* CLAUDE.

Mal. (*after doing silent obeisance to the Provost and* GRAHAM, *who,
  with* ALICE, *come forward to meet them, speaks in a low voice to*
  CLAUDE).
  And here, night after night, in all her beauty,
  She took her curtain'd rest, and here she died!
  But that which I expected is not here:
  Is this the very chamber?

Alice (*overhearing him, and in a low voice*).
  It is: but what thou lookst for is removed. (*Pointing.*)
  Upon that spot it stood.

Mal. Yes, thou hast read my thought, most gentle Alice!
          [*Goes to the spot, where he remains in silence, covering his
          face with his hands.*

Provost. Shall we not now proceed upon the business
  For which we are convened?
  (*To* GRAHAM.) To you, my ancient friend, I have explain'd it.
  Malcolm and Claude, know ye why in this chamber
  Your presence has been solemnly requested.

Claude. I guess it well. My sister has inform'd me
  Of Emma's last request; and I to Malcolm,
  As we came hither, have repeated it.

Provost (*to* ALICE). Now, dearest child! it is for thee to act.
          [*Leads* ALICE *to the bottom of the stage, where, taking aside
          the arras which covers the wall, a small door is discovered.*

Claude (*to* MALCOLM, *seeing him take a book from a book-case*).
  Why dost thou snatch that book so eagerly?

Malcolm. It is the book I praised to her so much
  A short while since; and see, she has procured it!

Claude. Ah! thou mayst well be proud. But how is this?
   Thy countenance all o' the sudden changed!
         [MALCOLM *lets the book drop from his hand, and* CLAUDE
         takes it up eagerly, and opens it, reading.
   "The gift of one most dear."—Of one most dear!
   Thou didst not give it to her?
Mal.   No; nor thou!
Marian. Hush, hush! words of ungentle rivalry
   Do ill become this solemn place. Be calm.
   See! Alice in the cabinet hath found
   That which the vision'd form so earnestly
   Directed her to search for.
         [ALICE, *returning to the front with a small box in her hands,*
         places it on a table, the rest gathering eagerly round her, and
         endeavours to open it.
Alice. I know this box: alas! I know it well,
   And many a time have open'd it; but now—
Provost. Thy hands have lost all power, thou tremblest so.
         [*Taking it from her and from Graham, who attempts to*
         assist her.
   Nay, friend, thou tremblest also: I will do it.
                     [*Opens the box, and takes out a written paper.*
Omnes. What is it?
Provost.   Give me time to look upon it.
Gra. Some deed or testament. Alas, poor child!
   Had she prepared for such an early death?
Provost. It is no testament.
Mal. (*impatiently*).   What is it then?
Claude. Nay, father, do not keep us in suspense!
Provost. It is a formal contract of betrothment;
   Vows sworn between herself and Basil Gordon.
Gra. That popish cadet of a hostile house
   To me and mine!—Let mine own eyes examine it.
   Contracted secretly! to him contracted!
   But she is in her grave, and I——O God!
   Grant me with patience to endure Thy chastening!
   Contracted! married!

Provost. Not married; no,—a mutual solemn promise,
　　Made to each other in the sight of heav'n.
　　Thus run the words:—
　　(*Reads.*) "I, Basil Gordon, will no woman wed
　　But Emma Graham."—Then follows her engagement:—
　　"I, Emma Graham, will wed no other man
　　Than Basil Gordon: yet will never marry
　　But with consent of my much honour'd father,
　　When he, less prejudiced, shall know and own
　　The worth of him I love."

　　　　　　　　　　　　　　　[*Spreading out the paper.*

　　This is her writing, as you plainly see;
　　And this is Gordon's, for I know it well.
Gra. (*beating his breast*). This blow! this blow! a Gordon and a papist!
Provost. True, he is both: the last, I must confess,
　　No trivial fault. Howbeit he is, in truth,
　　A brave and noble gentleman.
Alice. Indeed he is, dear sir. Your gentle Emma
　　Could love no other. Valiant in the field,
　　As frequent foreign records have attested:
　　In private conduct good and honourable;
　　And loving her he loved, as he has done,
　　With ardent, tender constancy—
Mal. 　　　　　　　　　　　Hold! hold!
　　He loved her not—by heav'n he loved her not!
　　When all who ever knew her, drown'd in sorrow,
　　Follow'd her hearse, he—he alone was absent.
　　Where was he then, I pray?
Provost. 　　　　　　　　I'll tell thee where:
　　Stretch'd on a sick-bed—smitten by the same
　　Most pestilent disease that slew his mistress.
Mal. Ha! is it so! (*Turning to* CLAUDE.) Then we must hold our
　　peace.
Claude. And with each other be at peace, dear Malcolm:
　　What is there now of rivalry between us?
Mal. Speak not so gently to me, noble Claude!
　　I've been to thee so wayward and unjust,
　　Thy kindness wrings the heart which it should soften.

(*After a pause.*) And all our fond delusion ends in this!
We've tack'd our shallow barks for the same course!
And the fair mimic isle, like Paradise,
Which seem'd to beckon us, was but a bank
Of ocean's fog, now into air dissolved!

Alice. No; say not beckon'd. She was honourable
As she was fair: no wily woman's art
Did e'er disgrace her worth:—believe me, Malcolm.

Mal. Yes; I believe thee, and I bless thee too,
Thou best and loveliest friend of one so lovely!
Pardon me, dearest Alice! generous Alice!
Pardon the hasty error of a word
Which had no meaning—no intended meaning
To cast one shade of blame on thy dear friend;
For henceforth by no other appellation
But thy dear friend shall she be named by me.

[*Turning to* GRAHAM.

And you, dear sir! look not so sternly sad.
Her love outran her duty one short step,
But would no farther go, though happiness
Was thereby peril'd. Though his house and yours,
His creed and yours, were so at variance, still,
She might expect his noble qualities
Would in the end subdue a father's heart,
Who did so fondly love her.

Gra. Cease! I am weak, bereft, and desolate,—
A poor old man, my pride of wisdom sear'd
And ground to dust: what power have I to judge?
May God forgive me if I did amiss!

Claude (*to Provost*). Did Gordon see her ere she breathed her last?

Provost. He did. The nurse, who was her close attendant,
Says, that he came by stealth into her chamber,
And with her words and looks of tenderness
Exchanged, though near her last extremity.
And there he caught the fatal malady.

Claude. A happy end for him, if it should prove so.

Enter a Servant, who draws the Provost aside.

Provost (aside to servant). Thou hast a woeful face! what has befallen?

[*Servant speaks to him in a whisper.*

Marian (to ALICE). Thy father has received some woeful tidings.

Alice. I fear he has; he stands in thoughtful silence.

Father, how is't? your thoughts are very sad.

Provost. Ay; were this span of earthly being all,

'Twere sad to think how wealth and domination,

Man's valour, landed pride, and woman's beauty,

When over them the blighting wind hath pass'd,

Are turned to vanity, and known no more!

[*The bell of a neighbouring church tolls five times.*

Mal. What bell is that?

Claude. Some spirit is released from mortal thraldom.

Alice. And passing on its way, we humbly hope,

To endless happiness.

Provost. I trust it is, though stern divines may doubt:

'Tis Basil Gordon's knell!

[*The bell tolls again at measured intervals, and, after a solemn pause, the curtain drops.*

WITCHCRAFT

A TRAGEDY IN PROSE.

IN FIVE ACTS.

PERSONS OF THE DRAMA.

MEN.

ROBERT KENNEDY OF DUNGARREN (*commonly called* DUNGARREN).
MURREY.
RUTHERFORD, *minister of the parish.*
FATHERINGHAM, *friend of* MURREY.
The Sheriff of Renfrewshire.
The Baillie or Magistrate of Paisley.
BLACK BAWLDY, *the herdboy of* DUNGARREN.
ANDERSON, *the principal domestic of* Dungarren.
Wilkin, an idiot.

Crowd, gaoler, landlord, &c.

WOMEN.

LADY DUNGARREN (*commonly so called*), mother of ROBERT KENNEDY.
VIOLET, *daughter of* MURREY.
ANNABELLA, the rich relation of Lady Dungarren.
GRIZELD BANE,
MARY MACMURREN, } *reputed witches.*
ELSPY LOW,
PHEMY, *maid to* ANNABELLA.

Nurse, maidservants, crowd, &c.

Scene in Renfrewshire, *in* Scotland.

ACT I.

SCENE I.

A parlour in the house or tower of DUNGARREN.

Enter LADY DUNGARREN *and* ANNABELLA, *by different sides.*

Anna. You must be surprised, my dear cousin, at my unexpected return.

Lady Dun. I will frankly confess that I am. How did you find your friends in Glenrowan?

Anna. With their house full of disagreeable visitors and discomfort: another day of it would have cast me into a fever; so I will trespass on your hospitality a week longer, knowing how kindly disposed you have always been to the child of your early friend.

Lady Dun. It would be strange, indeed, if the daughter of Duncan Gordon were not welcome here.

Anna. How has poor Jessie been since I left you?

Lady Dun. (*shaking her head*). I have but a sorrowful account to give of her.

Anna. Had she any rest last night? Does she look as wildly as she did? Were any strange noises heard in the chamber during the night?

Lady Dun. Ay; noises that made me start and tremble, and feel a horrid consciousness that some being or other was in the room near me, though to the natural eye invisible.

Anna. What kind of sounds were they? Why did you think they were so near you?

Lady Dun. I was sitting by the table, with my head resting on my hand, when the door leading from the back staircase, which I am certain I had bolted in the evening, burst open.

Anna. And what followed?

Lady Dun. I verily thought to see some elrich form or other make its appearance, and I sat for some moments rivetted to my chair, without power to move hand or foot, or almost to breathe.

Anna. Yet you saw nothing?

Lady Dun. Nothing.

Anna. And heard only the bursting of the door?

Lady Dun. Only that for a time: but afterwards, when I listened intently, I heard strange whisperings near me, and soft steps, as of unshod feet, passing between me and the bed.

Anna. Footsteps?

Lady Dun. Ay; and the curtains of the bed began to shake as if touched by a hand, or the motion of some passing body. Then I knew that they were dealing with my poor child, and I had no power to break the spell of their witchcraft, for I had no voice to speak.

Anna. You had no power to speak?

Lady Dun. No; though the Lord's prayer was on my lips, I was unable to utter it.

Anna. Heaven preserve us! what a dreadful situation you were in! Did the poor child seem to notice any thing?

Lady Dun. I cannot say how she looked when the door burst open; but as soon as I could observe her, her eyes were wide open, gazing fixedly, as if some ugly visage were hanging over her, from which she could not turn away, and presently she fell into a convulsion, and I at that instant recovered my voice and my strength, and called nurse from her closet to assist her.

Anna. What did nurse think?

Lady Dun. Nurse said she was sure that both Grizeld Bane and Mary Macmurren had been in the room. And this I will take my oath to, that afterwards, when she fell quiet, she muttered in her sleep, in a thick untuneable voice, and amongst the words which she uttered, I distinctly heard the name of Mary Macmurren.

Anna. What an awful thing it is if people can have power from the evil spirit to inflict such calamity!

Lady Dun. Awful indeed!

Anna. How can they purchase such power?

Lady Dun. The ruin of a Christian soul is price enough for any thing. Satan, in return for this, will bestow power enough to do whatever his bondswoman or bondsman listeth.

Anna. Yet they are always miserable and poor.

Lady Dun. Not always; but malignant gratifications are what they delight in, and nothing else is of much value to them.

Anna. It may be so:—it is strange and fearful!

Lady Dun. I must go to my closet now, and mix the medicine for poor Jessie, to be ready at the proper time; for I expect the minister to pray by her to-night, and would have every thing prepared before he comes.

[*Exit.*

Annabella (*alone, after a thoughtful pause*). Ay, if there be in reality such supernatural agency, by which a breast fraught with passion and misery may find relief. (*Starting back.*) Dreadful resource! I may not be so assisted. (*After walking to and fro in great perturbation.*) Oh, Dungarren, Dungarren! that a paltry girl, who is not worthy to be my tirewoman, the orphan of a murderer—a man disgraced, who died in a pit and was buried in a moor; one whose very forehead is covered with blushing shame when the eye of an irreproachable gentlewoman looks upon her; whose very voice doth alter and hesitate when a simple question of her state or her family is put to her,—that a creature thus naturally formed to excite aversion and contempt should so engross thy affections! It makes me mad!—"May not be so assisted!" Evil is but evil, and torment is but torment!—I have felt both—I have felt them to extremity? what have I then to fear? (*Starts on hearing the door open behind her, as* PHEMY *enters.*) Who is there?

Phemy. Only me, madam.

Anna. What brings thee here?

Phemy. I came to know if you will trust the Glasgow carrier, who is just come for the orders of the family, with your commission to the silk shop.

Anna. What art thou telling me?

Phemy. Of your commission to the silk shop.

Anna. I don't understand thee.

Phemy. The additional yards of silk that are wanted.

Anna. I want none, fool! Thy wits are bewildered.

Phemy. Not my wits, madam. What will you please to have, then, for the trimming of your new mantua?

Anna. Newt skins and adder skins, an thou wilt.

Phemy. That might do for a witch's gown, indeed: Grizeld Bane might have a garniture of that sort.

Anna. What dost thou know of Grizeld Bane?

Phemy. Stories enow, if they be true. It is she, or Mary Macmurren, who has, as they say, bewitched the poor young lady here; and it was a spell cast by her, that made the farmer's pretty daughter fall over the crag and break her leg, the week before her wedding.

Anna. Before her wedding?

Phemy. Yes, truly, madam; and no wedding at all will ever follow such an untoward mischance.

Anna. Who told thee this?

Phemy. Everybody tells it, and knows it to be true.—(*After a pause.*) But the carrier is waiting.—She does not heed me. (*Aside.*) What is the matter, madam? Are you not well?

Annabella (rousing herself suddenly). Dost thou know Grizeld Bane?

Phemy. Heaven forfend!

Anna. Dost thou know where she lives?

Phemy. Somewhere not far distant, I believe: Black Bawldy the herd knows her den well enough.

Anna. Is he in the house at present?

Phemy. Very likely; for this is the time when his cows are brought in for the milking.

Anna. Go find him, if thou canst, and send him to me immediately.

[*Exit* PHEMY.

If there be a spell to break wedlock, and to break affection also, it were well worth its purchase at any price; yea, though the soul's jeopardy were added to the gold.

Re-enter PHEMY, *followed by* BAWLDY.

Phemy. I had not far to seek for him: he stood waiting in the passage, for the cooling of his brose.

Anna. Come nearer, Bawldy. Dost thou know where Grizeld Bane lives?

Bawldy. Ay, that I do, to my cost. She and her black cat, too, live owre near my milk kye. Brindle and Hawky gi' but half the milk they should gi', and we wat weel whare the ither half gangs to.

Anna. Never mind that, my good lad! Hie to her immediately, and tell her to come to me.

Bawldy. To you, leddy?

Anna. Yes: to come to me without loss of time.—There is money for thee. (*Giving money.*) Do thy errand speedily and secretly: let nobody know that I have sent thee.

Bawldy. An' she's to come to you here, hidlings, as it war?

Anna. Yes, Bawldy; and when she comes, let her wait for me in the cattle shed, by the wood, and I'll meet her there. Dost thou understand me, man? Go quickly.

Bawldy. The night, leddy?

Anna. Yes, to-night. Why dost thou look so scared?

Bawldy. I darna gang to her at night.—Gude be wi' us! an I war to find her at her cantrips, I had better be belaired in a bog, or play coupcarling owre the craig o' Dalwhirry.

Anna. She must be very terrible to make thee so afraid.

Bawldy. When she begins to mutter wi' her white wuthered lips, and her twa gleg eyen are glowering like glints o' wildfire frae the hollow o' her dark bent brows, she's enough to mak a trooper quake; ay, wi' baith swurd and pistol by his side.—No, no, Leddy! the sun maun be up in the lift whan I venture to her den.

Anna. Thou wilt get there before it be dark, if thou make good speed.

Bawldy. No, though I had the speed o' a mawkin. It is gloaming already; black clouds are spreading fast owre the sky, and far-off thunner is growling. There is a storm coming on, and the fiends o' the air are at wark; I darna gang till the morning.

Anna. Timid loon! retire then, and go in the morning. But see that thou keep the secret. I'll give thee more money, if thou prove trusty and diligent.

[*Exit* BAWLDY.

Phemy. The carrier will set off in a trice, madam.

Anna. Let him go.

Phemy. And no orders given?

Anna. Give him what orders thou wilt, and plague me no more.

[*Exeunt severally.*

SCENE II.

Before the gate of DUNGARREN *tower:* ANDERSON *and other servants are seen loitering within the gate.*

Enter DUNGARREN, *with a fowling-piece in his hand, and a pouch or bag swung from his shoulder, as returned from sport.*

And. (*advancing to meet him.*) I'm right glad to see your honour returned; for the night draws on, and it wad hae been nae joke, I trow, to hae been belated on a haunted warlock moor, and thunner growling i' the welkin.

Dun. The sky indeed looks threatening.

And. And what sport has your honour had the day? The birds grow wilder every year, now.

Dun. Think you so, Anderson?

And. Trowth do I! There's something uncanny about them too. It's a fearfu' time we live in.

Dun. I have done pretty well, however. Give this to the housekeeper to increase the stores of her larder. (*Unfastening the bag, and giving it to* ANDERSON.)

And. By my faith! she'll be glad enough o' sick a supply; for Madam Annabell is come back again, wi' that Episcopal lassie frae the Isle o' Barra, that reads out o' a prayer book, and ca's hersell her leddy's gentlewoman. Lord be mercifu' to us! the leddy's bad enough, but Job himsell could hardly thole the gentlewoman.

Dun. What has brought her back so soon? She was to have staid a week in Dumbartonshire.

And. That's more than I can say: but here comes Black Bawldy, wha was sent for to speak to her; ay, and gaed into the very parlour till her. He, maybe, kens what has brought her back.

Dun. That's strange enough.

And. Nae mair strange than true. Into the very parlour: I saw him set his dirty feet on the clean floor wi' my ain eyen.

Enter BAWLDY.

Dun. So, Bawldy, thou'rt become company for ladies in a parlour.

Bawldy. Toot, your honour! ony body's gude enough to haver wi' them, when they're wearying.

Dun. What makes Mrs. Annabell return to us so soon, if she be wearying?

Bawldy. She'll no weary now, when your honour's come hame.

Dun. Has any thing happen'd? She was to have staid a week in Dumbartonshire.

Bawldy. Maybe she has been a week there, o' her ain reckoning, tho' we ca' it only twa days. Folks said when she gaed awa', that she wou'd na be lang awa'. It wou'd be as easy to keep a moth frae the can'le, or a cat frae the milk-house, as keep her awa' frae the tower o' Dungarren (*lowering his voice*) when the laird is at hame.

Dun. What say'st thou, varlet?

Bawldy. Only what I hear folks say, your honour.

Dun. Go thy ways to thy loft and thy byre. Folks are saucy, and teach lads to forget themselves.

[*Exit* BAWLDY.

(*Pointing to the bag.*) Take it in, Anderson.

[*Exit* ANDERSON.

Dun. (*alone, turning impatiently from the gate.*) I thought to have crossed the threshold of my own house in peace.—To be pestered with the passion of an indelicate vixen!—She fastens her affection upon me like a doctor's blister-sheet, strewed with all the stinging powders of the torrid zone, for daring and desperate medication. (*After pacing to and fro in a disturbed manner.*) And my gentle Violet, too: must she be still subjected to her scornful looks and insulting insinuations? A noble spirit like hers, under such painful circumstances to be exposed to such insolence! It shall not be: I will not suffer it. (*A thoughtful pause.*) To affront a lady in my own house? Not to be thought of! To leave the country at once, and let the sea and its waves roll between us? Ay, this were well, were not all that is dear to me left behind;—my mother, my poor afflicted sister, my dear, dear Violet, the noble distressed Violet Murrey.—No; I will stay and contend with the termagant, as I would with an evil spirit. Had she the soul of a woman within her, though the plainest and meanest of her sex, I would pity and respect her; but as she

is—O! shame upon it! she makes me as bad as herself. I know
not what to do: I dare not enter yet.

[*Exit the way by which he came.*

SCENE III.

*A wild moor, skirted on one side by a thick tangled wood, through which
several open paths are seen. The stage darkened to represent faint moonlight
through heavy gathering clouds. Thunder and lightning.*

Enter by the front ELSPY LOW, MARY MACMURREN, *and her son,* WILKIN,
who stop and listen to the thunder.

Mary Mac (*spreading her arms exultingly.*) Ay, ay! this sounds like the
   true sound o' princedom and powerfu'ness.

Elspy Low (*clapping her hands as another louder peal rolls on.*) Ay; it
   sounds royally! we shall na mare be deceived; it wull prove a'
   true at last.

Mary Mac. This very night we shall ken what we shall ken. We shall
   be wi' the beings of power—be wi' them and be of them.

[*Thunder again.*

Elspy Low. It is an awfu' din, and tells wi' a lordly voice wha is coming
   and at hand: we shall na mare be deceived.

Mary Mac (*to* WILKIN, *as he presses closer to her side*). Dinna tug at me
   sa wickedly, Wilkin; thou shalt ha' a bellyfu' soon o' the fat o'
   the lawn, my poor glutton.

Wilkin. Fou! fou! meat! great meat!—hurr, hurr! (*making a noise in his
   throat to express pleasure*) it's a-coming!

Mary Mac. We shall ha' what we list at last,—milk and meat! meat
   and malt!

Elspy Low. Mingling and merry-making; and revenge for the best
   sport of a'!

Mary Mac. Ay; the hated anes will pay the cost, I trow. We'll sit at our
   good coags of cream, and think o' the growling carle's kye wi'
   their udders lank and sapless, and the goodwife greeting ow'r
   her kirn.

Elspy Low. Ha, ha, ha! there's good spice in that, woman, to relish far
poorer fare.

Mary Mac. They refused us a han'fu' in our greatest need, but now it
wull be our turn to ha' fou sacks and baith cakes and kebbucks
at command, while their aumery is bare.

Elspy Low. Ha, ha, ha! there's good spice in that, kimmer.

[*A very loud peal, &c.*

Mary Mac. Hear ye that! the thunner grows louder and louder; and
here she comes wi' her arms in the air and her spirit as hie as
the clouds. Her murky chief and his murky mates wull soon fra
a' quarters o' the warld, I warrant ye, come trooping to their
tryste.

Enter GRIZELD BANE *from the wood by the bottom of the stage, advancing
with wild frantic gestures.*

Grizeld Bane (*stopping on the middle of the stage, and spreading wide her
raised arms with lofty courtesy*). Come, come, my mighty master!
Come on the clouds; come on the wind! Come for to loosen,
and come for to bind! Rise from the raging sea; rise from the
mine! There's power in the night storm for thee and for thine.

Mary Mac (*very eagerly to* GRIZELD). Dost thou really see him?

Elspy Low (*in the same manner*). Dost thou see him? or hear him?

Mary Mac. Is he near us?

Elspy Low. Is he on the moor?

Grizeld Bane. Hold your peace, wretches! he may start up by your
side in an instant, and scare the very life from your body, if ye
forget what I told you.

Elspy Low. I have na' forgotten it.

Mary Mac. Nor I neither. We're to tak' han's first of a'. (*Takes* ELSPY
by the hand, and then turns to WILKIN.) And thine, too, Wilkin.

Wilkin. Meat, meat!

Mary Mac. No, glutton; thou mun gi' me thy haun and go round, as
I told thee.

Wilkin. Round! round! pots be round, dishes be round; a' fou for
Wilkin! hurr, hurr!

[GRIZELD BANE *joins them, and they all take hands, moving in a circular direction, and speaking all together in a dull chanting measure.*

To the right, to the right, to the right we wheel;
Thou heaving earth, free passage give, and our dark prince
    reveal.
To the right, &c. (*three times, then turning the contrary way.*)
To the left, to the left, to the left we go;
Ye folding clouds, your curtain rend, and our great master
    show.

[*Loud thunder.*

Elspy Low (*after a pause*). Is he coming yet?
Mary Mac. Is he coming, Grizeld Bane? I see nothing.
Grizeld Bane (*seizing her by the throat*). Hold thy peace, or I'll strangle thee! Is it for a wretch like thee to utter earthly words on the very verge of such an awful presence?
Mary Mac. For God's sake!—for Satan's sake!—for ony sake, let gang thy terrible grip.

[*A tremendous loud peal.*

Grizeld Bane (*exultingly.*) There's an astounding din to make your ears tingle! as if the welkin were breaking down upon us with its lading of terror and destruction! The lightning has done as I bade it. I see him, I see him now.
Mary Mac. Where, where? I see nothing.
Elspy Low. Nor I either, Grizeld.
Grizeld Bane. Look yonder to the skirt of that cloud: his head is bending over it like a knight from the keep of a castle. Hold ye quiet for a space; quiet as the corse in its coffin: he will be on the moor in a trice.
Elspy Low. Trowth, I think he will; for I'm trembling sa.
Mary Mac. I'm trem'ling too, woman; and sa is poor Wilkin.
Grizeld Bane (*exultingly, after another very loud peal, &c.*). Ay, roar away! glare away! roar to the very outrage of roaring! Brave heralding, I trow, for the prince of the power of the air!—He will be here, anon.
Mary Mac. I'm sure he will, for my legs bend under me sa, I canna' stand upright.

Grizeld Bane. Hold thy tongue! he is on the moor. Look yonder, where he is moving with strides like the steps of a man, and light by his side. Dost thou see it? (*To* MARY MACMURREN.)

Mary Mac. Preserve us from scath! I see like a man wi' a lantern. Dost thou see it, Elspy?

Elspy Low. Distinctly: and wi' what fearfu' strides he comes on!

Grizeld Bane. It is him; he approaches. Bow your heads instantly to the earth, and repeat the Lord's Prayer backwards, if you can.

> [*They all bow their bodies and begin an inarticulate muttering; and presently enters* MURREY, *bearing a lantern, which he hastily darkens upon discovering them, and tries to avoid them.*]

Grizeld Bane. Do not pass from us! stay with us; speak to us, Satan! Our spells are shrewd and sure, and thou knowest we have served and will serve thee. Turn not away! Give us power and we'll worship thee. Art thou not come to our tryste?

Mur. Miserable women! what brings you here at this hour in this place? With whom have you made a tryste?

Grizeld Bane. With thyself, mighty Satan! for we know thee well enough for all the screen of darkness that encircles thee.

Mur (*in a deep, strong, feigned voice*). What is your will with me?

Grizeld Bane. Give us power, and we'll worship thee.

Mur. What power do you covet? Power over goods and chattels, or power over bodies and spirits? Say which, by your compact, you would purchase?

Grizeld Bane (*eagerly*). Both, both!

Mur. Ye ask too much; take your choice of the one or the other.

Mary Mac. What say'st thou, Elspy?

Elspy Low. I'll consider first.

Mary Mac. Goods and chattels for my compact.

Grizeld Bane (*to her disdainfully*). Sordid caitiff! Bodies and spirits for mine!

Mur. I will see to that at convenient season.

Grizeld Bane, Mary Mac, and *Elspy Low* (*speaking at once*). Now, now!

Grizeld Bane. Let us have it now, mighty master, and we'll swear to the compact on this spot.

Mur. Have ye considered it? Ye shall have your will on earth for a
term, and then ye must serve my will in the pit of fire and
brimstone for ever.

Grizeld Bane. Be it so! and make this very night the beginning of our
power.

Mur. Ye are rare mates, indeed, to be so eagerly set upon evil.

Grizeld Bane. Are we not, master? Swear us forthwith, and remove
that dull darkness from thy presence. Call round thy liege imps
and begin. Ay, ay; they are all coming.

Mary Mac. Where, where, Grizeld?

Grizeld Bane. A score of grinning faces to the right and the left. Dost
thou not see them, blind mole that thou art? But where is he
who was wont to attend thee, great chieftain? Thou hast never
a liege man like him.

Mur. Whom dost thou mean, haggard dame?

Grizeld Bane. He with the wreath round his throat; the fellest and
bravest of them all.

Mur. He shall be with me when I meet you again.

Grizeld Bane. Do not leave us now, princely master! do not deceive us
again: bind us and give us power ere we part.

Mur. Go to the further side of the wood, and I'll follow you: I may
not bind you here, for I hear the sound of horses approaching.
Begone; mortal man must not disturb our rites.

> [*As the women are about to go off,* RUTHERFORD, *as if just
> dismounted, holding his horse by the bridle, appears from
> behind a rocky hillock which forms one of the side scenes,
> near the front, whilst the lightning, coming in a broad flash
> across the stage, shows every thing upon it distinctly for a
> moment. A loud peal follows:* RUTHERFORD *and his horse
> draw back and disappear; and exeunt by the opposite side*
> GRIZELD BANE, &c., *leaving* MURREY *alone.*]

And so there be verily such wretched creatures in the world,
who are, or desire to be, in league with the wicked one! It is a
fearful and mortifying glimpse of human nature. I hope they
have not scared my poor child upon her way; or rather, that this
awful storm has prevented her from coming abroad. O, would
I had not requested her to meet me! for I know her brave spirit
and the strength of her affection; neither storm nor danger will

deter her. Why did I tempt her? Alas, my gentle child! is this the love of a parent? Here she is!

Enter VIOLET *from the same side by which* RUTHERFORD *disappeared, and he runs to her and locks her in his arms, both remaining silent for a time.*

Vio. My father! my dear, dear father!

Mur. My own sweet Violet! all that I can call my own, and worth all that I have lost. But for thee, my dear child, I should in truth be, what I am now, by all but thyself, believed to be,—no longer a being of this world.

Vio. Say not so, my dear father! are there not kindness and humanity every where, whether you receive it under one name or another? And if this be not the case, take me with you, and you shall be no longer friendless and bereft.

Mur. No, Violet; that I will never do. To see thee by stealth, were it but a few times in the course of years, with sad dreary intervals between, is still worth living for; and more than a man, stained with the blood of a fellow creature, deserves.

Vio. Ah, why will you tax yourself so harshly! The quarrel was fastened on you.

Mur. Fool that I was, to let the angry reproaches of a fool get such mastery over me! were reason and prowess bestowed upon me for such a despicable use? Oh! had Fatheringham, who stood by, and was the only witness of the combat, endeavoured, as he might have done, to reconcile us, that blood had never been shed.

Vio. But what is past is past; let us think of the lot which is our portion now—of that which lies before us. I will love you always, and think of you always, and be with you always, if you will permit me. The rank and the fare and the home that are good enough for you are good enough for me. And if Fatheringham be still in life, he may again appear to clear you from this crime. In the mean time, your supposed death and your supposed body being found and buried by your friends, give you in any distant retreat a complete security. Let me then, my dear father, go with you now, or follow you soon.

Mur. Is there not one to be left behind who is dear to you?

Vio. No one who is or ought to be so dear as you. And I shrink from the thought of being received into a family who will despise me.

Mur. Violet, thou art too proud: thou hast got my infirmity by inheritance. Yes, I was proud once: but, dead in men's belief, and separated from the social world, I am now, as it were, a dead man in my own feelings. I look on the things of this earth as though I belonged not to it. I am meek and chastened now, and will not encourage thee in the cherishing of imprudent unreasonable pride. But we will talk of this elsewhere: I hear voices from the wood.

[*Wild cries from the women heard at a distance, and then nearer.*
I fear they will return when they find I do not join them.

Vio. Whom do you mean?

Mur. Didst thou meet nobody on the way?

Vio. Nobody but our good minister and his man, going, as I suppose, to the tower of Dungarren, to pray by the sick child.

Mur. I hope he did not see you.

Vio. I hope he did not: for I tried to conceal myself behind a bush; and he and the servant passed me in silence.

[*Wild cries without, nearer than before.*]

Mur. Let us leave this spot: those creatures are returning to it. I will tell thee about them when we are in safety.

[*Exeunt in haste.*

SCENE IV.

A narrow passage hall or lobby. Enter PHEMY, *meeting* ANDERSON, *who carries a light in his hand.*

And. We may a' gang to our beds now, that are nae appointed to sit up.

Phemy. What a terrible storm we have had! The brazen sconces in the hall, with the guns, pistols, pikes, and claymores, made such a clattering, as if they were coming down upon our heads altogether, with the slates and rafters of the old roof on the top of all. I'm certain a thunderbolt struck somewhere or other on this unlucky house: I wish I were out of it.

And. It's pity ye dinna get your wish, then. I'm sure there's naebody rightfully belanging to this family that has ony mind to baulk it.

Phemy. Don't be so hasty, Mr. Anderson: I had no intention to disparage the house of Dungarren, though there be neither silk nor tapestry on its walls, like the houses that I have lived in.

And. Weel, weel! be it sae! Silk and tapestry may be plentier than manners in the rich island of Barra.

Phemy. I have lived in other places than Barra, I assure you.

And. I dinna doubt ye hae; but let us mak nae mair quarrelling about it now, whan we shou'd a' be thankfu' that we war sheltered frae sic a storm in ony house.—Grizeld Bane and her mates war on the moor the night, I'll tak my aith on't. God help ony poor wanderer wha may hae been belated near their haunts! I wadna hae been in his skin for the best har'st fee that ever was paid into a Lowlander's purse or a Highlander's spleuchan.

Phemy. Was not the minister expected?

And. O! he, belike, might cross the moor unscathed. It wad be a bauld witch or warlock either, that wad meddle wi' the minister. And that is the reason, I reckon, why he winna believe there is ony sic thing in a' the country about.

Enter BAWLDY.

Phemy. Here comes Bawldy. What keeps thee up, man?

Bawldy. I'm waiting for the minister.

And. Wha bade thee wait? What is Duncan about?

Bawldy. He's about a Highlandman's business, just doing naething at a'; and wad be snoring on the settle in the turning o' a bannock, if fear wad let him sleep.

Phemy. Is he more afraid than the rest of you?

Bawldy. He has mair cause, mistress: he has seen bogles enow in his time, and kens a' the gaits and fashions o' them.

Phemy. Has he indeed.

Bawldy. Ay, certes; by his ain tale, at least. We hae heard o' mawkins starting up in the shapes of auld women, whan chased to a cross running burn, but Duncan has seen it. Nae wonner if he be feared!

And. Weel, than, an thou will sit up, he'll tell thee stories to keep thee frae wearying; and I dinna care if I join ye mysell for an hour or sae, for I'm naewise disposed for my ain bed in that dark turret-chaumer.

Bawldy. But gin ye keep company wi' stable loons and herds, Mr. Anderson, ye'll gi' them, nae doubt, a wee smack o' your ain higher calling. Is the key o' the cellar in your pouch? My tongue's unco dry after a' this fright.

And. Awa', ye pawky thief! Dost tu think that I'll herrie the laird's cellar for thee or ony body?—But there's the whisky bottle in my ain cupboard, wi' some driblets in it yet, that ye may tak; and deil a drap mair shall ye get, an thy tongue were as guizened as a spelding. I wonder wha learnt sic a youngster as thee to be sae pawky.

Phemy. Bawldy has by nature cunning enough to lose nothing for want of asking; and Mr. Anderson, too, has his own natural faculty for keeping what he has got.—Good night to you both.

And. Good night to ye. (*Half aside.*) I'm sure I wad rather bid you good night than good morrow, at ony time.

[*Exeunt severally.*

SCENE V.

A large chamber, with a bed at the bottom of the stage, on which is discovered a sick child, and LADY DUNGARREN *seated by it.*

Enter DUNGARREN *by the front, stepping very softly.*

Dun. Is she asleep?

Lady Dun. Yes; she has been asleep for some minutes.

Dun. Let me watch by her then, and go you to rest.

Lady Dun. I dare not: her fits may return.

Dun. The medicine you have given her will, I trust, prevent it: so do go to rest, my dear mother!

Lady Dun. No, dear Robert; her disease is one over which no natural medicine has any power. As sure as there are witches and warlocks on earth—and we know there are—they have been dealing with her this night.

Dun. Be not too sure of this. The noise of the storm, and the flashes of lightning, might alarm her, and bring on convulsions.

Lady Dun. Ah, foolish youth! thou art proud of the heathenish learning thou hast gleaned up at college, and wilt not believe what is written in Scripture.

Dun. Nay, mother, say only that I do not believe—

[*Enter* ANNABELLA *behind them, and stops to listen.*
—such explanations of Scripture as have given countenance to superstitious alarm. Our good pastor himself attaches a different meaning to those passages you allude to, and has but little faith in either witches or apparitions.

Lady Dun. Yes, he has been at college, good man as he is. Who else would doubt of it?

Dun. But Violet Murrey has not been at college, and she has as little faith in them as Mr. Rutherford.

Anna. (*advancing passionately*). If Violet Murrey's faith, or pretended faith, be the rule we are to go by, the devil and his bondsfolk will have a fine time of it in this unhappy county of Renfrew. She will take especial care to speak no words for the detection of mischief which she profits by.

Dun. Profits by! What means that foul insinuation?

Lady Dun. Be not so violent, either of you. Soften that angry eye, Robert; and remember you are speaking to a lady.

Dun. And let her remember that she is speaking of a lady.

Anna. What rank the daughter of a condemned malefactor holds in the country, better heralds than I must determine.

Dun. Malignant and heartless reproach! Provoke me not beyond measure, Annabella. For this good woman's sake, for thy own sake, for the sake of female dignity and decorum, provoke me no more with words so harsh, so unjust, so unseemly.

Anna. Not so unseemly, Dungarren, as degrading the heir of an honourable house, with an attachment so—But I will say no more.

Dun. You have said too much already.

Lady Dun. Hush, hush! for Heaven's sake be peaceable! You have
wakened the child from her sleep. Look how she gazes about.
Nurse! nurse! ho! (*Calling loud off the stage.*)

Enter Nurse.

Nurse. Are they tormenting her again? They hae time now, when
their storm and their revelry is past, to cast their cantrips here,
I trow. (*Shaking her fist angrily.*) O you ugly witch! show your
elrich face from behint the hangings there, an' I'll score you
aboon the breath wi' a jocteleg.

Lady Dun. (to Nurse). Dost thou see any thing?

Nurse. I thought I just saw a waft o' her haggart visage in the dark
shadow o' the bed hangings yonder. But see or no see, she is in
this room, as sure as I am a Christian saul. What else shou'd mak
the bairn stare sae, and wriggle wi' her body sae miserably?

Dun. But are not you a bold woman, Nurse, to threaten a witch so
bloodily?

Nurse. I'm bauld enough to tak vengeance at my ain haun upon
ony body that torments my bairn, though it war Satan himsel.
Howsomever, I carry about a leaf o' the bible sewed to my
pouch, now; for things hae come to sic a fearfu' pitch, that
crooked pins and rowan-tree do next to nae good at a'.—Bless
us a'! I wush the minister war come.

Dun. And you have your wish, Nurse; for here he is.

Enter RUTHERFORD, *in a hurried, bewildered manner.*

Lady Dun. My good sir, you are welcome: but my heart reproaches
me for having brought you from home in such a dreadful
night.—What is the matter with you?

Dun. He cannot speak.

Lady Dun. Sit down in this chair, my good sir. He is going to faint.
            [DUNGARREN *supports him, and places him in an easy chair;*
                then fetches him a glass of water, which he swallows hastily.

Dun. Has the lightning touched you, dear sir?

Ruth. Not the lightning.

Lady Dun. Has aught happened to you on the moor?

Anna. Have you seen any thing?—He has seen something.

Dun. Have you seen any thing, my good sir?

Ruth. Nought, by God's grace, that had any power to hurt me.

Dun. But you have seen something which has overcome your mind to an extraordinary degree. Were another man in your case, I should say that superstitious fears had o'ermaster'd him, and played tricks with his imagination.

Ruth. What is natural or unnatural, real or imaginary, who shall determine? But I have seen that, which, if I saw it not, the unassisted eyesight can give testimony to nothing.

Lady Dun. and Anna. (both speaking together). What was it? What was it?

[RUTHERFORD *gives no answer.*

Dun. You saw, then, what has moved you so much, distinctly and vividly?

Ruth. Yea, his figure and the features of his face, as distinctly, in the bright glare of the lightning, as your own now appear at this moment.

Dun. A man whom you knew, and expected not to find at such an hour and in such a place. But what of this? Might not such a thing naturally happen?

Ruth. (lowering his voice, and drawing DUNGARREN *aside, while* ANNABELLA *draws closer to him to listen).* No, Robert Kennedy: he whose form and face I distinctly saw, has been an indweller of the grave these two years.

Dun. (in a low voice also). Indeed! Are you sure of it?

Ruth. I put his body into the coffin with mine own hands, and helped to carry it to the grave; yet there it stood before me, in the bright blazing of the storm, and seemed to look upon me, too, with a look of recognition most strange and horrible.

Annabella (eagerly). Whose ghost was it? Who was the dead man you saw?

Ruth (rising from his chair, and stepping back from her with displeasure). I reckoned, madam, but upon one listener.

Lady Dun. Nay, be not angry with her. Who can well refrain from listening to such a tale? And be not angry with me neither, when I ask you one question, which it so much concerns me to know. Saw you aught besides this apparition? any witches or creatures of evil?

Ruth. I will answer that question, lady, at another time, and in greater privacy.

Annabella (to LADY DUNGARREN). He has seen them; it is evident he has. But some of his friends might be amongst them: there may be good cause for secrecy and caution.

Dun. (to ANNABELLA). Why do you press so unsparingly upon a man whose spirits have, from some cause or other, received such a shock?

Ruth. I forgive her, Dungarren: say no more about it. It is God's goodness to me that I am here unhurt, again to do the duty of a Christian pastor to my dear and friendly flock now convened. Let me pray by the bed of that poor suffering child, for her, for myself, and for all here present.

Lady Dun. (to ANNABELLA). Let us put her in a different position before he begin: she must be tired of that; for see, she moves again uneasily.

> [LADY DUNGARREN *takes* ANNABELLA *to the bottom of the stage, and they both seem employed about the child, while* DUNGARREN *and* RUTHERFORD *remain on the front.*

Dun. It is a most extraordinary and appalling apparition you have seen. What do you think of it?

Ruth. What can I think of it, but that the dead are sometimes permitted to revisit the earth, and that I verily have seen it.

Dun. I would more readily believe this than give credit to the senseless power and malevolence of witchcraft, which you have always held in derision.

Ruth. It is presumption to hold any thing in derision.

Dun. Ha! say you so, in this altered tone of voice! Have you met with any thing to-night to change your opinions on this subject? Have you seen any of the old women, so strangely spoken of, on the moor?

Ruth. Would that I had only seen such!

Dun. The voice in which you speak, the expression with which you look upon me, makes me tremble. Am I concerned with aught that you have seen?

Ruth. You are, my dear Robert, and must think no more of Violet Murrey. (*A deep silence.*) Yes; it has stricken you to the heart. Think upon it as you ought. I expect no answer.

Dun. (*endeavouring to recover speech*). But I must—I will try—I must answer you, for I— (*tearing open his waistcoat, and panting for breath,*) —I can believe nothing that accuses her.

Ruth. Were a daughter of my own concerned, I could not be more distressed.

Dun. It makes me distracted to hear thee say so!

Ruth. Go to thine own room, and endeavour to compose thy mind, and I will pray for thee here. Pray for thyself, too, in private: pray earnestly, for there is, I fear, a dreadful warfare of passion abiding thee.

> [*Exit* DUNGARREN *by the front, while* RUTHERFORD *joins the ladies by the sickbed, where they prepare to kneel as the scene closes.*

ACT II.

SCENE I.

The inside of a miserable cottage, with a board or coarse table by the wall, on which stand some empty wooden bickers or bowls. Enter WILKIN, *who runs eagerly to the board, then turns away disappointed.*

Wilkin. Na, na! tuim yet! a' tuim yet! Milk nane! parritch nane! (*Pointing to the bowls, and then pressing his stomach.*) Tuim there! tuim here! Woe worth it! to say they wad be fou, an' they're no fou! Woe worth it! woe worth them a'!

Enter BAWLDY, *and* WILKIN *runs to take hold of him.*

Bawldy (*frightened*). Han's aff, I tell thee!

Wilkin. Hast brought ony thing? Gie me't, gie me 't.

Bawldy (*pulling out a horse-shoe from his pocket*). Stan' aff, I say! Nane o' your witch nips for me! I hae, maybe, brought what thou winna like, an tu hae wit enough to ken what it is.

Wilkin. Will 't kill me?

Bawldy. Ay; fule as he is, he's frightened for 't;—the true mark of
warlockry. They hae linket him in wi' the rest: naething's owre
waff for Satan, an it hae a saul o' ony kind to be tint.

Wilkin. Will 't kill me?

Bawldy. No: but I'll score thy imp's brow wi 't,—that's what I'll do,—
an tu lay a finger on me. But dinna glow'r sae: stan' aff a bit,
an answer my quastions, and there's siller for thee. (*Throwing
him some pence.*) Was tu on the moor i' the night-time, wi' thy
mither?

Wilkin. Mither?

Bawldy. Ay; was tu on the moor wi' her, whan the thunner roared?

Wilkin. Thunner roared, fire roared, thunner roared! hurl! hurl! hurl!
(*Imitating the noise of thunder.*)

Bawldy. Ay; an' ye ware there?

Wilkin. Ay, there. (*Nodding his head.*)

Bawldy. An' wha was there beside?

Wilkin. Beside?

Bawldy. Beside thee an' thy mither. What saw ye there?

Wilkin. Black man an' fire: hurl! hurl! (*Making a noise as before.*)

Bawldy. Gude saf' us! has tu seen the deil then, bodily?

Wilkin. Deil, deil!

Bawldy (*shrinking back from him*). Keep me frae scathe! That I should
stan' sae near ane that has been wi' Satan himsel! What did tu
see forbye?

Wilkin. Saw? Saw folk.

Bawldy. What folk? Auld women?

Wilkin. Auld women; young women. Saw them a' on fire. Hurl!
hurl! hurl!

Bawldy. Saw a young woman? Was it Maggy Kirk's crooket
daughter?

Wilkin. Na, joe! young woman.

Bawldy. What's her name? What did they ca' her?

Wilkin. Leddy—young leddy, on fire.

Bawldy. Gude saf' us a'! can this be true!

[*Voices without.*

1st voice. I'll tak amends o' her for cheating us again.

2d voice. An' sae will I, spitefu' carlin! Maun naebody hae power but
    hersel?

Enter MARY MACMURREN *and* ELSPY LOW, *and* BAWLDY *hides himself
behind the door.*

Mary Mac. There's power to be had, that's certain: power that can
    raise the storm and the fiend; ay, that can do ony thing. But
    we're aye to be puir yet: neither meat nor money, after a's
    dune!
Elspy Low. Neither vengeance nor glawmery, for a' the wicket
    thoughts we hae thought, for a' the fearfu' words we hae
    spoken, for a' the backward prayers we hae prayed!—I'll rive
    her eyen out o' her head, though they shou'd glare upon us frae
    their hollow sconces, like corpse-can'les frae a grave-stane.
Mary Mac (pointing to the board). Even thay puir cogs are as toom as
    before, and my puir idiot as hungry. Hast tu had ony thing,
    Wilkin? (*Turns round to him and discovers* BAWLDY.) Ha! wha has
    tu wi' thee? (*To* BAWLDY.) What brought thee here, in a mischief
    to thee! Thou's Dungarren's herd, I reckon.
Bawldy. I came frae the tower of Dungarren wi' an errand, I wou'd
    hae ye to wit.
Mary Mac. Tell thy errand, then, and no lurk that gate, in a nook,
    like a thoumart in a dowcot: for if tu be come here without an
    errand, thou shalt rue it dearly to the last hour o' thy life.
Bawldy. Isna this Grizeld Bane's house?
Mary Mac. No, silly loon! it's my house. She's but a rinagate rawny,
    frae far awa' parts, that came to be my lodger. Ay; and she may
    gang as she came, for me: I'll no harbour her ony mair. Nae
    mair Grizeld Banes in my house, to reeve an' to herrie me sae!
    She maun pack aff wi' hersel this very day.

Enter GRIZELD BANE.

Grizeld Bane (looking on her with stern contempt). Who speaks of
    Grizeld Bane with such unwary words? Repeat them, I pray
    thee. (MARY *stands abashed.*) Thou wilt not.— (*To* ELSPY, *in like*

manner.) And what hast thou to say of Grizeld Bane? (*A pause*.)
And thou, too, art silent before my face.

Elspy Low. There's a callant frae Dungarren, i' the nook, that comes
on an errand to thee.

Grizeld Bane (*to* BAWLDY). Do not tremble so, silly child! What is thine
errand?

Bawldy. She bade me—she bade me say—ye maun come to her.

Grizeld Bane. To whom, and where? Thou speakest as if my hand
were already on thy throat, where it shall very soon be, if thou
tell not thy errand more distinctly.

Bawldy. The stranger leddy at the tower, the leddy Annabell, desires
that ye wad meet her in the lone shed, near the outer gate, in
the afternoon. Gi' me an answer, an please ye.

Grizeld Bane (*in a kind of chant*).

Where there be ladies and where there be lords,
Mischief is making with glances and words,
Work is preparing for pistols and swords.

Bawldy. Is that an answer?

Grizeld Bane. She may take it for one; but if it please thee better, thou
may'st say to her, I will do as she desires. And take this token
with thee, youngster. (*Going close to him*.)

Bawldy. Na, na, I thank ye; I have answer enough.

[*Exit in a fright*.

Grizeld Bane (*turning to* MARY MACMURREN *and* ELSPY LOW). And ye
are dissatisfied, forsooth! you must have power as you will and
when you will.

Elspy Low. Thou hast deceived us.

Grizeld Bane. Was there not storm enough to please ye?

Elspy Low. Enough to crack the welkin; but what got we by it?

Grizeld Bane. Did he come in the storm? Did you not see him and
hear him?

Mary Mac. Certes did he; but what gat we by it? He keepit na' his
tryste wi' us the second time; an' we gaed wearily hame on our
feet, as wat and as puir as we came.

Grizeld Bane. O that false tongue! ye rode upon clouds: I saw you
pass over my head, and I called to you.

Mary Mac. The woman is a fiend or bereft a' thegether! I walket hame on my feet, en' gaed to my miserable bed, just as at ony ither time, an' sa did she.

Grizeld Bane. But rode ye not afterwards, my chucks? I saw you both pass over my head, and I called to you.

Elspy Low. If we ware upon clouds, we ware sleeping a' the while, for I ken naething anent it. Do ye, neighbour? (*To* MARY MACMURREN.)

Mary Mac. I dare na' just say as ye say, kimmer, for I dreamt I was flying in the air and somebody behint me.

Grizeld Bane. Ay, ay, ay; ye will discern mist and mysteries at last. But ye must have power, forsooth! as ye list and when ye list. If he did not keep tryste in the night, let us cast a spell for him in the day. When doors and windows are darkened, mid-day is as potent as midnight. Shut out the light and begin. But if he roar and rage at you when he does come, that is no fault of mine. (*Draws a circle on the floor.*)

Mary Mac and *Elspy Low* (*at once*). Na, na! dinna bring him up now.
[*Exeunt hastily, leaving* GRIZELD *alone.*

Grizeld Bane (*chanting to herself after having completed the circle*).

> Black of mien and stern of brow,
> Dark one, dread one, hear me now!
> Come with potency and speed;
> Come to help me in my need.
> Kith and kindred have I none,
> Ever wand'ring, ever lone.
> Black of mien and stern of brow,
> Dark one, dread one, hear me now!

He is now at hand; the floor yawns under my feet, and the walls are running round; he is here! (*Bending her head very low and then raising it.*) Ha! is it thou? art thou risen in thy master's stead? It becomes thee to answer my call; it is no weak tie that has bound us together. I loved thee in sin and in blood: when the noose of death wrung thee, I loved thee. And now thou art a dear one and a terrible with the prince of the power of the air. Grant what I ask! grant it quickly. Give me of thy power; I have earned it. But this is a mean, narrow den; the cave of the lin is near, where water is soughing and fern is waving; the bat-bird clutching o'er head, and the lithe snake stirring below; to the cave, to the cave! we'll hold our council there.

> [*Exit with frantic gestures, as if courteously showing the way to some great personage.*

SCENE II.

A flower garden by the cottage of VIOLET MURREY, *with the building partly occupying the bottom of the stage, and partly concealed.*

Enter DUNGARREN, *who stops and looks round him, then mutters to himself in a low voice, then speaks audibly.*

Dun. The lily, and the rose, and the gillyflower; things the most beautiful in nature, planted and cherished by a hand as fair and as delicate as themselves! Innocence and purity should live here; ay, and do live here: shall the ambiguous whisper of a frightened night-scared man, be his understanding and learning what they may, shake my confidence in this? It was foolish to come on such an errand. (*Turns back, and is about to retire by the way he entered, then seems irresolute, and then stops short.*) Yet being here, I had better have some parley with her: I may learn incidentally from her own lips, what will explain the whole seeming mystery. (*Looking again on the flowers as he proceeds towards the house.*) Pretty pansey! thou hast been well tended since I brought thee from the south country with thy pretty friend, the carnation by thy side. Ay, and ye are companions still; thou, too, hast been well cared for, and all thy swelling buds will open to the sun ere long.

Enter VIOLET *from the house, while he is stooping over the flowers.*

Vio. You are come to look after your old friends, Dungarren?
Dun. I have friends here worth looking after, if beauty and sweetness give value. Thou art an excellent gardener, Violet; things thrive with thee wonderfully, even as if they were conscious whose flowers they are, and were proud of it.

Vio. Ah! that were no cause for pride. Methinks, if they were conscious whose flowers they are, they would droop their heads and wither away.

Dun. Say not so: thou art melancholy; the storm has affected thy spirits. Those who were abroad in it say that the lightning was tremendous.

Vio. It was tremendous.

Dun. And the rolling of the thunder was awful.

Vio. It was awful.

Dun. And the moor was at times one blaze of fiery light, like returning bursts of mid-day, giving every thing to view for an instant in the depth of midnight darkness. (*A pause.*) One who was there told me so. (*Another pause, and she seems uneasy.*) And more than that, a strange unlikely story. (*A still longer pause, and she more uneasy.*) But thou hast no desire to hear it: even natural curiosity has forsaken thee. What is the matter?

Vio. Nothing is the matter: tell me whatever you please, and I will listen to it. Were witches on the moor?

Dun. Yes, witches were there, but that is not my story. There was a form seen on the moor most unlike any thing that could be evil. Thou art pale and disturbed; hast thou a guess of my meaning?

Vio. The moor is wide, and benighted wanderers might be upon it of different forms and degrees.

Dun. But none who could look like one, whom, nevertheless, 'tis said, it did resemble.

Vio. (*endeavouring to recover herself*). Nay, nay, Dungarren! do not amuse yourself with me: if the devil has power to assume what form he pleases, that will account for your story at once. If he has not, you have only to suppose that some silly girl, with her plaid over her head, was bewildered by the storm at her trysting place, and that will explain it sufficiently.

Dun. These are light words, methinks, to follow upon melancholy gravity so suddenly.

Vio. If my words displease you, Dungarren, there is more cause for sorrow than surprise, and the sooner I cease to offend the better.

Dun. Violet Murrey of Torewood!!!

Vio. Robert Kennedy of Dungarren!!!

Dun. What am I to think?

Vio. Thoughts are free: take your range. Thinking is better than speaking for both of us; and so, if you please, we shall wish each other good morning. (*Turning from him with a hurried step towards the house.*)

Dun. (*following her*). We must not so part, my Violet. Had any woman but thyself used me thus,—but what of that! I love thee and must bear with thee.

Vio. No, Robert Kennedy; thou lovest me not: for there is suspicion harboured in thy mind which love would have spurned away.

Dun. Say not harboured. O no! Spurned and rejected, yet, like a trodden adder, turning and rearing again. I ask to know nothing that thou seekest to conceal. Say only that thou wert in thy own home during the night, as I am sure thou wert, and I will be satisfied, though all the diabolical witnesses of Renfrewshire were set in array against thee.

Vio. Must I be forced to bear witness in my own behalf? There is one who should bear witness for me, and lacking that evidence, I scorn every other.

Dun. And where is that witness to be found?

Vio. In the heart of Dungarren.

Dun. Thou wring'st it to the quick! I am proud and impetuous, but have I deserved this haughty reserve? Dost thou part with me in anger?

Vio. I am angry, and must leave thee; but perhaps I am wrong in being so.

Dun. Indeed thou art wrong.

Vio. Be thou charitable, then, and forgive me; but for the present let us part.

[*Exit into the house.*

Dun. (*alone*). Her behaviour is strange and perplexing. Was her anger assumed or sincere? Was she, or was she not, on that accursed moor? "Some silly girl bewildered by the storm at her trysting place,"—were not these her words? Ay, by my faith! and glancing at the truth too obviously; at the hateful, the distracting, the hitherto unsuspected truth. It is neither witch, warlock, nor devil, with whom she held her tryste. Yea, but it is a devil, whom I will resist to perdition! It is a devil who will make me one also. O, this proud rising of my heart! it gives the cruelty of distraction; and, but for the fear of God within me, would nerve my hand for blood.

Re-enter VIOLET, *in alarm, from the house.*

Vio. Oh Robert, Robert! what mean those tossings of the arms—those gestures of distraction? You doubt my faith, you think me unworthy, and it moves you to this fearful degree. If I deserve your attachment I deserve to be trusted. Think of this, dear Robert, for it kills me to see you so miserable.

Dun. Dear! you call me dear, only because you pity me.

Vio. I call thee dear, because—because—Out on thee, Robert Kennedy! hast thou no more generosity than this?

[*Bursting into tears.*

Dun. (*catching her in his arms, then unclasping her suddenly and dropping on his knee*). O forgive me, forgive me! I have treated thee ungenerously and unjustly: forgive me, my own sweet girl!

Vio. I will not only forgive thee, but tell thee every thing when I am at liberty to do so. Let us now separate; I have need of rest.

[*He leads her towards the house, caressing her hand tenderly as they go; then exeunt severally.*

SCENE III.

A passage or entrance-room in the tower. Enter ANDERSON.

And. (*looking off the stage*). What's the cunning loon standing, wi' his lug sae near that door for? (*Calling loud.*) What's tu doing there, rascal?

Enter BAWLDY.

Wha gies thee leave to come near the chambers o' gentle folks, and lay thy blackened lug sae close to the key-hole?

Bawldy. As for gentle folks, they come to me oftener nor I gang to them; and as for my lug, there was nae need to lay it to the keyhole whan the door was half open.

And. Catch thee who can unprovided wi' a ready answer! Thou hast the curiosity o' the deevil in thee and his cunning to boot: what business hast thou to pry into people's secrets?

Bawldy. A secret, forsooth, tauld wi' an open door and voices as loud as twa wives cracking in the lone! And gude be wi' us a'! they war only talking o' what we are a' talking or thinking o' fra' morning till night and fra' Sabbath day till Saturday.

And. And what is that, ne'er-do-weel?

Bawldy. What should it be but witchcraft and the young leddy? But this last bout, I trow, is the strangest bout of a'.

And. What has happened now?

Bawldy. As I was passing by the door, I heard nurse tell the Leddy Annabell how the young leddy was frightened frae her rest, as she lay in her bed, wi' the room darkened.

And. And how was that?

Bawldy. Witches cam' into the room, I canna tell how mony o' them, and ane o' them cam' upon the bed, and a'maist smoored her.

And. The Lord preserve us!

Bawldy. Ay; and she would hae been smoored a'thegither, gin she had na claught haud of the witch's arm, and squeezed it sae hard that the witch ran awa', and left a piece o' her gown sleeve in the young leddy's han'.

And. It was Grizeld Bane or Mary Macmurren, I'll be bound for't.

Bawldy. Wha it was she could na say, for she could na see i' the dark.

And. But the piece of the gown sleeve will reveal it. Show me that, and I'll ken wha it was, to a certainty. I ken ilka gown and garment belanging to them.

Bawldy. So does nurse, too: but the young leddy took a fit, as the roodies left the chaumer, and she has lost the clout.

And. That was a pity. The chamber maun be searched for it carefully, else they'll come again, and wi' some cantrup or ither, join it into the sleeve it was riven frae, as if it ne'er had been riven at a'. But gang to thy crowdy, man, and dinna tine a meal for a marvel. Thou hast nae business here: the kitchen and the

byre set thee better than lobbies and chambers. (*Exit* BAWLDY.)
That callant lurks about the house like a brownie. He's a clever
varlet, too: he can read the kittle names in the Testament, and
ding the dominie himsel at the quastions and caratches. He's
as cunning and as covetous as ony gray-haired sinner i' the
parish;—a convenient tool, I suspect, in the hands of a very
artful woman.

[*Exit.*

SCENE IV.

The apartment of ANNABELLA, *who enters, and throws herself into a chair,
remaining silent for a short time, and then speaks impatiently.*

Anna. What can detain her so long? Could she miss finding him?
He is seldom far off at this hour of the day, when broth and
beef are on the board; and he can send a boy to the hill as his
substitute. I wish the sly creature were come; for time passes
away, and with it, perhaps, opportunity.

Enter PHEMY.

Phemy. He's here, madam.
Anna. That's well. Let him enter immediately, and do thou keep
watch in the outer room.
[*Exit* PHEMY, *and presently* BAWLDY *enters.*
I want thee to do an errand for me again, Bawldy. Do not look
so grave and so cowed, man: thou shalt be well paid for it.
Bawldy. A'tweel, I'm ready enough to do ony errand, gin there be
nae witchery concerned wi't.
Anna. And what the worse wilt thou be if there should? Didst thou
not go to Grizeld Bane this morning, and return safe and sound
as before, both soul and body, with a good crown in thy pocket
to boot?
Bawldy. Certes my body cam' back safe enough; but for my puir saul,
Lord hae mercy on it! for when I gaed to my kye on the hill
again, I tried to croon o'er to mysel the hunder and saxteen

psalm, and second commandment, and could hardly remember a word o' them. Oh! she's an awfu' witch, and scares the very wit frae ane's noddle.

Anna. Never fear, Bawldy: she has left thee enough of that behind to take care of thine own interest. Thou hadst wit enough, at least, to do thy business with her; for she came to me in good time, to the spot which I appointed.

Bawldy. If she kens the place, she may meet you there again, without my ganging after her. The Lord preserve us! I wadna enter that house again for twa crowns.

Anna. Be not afraid, man: it is not to that house I would send thee; and thou shalt have two crowns for thy errand, though it be both an easy and a short one.

Bawldy. As for that, madam, an it war baith lang an' hard, I wadna mind it, so as it be an errand a Christian body may do.

Anna. A Christian body may go and speak a few words privately to Mrs. Violet Murrey's pretty maid, I should think.

Bawldy (sheepishly). There's nae great harm in that, to be sure.

Anna. And a Christian body may slip a crown quietly into her hand, and—

Bawldy (interrupting her in a low murmuring voice). Ay, ane o' the twa ye spak o'.

Anna. No, indeed, Bawldy; a third crown, which I will give thee to take from thine own pocket, and put into her pretty hand.— Perhaps it may prove the forerunner of some other token between you. She is a good tight girl, but a few years older than thyself: she may take a fancy to thee.

Bawldy. Ah! madam Annabell, somebody has been telling you that I hae a fancy for her; for they never devall wi' their havers.—But what is she to do for the crown? for I reckon she maun won it some way or anither.

Anna. In a very easy way. Tell her to send me her mistress's striped lutestring gown, for I want to look at the pattern of it, and will restore it to her immediately.

Bawldy. Is that a'?

Anna. Only thou must make her promise to conceal, from her mistress and from every body, that I borrowed the gown. Be sure to do that, Bawldy.

Bawldy. That's very curious, now. Whaur wad be the harm o' telling that ye just looket at it.

Anna. Thou'rt so curious, boy, there's no concealing any thing from thee. Art thou silly enough to believe that I only want to look at it?

Bawldy. Na, I guessed there was somewhat ahint it.

Anna. And thou shalt know the whole, if thou wilt promise to me solemnly not to tell any body.

Bawldy. I'll tell naebody. Gif my ain mither war to speer, she wad ne'er get a word anent it frae me.

Anna. I have been consulting with Grizeld Bane, about what can be done to relieve our poor sick child from her misery,—for those who put her into it can best tell how to draw her out of it,—and she says, a garment that has been upon the body of a murderer, or the child of a murderer,—it does not matter which,—put under the pillow of a witched bairn, will recover it from fits, were it ever so badly tormented. But, mark me well! should the person who owns the garment ever come to the knowledge of it, the fits will return again, as bad as before. Dost thou understand me?

Bawldy. I understand you weel enough: but will witches speak the truth, whan the deil is their teacher?

Anna. Never trouble thy head about that: we can but try. Fetch me the gown from thy sweetheart, and thou shalt have more money than this, by and by.

[*Gives him money.*

Bawldy. Since you will ca' her my sweetheart, I canna help it; though I ken weel enough it's but mocking.

Anna. Go thy ways, and do as I bid thee, without loss of time, and thou wilt soon find it good, profitable earnest. She will make a very good thrifty wife, and thou a good muirland drover, when thou'rt old enough.

[*Exit* BAWLDY.

Annabella (alone). Now shall I have what I panted for, and far better, too, than I hoped. To be tormented by witchcraft is bad; but to be accused and punished for it is misery so exquisite, that, to purchase it for an enemy, were worth a monarch's ransom. Ay, for an enemy like this, who has robbed me of my peace, stolen the affections of him whom I have loved so ardently and so long; yea, who has made me, in his sight, hateful and despicable. I will bear my agony no longer. The heart of Dungarren may be lost for ever; but revenge is mine, and I will enjoy it.—It is a fearful and dangerous pleasure, but all that is left for me.—Oh, oh! that I should live to see him the doating lover of a poor, homely—for homely she is, let the silly world call her what they please—artful girl, disgraced and degraded; the daughter of a murderer, saved only from the gibbet by suicide or accident! That I should live to witness this!—But having lived to witness it, can revenge be too dearly purchased? No; though extremity of suffering in this world, and beyond this world, were the price—Cease, cease! ye fearful thoughts! I shall but accuse her of that of which she is, perhaps, really guilty. Will this be so wicked, so unpardonable? How could a creature like this despoil such a woman as myself of the affections of Dungarren, or any man, but by unholy arts?

Enter PHEMY *in alarm.*

Phemy. Madam, madam! there are people in the passage.

Anna. And what care I for that?

Phemy. You were speaking so loud, I thought there was somebody with you. (*Looking fearfully round.*)

Anna. Whom dost thou look for? Could any one be here without passing through the outer room?

Phemy. I crave your pardon, madam, they can enter by holes, as I have heard say, that would keep out a moth or a beetle.

Anna. Go, foolish creature! Thy brain is wild with the tales thou hast heard in this house.—Did I speak so loud?

Phemy. Ay, truly, madam, and with such violent changes of voice, that I could not believe you alone.

Anna. I was not aware of it. It is a natural infirmity, like talking in one's sleep: my mother had the same.—I'll go to the garden, where the flowers and fresh air will relieve me.

Phemy. Are you unwell?

Anna. Yes, girl; but say so to no one, I pray thee.

[*Exeunt.*

ACT III.

SCENE I.

A half-formed cave, partly roofed with rock and partly open to the sky, which is seen through the overhanging bushes; a burn or brook crossing the mouth of it, at the bottom of the stage, banked by precipitous rocks mixed with wood and fern.

Voice (heard without). Indeed, thou canst not pass this way.

2d voice (without). I don't mind it at all; the water will do me no harm.

1st voice (without). Thou shalt not wet thy feet, my dear child, when a father's arms are here, so able and so happy to carry thee.

Enter Murrey *by the mouth of the cave, bearing* Violet *in his arms, whom he sets down by some loose rocks near the front of the stage.*

Vio. Set me down, my dear father; I am heavy.

Mur. I could carry thee to the world's end, my own dear girl. O that thou wert again a baby, and mine arms lock'd round thee as of yore!

Vio. I remember it, father.

Mur. Dost thou, sweet one? Ah, ah! thee in my arms, and she whom I loved by my side, and thy pretty worldless lips cooing to us by turns—an utterance that made all words contemptible! Alas, alas! such days, and many bright succeeding days have been and are gone. The fatal passion of a few short moments has made me a homeless outlaw, while reproach, instead of protection, is a father's endowment for thee. (*Sits down on a low detached rock, and buries his face in the folds of his plaid.*)

Vio. Dear, dear father! do not reproach yourself so harshly. If the world call what you have done by a very dreadful name, it is not a true one: equal fighting, though for a foolish quarrel, deserves not that appellation.

Mur. Whatever it may deserve, it will have it, when there is no witness to prove the contrary. Fatheringham alone was present, and he disappeared on the instant. When my trial came, I could not prove that the man I had slain fell in equal combat; nay, was the real aggressor in first attacking me.

Vio. It was cowardly and strange,—it was not the act of a friend to disappear and leave you so exposed.

Mur. Some evil fate befell him: he was not alive, I am certain, when I was apprehended, else he would have come forward like an honest, manly friend in my justification. The sentence of death is upon me; the mark of Cain is on my forehead; I am driven from the fellowship of men.

Vio. Say not so; for you have by the accidental death of your servant been, as it were, providentially saved from a fearful end; and being so saved, I must needs believe that some better fortune is in reserve for you.

Mur. Ay, poor Donald! I believe he would willingly have died for my sake, and Providence did so dispose of him. I little thought, after my escape from prison, when I had changed apparel with him, how completely our identity was to be confounded. He lies in the grave as James Murrey of Torwood,—in an unhallowed grave, as a murderer.

Vio. Were you near him when he fell into the pit?

Mur. Dear Violet, thou art bewildered to ask me such a question! When we had changed clothes completely, and I had even forced upon him as a gift, which he well deserved, the gold watch and seals of my family, we parted; and when his body was discovered, many weeks afterwards, the face, as I understand, from the mutilations of bruises and corruption, was no longer recognizable. But this is a mournful subject, and it is useless to dwell upon it now.

Vio. Very true; let us speak of those things for which there is still cause of thankfulness. The Irish home you have found on the mountains of Wicklow, is it not a pleasant one?

Mur. Pleasant to those who look on sky and cliff, on wood and torrent, to rouse and refresh the mind, in the intervals of such retirement as hath a purpose and a limit. To the lonely outcast what scene is pleasant? The meanest man who plies his honest trade in the narrow lane of a city, where passers-by may wish him a good day, or bid God speed him, has a domicile and a home which I think of with envy.

Vio. O do not, then, live any longer in this deserted situation!

Mur. I know what thou wilt offer, but it must not be.

Vio. Why so? Since I have lost my dear mother, and have no farther duties to detain me here, may I not cross the sea with you now, and spend some time with you in Wicklow. It will be thought that I am gone to visit our Irish relation.

Mur. No, my affectionate child, that may not be.

Vio. I should go to our relation first, and nobody should know that I went anywhere else but Dungarren; nor should I even tell it to him without your permission.

Mur (*rising quickly from his seat*). Which thou shalt never have.

Vio. Why do you utter those words so vehemently? He is honourable and true.

Mur. He is thy lover, and thou believest him to be so.

Vio. Are you displeased that he is my lover?

Mur. Yes, I am displeased, for he will never be thy husband.

Vio. O think not so hardly of him! in his heart there is honour even stronger than affection. And if I might but tell him of your being alive—

Mur. Art thou mad? art thou altogether bereft of understanding? Swear to me, on the faith of a Christian woman, that thou wilt never reveal it.

Vio. He is incapable of betraying any one, and far less—

Mur. Hold thy tongue! hold thy tongue, simple creature! Every man seems true to the woman whose affections he hath conquered. I know the truth of man and the weakness of woman. Reason not with me on the subject, but solemnly promise to obey me. I should feel myself as one for whom the rope and the gibbet are preparing, should any creature but thyself know of my being alive.

Vio. Woe is me! this is misery indeed.

Mur. Do not look on me thus with such mingled pity and surprise. Call what I feel an excess of distrust—a disease—a perversion of mind, if thou wilt, but solemnly promise to obey me.

Vio. Let my thoughts be what they may, I dare not resist the will of a parent; I solemnly promise. (*Looking up to heaven, and then bending her head very low*).

Mur. I am satisfied, and shall return to my boat, which waits for me on the Clyde, near the mouth of this burn, with a mind assured on so important a point, and assured of thy good conduct and affection. (*Looking about, alarmed.*) I hear a noise.

Vio. 'Tis the moving of some owlet or hawk in the refts of the rock over-head. To this retired spot of evil report no human creature ever ventures to come, even at mid-day.

Mur. Yes, I remember it used to be called the Warlock's den, and had some old legendary pretensions to the name. But there is a noise. (*Looks up to the open part of the cave, and discovers* DUNGARREN *above, looking down upon them.*)

Vio. It is Dungarren; what shall we do? Begone, father?

Mur. I must stand to it now; he will be down upon us in an instant: it is too late to avoid him.

Vio. No, it is not; he shall not come down. (*Calling up to him.*) Robert Kennedy, is it thou?

Dun. (*above*). Does the voice of Violet Murrey dare to ask me the question?

Vio. Stay where thou art, and come no farther; I dare ask of thee to be secret and to be generous.

Dun. (*above*). Distracting and mysterious creature, I obey thee. (*Retires.*)

Vio. He retires, and we are safe. Let us now separate. (*In a low voice.*) Farewell, my dear father! you will come and see me again?

Mur. I hope next summer to pay thee another and a less hurried visit. Farewell. (*Holding her back.*) No, no! do not embrace me.

Vio. He has retired, and will not look again.

Mur. Be not too confident. Farewell, and remember thy solemn promise. My ship will sail for Ireland to-morrow morning early, and thou shalt hear from me soon.

[*Exit by the way he entered.*

Vio. (*alone*). If they should meet without, and they may do so!— But that must not be. (*Calling in a loud voice.*) Dungarren, Dungarren! art thou still within hearing? (DUNGARREN *reappears above.*) I cannot speak to thee in so loud a voice; come down to me here.

[*He descends by the jutting rocks into the bottom of the cave in the dress and accoutrements of an angler, with a fishing-*

rod in his hand, and stands before her with a stern and serious look, remaining perfectly silent.]

O Robert Kennedy! look not on me thus! I meant to thank you for your friendly forbearance, but now I have no utterance: I cannot speak to you when you so look upon me.

Dun. Silence is best where words were vain and worthless.

Vio. You deserve thanks, whether you accept them or not.

Dun. To obey the commands of a lady deserves none.

Vio. Nay, but it does, and I thank you most gratefully. He who was with me is gone, but—but—

Dun. But will return again, no doubt, when the face of a casual intruder will not interrupt your conference.

Vio. O no! he will not return—may never return. Who he is, and where he goes, and how I am bound to him, O how I long to tell thee all, and may not!

Dun. What I have seen with mine eyes leaves you nothing to tell which I am concerned to hear.

Vio. Be it so, then; since the pride of your heart so far outmates its generosity.

Dun. You have put it out of my power to be generous; but you desire me to be secret, and shall be obeyed. Is it your pleasure, madam, that I should conduct you to your home, since he who was with you is gone?

Vio. That I accept of a service so offered, shows too well how miserably I am circumstanced. But I do accept it: let me leave this place. (*Goes toward the mouth of the cave.*)

Dun. Not by the burn, the water is too deep.

Vio. I came by it, and there is no other way.

Dun. Came by it, and dry-shod too! (*Looking at her feet.*) He who was with thee must have carried thee in his arms.

Vio. Yes, he did so; but now I will walk through the stream: wet feet will do me no injury.

Dun. There is another passage through a cleft rock on this side, concealed by the foxglove and fern.

Vio. Lead on, then, and I'll follow.

[*Exeunt.*

SCENE II.

A large hall or entrance-room, with deer's horns and arms hanging on the walls. Enter Nurse with a tankard in her hand, followed presently by ANDERSON, *who calls after her as she is about to disappear by the opposite side.*

And. Nurse, nurse, I say! Is the woman deaf?

Nurse. What are ye roaring after me for? Can a body get nae peace or comfort ony time o' the day or night? Neither o' them, by my trouth, bring muckle rest to me.

And. That may be, but ye'r tankard comforts, that belang, as it wad seem, to baith day and night, maun be stinted at present; for the sheriff and a' his rascally officers frae Paisley are at the yett, and writers beside, Lord preserve us! wi' inkhorns at their buttons and paper in their hands. Gae tell the leddy quickly, and set ye'r tankard down.

Nurse. For the sheriff officers to lay their lugs in. Na, na! sma'er browst may serve them; I'll mak' sure o'some o't.

> [*Takes a drink, and exit.*

And. I wonder whaur the laird is: its an unchancy time for him to be out of the gaet. Donald, Donald!

Enter DONALD.

Whaur's the laird? He should be here to receive the sheriff.

Don. He's no in the house.

And. Gang and find him in the fields, then.

Don. He's no in the fields, neither.

And. Whaur is he, then?

Don. He'll be a clever fellow, I reckon, that finds him on the hither side o' Dumbarton.

And. How dost tu ken that sa weel? What suld tak him to Dumbarton?

Don. His ain ill humour, I believe, for he returned fra' the fishing wi' his knit brows as grumly as a thunner cloud on the peak o' Benloman, and desired me to saddle his meir: and he took the road to the ferry without speaking anither word; and the last sight I gat o' the meir and him was frae the black craig head, whan they war baith in the boat thegether, half way over the Clyde.

And. That's unlucky: I maun gang to the yett and receive the sheriff mysel, as creditably as I can.

Don. Ye may save yoursel that trouble, I trow, for he has made his way into the house already.

Enter the sheriff with his officers and attendants, and servants of the family following them.

Sheriff (to ANDERSON). We would see the Laird of Dungarren.

And. He's frae hame, an please your honour.

Sheriff. From home! are you sure of this? we come on no unfriendly errand.

And. I mak' nae dout o' that, your honour: but he is frae hame, and far a-field, too.

Sheriff. That is unfortunate; for I am here officially to examine the members of his household. His mother, I presume, is at home?

And. Yes, your honour; the leddy is at hame, and will come to you immediately.

Sheriff. It is said you have been disturbed with strange noises and visitations in this family, and that the young lady is more tormented than ever. What kind of noises have been heard?

And. O Lord, your honour, sic elrich din! I can compare it to nothing. Sometimes it's like the soughing o' wind; sometimes like the howling o' dogs.

Donald (taking the word from him). Sometimes like the mewling o' cats; sometimes like the clattering o' broomsticks.

1st serv. (pressing forward, and taking the word from DONALD). Sometimes like the hooting o' howlets; and sometimes like a black sow grunting.

Sheriff. A black sow grunting!

Don. Ay, please your honour. The grunt of a black sow is as deil-like as its colour: I wad ken't, in the dark, frae ony white sow that ever wore a snout.

Sheriff. Well, sometimes hooting of owlets, and the grunting of a black sow.

And., Donald, and 1st *serv. (all speaking at once).* And sometimes like a—

Sheriff. Spare me, spare me, good folks! I can listen but to one at a time.

Enter LADY DUNGARREN, ANNABELLA, PHEMY, *nurse, and maid-servants.*

Good day, and my good service to you, Lady Dungarren. I'm sorry the laird is from home: my visit may perhaps disturb you.

Lady Dun. Do not say so, Sheriff; I am at all times glad to see you; but were it otherwise, we are too well accustomed to be disturbed in this miserable house, to think much of any thing.

Sheriff. I am very sorry for it,—very sorry that your daughter continues so afflicted.—(*Showing her a paper.*) Have you any knowledge of this paper? The information contained in it is the cause of my present intrusion.

Lady Dun. (after having looked over it attentively). I know nothing of the paper itself; but the information it conveys is true.

Sheriff. Have you ever seen the hand-writing before?

Lady Dun. No—yes—I think I have. Look at it, Annabella: it is somewhat like your own.

Annabella (in a hurried manner). Dear madam, how can you say so? The l's, and the m's, and the n's are all joined stiffly together, and you know very well that I never join my letters at all.

Lady Dun. Very true, cousin; I see there is a great difference now, and I don't know whose hand it is, though doubtless the hand of a friend; for we cannot remain in this misery much longer. It should be examined into, that the guilty may be punished, and prevented from destroying my poor child entirely.

Sheriff. Has any person of evil repute been admitted to see her? Who has been in her chamber?

Lady Dun. Who has been visibly in her chamber, we can easily tell; but who has been invisibly there, the Lord in heaven knows.

Sheriff. Have they never been visible to the child herself whom they torment?

Lady Dun. She has stared, as though she saw them.

Anna. She has shrieked, as though they laid hold of her.

Nurse. She has clenched her hands, as if she had been catching at them, in this way. (*Showing how.*)

Phemy. Ay, and moved her lips so (*showing how*), as if speaking to them. I saw her do it.

Nurse. And so did I; and saw her grin, and shake her head so, most piteously.

Phemy, nurse, and maid-servant (all speaking at once). And I saw her—

Sheriff. Softly, softly, good women! Three tellers are too many for one tale, and three tales are too many for one pair of ears to take in at a time.—(*Turning to the* LADY.) Has she ever told you that she saw witches by her bed-side?

Lady Dun. Yes; several times she has told me so, in wild and broken words.

Sheriff. Only in that manner.

Anna. You forget, madam, to mention to the Sheriff, that she told us distinctly, a few hours ago, how a witch had been sitting on her breast, as she lay in bed; and that, when she struggled to get rid of her, she rent a piece from the sleeve of her gown.

Sheriff. The witch rent the sleeve from her gown?

Nurse. No, no, your honour; our poor child rent a piece frae the sleeve o' the witch's gown.

Sheriff. Has the piece been found? A great many, speaking at once. Ay, ay! it has! it has!

Sheriff. Silence, I say!—(*To* ANNABELLA.) Have the goodness to answer, madam: has the rag been preserved?

Anna. It has, sir; but it is no rag, I assure you.

Nurse. As good silk, your honour, as ever came frae the Luckenbooths of Edinburgh.

Sheriff. Are not witches always old and poor? The devil must have helped this one to a new gown, at least; and that is more than we have ever heard of his doing to any of them before.

Anna. We have read of witches who have been neither old nor poor.

Sheriff. Ha! is there warranty, from sober sensible books, for such a notion? I am no great scholar on such points: it may be so.—But here comes the minister: his better learning will assist us.

ENTER *Mr. Rutherford.*

I thank you, my reverend sir, for obeying my notice so quickly.
Your cool head will correct our roused imaginations: you
believe little, I have heard, of either apparitions or witches.

Ruth. My faith on such subjects was once, indeed, but weak.

Sheriff. And have you changed it lately?—(*A pause for* RUTHERFORD
to answer, but he is silent.) Since when has your faith become
stronger?

After a short pause as before, several voices call out eagerly.—Since the
storm on Friday night; when Mary Macmurren and a' the crew
were on the moor.

Sheriff. Silence, I say again! Can the minister not answer for himself,
without your assistance?—You heard my question, Mr.
Rutherford: were you upon the moor on that night?

Ruth. I was.

Sheriff. And saw you aught upon the moor contrary to godliness and
nature?

Ruth. What I saw, I will declare in fitter time and place, if I must
needs do so.

Sheriff. Well, well, you are cautious, good sir; and, perhaps, it is wise
to be so.—Lady Dungarren, with your permission, I will go
into the sick chamber and examine your daughter myself.

Lady Dun. You have my permission most willingly. Follow me
immediately, if you please, and ask the poor child what
questions you think fit. Mr. Rutherford, do you choose to
accompany us?

> [*Exeunt* LADY DUNGARREN, ANNABELLA, SHERIFF, *and*
> RUTHERFORD; ANDERSON, *nurse,* DONALD, *&c. &c.
> remaining.*

And. And he'll gie nae answer at a', even to the Sheriff.

Nurse. Certes, were he ten times a minister, he should hae tauld what
he saw to the Sheriff of the county.

Don. A gentleman born and bred, and the king's appointed officer
into the bargain.

Nurse. And he winna tell what he saw afore us, forsooth—for
that's what he means by fitter time and place—foul befa' his

discretion! He wadna believe in witches, I trow; but they hae cowed him weel for't at last.

And. To be sure, he looket baith ghastly and wan, when the sheriff speered what he saw upon the moor.

Nurse. Ay, ay, it was some fearfu' sight, nae doubt. God's grace preserve us a'! the very thought o' what it might be gars my head grow cauld like a turnip.

Don. It was surely something waur than witches dancing that frightened the minister.

Nurse. As ye say, Donald: either Highlander or Lowlander has wit enough to guess that. I like nane o' your ministers that'll speak naewhere but in the pu'pit. Fitter time and place, quotha!

And. Hoot, toot, woman! he has gotten his lear at the college, and he thinks shame to be frightened.

Nurse. Foul befa' him and his lear too! It maun be o' some new-fangled kind, I think. Our auld minister had lear enough, baith Hebrew and Latin, and he believed in witches and warlocks, honest man, like ony ither sober, godly person.

And. So he did, nurse; ye're a sensible woman, but somewhat o' the loudest, whan ye're angry. Thae gude folks want some refection, I trow; and there's gude yill and ham in the buttery.—Come, Sirs, follow me.

> [*Exit, with a courteous motion of the hand, followed by the Sheriff's officers, &c. Phemy and Nurse remaining.*

Nurse. Whaur can Black Bauldy be a' this while? His smooty face is seldom missing whan ony mischief is ganging on?

Phemy. What do you want with him?

Nurse. To send him owre the craft for the new-laid eggs, that the ploughman's wife promised us.

Phemy. He has been sent further off on another errand already.

Nurse. And wha sent him, I should like to ken, whan we are a' sae thrang?

Phemy. My lady sent him.

Nurse. Your leddy, say ye! She has grown unco intimate wi' that pawky loon o' late: I wish gude may come o't. I maun gang for the eggs mysel, I warrant.—But I maun e'en gang first to the chaumer door, and listen a wee; though we'll only hear the hum o' their voices, an our lugs war as gleg as the coley's.

Phemy. And I'll go with you too: the hum of their voices is worth
listening for, if nothing more can be heard.

[*Exeunt.*

ACT IV.

SCENE I.

An open space before the abbey church of Paisley. Enter the Sheriff and
RUTHERFORD, *in earnest discourse.*

Sheriff. Yes, you may, indeed, be well assured that I have never, during
all the years in which I have served the office of sheriff of this
county, performed a duty so painful; and I am very sensible that
what I am compelled to summon you to perform, is still more
distressing.

Ruth. Were it not sinful, I could wish myself incapable, from disease
or disaster, or any other let, of giving legal testimony. Oh! to
think of it clouds my brain with confusion, and makes me sick
at heart! Violet Murrey, the young, the unfortunate, the gentle,
and, I firmly believe, the innocent,—to give evidence to her
prejudice,—it is a fearful duty

Sheriff. It is so, good Sir; yet it must be done. I have taken into custody,
on accusation of witchcraft, the fairest woman in the west of
Scotland; and you must answer on oath to the questions that
may be put to you, whether it be for or against her. If she be
innocent, Providence will protect her.

Enter the chief baillie of Paisley behind them, and listens to the conclusion
of the above speech.

Baillie. If she be innocent! Can any one reasonably suppose that
such a creature would be accused, or even suspected, but on
the strongest proofs of guilt? Some old haggard beldame, with
an ill name at any rate, might be wrongfully suspected; but
Violet Murrey, good sooth! must have been where she should

not have been, ere a tongue or a finger in the county would
have wagged to her prejudice.

Sheriff. That's what your wife says, I suppose.

Baillie. By my faith, sheriff, it's what every body says; for it stands to
reason.

Ruth. That it stands to folly, would be an apter cause for every body's
saying it, my worthy baillie.

Baillie. Grace be with us all! does a minister of the gospel set his
face against that for which there be plain texts of Scripture?
And when cattle are drained dry, children possessed, storms
raised, houses unroofed, noises in the air, and every one's heart
beating with distrust and fear of his neighbour,—is this a time
for us to stand still, and leave free scope for Satan and his imps
to lord it over a sober and godly land? By my certes! I would
carry faggots with my own hands to burn my nearest of kin,
though her cheeks were like roses, and her hair like threads of
gold, if she were found, but for one night, joining in the elrich
revelry of a devil's conventicle. (*A distant trumpet heard.*) Ha! the
judges so near the town already!

Sheriff. Would they were further off! they come sooner than I
reckoned for.

Baillie. Soon or late, we must go to meet them, as in duty bound.—
You take precedence, sheriff: I will follow you.

　　　　　　　　　　　　　　　　[*Exeunt sheriff and baillie.*

Ruth (alone). What is or is not in this mysterious matter, lies beyond
human reason to decide. That I must swear to the truth of what
I have seen, when questioned thereupon by authority, is my
only clear point of discernment. Hard necessity! My heart, in
despite of every proof, whispers to me she is innocent. (*A loud
brawling and tumult heard without.*) What noise is this?—The
senseless exasperated crowd besetting one of those miserable
women who held orgies on the heath on that dreadful night.

Enter MARY MACMURREN *and* WILKIN, *in the custody of constables, and
surrounded by a crowd, who are casting dust at her, &c. The constables
endeavouring to keep them off.*

1st woman. Deil's hag! she'll pay for her pastime now, I trow.

2d woman. For a' the milk kye she has witched.

1st woman. For a' the bonnie bairns she has blasted.

1st man. She girns like a brock at a terry-dog.

2d man. Score her aboon the breath, or she'll cast a cantrup, and be out o' your han's in a twinkling.

Mary Mac. What gars ye rage at me sae? I ne'er did nae harm to nane o' ye.

1st woman. Hear till her! hear till her! how she lees!

1st man. And what for no? Leeing is the best o' their lear, that hae the deel for their dominie.

2d man. Ay, wicket witch; leeing's nought to her: but we'll gie her something forbye words for an answer. Wha has gotten a jocteleg to score the wrinkled brow o'her?

3d man (offering a knife). Here! here!

> [*The crowd rush furiously upon her, and are with difficulty kept off by the constables.*

1st con. Stand back, I say, every mither's son o' ye, an' every faither's daughter to boot. If the woman be a witch winna she be burnt for 't, as ithers o' that calling hae been afore her? Isna that enough to content ye?

1st man. Ay, we'll soon see that ugly face, glowering through the smoke o' her benfire, like a howlet in the stour of an auld cowping barn.

2d man. An that piece o' young warlockry by her side, see how he glow'rs at us! Can tu squeek, imp? (*Trying to pinch* WILKIN, *who calls out.*)

Wilkin. O dull, o' dear! the're meddling wi' me.

1st con. Shame upon ye, shame upon ye a'! Ha' ye nae better way o' warring wi' the deel than tormenting a poor idiot?

Mary Mac. Shame upon ye! he's a poor fatherless idiot.

1st woman. Fatherless, forsooth! He's a fiend-begotten imp I warrant ye, and should be sent to the dad he belongs to. (*Trumpet heard nearer.*)

1st con. Red the way, I say, and gang out o' our gait, ilka saul and bouk o' ye! The judges are at han', and my prisoner maun be kary'd or they come, else they'll order ye a' to the tolbooth at a swoop.

[*Exeunt constables with* MARY MACMURREN *and* WILKIN, *followed by some of the crowd, while others remain; the trumpet heard still nearer.*]

1st man. What a braw thing it is to hear the trumpet sound sae nobly! There they come now; the judges, and the sheriff, and the baillies, and the deacons—a' the grand authorities o' the country.

1st woman. Hegh saf' us, what a gurly carle that judge is on the left! nae witch that stan's before him wull escape, I trow, war' she as young and as bonny as the rose-buds in June.

Young woman. Hau'd your tongue, mither, that a body may see them in peace. It's an awfu' thing but to look upon them here: the Lord help them that maun face them in condemnation!

1st woman. Daft bairn! wull the Lord help witches, think'st tu?

Enter judges in procession, followed by the sheriff, baillies, gentlemen of the county, and attendants, &c. &c. and passing diagonally across the stage, exeunt.

SCENE II.

A poor, mean room in a private house in Paisley. Enter ANNABELLA, *throwing back her hood and mantle as she enters.*

Anna. Now let me breathe awhile, and enjoy my hard-earned triumph unconstrainedly.—Revenge so complete, so swift-paced, so terrible! It repays me for all the misery I have endured.—May I triumph? dare I triumph?—Why am I astounded and terrified on the very pinnacle of exultation? Were she innocent, Providence had protected her. What have I done but contrived the means for proving her guilt? Means which come but in aid of others that would almost have been sufficient.

Enter BLACK BAWLDY.

Bawldy. O dool, O dool! she's condemned! she'll be executed, she'll be burnt, she'll be burnt the morn's morning at the cross, and a' through my putting that sorrowfu' gown into your hands, and by foul play, too, foul befa' it! O hone, O hone!

Anna. What's all this weeping and wringing of hands for? Art thou distracted?

Bawldy. I kenna how I am, I care na how I am; but I winna gang to hell wi' the death of an innocent leddy on my head, for a' the gowd in Christentie.

Anna. Poor fool! what makes thee think that the gown thou gottest for me had any thing to do with her condemnation?

Bawldy. O you wicked woman! I ken weel enough; and I ken what for you confined me in that back chammer sae lang, and keepet my brains in sic a whirlegig wi' whiskey and potations.

Anna. Thou knowest! how dost thou know?

Bawldy. I set my lug to a hole in the casement, and heard folks below in the close telling a' about the trial. It was that gown spread out in the court, wi' a hole in the sleeve o't, matching precisely to a piece o' the same silk, which na doubt you tore out yoursel whan it was in your hands, that made baith judge and jury condemn her.

Anna. Poor simpleton! did'st thou not also hear them say, that the minister, sore against his will, swore he saw her on the moor, where the witches were dancing, in company with a man who has been in his grave these three years? was not that proof enough to condemn her, if there had been nothing more?

Bawldy. It may be sae.

Anna. And is so. Is not Mary Macmurren a witch? and has not she been condemned upon much slighter evidence? Thou'rt an absolute fool, man, for making such disturbance about nothing.

Bawldy. Fool, or nae fool, I'll gang to the sheriff and tell him the truth, and then my conscience wull be clear frae her death, whate'er she may be.

Anna. Her death, frightened goose! Dost thou think she will really be executed?

Bawldy. I heard them say, that she and Mary Macmurren are baith to be brunt the morn's morning.

Anna. They said what they knew nothing about. Mary Macmurren will be burnt, for an example to all other witches and warlocks, but a respite and pardon will be given to Violet Murrey: it is only her disgrace, not her death, that is intended; so thy conscience may be easy.

Bawldy. If I could but believe you!

Anna. Believe me, and be quiet; it is the best thing thou canst do for thyself, and for those who are dearest to thee. Be a reasonable creature, then, and promise to me never to reveal what thou knowest.

Bawldy. I will keep the secret, then, since she is not to suffer. But winna you let me out the morn to see the burning o' Mary Macmurren? It wad be a vexatious thing to be sae near till't, and miss sic a sight as that.

Anna. Thou shalt have all reasonable indulgence. But what scares thee so?

[*Voice heard without.*

Bawldy (*trembling*). I hear the voice o' Grizeld Bane. She mun ha' been below the grund wi' her master sin' we last gat sight o' her at the tower, else the sheriff officers wad ha' grippet her wi' the rest.—Lord preserve us! is she coming in by the door or the winnoch, or up through the boards o' the flooring? I hear her elrich voice a' round about us, an my lugs ring like the bell o' an amos house.

Enter GRIZELD BANE.

Grizeld Bane. Now, my brave lady, my bold lady, my victorious lady! Satan has many great queens in his court, many princesses in his court, many high-blooded beauties in his court; I saw them all last night, sweeping with their long velvet robes the burning pavement of it: thou wilt have no mean mates to keep thee company, and thou wilt match with the best of them too; there is both wit and wickedness in thee to perfection.

Anna. Hush, hush, Grizeld Bane! What brings thee here? Is there not good ale and spirits in thy cellar, and a good bed to rest upon? What brings thee here?

Grizeld Bane. Shame of my cellar! think'st thou I have been there all this time? I have been deeper, and deeper, and deeper than a hundred cellars, every one sunken lower than another.

Bawldy (*aside to* ANNABELLA). I tauld you sae, madam.

Annabella (aside to BAWLDY). Go to thy chamber, if thou'rt afraid.

Grizeld Bane. Ay, deeper and deeper—

Anna. Thou need'st not speak so loud, Grizeld Bane: I understand thee well enough. I hope thou hast been well received where thou wert.

Grizeld Bane. Ay; they received me triumphantly. They scented the blood that will pour and the brands that will blaze; the groans and the shrieks that will be uttered were sounding in their ears, like the stormy din of a war-pipe. What will be done to-morrow morning! Think upon that, my dainty chuck! and say if I did not deserve a noble reception.

Anna. No doubt, with such society as thy imagination holds converse with.

Grizeld Bane. Yes, dearest! and thou, too, hast a noble reception abiding thee.

Annabella (shrinking back). Heaven forfend!

Grizeld Bane. Ha, ha, ha! Art thou frighten'd, dearest? Do not be frightened! it is a grand place: my own mate is there, and the cord about his neck changed into a chain of rubies. There is much high promotion abiding thee.

Anna. And will have long abiding, I trust, ere I am invested with it.

Grizeld Bane. Not so long; not so long, lady: whenever thou wilt it may be. Dost thou love a clasp'd gorget for thy pretty white neck? (*Going up to her with a sly grin of affected courtesy, and attempting to grasp her throat.*)

Bawldy (springing forward and preventing her). Blasted witch! wad ye throttle her?

Grizeld Bane. Ha! imp! hast thou followed me so fast behind? Down with thee! down with thee! There is molten lead and brimstone a-cooking for thy supper; there's no lack of hot porridge for thee, varlet.

Bawldy. Oh madam, oh madam! what hae ye brought on yoursel and on me, that was but a poor ignorant callant! O send for the minister at once, and we'll down on our knees, and he'll pray for us. The damnation of the wicked is terrible.

Anna. She is but raving: the fumes of her posset have been working in her brain; be not foolish enough to be frightened at what she says.

Bawldy. I wish, O I wish I had never done it! I wish I had never set eyes or set thoughts on the mammon of unrighteousness. Oh, oh!

Grizeld Bane (to BAWLDY). Ha, ha, ha! Thou'rt frighten'd, art thou?

Anna. Thou see'st she is in jest, and has pleasure in scaring thee. Go to thy chamber, and compose thyself. (*Calling him back as he is about to go, and speaking in his ear.*) Don't go till she has left me. Hie to thy cellar, Grizeld Bane.

Grizeld Bane. And leave thy sweet company, lady?

Anna. For a good savoury meal, which is ready for thee; I hear them carrying it thither. Go, go! I have promised to visit Lady Dungarren at a certain hour, and I must leave thee. (*Calling very loud.*) Landlord! Landlord!

Enter Landlord (a strong determined-looking man).

Is Grizeld Bane's meal ready? (*Significantly.*)

Land. Yes, madam, and with as good brandy to relish it as either lord or lady could desire. (*To* GRIZELD BANE.) Come, my lofty dame, let me lead you hence. (*Fixing his eyes stedfastly on her face, while she sullenly submits to be led off.*)

Manent ANNABELLA *and* BAWLDY.

Bawldy. The Lord be praised she is gone! for she has been in the black pit o' hell since yestreen, and wad pu' every body after her an she could. Dear leddy, send for the minister.

Anna. Hold thy foolish tongue, and retire to thy chamber. Violet Murrey's life is safe enough, so thy conscience may be easy. Follow me, for I must lock thee in.

Bawldy. Mun I still be a prisoner?

Anna. Thou sha'n't be so long; have patience a little while, foolish boy.

[*Exeunt.*

SCENE III.

A prison. Violet Murrey *is discovered sitting on the ground, by the light of a lamp stuck in the wall; her face hid upon her lap, while a gentle rocking motion of the body shows that she is awake.*

Enter Dungarren *by a low arched door, which is opened cautiously by a turnkey, who immediately shuts it again and disappears.*

Dun. (*going close to her, and after a sorrowful pause*). Violet, O Violet, my once dear Violet! dost thou know my voice? Wilt thou not raise thy head and look upon me?

Vio. I know your voice: you are very kind to come to me in my misery.

Dun. Misery, indeed! Oh that I should see thee thus,—the extremity of human wretchedness closing around thee!

Vio. (*rising from the ground and standing erect*). Say not the extremity, Robert Kennedy, for I am innocent.

Dun. I will believe it. Ay, in despite of evidence as clear as the recognition of noon-day,—in despite of all evidence, I would believe it. The hateful sin of witchcraft, if such a sin there be, thou hast never committed; it is impossible.

Vio. I know thou wilt believe it: and O! that thou could'st also believe that I am innocent of all falsehood and fickleness of affection! But thou canst not do so; it were unreasonable to expect it. Thou wilt think of me as an ungrateful, deceitful creature; and this is the memory I must leave behind me with Robert of Dungarren.

Dun. I forgive thee! I forgive thee, dear Violet! for so in thy low estate I will call thee still, though thou lovest another as thou hast never loved me.

Vio. I love him, full surely, as I cannot love thee, but not to the injury of that affection which has always been thine.

Dun. I came not here to upbraid: we will speak of this no more.

Vio. Alas, alas! I should speak and think of things far different, yet this lies on my heart as the heaviest load of all. May God forgive me for it!

Dun. And he will forgive thee, my dear friend! for such I may and will call thee, since I may not call thee more.

Vio. Do, my noble Robert! that is best of all. And, resting in thy mind as a friend, I know—I am confident, that something will happen, when I am gone, that will discover to thee my faithfulness. Death will soon be past, and thou wilt live to be a prosperous gentleman, and wilt sometimes think of one—my evil fame will not—thou wilt think, ay, wilt speak good of Violet Murrey, when all besides speak evil. Thou wilt not—(*Bursts into tears.*)

Dun. (*embracing her passionately*). My dear, dear creature! dear as nothing else has ever been to me, thou shalt not die: the very thought of it makes me distracted!

Vio. Be not so: it is the manner of it that distresses thee. But has it not been the death of the martyrs, of the holy and the just; of those, the dust of whose feet I had been unworthy to wipe? Think of this, and be assured, that I shall be strengthened to bear it.

Dun. Oh, oh, oh! If deliverance should be frustrated!

Vio. What art thou talking of? thou art, indeed, distracted. Nay, nay! let not my execution terrify thee so much. I, too, was terrified; but I have learnt from my gaoler, who has been present at such spectacles, that the sentence, though dreadful, is executed mercifully. The flames will not reach me till I have ceased to breathe; and many a natural disease doth end the course of life as mine will be terminated.

Dun. God forbid! God help and deliver us! (*Runs impatiently to a corner of the dungeon, and puts his ear close to the ground.*) I do not hear them yet: if they should fail to reach it in time, God help us!

Vio. What dost thou there? What dost thou listen for? What dost thou expect?

Dun. Means for thy deliverance,—thy escape.

Vio. Say not so; it is impossible.

Dun. It is possible, and will be, if there's a Providence on earth—if there's mercy in heaven. (*Puts his ear to the ground as before.*)

Vio. (*stooping and listening*). I hear nothing. What is it thou expectest to hear?

Dun. I do hear it now: they are near; they will open upon us presently.

Vio. What dost thou hear?

Dun. The sound of their spades and their mattocks. O my brave miners! they will do their work nobly at last.

Vio. A way to escape under ground! my ears ring and my senses are confounded. Escape and deliverance?

Dun. Yes, love, and friend, and dear human creature! escape and deliverance are at hand.

Vio. How good and noble thou art to provide such deliverance for me, believing me unfaithful!

Dun. Come, come; that is nothing: be what thou wilt, if I can but save thee!—Life and death are now on the casting of a die.— The ground moves; it is life! (*Tossing up his arms exultingly.*)

Vio. The ground opens: wonderful, unlooked-for deliverance! Thank God! thank God! his mercy has sent it.

> [*The earthen floor of the dungeon at one corner falls in, making a small opening, and the miners are heard distinctly at work.*

Dun. (*calling down to them*). May we descend? are you ready?

Voice (*beneath*). In two minutes the passage will be practicable.

Dun. (*as before*). Make no delay; we will pass any how.

Vio. How quickly they have worked, to mine so far under ground since yesterday!

Dun. That mine was completed many months ago to favour the escape of a prisoner, who died suddenly in prison before his projected rescue. The secret was revealed to me yesterday, by one of the miners, who had originally conducted the work.

Voice (*beneath*). We are ready now.

Dun. Heaven be praised! I will first descend, and receive thee in my arms.

> [*As they are about to descend, the door of the dungeon opens, and enter* RUTHERFORD *and* LADY DUNGARREN, *accompanied by the sheriff and gaoler.*

Sheriff. Ha! company admitted without due permission! Dungarren here! Your underling, Mr. Gaoler, is a rogue. How is this?

Gaoler. As I am a Christian man, I know no more about it than the child that was born since yestreen.

Sheriff. It is only one born since yestreen that will believe thee. A hole in the floor, too, made for concealment and escape! Dungarren, you are my prisoner in the king's name. To favour the escape of a criminal is no slight offence against the laws of the land.

Dun. You distract me with your formal authorities: the laws of the land and the laws of God are at variance, for she is innocent.

Sheriff. She has abused and bewitched thee to think so; and a great proof it is of her guilt.

Dun. It is you and your coadjutors who are abused, dreadfully and wickedly abused, to hurry on, with such unrighteous obduracy, the destruction of one whom a savage would have spared. Tremble to think of it. At your peril do this.

Sheriff. I am as sorry as any man to have such work to do, but yet it must be done; and at your peril resist the law. Holloa, you without! (*Calling loud.*)

Enter his officers, armed.

Take Robert Kennedy, of Dungarren, into custody, in the king's name.

  [*The officers endeavour to lay hold of* DUNGARREN, *who paces about in a state of distraction.*

Dun. Witchcraft! heaven grant me patience! her life to be taken for witchcraft? senseless idiotical delusion!

Sheriff (*to officers*). Do your duty, fellows: he is beside himself; distracted outright.

Vio. Noble Dungarren! submit to the will of heaven. I am appointed to my hard fate; and God will enable me to bear it. Leave me, my dear friend! be patient, and leave me.

Dun. They shall hack me to pieces ere I leave thee.

Vio. Dear Robert, these are wild distracted words, and can be of no avail.—Good Mr. Rutherford, and Lady Dungarren, too; ye came here to comfort me: this I know was your errand, but O comfort him! speak to him, and move him to submission.

Ruth. Your present vain resistance, Dungarren, does injury to her whom you wish to preserve.

Lady Dun. My son, my Robert, thou art acting like a maniac. Retire with these men, who are only doing their duty, and neither wish to injure nor insult you. I will stay with Violet, and Mr. Rutherford will go with you.

Dun. Leave her, to see her no more!

Lady Dun. Not so; the sheriff will consent, that you may see her again in the morning, ere—

Sheriff. I do consent: you shall see her in the morning, before she goes forth to—to the—to her—

Dun. To that which is so revolting and horrible, that no one dare utter it in words. Oh! oh, oh!

> [*Groans heavily, and leans his back to the wall, while his arms drop listlessly by his side, and the officers, laying hold of him, lead him out in a state of faintness and apathy.*

Ruth. His mind is now exhausted, and unfit for present soothing; attempts to appease and console him must come hereafter; there is time enough for that. (*To* VIOLET, *with tenderness.*) But thy time is short; I would prepare thee for an awful change. Unless thou be altogether hostile to thoughts of religion and grace, which I can never believe thee to be.

Vio. O no, no! that were a dreadful hostility; and thou, even thou, the good and enlightened Rutherford, my long-tried monitor and friend, can express a doubt whether I am so fearfully perverted. Alas! death is terrible when it comes with disgrace,—with the execration of Christian fellow-creatures! O pray to God for me! pray to God fervently, that I be not overwhelmed with despair.

Ruth. I will pray for thee most fervently; and thou wilt be supported.

Vio. I have been at times, since my condemnation, most wonderfully composed and resigned, as if I floated on a boundless ocean, beneath His eye who says, "Be calm, be still; it is my doing." But, oh! returning surges soon swell on everyside, tossing, and raging, and yawning tremendously, like gulfs of perdition, so that my senses are utterly confounded. My soul has much need of thy ghostly comfort.

Lady Dun. Comfort her, good Rutherford! I forgive her all that she has done against my poor child, and may God forgive her!

Vio. And will nothing, dear madam, remove from your mind that miserable notion, that I have practised witchcraft against the health and life of your child? Can you believe this and pity me? No, no! were I the fiend-possessed wretch you suppose me to be, a natural antipathy would rise in your breast at the sight of me, making all touch of sympathy impossible. I am innocent of this, and of all great crime; and you will know it, when I am laid in a dishonoured grave, and have passed through the fearful pass of death, from which there is no return.

Lady Dun. You make me tremble, Violet Murrey: if you are innocent, who can be guilty?

Vio. Be it so deem'd! it is God's will: I must be meek when such words are uttered against me. (*After a pause.*) And you think it possible that I have practised with evil powers for the torment and destruction of your child; of poor Jessie, who was my little companion and play-fellow, whom I loved, and do love so truly; who hung round my neck so kindly, and called me—ay, sister was a sweet word from her guileless lips, and seemed to be— (*Bursts into an agony of tears.*)

Lady Dun. (*to* RUTHERFORD). She may well weep and wring her hands: it makes me weep to think of the power of the Evil One over poor unassisted nature. Had she been less gentle and lovely, he had tempted her less strongly. I would give the best part of all that I possess to make and to prove her innocent. But it cannot be; O no! it cannot be!

Ruth (*to* LADY DUNGARREN). Forbear! forbear! Prayer and supplication to the throne of mercy for that grace which can change all hearts, convert misery into happiness, and set humble chastised penitence by the side of undeviating virtue,—prayer and supplication for a poor stricken sister, and for our sinful selves, is our fittest employment now.

Vio. Thanks, my good Sir; you are worthy of your sacred charge. I am, indeed, a poor stricken sister; one of the flock given you to lead, and humbly penitent for all the sins and faults I have really committed. Pray for me, that I may be more perfectly penitent, and strengthened for the fearful trial that awaits me.

Ruth. Thou wilt be strengthened.

Vio. O! I have great need! I am afraid of death; I am afraid of disgrace; I am afraid of my own sinking pusillanimous weakness.

Ruth. But thou need'st not be afraid, my dear child; trust in his Almighty protection, who strengthens the weak in the hour of need, and gives nothing to destruction which in penitence and love can put its trust in Him.

Vio. (*weeping on his shoulder*). I will strive to do it, my kind pastor; and
    the prayers of a good man will help me.

Ruth. Let us kneel, then, in humble faith.

Sheriff (*advancing from the bottom of the stage*). Not here, good Sir; I
    cannot leave her here, even with a man of your cloth, and that
    opening for escape in the floor.

Ruth. As you please, sir; remove her to another cell: or, if it must be,
    let a guard remain in this.

Enter an attendant.

Att. (*to Sheriff*). It is ready, sir.

Sheriff (*to* VIOLET). You must be removed to another prison-room.

Vio. As you please, Sheriff.

Sheriff. Lean upon me, Madam: woe the day that I should lodge so
    fair a lady in such unseemly chambers!

Vio. I thank you for your courtesy, good Sheriff:—you do what you
    deem to be your duty; and when you are at last undeceived,
    and convinced of my innocence, as I know you will one day be,
    you will be glad to remember that you did it with courtesy.

Sheriff. Blessing on thy lovely face, witch or no witch! dost thou
    speak to me so gently!

                [*Exit* VIOLET, *leaning on the sheriff.*

Manet gaoler, who mutters to himself as he prepares to follow them.

Gaoler. A bonny witch, and a cunning ane, as ever signed compact
    wi' Satan! I wonder what cantrap she'll devise for the morn,
    whan the pinching time comes. I wish it were over.

                [*Exit, locking the door.*

ACT V.

SCENE I.

A mean chamber, with a window looking upon the market-place of Paisley. Enter ANNABELLA *and the landlord of the house.*

Land. Here, Madam, you can remain concealed from every body, and see the execution distinctly from the window.

Anna. Yes; this is what I want. And you must let no creature come here, on any account. Keep your promise upon this point, I charge you.

Land. Trust me, madam, nobody shall enter this room, though they carried a bag of gold in their hand. I have refused a large sum for the use of that window; and excepting some schoolboys and apprentices who have climbed up to the roof of the house, there is not a creature in the tenement, but Grizeld Bane and Black Bawldy, each in their place of confinement.

Anna. I thank thee, landlord, and will reward thee well: thou shalt be no loser for the money thou hast refused on my account. What is the hour?

Land. The abbey church struck eight, as I reckon, half an hour ago.

Anna. Longer than that—much longer. The time should be close at hand for leading out the criminals. (*Going to the window.*) What a concourse of people are assembled! and such a deep silence through the whole!

Land. Ay; in the day of doom they will scarcely stand closer and quieter.

Anna. Hold thy tongue: we know nothing of such matters.

Land. But what the holy book reveals to us.

Anna. Leave me, I pray thee. I would be alone. (*Landlord retires.*) Half an hour! no half hour was ever of such a length.—Landlord! ho! Landlord!

Re-enter Landlord.

Land. What is your pleasure, madam?

Anna. Art thou sure that no reprieve has arrived? It must be past the hour. (*Bell tolls.*) Ha! the time is true.

Land. That awful sound! It gives notice that the prisoners will soon be led forth. Lord have mercy on their sinful souls! on all sinful souls!

Anna. Thou may'st go: I would be alone.

[*Exit Landlord.*

[*Bell tolls again, and at intervals through the whole scene.*

Anna. (*alone*). Now comes the fearful consummation! Her arts, her allurements, her seeming beauty, her glamour, and her power,—what will they all amount to when the noon of this day shall be past? a few black ashes, and a few scorched bones.—Fye upon these cowardly thoughts,—this sinking confidence! Revenge is sweet; revenge is noble; revenge is natural; what price is too dear for revenge?—Why this tormenting commotion? To procure false evidence for the conviction of one whom we know or believe to be guilty,—is this a sin past redemption? No; it is but the sacrifice of truth for right and useful ends. I know it is; reason says it is; and I will be firm and bold, in spite of human infirmity.

Enter Grizeld Bane.

Grizeld Bane. Yes, dearest; thou art very bold. There is not a cloven foot, nor a horned head of them all, wickeder and bolder than thou art.

Annabella (*shrinking back*). What brings thee here?

Grizeld Bane. To be in such noble company.

Anna. What dost thou mean by that?

Grizeld Bane. Every word hath its meaning, Lady, though every meaning hath not its word, as thou very well knowest. I am great; thou art great; but the greatest of all stands yonder. (*Pointing to the farther corner of the room.*)

Anna. What dost thou point at? I see nothing.

Grizeld Bane. But thou wilt soon, dearest. The master we both serve is standing near us. His stature is lofty; his robe is princely; his eyes are two flames of fire. And one stands behind him, like a chieftain of elrich degree.—But why is he thus? Can no power undo that hateful noose? It wavers before my eyes so distractingly!

Anna. Thou art, indeed, distracted and visionary. There is nobody here but ourselves.

Grizeld Bane. The master of us all is waiting yonder; and he will not sink to his nether court again till the fair lady is with him.

Anna. O! I understand thy moody fancy now. The master thou meanest is waiting for Violet Murrey.

Grizeld Bane. Yes, dearest, if he can get her. If not, he will have some one else, who is worthy to bear him company. He must have his meed and his mate: he will not return empty-handed, when a fair lady is to be had.

Anna. Heaven forfend! (*The bell now sounds quicker.*) That bell sounds differently: they are now leading them forth.

Grizeld Bane (*running to the window, and beckoning her*). Come, come here, darling: here is a sight to make the eyes flash, and the heart's blood stir in its core. Here is a brave sight for thee!

[*They both go to the window, and the scene closes.*

SCENE II.

The market-place prepared for the execution, with two stakes, and faggots heaped round them, erected in the middle, but nearer the bottom than the front of the stage. A great crowd of people are discovered. The bell tolls rapidly, and then stops.

Enter the sheriff and magistrates, and MARY MACMURREN, *supported by a clergyman, and guarded.*

Cler. Now, prisoner, may God be merciful to thee! Make use of the few moments of life that remain, by making confession before these good people of the wickedness thou hast committed, and the justice of the sentence that condemns thee. It is all the reparation now in thy power; and may God accept it of thee!

Mary Mac. Oh, hone! oh, hone!

Cler. Dost thou not understand what I say? Make confession.

Mary Mac. Oh, hone! oh, hone!

Cler. Dost thou hear me, woman? Make confession.

Mary Mac. Confession?

Cler. Yes, confession, woman.

Mary Mac. Tell me what it is, an' I'll say't.

Baillie. How cunning she is to the last!

Cler (*to* MARY MACMURREN). Didst thou not confess on thy trial that thou wert a witch, and hadst tryste-meetings and dealings with the devil?

Mary Mac. Lord hae mercy on me: I said what I thought, and I thought as ye bade me. The Lord hae mercy on a wicked woman! for that, I know, I am.

Baillie. How cunning she is again! She calls herself wicked, but will not call herself witch.

Cler. Mary Macmurren, make confession ere you die, and God will be more merciful to you.

Mary Mac. Oh, hone! oh, hone! miserable wretch that I am! Do ye mak confession for me, Sir, and I'll say't after you, as weel as I dow. Oh, hone! oh, hone!

Sheriff (*to clergyman*). There is no making any thing of her now, miserable wretch! Lead her on to the stake, and make her pray with you there, if the Evil One hath not got the entire mastery over her to the very last. (*The clergyman leads* MARY MACMURREN *to the stake.*) And now there is a sadder duty to perform; the fair, the young, and the gentle must be brought forth to shame and to punishment.

> [*He goes to the gate of the prison, and returns, conducting* VIOLET MURREY, *who enters, leaning on the arm of* RUTHERFORD.

Sheriff. Now, Madam, it is time that I should receive from you any commands you may wish to entrust me with: they shall be faithfully obeyed.

Vio. I thank you, Mr. Sheriff. What may be allowed for mitigating my sufferings, I know you have already ordered: have you also given similar directions in behalf of my miserable companion?

Sheriff. I have, Madam.

Vio. Thanks for your mercy! My passage to a better state will be short: and of God's mercy there I have no misgivings; for of the crime laid to my charge I am as innocent as the child newly born; as you yourself, worthy sir, or this good man on whose arm I now lean.

Sheriff. If this be so, lady, woe to the witnesses, the judges, and the jury by whom you are condemned!

Vio. Say not so. I am condemned by what honest, though erring men, believed to be the truth. What God alone knows to be the truth, is not for man's direction.—(*To* RUTHERFORD.) Weep not for me, my kind friend. You had good cause to believe that you had seen me in company with a creature not of this world, and you were compelled to declare it.

Ruth. I wish I had died, ere that evidence had been given!

Vio. Be comforted! be comforted! for you make me good amends, in that your heart refuses, in spite of such belief, to think me guilty of the crime for which I am to suffer. There is another— you know whom I mean—who thinks me innocent. When I am gone, ye will be often together, and speak and think of Violet Murrey. This is the memory I shall leave behind me: my evil fame with others is of little moment. And yet I needs must weep to think of it; 'tis human weakness.

Ruth. God bless and strengthen thee, my daughter, in this thy last extremity!

Vio. Fear not for that: I am strengthened. You have prayed for me fervently, and I have prayed for myself; and think ye I shall not be supported? (*Looking round on the crowd.*) And these good people, too, some of them, I trust, will pray for me. They will one day know that I am innocent.

Several voices (*from the crowd, calling out in succession*). We know it already.—She must be so.—She is innocent.

Baillie. I command silence!—Mr. Sheriff, your duty calls upon you.

Sheriff (*to* VIOLET). Madam. (*Turns away.*)

Vio. You speak, and turn from me: I understand you.

Sheriff. I am compelled to say, though most unwillingly, our time is run.

Vio. And I am ready.—(*Turning to* RUTHERFORD.) The last fearful step of my unhappy course only remains: you have gone far enough, my good sir. Receive my dying thanks for all your kindness, and let us part. Farewell! till we meet in a better world!

Ruth. Nay, nay; I will be with thee till all is over, cost what it may,—
though it should kill me.

Vio. Most generous man! thou art as a parent to me, and, woe the
day! thy heart will be wrung as though thou wert so in truth.

Baillie (to sheriff). Why so dilatory? Proceed to the place of
execution.

Sheriff. Not so hasty, sir! The psalm must first be sung.

Baillie. It will be sung when she is at the stake.

Sheriff (aside). Would thou wert there in her stead, heartless bigot!—
(*Aloud.*) Raise the psalm here.

Vio. You are very humane, good sheriff, but we shall, if you please,
proceed to the place appointed.

> [*She is led towards the stake, when a loud cry is heard without.*

Voice. Stop! stop! stop the execution.

Enter MURREY, *darting through the crowd, who give way to let him pass.*

Mur. She is innocent! she is innocent! Ye shall not murder the
innocent!

Sheriff (to MURREY). Who art thou, who wouldst stop the completion
of the law?

Mur. One whom you have known; whom you have looked on often

Sheriff. The holy faith preserve us! art thou a living man?

Ruth. Murrey of Torwood! doth the grave give up its dead, when the
sun is shining in the sky?

Sheriff. Look to the lady, she is in a swoon.

Mur (supporting VIOLET). My dear, my noble child! thine own misery
thou couldst sustain, but mine has overwhelmed thee: dear,
dear child!

Enter DUNGARREN, *running distractedly.*

Baillie (fronting him). Dungarren broke from prison, in defiance of
the law!

Dun. In defiance of all earthly things. (*Pushing the Baillie aside, and
rushing on to* VIOLET.) Who art thou? (*Looking sternly at* MURREY.)
What right hast thou to support Violet Murrey?

Mur. The right of a father; a miserable father.

Dun. Her father is dead.

Mur. Not so, Dungarren: I would I were dead, if it could save her life.

Dun. (*pointing to* RUTHERFORD). This good man, whose word is truth itself, laid Murrey of Torwood in the grave with his own hands.

Mur. Did he examine the face of the corse which he so piously interred? I had changed clothes with my faithful servant.— But it is a story tedious to tell; and can ye doubt his claims to identity, who, in the very act of making them, subjects his own life to the forfeit of the law?

Baillie (*aside to the Sheriff's officers*). By my faith! he is a condemned murderer, and will be required of our hands; keep well on the watch, that he may not escape.

Dun. She seems to revive; she will soon recover. (*To* MURREY.) And it was you who were with her on the heath, and in the cave?

Mur. It was I, Dungarren.

Dun. No apparition, no clandestine lover, but her own father!

Vio. (*recovering, and much alarmed*). Call him not father! I own him not! Send him away, send him away, dear Robert!

Mur (*embracing her*). My generous child! the strength of thy affection is wonderful, but it is all vain: I here submit myself willingly to the authority of the law, though innocent of the crime for which I am condemned—the wilful murder of a worthy gentleman. And now, Mr. Sheriff, you cannot refuse to reprieve her, who is mainly convicted for that, in being seen with me, she seemed to hold intercourse with apparitions, or beings of another world.

Sheriff. You speak reason: God be praised for it!

Dun. God be praised, she is safe!

Baillie. There be other proofs against her besides that.

Dun. Be they what they may, they are false!

Enter BLACK BAWLDY, *letting himself down from the wall of a low building, and running eagerly to the sheriff.*

Bawldy. Hear, my Lord Sheriff,—hear me, your honour—hear me, Dungarren;—hear me, a' present! She's innocent;—I stole it, I stole it mysel: the Lady Annabel tempted me, and I stole it.

Sheriff. Simple fool! it is not for theft she is condemned.

Bawldy. I ken that weel, your honour. She's condemned for being a witch, and she's nae witch: I stole it mysel and gied it to the Lady Annabel, wha cuttet the hole i' the sleeve o't, I'll be sworn. Little did I think what wicked purpose she was after.

Sheriff. Yes, yes, my callant! I comprehend thee now: it is that gown which was produced in Court, thou art talking of. Thou stole it for the Lady Annabel, and she cut a piece out of it, which she pretended to have found in the sick-chamber?

Bawldy. E'en sae, your honour. Whip me, banish me, or hang me, an' it man be sae, but let the innocent leddy abee.

Sheriff. Well, well; I'll take the punishing of thee into my own hands, knave. What shrieks are these?

> [*Repeated shrieks are heard from the window of a house, and two figures are seen indistinctly within, struggling: a dull stifled sound succeeds, and then a sudden silence.*

There is mischief going on in that house.

Baillie (*running to the door of the house, and knocking*). Let me enter: I charge you within, whoever ye be, to open the door. No answer! (*Knocks again.*) Still no answer! Open the door, or it shall be forced open.

Grizeld Bane (*looking over the window*). Ha, ha! what want ye, good Mr. Magistrate?

Baillie. Some body has suffered violence in this house; open the door immediately.

Grizeld Bane. And what would you have from the house that ye are so impatient to enter? There be corses enow in the churchyard, I trow; ye need not come here for them.

Sheriff. She is a mad woman, and has murdered somebody.

1st off. Mad, your honour! she's the witch we ha' been seeking in vain to apprehend, and the blackest, chiefest hag o' them a'.

2nd off. By my faith, we mun deal cannily wi' her, or she'll mak her escape fra' us again through the air.

Baillie (calling up to her). Open the door, woman, and you sha'n't be forced; we want to enter peaceably. Who is with you, there? Who was it that shrieked so fearfully?

Grizeld Bane. Never trouble thy head about that, Mr. Magistrate; she'll never disturb you more.

Sheriff. Who is it you have with you?

Grizeld Bane (throwing down to them the scarf of Annabella). Know ye that token? It was a fair lady who owned it, but she has no need of it now: hand me up a winding sheet.

Sheriff. The cursed hag has destroyed some lady.—Officers, enter by force, and do your duty. Witch or no witch, she cannot injure strong men like you, in the open light of day.

> [*The door is burst open, and the officers go into the house, and presently re-enter, bearing the dead body of* ANNABELLA, *which they place on the front of the stage, the crowd gathering round to stare at it.*]

Baillie. Stand back, every one of you, and leave clear room round the body. It is the Lady Annabella. She has been strangled:— she has struggled fearfully; her features are swollen, and her eyes starting from her head; she has struggled fearfully.—Stand back, I say; retire to your places, every one of you, or I'll deal with you as breakers of the peace.

Sheriff. Be not so angry with them, good Baillie: they must have some frightful sight to stare at, and they will be disappointed of that which they came for.

Baillie. Disappointed, sheriff! You do not mean, I hope, to reprieve that foul witch at the other stake: is not one execution enough for them? It makes me sick to see such blood-thirsting in a Christian land.

Sheriff. Ay, you say true; that poor wretch had gone out of my head.

Baillie. Wretch enough, good sooth! the blackest witch in Renfrewshire, Grizeld Bane excepted.

Sheriff. But we need not burn her now: her evidence may be wanted to convict the other.

Baillie. Not a whit! we have evidence at command to burn her twenty times over. A bird in hand is a wise proverb. If we spare her now, she may be in Norway or Lapland when we want her again for the stake.

Dun. (*approaching the body of* ANNABELLA). And this is thy fearful end, most miserable woman! It wrings my heart to think of what thou wert, and what thou mightst have been.

Mur. (*to sheriff*). Your authority having, on these undoubted proofs of her innocence, reprieved her, may I request that she be now withdrawn from the public gaze? It is not fit that she should be further exposed.

Sheriff. True, Torwood; you shall lead her back to prison, where she shall only remain till safe and commodious apartments are prepared for her. As for yourself, I am sorry to say, we have no power to lodge you otherwise than as a condemned man, obnoxious to the last punishment of the law.

Vio. O say not so, dear sir! He had made his escape, he was safe, he was free, and he surrendered himself into your hands to save the life of his child. Will ye take advantage of that? it were cruel and ungenerous.

Sheriff. We act, lady, under authority, and must not be guided by private opinions and affections.

Baillie. Most assuredly! it is our duty to obey the law and to make it be obeyed, without fear or favour.

Vio. On my knees, I beseech you! (*Kneeling and catching hold of the Baillie and sheriff.*) I beseech you for an innocent man! Royal mercy may be obtained if ye will grant the time—time to save the life of the innocent—innocent, I mean, of intentional murder.

Sheriff. Has he further proof of such innocence to produce than was shown on his trial?

Baillie. If he has not, all application for mercy were vain. He slew the man with whom he had a quarrel, without witnesses. If he is innocent, it is to God and his own conscience, but the law must deem him guilty.

Vio. He did it not without witnesses, but he who was present is dead. Alas, alas! if Fatheringham had been alive, he had been justified.

Baillie. Forbear to urge that plea, lady: that the only person who was present at the quarrel or combat is dead or disappeared, throws a greater shade of darkness on the transaction.

Sheriff. These are hard words, Baillie, and unnecessary.

Baillie. You may think so, Sheriff, but if you yield on this point, I entirely dissent from it; ay, from granting any delay to the execution of his sentence. Shall a man be made gainer for having defied the law and broken from his prison?

Sheriff (to MURREY *sorrowfully).* I am afraid we can do nothing for you. You must prepare for the worst.

Mur. I came here so prepared, worthy sir: I knew you could do nothing for me. (*To* VIOLET, *who again kneels imploringly).* Forbear, dearest child! thou humblest thyself in vain. I will meet fate as a man: do not add to my suffering by giving way to such frantic humiliation. (*Raising her from the ground.*) Dungarren, I commit her to your protection. You will be her honourable friend.

Dun. Ay, and her devoted husband, also, if you esteem me worthy to be so.

Mur. Worthy to be her husband, were she the daughter of a king, my noble Robert Kennedy. But thou must not be the son-in-law of such a one as I am,—one whose life has been terminated by—

Dun. I despise the prejudice!

Vio. But I do not! O! I cannot despise it! If my father must suffer, I will never marry thee, and I will never marry another.—My fate is sealed. Thou and this good man (*pointing to* RUTHERFORD) will be my friends, and Heaven will, in pity, make my earthly course a short one. A creature so stricken with sorrow and disgrace has nothing to do in this world but to wait, in humble patience, till God in his mercy takes her out of it.

Mur. Come from this hateful spot, my sweet child! Cruel as our lot is, we shall be, for what remains of this day, together.

> [*Endeavours to lead her out, but is prevented by the crowd, who gather close on the front of the stage, as* GRIZELD BANE *issues with frantic gestures from the house.*

Voices (from the crowd in succession). Ay, there she comes, and the de'il raging within her.—The blackest witch of a'.—Let her be brunt at the stake that was meant for the leddy.—Hurra! hurra! mair faggots and a fiercer fire for Grizeld!—Hurra! and defiance to Satan and his agents!

> [*A trumpet sounds without, and the tumult increases, till a company of soldiers appears under arms, and enter an officer, accompanied by* FATHERINGHAM.

Off. (*giving a paper to the Sheriff.*) You will please, Mr. Sheriff, to make the contents of this paper public.

Sheriff. I charge every one here, at his peril, to be silent. (*Reading.*)

"Be it known unto all men, that the King's Majesty, with the Lords and Commons in Parliament assembled, have decreed that the law punishing what has been called the crime of witchcraft as a felonious offence be repealed; and it is therefore repealed accordingly. Henceforth there shall no person be prosecuted at law as a wizard or witch, throughout these realms; and any person or persons who shall offer injury to any one, as being guilty of the supposed crime of witchcraft, shall be punished for such aggression. God save the King!"

> [*A pause of dead silence, followed by low, then loud murmurs, and then voices call out in succession.*

Voices. My certes! the de'il has been better represented in the house of Parliament than a' the braid shires in the kingdom.—Sic a decree as that in a Christian land!—To mak Satan triumphant!—There'll be fine gambols on moors and in kirkyards for this, I trow.—Parliament, forsooth! we hae sent bonnie members there, indeed, gin thae be the laws they mak.—And will Mary Macmurren escape after a'?—Out upon't! She may be brunt at ony rate, for she is condemned by the gude auld law of our forefathers.—Ay, so she may; that stands to reason.

> [*Crowd close round the stake where* MARY MACMURREN *is bound.*]

Sheriff (*to the crowd*). Desist, I say, or the soldiers shall disperse you forthwith.

Fath. Would they burn the miserable creature for an imaginary crime; one may say, for a pastime!

Baillie (*to* FATHERINGHAM). No, good sir; not imaginary. She is a witch by her own confession. And that woman (*pointing to* GRIZELD BANE) is also, by her own words, convicted of consorting and colleaguing with Satan,—an awful and mischievous witch.

Fath. Is she so?

Grizeld Bane (looking at him fiercely). Who says otherwise? The sun shines now, and that makes thee bold; but my time of power is coming.

Fath (approaching her). Is this you, Grizeld Bane? What brought you to this part of the country?

Grizeld Bane. The prince of the power of the air.

Baillie. There, sir! you hear her confess it. And who is she? for you seem to know her.

Fath. A miserable woman whose husband was hanged for murder, at Inverness, some years ago, and who thereupon became distracted. She was, when I left that country, kept in close custody. But she has, no doubt, escaped from her keepers, who may not be very anxious to reclaim her.

Baillie. We must secure her, then, and send her back to the north.

Grizeld Bane. Lay hands on me who dare! I defy you: my master is stronger than you all, since you sent him to his kingdom of darkness. Ye cannot stop the breath of a spirit, though you had a score of executioners at your beck. Lay hands upon me who dare!

Fath. Nobody will do you any violence, dame; but you will quietly retire with these two friends of yours (*motioning significantly to two soldiers, who advance and take charge of her*). Nay; make no resistance: look steadfastly in my face, and you will plainly perceive that you must go.

> [*Fixes his eyes upon her sternly, while she suffers herself to be led off.*

Off. Now, Mr. Sheriff, release your prisoners, since the laws against witchcraft are abrogated.

Sheriff. I do it most gladly. Would you had authority to command the release of all my prisoners.

Off. It is only those condemned for witchcraft, whose enlargement I have authority to command.

Mur. (*stepping sternly from the opposite side of the stage, and fronting Fatheringham closely*). But there is a prisoner condemned for murder whom thou, James Fatheringham, knowest to be innocent, and therefore thou art by nature authorised, yea, compelled, to demand his release,—I mean, the reversion of his sentence.

Fath (*starting back*). Murrey of Torwood in the land of the living!

Mur. No thanks to thee that I am so! To desert me, and leave the country too, circumstanced AS thou knewest me to be,—the only witness of that fatal quarrel,—was it the act of a friend, of a Christian, of a man?

Fath. No, neither of a Christian, nor a heathen, had it been a voluntary act. But you were not yet in custody, when I left the country, with no intention of going further than the southern coast of Ireland, to visit a dying relation.

Mur. In Ireland all these years?

Fath. Be not so hasty. That coast I never reached: a violent storm drove our vessel out to sea, where she was boarded and captured by a pirate. My varied tale, dear Murrey, you shall hear on a fitter occasion. Thank God that I am now here! and have this day accompanied my friend (*pointing to the officer*) on his public errand, still in time to save thee. For hearing, on my return to England, some weeks ago, thy sad story, how thou hadst been condemned, hadst made thy escape from prison, how thy dead body was found in a pit, and interred,—I was in no hurry to proceed northwards, as the justification of thy memory could not be disappointed.

Mur. Thou shouldst not have suffered even my memory to rest under such imputation,—no, not an hour.

Vio. Dear father, be not so stern when deliverance,—a blessed deliverance,—is sent to thee. See; there is a tear in his eye. It was not want of friendship that detained him.

Fath. I thank thee, sweet lady, for taking my part. It was not want of friendship that detained me; though Murrey has always been so hasty and ardent, and I so deliberate and procrastinating, it is wonderful we should ever have been friends.

Dun. No, not wonderful: though slow yourself, you loved him, perhaps, for his ardour.

Fath. Yes, young man, you are right. But how was it that he loved me? if, indeed, he ever loved me. Perhaps he never did.

Mur. (*rushing into his arms*). I did—I do—and will ever love thee, wert thou as slow and inert as a beetle.

Dun. Now ye are friends, and this terrible tempest has past over us!
May such scenes as we have this day witnessed never again
disgrace a free and a Christian land!

[*A murmur amongst the crowd.*

Sheriff. Good people, be pacified; and instead of the burning of a
witch, ye shall have six hogsheads of ale set abroach at the
cross, to drink the health of Violet Murrey, and a grand funeral
into the bargain.

Dun. Forbear, sheriff: the body of this unhappy lady is no subject for
pageantry. She shall be interred with decent privacy; and those
who have felt the tyranny of uncontrolled passions will think,
with conscious awe, of her end.

[*The curtain drops.*

Printed in the United States
126181LV00002B/181/A